EUSEBIUS
THE CHURCH HISTORY

Books by Paul L. Maier

FICTION

The Flames of Rome

More Than a Skeleton: It Was One Man Against the World

Pontius Pilate

A Skeleton in God's Closet

NONFICTION

The Best of Walter A. Maier (ed.)

*Caspart Schwenckfeld on the Person and Work of Christ:
    A Study of Schwenckfeldian Theology at Its Core*

The Da Vinci Code: Fact or Fiction? (with H. Hanegraaff)

Eusebius—The Church History (ed., trans.)

First Christians

First Christmas

First Easter

In the Fullness of Time

Josephus—The Essential Writings (ed., trans.)

Josephus—The Essential Works (ed., trans.)

Josephus—The Jewish War (ed., trans. with G. Cornfeld)

A Man Spoke, a World Listened

Martin Luther: A Man Who Changed the World

The New Complete Works of Josephus (ed.)

EUSEBIUS

THE CHURCH HISTORY

Translation and commentary by
PAUL L. MAIER

Kregel
Academic & Professional

Eusebius: The Church History
Copyright © 1999, 2007 by Paul L. Maier

Published by Kregel Publications, a division of Kregel, Inc., P.O. Box 2607, Grand Rapids, MI 49501.

Library of Congress Cataloging-in-Publication Data
Eusebius, of Caesarea, Bishop of Caesarea, ca. 260–ca. 340.
  [Ecclesiastical history, English]
Eusebius: the church history / by Paul L. Maier.
p. cm.
    1. Church history—Primitive and early church, ca. 30–600.
    I. Maier, Paul L. II. Title.
BR160.E5E5   1999   270.1–dc21   98-13442
CIP

ISBN 978-0-8254-3307-8

10 11 12 13 / 7 6 5 4

To the faculty of Concordia Seminary

in appreciation
for their conferral
of the degree of
Doctor of Letters, *honoris causa*

CONTENTS

Introduction   9

Book 1 THE PERSON AND WORK OF CHRIST   21
            Commentary: Eusebius on Jesus   49

Book 2 THE APOSTLES   52
            Commentary: Eusebius on the Apostles   77

Book 3 MISSIONS AND PERSECUTIONS   80
            Commentary: Eusebius's Sources   115

Book 4 BISHOPS, WRITINGS, AND MARTYRDOMS   118
            Commentary: Defenders and Defamers
            of the Faith   147

Book 5 WESTERN HEROES, EASTERN HERETICS   150
            Commentary: Christian Agonies
            and Arguments   185

Book 6 ORIGEN AND ATROCITIES AT ALEXANDRIA   188
            Commentary: Eusebius's Horizons   223

Book 7 DIONYSIUS AND DISSENT   227
            Commentary: Dionysius of Alexandria   255

Book 8 THE GREAT PERSECUTION   259
            Commentary: The Four Emperors   283

Book 9 THE GREAT DELIVERANCE   286
            Commentary: The End of Persecution?   304

Book 10 CONSTANTINE AND PEACE   308
            Commentary: Eusebius and Constantine   333

Appendix 1: Eusebius's Citation of Josephus on Jesus   336

Appendix 2: The Successions of Emperors and Bishops   339

Bibliography   344

Indexes   348

INTRODUCTION

If Herodotus is the father of history, then Eusebius of Caesarea (c. A.D. 260–339) is certainly the father of church history. He was the first to undertake the task of tracing the rise of Christianity during its crucial first three centuries from Christ to Constantine. Since no other ancient author tried to cover the same period, Eusebius is our principal primary source for earliest Christianity, and his *Church History* is the cornerstone chronicle on which later historians would build. The Jewish historian Flavius Josephus provides fascinating addenda to our information about the people, places, and events of the biblical world, and Eusebius does the same for the period up to A.D. 324.

What happened to Jesus' apostles later in life? Did Simon Peter ever go to Rome? Where did John spend the rest of his days? Did Paul survive his trial before Nero? When were the Gospels written? Who wrote them, and where? How did the New Testament canon develop? Why and how were the early Christians persecuted? These questions and many more involve an era no longer covered by the New Testament and could hardly be answered were it not for Eusebius.

The ten books[1] of his *Church History* are a treasure trove of data on the fledgling faith, whose survival and purity were sorely tested by persecution without and heresy within. Today Christianity is the most successful single phenomenon, statistically considered, in all of history. During its early years, however, it was fragile, fragmented, harried, tortured, and seemingly doomed by a hostile Roman Empire. Equally destructive were the internal attacks by renegade religionists who tried to seduce the saints through arcane distortions of doctrine or corral them into schismatic groups that foreshadowed contemporary cults.

Eusebius tells it all, but he also reports the heroic stance of the martyrs, whose blood indeed became the "seed of the church," as Tertullian put it. Eusebius writes of the fearless defenders of the faith who had the courage to face emperors and face down heretics, of bishops and elders who guided the church through

---

1. The modern equivalent for "books" in the ancient world would be "long book chapters," since the term referred originally to scrolls. Such "books" might range in length from a modern lengthy chapter to a seventy-page booklet.

horrendous adversity, and of writers whose crucial statements preserving orthodoxy would in many cases have been lost had Eusebius not reported them word for word. These pages, then, show how Christianity's tragedies turned into triumph in the course of its first three centuries.

The Life of Eusebius

Eusebius in Greek means one who is reverent, pious, or devout—a proper name (nearly equivalent to *Pius* in Latin) that was shared by a half dozen other famed figures in Christian history. A geographical suffix distinguishes them from one another. Just as Jesus *of Nazareth* differentiated him from the twenty other Jesuses in biblical times, so Eusebius *of Caesarea* designates the church historian.

Ancient Caesarea, looking toward the southeast. Herod the Great constructed the city in the years 25 to 13 B.C., including the semicircular seawall opening to the north (*George Beattie*).

Although there were also a number of Caesareas in antiquity—all named in honor of Augustus, the first Roman emperor—Eusebius's is Caesarea Maritima, the famous city of Palestine constructed by Herod the Great on the Mediterranean shore, at a site previously called Strato's Tower. This Caesarea is mentioned frequently in the New Testament as the Roman capital of Judea, the headquarters of Pontius Pilate, Cornelius, Herod Agrippa, Felix, and Festus, as well as the place where Paul was imprisoned for two years. Here, too, the riot broke out in A.D. 66 that led to the great Jewish War against Rome and the destruction of Jerusalem. The last only enhanced the importance of Caesarea, and by the third century it was virtually the capital of Syria, a very large, cosmopolitan city with a Jewish, Greek, Samaritan, and Christian populace.

Eusebius was probably born around 260. His biography, written by Acacius, his successor as Bishop of Caesarea, has not survived to provide more exact detail. His ancestry and the story of his youth are unknown. His education may be adduced from the fact that the great Eastern scholar-theologian Origen spent his later years in Caesarea, dying several years before Eusebius was born. Origen's influence persisted strongly in the theological school founded there by the learned Pamphilus, presbyter in the church at Caesarea, who taught Eusebius and influenced him most. Eusebius joined Pamphilus in writing a defense of Origen, made use of his great library, and wrote a *Life of Pamphilus* (now lost), whom he valued so highly that he was often known as Eusebius Pamphili. In the final Great Persecution of the Christians under Diocletian, Pamphilus was imprisoned and martyred in 310.

Upon the death of his mentor, Eusebius went to Tyre in Phoenicia and Alexandria in Egypt, where he was imprisoned in the Diocletianic persecution but released shortly afterward. Many years later an opponent accused him of having gained his release by pagan sacrifice, but no evidence for this was adduced at the time or since. Had such evidence existed, it surely would have been used in the theological turmoil of the day. Just after Constantine's edict of toleration was issued in 313, Eusebius was elected Bishop of Caesarea, where he remained until his death, despite being offered (and declining) the patriarchate of Antioch in 331.

About 316, he gave the dedicatory address at the new cathedral in Tyre, which he published in Book 10 of his *Church History*. Two years later the Arian controversy exploded in Eastern Christendom, and Eusebius soon found himself embroiled in it. He favored a mediating position between the theological extremes of Arius, presbyter in Alexandria ("Jesus is more than man but less than God, who existed before the Son"), and Alexander, Bishop of Alexandria ("Jesus is God, of the same essence and co-eternal with the Father"). Although Eusebius did not endorse the full subordinationism of Arius, he was somewhat sympathetic to the Arian cause, for which the Council of Antioch provisionally excommunicated him and two others in 324. His case, however, was transferred to the great Council of Nicea the following year, where he sat at Constantine's right hand and served as a prominent theological adviser, delivering a panegyric in honor of the emperor.

As leader of the moderate party at the council, Eusebius presented the creed used by his church at Caesarea and was exonerated of any heresy. Constantine stated that the creed reflected his own views, and it seems to have served as basis for that adopted at Nicea, but this creed was adopted only after important addenda had been made by the Alexandrian party, including Jesus being defined as *homoousios* ("of one substance" or "essence") with the Father. Although Eusebius finally voted with the overwhelming majority for what would emerge as the Nicene Creed, he wrote a letter to his church explaining his hesitations and voicing concerns that the Alexandrian party was verging on Sabellianism, a heresy that claimed unity over trinity (i.e., that the Son of God was only God acting in a saving mode or capacity).

This concern followed Eusebius to the Council of Antioch in 331, which deposed Eustathius, a leading anti-Arian, and to the Synod at Constantinople in 336, which condemned Marcellus, Bishop of Ancyra (modern Ankara), for extreme anti-Arianism. This does not, however, mean that Eusebius remained a pro-Arian. Eusebius's orthodoxy later in life is confirmed by his rejection of two cardinal principles of Arianism: that there was a time when the Son of God was not and that he was created out of nothing.

Just after the Synod of Constantinople, Eusebius was chosen to deliver an oration on the *tricennalia* of Constantine, the celebration marking his thirtieth year as emperor. Constantine died in the following year (337), and Eusebius two years after that, most probably on May 30, 339, a date known with considerable certainty from the Syriac martyrology of the fourth century. Nothing is known of Eusebius's two final years, other than that he published a *Life of Constantine* in four books, a panegyric rather than a strict history.

The Writings of Eusebius

Eusebius was a prolific author, writing books, chronologies, treatises, dictionaries, and orations in many different areas, not to mention his extensive correspondence. The most complete edition of his works (vols. 19–24 of J. P. Migne, ed., *Patrologia Graeca* [Paris: 1857]) fills six large volumes, and these are merely some, not all, of his writings that have survived in Greek. Following is a partial catalogue of his works in categories suggested by A. C. McGiffert in his magisterial introduction to Eusebius in *The Nicene and Post-Nicene Fathers*. Some of these titles have been lost or survive only in fragments.

1. Historical Writings. Aside from the *Church History*, which will be discussed in the next section, Eusebius wrote about his mentor in the *Life of Pamphilus;* two separate works on persecution in the *Martyrs of Palestine* and *Collection of Ancient Martyrdoms;* an important work on chronology, the *Chronicon* or *Chronicle;* and the *Life of Constantine*.

2. Apologetic Works. In defending the faith, Eusebius wrote *Against Hierocles*, opposing a Neoplatonist governor in Bithynia and Egypt who persecuted the Christians; and *Against Porphyry*, refuting another Neoplatonist philosopher who launched a formidable attack on Christianity. *On the Numerous Progeny of the Ancients* was Eusebius's explanation of the polygamy of the patriarchs. His greatest apologetic writings, however, are the *Preparation for the Gospel*, in which he shows how superior a base for Christianity were the Scriptures of monotheistic Judaism rather than the pagan polytheisms of the Greeks; and the *Proof of the Gospel*, which shows how Jesus was indeed the Messiah predicted in the Hebrew Scriptures. Unlike these major works, the *Praeparatio Ecclesiastica* and the *Demonstratio Ecclesiastica*, which concerned the life of the church rather than its doctrines, have not survived. In the *Theophany* he defends God's manifestation in Christ; his *Two Books of Objection and Defense* have been lost.

3. Polemic Writings. As mentioned earlier, Eusebius and his mentor Pamphilus jointly wrote the *Defense of Origen*, against attackers who faulted Origen's allegorizing theology. Only the first of the six books of the *Defense* has survived, and that in a Latin translation by Rufinus.

Eusebius seems to have been provoked most by the Sabellian heresy of his day, which stressed unity in the Trinity to such an extent as to teach that the one God appeared in three different modes, not persons, and it might thus be said that the Father suffered in the Christ mode (Patripassianism). He wrote two works against the Sabellian views of the Bishop of Ancyra: *Against*

Marcellus and *On the Theology of the Church: A Refutation of Marcellus.*

He also wrote *Against the Manicheans,* opposing followers of Mani, who preached in Persia a dualistic Gnosticism that divided reality into two principles—Light and Dark, God and Matter—and ensnared even the later Augustine for a decade.

4. Doctrinal Works. As an opening guide to theological study, Eusebius wrote ten books entitled *General Elementary Introduction,* of which only fragments survive, except for Books 6-9, which formed an independent unit called *Prophetic Extracts,* dealing with messianic passages from the Old Testament.

On the Paschal Festival was Eusebius's contribution to the controversy over the date to celebrate Easter. It explains the decision made at the Council of Nicea.

5. Exegetical Writings. Eusebius was particularly active in transcribing biblical texts, especially Origen's edition of the Septuagint. Under commission from Constantine, he also had fifty elaborate copies of the Scriptures prepared for use by the churches in Constantinople.

In *Ten Evangelical Canons,* he wrote a comparative harmony of the New Testament Gospels, showing which passages were common to all or several of them and which were unique to each. *Gospel Questions and Solutions* deals with the different genealogies of Jesus given in Matthew and Luke, as well as with the divergences in the accounts of the Resurrection.

The following listing is in biblical, not chronological, order. His *Commentary on the Psalms* is complete to Psalm 118, but that for 119 to 150 survives only in fragments. Because of its good Hebrew scholarship and critical acumen, the work enjoyed high regard among his contemporaries and since. The same can be said of his *Commentary on Isaiah.* In contrast, the simpler interpretations in his *Commentary on Luke* suggest an earlier dating. Other writings, such as his *Commentary on First Corinthians,* are known only as names or have survived only in fragments.

6. Bible Dictionaries. Eusebius's range of learning surfaces also in his titles: *Interpretation of Ethnological Terms in the Hebrew Scriptures,* his *Chorography of Ancient Judea,* and *A Plan of Jerusalem and of the Temple,* all of which have been lost. Fortunately, this is not the case with his *Onomasticon,* or *On the Names of Places in Holy Scripture,* which lists and defines, in alphabetical order, the names of biblical cities, villages, rivers, mountains, and the like, very much like a modern Bible dictionary.

Finally, *On the Nomenclature of the Book of the Prophets* summarizes the lives and predictions of the Old Testament prophets.

7. Orations. Aside from the panegyric at Tyre contained in Book 10 of the *Church History,* Eusebius gave the following major addresses: The *Oration at the Vicennalia of Constantine,* commemorating the twentieth anniversary of Constantine's reign in 325, was delivered at the opening of the Council of Nicea. The *Oration on the Savior's Sepulcher* was also heard by Constantine a decade later, just after the dedication of the Church of the Holy Sepulcher in Jerusalem. A third was the *Oration at the Tricennalia of Constantine,* which Eusebius delivered at Constantinople in 336 for the emperor's thirtieth anniversary. He delivered other addresses: *In Praise of the Martyrs, On the Failure of Rain,* and on other topics.

8. Letters. Eusebius's surviving correspondence deals with the Arian controversy in letters to Alexandria, his own Caesarea, and elsewhere. But it includes also a letter *To Constantia Augusta,* Constantine's sister and the wife of his co-emperor, Licinius, in reply to her request that Eusebius send her a likeness of Christ about which she had heard. Eusebius objected that such images invite idolatry.

Even apart from his *Church History,* then, Eusebius was a prolific and wide-ranging author of much erudition. This list of his own publications exceeds most of those he recorded for other writers whom he admired in the first three centuries A.D.

The Church History

The title of this work in the original Greek is *Ekklesiastices Historias,* in Latin *Historia Ecclesiastica,* and in English *Ecclesiastical History,* the formal title by which it is still known (and usually abbreviated by scholars as *Hist. eccl.* or simply *H.E.*). The final version comprises ten books, of which the first deals with the life of Jesus as the incarnate Word of God. Books 2–7 cover the rise of Christendom from the ascension of Christ in A.D. 33 up to the reign of Diocletian, which began in 284. Book 8 tells of the Great Persecution under Diocletian that started in 303 and ended under his successor Galerius in 311. Book 9 reports Constantine's victory in the West and Maximin's renewed persecution in the East, while Book 10 celebrates the toleration, peace, and imperial favor finally accorded the church.

Eusebius added to his original work as time went on. The first edition most likely comprised Books 1–7 only and was probably published before 300 (though some scholars argue for a later dating). Books 8–10 differ from the previous ones in that the author is now a contemporary or an eyewitness of the events described, and they no longer continue lists of apostolic succession, a hallmark of the earlier books. It is clear that Eusebius published another edition of his history that included Books 8, 9, and 10 (through chapter 7) after his panegyric at the rededication of the basilica at Tyre in 314 and before Constantine's war with his co-emperor, Licinius, in 316. The final edition including all of Book 10 as we now have it appeared after the defeat of Licinius in 324 and before the death of Constantine's son Crispus in 326, hence late 324 or early 325, just prior to the Council of Nicea. The reasons will be obvious in Book 10.

Eusebius structured his *Church History* on a time grid of Roman emperors, a device used in nearly all histories of the Roman Empire to the present day. Within this framework the successions of bishops in the four great centers of the early church—Jerusalem, Antioch, Alexandria, and Rome—constitute subdivisions. Eusebius thus shares the annalistic tradition of such predecessor historians as Thucydides, Polybius, Tacitus, and Josephus, as we might expect from the author of the earlier *Chronicle*. Difficulties in this otherwise logical arrangement, however, develop when a theme or a personality extends into the reigns of several emperors. One such was Justin Martyr, who appears in Books 2, 3, 4, and 5, when one section dedicated to the apologist might better have served the reader.

His sources, which Eusebius often quotes, paraphrases, or condenses in Books 2–7, need not be listed here, since he is always scrupulous about crediting the fonts of his information and citations. His debt to Josephus, Hegesippus, Justin, Irenaeus, Dionysius of Alexandria, and others is open and acknowledged. He may have borrowed too heavily for modern tastes, but much of this material owes its very survival to its felicitous incorporation in Eusebius's record. He found much of his material in the vast library at his own Caesarea, founded by Origen and tended by Pamphilus, and that at Jerusalem established by Bishop Alexander, which accounts for the Greek and Eastern emphasis in his pages at the expense of the Latin and Western contributions, which somewhat upsets a balanced presentation in his *Church History*.

Other faults in Eusebius's historiography will become clear in the reading. Footnotes in the text will have to correct his occasional inaccuracies in matters of chronology and interpretation. In desultory fashion he often jumps from one theme to the next through abrupt transitions, and one hardly looks for literary elegance or logical precision in his copious prose. He seems to have written rapidly, with little thought given to subsequent refinement or revision. His coverage at places is superficial, where he seems content to describe effects but not causes or identifies either God or Satan as sufficient explanation of cause. Except for the persecutions, the events of history and its actors seem to interest him less than its writers and their books, for Eusebius is preeminently a literary historian. Even here, however, the central ideas of these literati receive only scant attention, as is the case with the basic teachings of the Fathers or the errors of the heretics.

Eusebius's merits, however, clearly outweigh these defects. Had his *Church History* never been written, our knowledge of the first three centuries of Christendom would be heavily pockmarked by missing figures, facts, documents, and data of major importance. With his vast erudition, the Bishop of Caesarea sifted through mountains of material to gather valuable information for subsequent ages that might explore it more deeply than he did. Unlike many authors of antiquity, he could usually discriminate between reliable and unreliable sources and was far less credulous than many historians before him and since. He was scrupulously honest not only in acknowledging his sources but also in confessing the trepidation with which he undertook this task, since no history of the church had been written before. He was blazing a theological-historical trail, and pioneers can be forgiven their rugged qualities. His *Church History* was never redone by another historian of antiquity but became a classic and has survived the centuries intact—facts that overcome all criticism.

This Edition

Unlike my *Josephus—The Essential Works* (Kregel Publications), which is necessarily a condensation of the vast writings of the Jewish historian, this volume is a full translation of Eusebius's *Church History*. It is based on the standard critical edition of the original Greek text of Eusebius published by the great German scholar Eduard Schwartz (in *Die griechischen christlichen Schriftsteller* [Leipzig: Hinrichs'sche Buchhandlung, 1897]). This text, which has superseded earlier versions, is most conveniently available in the *Loeb Classical Library* (Cambridge: Harvard University Press; and London: Heinemann, 1926, 1932), with

English translations by Kirsopp Lake (vol. 1) and J. E. L. Oulton (vol. 2). Other prominent English translations include a rather dated version by Christian Frederick Cruse from 1850 (reprint ed.; Grand Rapids: Baker, 1991); a text with excellent commentary by A. C. McGiffert from 1890, reprinted in *The Nicene and Post-Nicene Fathers*, volume 1 (Grand Rapids: Eerdmans, 1952); and the best recent translation: G. A. Williamson, *Eusebius—The History of the Church from Christ to Constantine* (London: Penguin, 1965; rev. ed., Andrew Louth, 1989).

A new edition, translation, and brief commentary on Eusebius, however, seems indicated for several reasons. The first is to make Eusebius clearer and more readable. His Greek, as Williamson points out, is quite difficult: "The first sentence of Book I is 166 words long, and we have to plough through 153 of them before we reach the one and only main verb. Sometimes there is no main verb at all, or the sentence is an anacoluthon, beginning in one way and ending in another" (xxxvii).

A word-for-word translation would be almost unreadable, and yet Eusebius must survive his translation intact. The problem of trying to remain faithful to an original text while rendering it readable in another language is one that has always beset translators. As someone has said (wickedly and in sexist days), "A translation is very much like a woman: if it is beautiful, it is not faithful; if it is faithful, it is not beautiful."

I have endeavored to clarify Eusebius's text by breaking up his long sentences into digestible segments, eliminating excess verbiage where it serves no purpose other than to obscure meaning, reducing parallel phraseology where it is clearly useless, and dropping any cloyingly repetitive phrases that add nothing to the record. In other words, *if Eusebius had had a good editor*, this is how his text might have appeared when adjusted for modern tastes. (Eusebius, it will be recalled, did not have an editor, not even himself in polishing or revising his work.) Not one datum of information has been surrendered in the process, and the results, I hope, have rendered Eusebius far more readable and usable today.

Several examples may illustrate my method. The first translation in the following couplets is from the Loeb edition, which faithfully renders all of Eusebius's verbiage, while the second is mine:

I have already summarized the material in the chronological tables which I have drawn up, but nevertheless in the present work I have undertaken to give the narrative in full detail (1.1).

Previously I summarized this material in my *Chronicle*, but in the present work I deal with it in the fullest detail.

Again:

Now while Origen was plying his accustomed tasks at Caesarea, many came to him, not only of the natives, but also numbers of foreign pupils who had left their own countries (6.30).

While Origen was teaching at Caesarea, many students, both local and from many foreign countries, studied under him.

And again:

It is not our part to commit to writing the conflicts of those who fought throughout the world on behalf of piety toward the Deity, and to record in detail each of their happenings; but that would be the especial task of those who witnessed the events (8.13).

To record in detail the ordeals of those who fought throughout the world for reverence toward the Deity would be a task for eyewitnesses rather than for me.

Another, though lesser, reason for this new translation is to correct occasional errors in previous versions. For example, Eusebius has an interesting passage concerning the fate of Pontius Pilate after Pilate's return to Rome in A.D. 37. According to one recent translation, Pilate committed suicide, "as the records show" (2.7), but Eusebius's Greek for the phrase in quotes is much less definite: *katexei logos*, "word has it" or "tradition holds"—a rather significant difference. (There is earlier evidence that Pilate was not a suicide.)

Finally, no edition of Eusebius, to my knowledge, is illustrated with documentary photographs of the sites he describes or with maps and charts that assist in interpreting the text. Sometimes these become very important in trying to understand Eusebius's meaning in full.

A word of caution may be appropriate here. Since Eusebius was eager to trace the episcopal succession in the four great sees of early Christendom—Jerusalem, Antioch, Alexandria, and

Rome—long lists of bishops' names and dates at these locations will clutter the text from time to time. The reader is urged to scan or to skip this material, since it can all be found in Appendix 2, where it is laid out much more clearly.

Several mechanical items should be mentioned. Greek versions of proper names have been rendered in their common English equivalents (e.g., "Peter" rather than "Petros"). Literary titles are treated similarly: hence Justin's *Defense,* for example, rather than his *Apologia;* Clement's *Outlines* rather than his *Hypotyposes.* Although each book (chapter) in this volume is lengthy, it was Eusebius himself who divided his work into these ten segments. Book titles and subtitles, however, are mine, as are chapter or section titles. Their numbering in each book has been standard since the early manuscripts of Eusebius, even if the placement of these numbers sometimes seems to have been the work of a madman. The Greek manuscripts also have lengthy indexes prior to each book, which are tedious and unnecessary and have not been included in this translation. Many of the chapter titles, however, directly reflect these.

Important dates are added in the margins, since the B.C./A.D. system was not yet in use at the time of Eusebius. Ellipses (. . .) do not indicate omissions in the text other than, for example, when Eusebius, in quoting Josephus twice in the same passage, strings citations together with an unnecessary "Josephus goes on to say." Brackets denote my addenda in Eusebius's text to improve its intelligibility.

Brief commentaries follow each chapter to elucidate the preceding material. The last part of each of these provides a summary of concurrent Roman imperial history to clarify the political framework of the times.

Going behind the works of digested or secondary history to primary sources like Eusebius is extremely rewarding. Even if historians have pored over this material for nearly seventeen hundred years, joining them in this process should be a refreshing experience for the lay reader or, in the case of the scholar, a challenge to find new nuggets of information. Here then is the most important work of the most voluminous extant author, pagan or Christian, of the late third and early fourth centuries: the first history of the church ever written.

PAUL L. MAIER
WESTERN MICHIGAN UNIVERSITY

BOOK 1

THE PERSON AND
WORK OF CHRIST

AUGUSTUS TO TIBERIUS

The Contents of These Books

1. It is my purpose to record

the successions from the holy apostles and the periods extending from our Savior's time to our own;

the many important events that occurred in the history of the church;

those who were distinguished in its leadership at the most famous locations;

those who in each generation proclaimed the Word of God by speech or pen;

the names, number, and ages of those who, driven by love of novelty to the extremity of error, have announced themselves as sources of knowledge (falsely so-called)[1] while ravaging Christ's flock mercilessly, like ferocious wolves;

the fate that overtook the whole Jewish race after their plot against our Savior;

---

1. The Gnostics, as prime representatives of heresy.

the occasions and times of the hostilities waged by heathen against the divine Word and the heroism of those who fought to defend it, sometimes through torture and blood;

the martyrdoms of our own time and the gracious deliverance provided by our Savior and Lord, Jesus the Christ of God, who is my starting point.

This project requires kindness on the part of the reader, since I feel inadequate to do it justice as the first to venture on such an undertaking, a traveler on a lonely and untrodden path. But I pray that God may guide me and the power of the Lord assist me, for I have not found even the footprints of any predecessors on this path, only traces in which some have left us various accounts of the times in which they lived. Calling as from a distant watchtower, they tell me how I must walk in guiding the course of this work to avoid error. I have gathered from the scattered memoirs of my predecessors whatever seems appropriate to this project, plucking, as it were, flowers from the literary fields of the ancient authors themselves. I shall incorporate them in a historical narrative, happy to rescue from oblivion at least the most distinguished of the successors of our Savior's apostles in the most famous churches. I deem this work especially necessary because I know of no Christian author who has taken interest in such writings, which, I hope, those who know the value of history will find most valuable. Previously I summarized this material in my *Chronicle*, but in the present work I deal with it in the fullest detail.

I will begin with a concept too sublime and exalted for human grasp: the ordering of events [by God] and the divinity of Christ. Anyone intending to write the history of the church must start with the Christ himself, from whom we derive our very name, a dispensation more divine than most realize.

The Nature of Christ

[Chapters (sections) 2–4 that follow are unlike the rest of the Church History *and deal with the preexistent Christ. Eusebius's regular history begins with section 5.]*

2. His character is twofold: like the head of the body in that he is regarded as God and yet comparable to the feet in that he put on humanity for the sake of our salvation, a man of passions like ours. If I begin his story with the principal and most basic points to consider, both the antiquity and divine character of Christianity will be demonstrated to those who suppose that it is recent and foreign, appearing only yesterday.

No language could adequately describe the origin, essence, and nature of Christ, as indeed the Holy Spirit says in prophecy: "Who shall declare his generation?" [Isa. 53:8]. For no one knows the Father except the Son, and no one has fully known the Son except the Father who begot him. And who but the Father could conceive of the Light that existed before the world, the Wisdom that preceded time, the living Word that was in the beginning with the Father and was God? Before all creation and fashioning, visible or invisible, he was the first and only offspring of God, the commander-in-chief of the spiritual host of heaven, the messenger of mighty counsel, the agent of the ineffable plan of the Father, the creator—with the Father—of all things, the second cause of the universe after the Father, the true and only begotten Child of God, the Lord and God and King of everything created, who has received lordship, power, honor, and deity itself from the Father. According to the mystic ascription of divinity to him in the Scriptures:

> In the beginning was the Word, and the Word was with God, and the Word was God. . . . All things were made by him, and apart from him nothing was made [John 1:1, 3].

Indeed, this is also the teaching of the great Moses, the earliest of all the prophets, when by the Holy Spirit he described the origin and ordering of the universe: the Creator gave over to none but Christ himself the making of subordinate things and discussed with him the creation of man: "For God said, 'Let us make man in our image and likeness' " [Gen. 1:26].

Another of the prophets confirms this ascription of divinity: "He spoke, and they were made; he commanded, and they were created" [Ps. 33:9; 148:5]. Here he introduces the Father and Maker as a supreme sovereign giving commands by a royal nod and, second to him, none other than the divine Word as carrying out his commands.

Ever since Creation, all those distinguished for righteousness and virtue—Moses, and before him Abraham and his children, as well as all the just men and prophets since—recognized him through the eyes of the mind and paid him the reverence due the Son of God, who taught all humanity the knowledge of the Father.

Thus the Lord God is said to have appeared as an ordinary man to Abraham as he sat by the oak of Mamre, yet he worshiped him as God, saying, "O Lord, judge of all the world, will you not do justice?" [Gen. 18:25]. Since reason would never permit that the immutable essence of the Almighty be changed into human form, even by illusion, or that Scripture would falsely invent such a story, who else could be so described as appearing in human form but the preexistent Word, since naming the First Cause of the universe would be inappropriate? Of him it is said in the Psalms:

> He sent his Word and healed them,
> And he rescued them from their destruction [107:20].

Moses clearly speaks of him as a second Lord after the Father when he says: "The Lord rained on Sodom and Gomorrah brimstone and fire from the Lord" [Gen. 19:24]. Holy Scripture again refers to him as God when he appeared to Jacob in the form of a man and said, "No longer shall your name be Jacob, but Israel . . . for you have prevailed with God." Then too: "Jacob called the name of that place 'the Vision of God,' saying, 'For I saw God face-to-face, and my life was spared' " [Gen. 32:28–29].

To suppose that these recorded theophanies were appearances of subordinate angels and ministers of God cannot be correct, for whenever these appear to people, Scripture distinctly declares in countless passages that they are called angels, not God or Lord.

Joshua, Moses' successor, names him commander-in-chief of the Lord's army, as leader of the angels and archangels and the heavenly powers and accorded the second place in universal rule as the power and wisdom of the Father, yet Joshua too saw him only in human form. For it is written:

> When Joshua was at Jericho, he looked up and saw a man standing before him with a drawn sword in his hand. Joshua approached him and said, "Are you for us or for our enemies?" He replied, "It is as commander of the Lord's army that I have come." Then Joshua fell to the ground, face downward, and asked, "Master, what do you command your servant?" The commander of the Lord's army replied, "Take off your shoes, for the place where you stand is holy" [Josh. 5:13–15].

The words themselves will show you here too that this was none other than the one who spoke also to Moses:

When the Lord saw that he approached to see, the Lord called out to him from the bush, "Moses, Moses!" He replied, "What is it?" He said, "Do not come near. Remove your sandals, for the place where you stand is holy ground." He continued, "I am the God of your father, the God of Abraham, the God of Isaac, and the God of Jacob" [Ex. 3:4-6].

There are additional proofs that this really is the being named the Word of God and Wisdom, who existed before the world and assisted the God of the universe in the fashioning of all created things. Wisdom clearly reveals her own secret through the mouth of Solomon:

> I, Wisdom, made counsel my dwelling and invoked knowledge and
> thought.
> By me kings reign and rulers decree justice;
> By me the great are enhanced and sovereigns rule. . . .
> In the beginning before time began and before the Lord made the
> earth
> He begot me, before springs gushed forth and the mountains arose.
> When he prepared the heavens, I was there, and when he secured
> the springs under heaven, I was with him, setting them in order.
> I was she in whom he daily delighted, and I always rejoiced in his
> presence when he rejoiced that he had completed the world.[2]

This, then, is a brief demonstration that the divine Word pre-existed and appeared to some, if not all, people.

Why he was not proclaimed long ago to all people and all nations, as now, is explained as follows. In the past humanity was not capable of grasping the teaching of Christ in all its wisdom and virtue. At the beginning, after the original state of blessedness, the first man disregarded the command of God and fell into this mortal state, exchanging the delight of heaven for the curse of earth. His descendants, who filled our world, showed themselves even worse, except for one or two, choosing a brutal existence and a life not worth living. City, state, art, knowledge, laws, virtue, or philosophy were not even names among them, and they lived as savage nomads in the desert, destroying reason and culture through excessive wickedness. Surrendering to total depravity, they corrupted, murdered, or cannibalized each

---

2. Selections from Prov. 8:12-31.

other and in their madness prepared for war with God himself and to fight the famed battles of the giants,[3] trying to fortify earth against heaven and, in their delirium, to do battle with the supreme Ruler himself.

In response, God sent them floods and conflagrations, famines and plagues, wars and thunderbolts—punishments progressively drastic—in order to restrain the noxious illness of their souls. Then, just when the vast flood of evil had nearly drowned humankind, the firstborn and first-created Wisdom of God, the preexistent Word himself, appeared in his great kindness, as an angelic vision or in person as God's saving power to one or two of the God-fearing men of old, yet always in human form, since they could receive him in no other way.

When they, in turn, had sown the seeds of true religion among many, an entire nation appeared, sprung from the Hebrews and practicing the true religion. To them, through the prophet Moses, he revealed images and symbols of a mystical Sabbath and of circumcision, as well as instruction in other spiritual principles, but no complete revelation of the mysteries, for they were still bound by old practices. Yet when their law became famous and penetrated everywhere like a fragrant breeze, the minds of most of the heathen were moderated by lawgivers and philosophers. Savage brutality changed into mildness, so that profound peace, friendship, and easy communication prevailed.

Then at last, when all humanity throughout the world was now ready to receive knowledge of the Father, that same divine Word of God appeared at the beginning of the Roman Empire in the form of a man, of a nature like ours, whose deeds and sufferings accorded with the prophecies that a man who was also God would do extraordinary deeds and teach all nations the worship of the Father. They also predicted the miracle of his birth, his new teaching, the wonder of his deeds, the manner of his death, his resurrection from the dead, and, finally, his restoration to heaven by the power of God. Through inspiration by the Holy Spirit, the prophet Daniel described his final sovereignty in human terms:

> As I looked, thrones were placed and an Ancient of Days was seated.
> His clothing was white as snow and his hair like pure wool. His

---

3. Eusebius combines the description of the *nephilim* (Gen. 6:4) with the account of the Tower of Babel (Gen. 11:1-9).

throne was a flame of fire. . . . A thousand thousand ministered to him, and ten thousand times ten thousand stood before him. The court sat in judgment, and the books were opened. . . . I looked, and behold, one like a Son of Man came with the clouds of heaven before the Ancient of Days. To him was given dominion, glory, and kingdom, that all peoples, nations, and languages should serve him. His is an everlasting sovereignty that shall not pass away, and his kingdom shall not be destroyed [Dan. 7:9–10, 13–14].

Clearly this could not apply to anyone but our Savior, the God-Word who was in the beginning with God, called "Son of Man" because of his ultimate incarnation. But since I have collected the prophecies concerning our Savior Jesus Christ in special commentaries, let this suffice.

The Names Jesus and Christ Known Earlier

3. The very names *Jesus* and *Christ* were honored even by the God-loving prophets of old. Moses himself was the first to announce how greatly sanctified and glorious was the name of Christ, using types and symbols in response to the oracle that told him, "Make everything according to the pattern shown you in the mount" [Ex. 25:40]. When describing God's high priest as a man of supreme power, he calls him and his office "Christ" as a mark of honor and glory,[4] understanding the divine character of "Christ."

He was also inspired by the Holy Spirit to foresee quite clearly the title *Jesus*. Although previously it had never been known, Moses gave the title *Jesus*, again as a type or symbol, only to the man he knew would succeed him after his death.[5] His successor had been known by another name, Hoshea, which his parents had given him [Num. 13:16], but Moses calls him Jesus—Joshua the son of Nun himself bearing the image of our Savior, who alone after Moses received authority over the true and pure religion. In this way Moses bestows the name of our Savior Jesus Christ as a supreme honor on the two men who in his time surpassed all others in merit and glory: the high priest and the man who would rule after him.

---

4. The high priest is described as "anointed" in Lev. 4:5, 16 and in 6:22. The words *Christ* and *anointed,* though different in English, are the same in Greek, as translations of the Hebrew *messiach* or "Messiah."

5. Num. 27:12–23 refers to *Joshua,* which is the Greek transliteration of "Jesus."

Later prophets also clearly foretold Christ by name, predicting also the plots against him by the Jewish people and the calling of the Gentiles through him. Jeremiah, for example, says:

> The spirit of our face, Christ the Lord, was caught in their pits; Of whom we said, "In his shadow we shall live among the Gentiles" [Lam. 4:20].

David, in his perplexity, asks:

> Why did the nations rage and the peoples imagine vain things?
> The kings of the earth arrayed themselves, and the rulers convened against the Lord and against his Christ [Ps. 2:1-2].

He adds, speaking in the person of Christ himself:

> The Lord said to me, "You are my Son; today I have begotten you.
> Ask me, and I will give you the Gentiles as your inheritance and the limits of the world as your possession" [Ps. 2:7-8].

Accordingly, it was not only the high priests, symbolically anointed with oil, who were designated among the Hebrews with the name *Christ*, but also the kings; for by divine directive they too were anointed by the prophets as symbolic Christs, since they carried in themselves the patterns of the regal and sovereign authority of the only true Christ, the divine Word, who rules over all. Similarly, some of the prophets themselves, by anointing, became types of Christ, so that all [three] refer to the true Christ, the divine Word, who is the only High Priest of the universe, the only King of all creation, and the only Archprophet of the Father.

Proof of this is the fact that none of those symbolically anointed of old, whether priest, king, or prophet, ever obtained the sort of divine power our Savior and Lord, Jesus—the only real Christ—demonstrated. None of them, however honored among their own people for so many generations, ever conferred the name *Christian* on their subjects from their symbolic title of *Christ*. None was worshiped by his subjects or held in such esteem after his death as to be ready to die for the person honored. None caused such a stir in all nations throughout the world, since the power of the symbol could not produce such an effect as the reality of our Savior. He did not receive the symbols of high priesthood from anyone or trace his physical descent from priests. Armed forces did not promote his rule, nor did he become a prophet like those of old. Jews accorded him no rank or precedence whatever. Yet he had been adorned with all these by the Father, not in symbols but in truth. Although he did not obtain the honors cited, he is called Christ more than all of them, for he is himself the one true Christ of God who has filled the entire world with his Christians. He no longer provides patterns or images for his followers but fully revealed truths, and he has received not material chrism but divine anointing by the Spirit of God through sharing in the unbegotten divinity of the Father.

Isaiah teaches this very point when he exclaims, as if Christ were speaking:

> The Spirit of the Lord is upon me, for he has anointed me to bring good news to the poor.
> He has sent me to proclaim liberty to the captives and recovery of sight to the blind [Isa. 61:1-2].

And not only Isaiah but David also refers to him in saying:

> Your throne, O God, is for ever and ever:
> Your royal scepter is a scepter of equity.
> You have loved righteousness and hated iniquity.
> Therefore God, your God, has anointed you
> With the oil of gladness above your fellows [Ps. 45:6-7].

The first verse calls him God, the second accords him a royal scepter. Honored with divine and royal attributes, he is presented, in the third place, as having become Christ, anointed not with material oil but divine, and far superior to his physically anointed predecessors. Elsewhere too the same writer explains his status:

> The Lord said to my Lord, "Sit at my right hand
> Till I make your enemies your footstool. . . .
> From the womb before the morning star, I begot you."
> The Lord swore and will not rescind: "You are a priest forever of the order of Melchizedek" [Ps. 110:1-4].

This Melchizedek is defined in the sacred books as priest of the most high God without his having received any material anointing or even as belonging to the Hebrew priesthood. That is why our Savior has been called, under oath, Christ and priest according to his order and not that of others who received symbols and patterns. Nor does the record state that he was anointed physically by the Jews or belonged to the tribe of those who held the priesthood but that he had his existence from God himself before the morning star, that is, before the creation of the world, and holds his priesthood to all eternity.

That his anointing was divine is proved by the fact that he alone, of all who have ever lived, is known throughout the world as Christ and is called thus by Greeks and non-Greeks alike and to this day is honored by his worshipers throughout the world as King, held in greater awe than a prophet, and glorified as the true and only High Priest of God and above all as the preexistent Word of God, having his being before all ages and worshiped as God. We who are dedicated to him honor him not only with voice and word, but also with all of our soul, so that we value testimony to him more than life itself.

The Antiquity of the True Faith

4. This introduction was necessary lest anyone think of our Savior and Lord, Jesus Christ, as novel, in view of the date of his incarnation, or his teaching new and strange, as crafted by a typical man of recent date. With his recent advent, it was admittedly a new people—neither small, weak, nor remote but the most numerous, pious, and invincible, with God's eternal help—that appeared at the appointed time, honored with the name of Christ. This so amazed one of the prophets when he foresaw the future through the eye of the Holy Spirit that he exclaimed:

Who has ever heard such things? And who spoke thus?
Was the earth in labor but one day, and was a nation born at once
 [Isa. 66:8]?

The same writer also hints at its future name, saying, "Those who serve me shall be called by a new name, which shall be blessed on the earth" [Isa. 65:15–16].

But although we are new and this clearly fresh name of Christians has only recently become known among all nations, our life, conduct, and religious principles are no recent invention of ours but stem from the natural concepts of men of old who were the friends of God, as we will demonstrate. The Hebrews are not a new people but are known by all and honored for their antiquity.

Now their oral and written records deal with men of an early age, few and scarce in number yet outstanding in piety, righteousness, and other virtues. Some of them lived before the Flood, others after—Noah's children and descendants—but Abraham in particular, whom the Hebrews boast as their own founder and ancestor. All of these credited for righteousness, going back from Abraham to the first man, could be described as Christians in fact if not in name, without exceeding the truth. For the name means that the Christian, through the knowledge and teaching of Christ, excels in self-control and righteousness, in discipline and virtue, and in the confession of the one and only God over all, and in all this they showed no less zeal than we.

They had no interest in bodily circumcision, nor do we; nor for keeping the Sabbaths, nor do we; nor for abstaining from some foods or other distinctions that Moses first delivered to their successors to be observed as symbols, nor do such things concern Christians now. But clearly they knew the Christ of God, since he appeared to Abraham, taught Isaac, spoke to Israel [Jacob], and conversed with Moses and the later prophets, as I have shown. Therefore you will find that these God-loving men even received the name of Christ, according to the word regarding them: "Touch not my Christs, and do no wickedness among my prophets" [Ps. 105:15]. Clearly then, the recent proclamation of Christ's teaching to all nations is none other than the very first and most ancient of all religions discovered by Abraham and those lovers of God who followed him. Even if they argue that Abraham long afterward received the command for circumcision, I reply that before this he had been deemed righteous through faith, as the divine Word says: "Abraham believed God, and it was accounted to him for righteousness" [Gen. 15:6]. The oracle given him before his circumcision by the God who showed himself to him—Christ himself, the Word of God—dealt with those who in the future would be justified in the same way as he and ran as follows: "In you shall all the nations of the earth be blessed" [Gen. 12:3]. And: "He shall become a great and mighty nation, and in him shall all the nations of the earth be blessed" [Gen. 18:18].

Now this has obviously been fulfilled in us, for it was by faith in the Word of God, the Christ who had appeared to him, that he was made righteous and gave up the superstition of his fathers to confess the one God, the God over all, serving him by right conduct and not by the law of Moses, who came later. To him, as he was then, it was said that all nations would be blessed in him. And currently, in deeds louder than words, Christians alone across the world practice their faith in the very way that Abraham practiced it. Accordingly, Christ's followers share the same life and religion as the God-loving men of old, and thus Christ's teaching is not new or strange but, in all honesty, ancient, unique, and true.

Jesus' Birth and the End of the Jewish Dynasty

5. Now then, after this necessary introduction to my *Church History*, let us begin with the appearance of our Savior in the flesh, first invoking God, the Father of the Word, and Jesus Christ himself to assist us in producing a truthful narrative. It was in the forty-second year of the reign of Augustus and the twenty-eighth after the conquest of Egypt and the deaths of Antony and Cleopatra,[6] the last of the Ptolemaic dynasty, that our Savior and Lord, Jesus Christ, was born in Bethlehem of Judea in accordance with the prophecies concerning him. This was at the time of the first census, which took place while Quirinius was governor of Syria, a registration mentioned also by Flavius Josephus, the most famous of the Hebrew historians, who adds an account of the Galilean sect that arose at the same time, to which our own Luke refers in the Acts:

> After him arose Judas the Galilean at the time of the census. He persuaded some of the people to follow him. But he too perished, and all his followers were scattered [Acts 5:37].

The historian previously cited [Josephus] supports the above in *Antiquities*, Book 18:

> Quirinius, a member of the senate who had passed through all the other offices to become consul and was a man of high distinction in other ways, arrived in Syria with a small staff. He had been sent by Caesar to govern the nation and to assess their property. . . . Judas, a Gaulonite from the city called Gamala, took with him Zadok, a Pharisee, and incited a revolt, for they claimed that the assessment

---

6. Eusebius calculates Augustus's reign as beginning with the death of Julius Caesar in 44 B.C., hence 2 B.C. for the birth of Jesus, which accords also with twenty-eight years after the deaths of Antony and Cleopatra in 30 B.C. This date, however, is too late, since Jesus was born in 4 B.C. at the latest and most probably in 5 B.C.

Statue of Augustus, emperor 27 B.C. to A.D. 14, in the garb of a priest (*Museo Nazionale, Rome*).

would lead to nothing but total slavery, and they called on the people to defend their freedom.[7]

And in the second book of his *Jewish War*, he writes about the same man:

At this time a Galilean named Judas stirred the natives to revolt, naming them cowards if, after serving God, they accepted mortal masters and submitted to paying taxes to the Romans.[8]

6. At this time Herod was the first foreigner to become king of the Jewish nation, fulfilling Moses' prophecy that "A ruler shall not be wanting from Judah, nor a leader from his loins, until he comes for whom it is reserved" [Gen. 49:10]. Moses also states that he will be "the expectation of the Gentiles." This prediction

---

7. *Antiquities* 18.1, 4. The census causing Judas's revolt took place in A.D. 6, ten years after Jesus' birth, a chronological problem long debated among scholars.

8. *Jewish War* 2.118.

could not be fulfilled as long as the Jews lived under rulers of their own race, beginning with Moses and continuing down to Augustus's reign. In his time, however, the Romans awarded the government of the Jews to Herod, the first foreigner. Josephus states that he was an Idumean on his father's side and an Arab on his mother's, but [Julius] Africanus—no ordinary historian—claims that Antipater, Herod's father, was the son of a certain Herod of Ascalon, one of the servants in the temple of Apollo. As a child, this Antipater was captured by Idumean bandits and stayed with them because his father was too poor to pay his ransom. He was brought up in their customs and later befriended by the Jewish high priest Hyrcanus. His [Antipater's] son was the Herod of our Savior's time.

When the Jewish kingship devolved on such a man, the expectation of the Gentiles, according to prophecy, was already at the door, for the regular succession of their rulers and governors from the time of Moses came to an end. Before their Babylonian captivity, they were ruled by kings, Saul and David being the first. And before the kings, rulers known as judges governed them, following Moses and his successor Joshua. After the return from Babylon, an oligarchic aristocracy of priests was in control until the Roman general Pompey laid siege to Jerusalem and defiled **63 B.C.** the holy places by entering the inner sanctuary of the temple. He sent as prisoner to Rome, together with his children, the king and high priest, Aristobulus, who had continued the succession of his ancestors up to that time, and transferred the high priesthood to his [Aristobulus's] brother, Hyrcanus, while making the whole Jewish nation tributary to Rome from then on. And when Hyrcanus was taken prisoner by the Parthians, Herod was the first foreigner, as I have said, to be placed over the Jewish nation by the Roman senate and the emperor Augustus. The advent of Christ clearly occurred in his time, and the anticipated salvation and calling of the Gentiles followed in accord with the prophecy.

When the line of Jewish rulers ceased, the orderly succession of high priests from generation to generation fell into instant confusion. The reliable Josephus reports that Herod, once made king by the Romans, no longer appointed high priests of the ancient line but obscure sorts instead, a practice followed by his son Archelaus and the Roman governors after him when they took over the government of the Jews. The same writer reports that Herod was the first to lock up the sacred vestment of the high priest and keep it under his own seal rather than priestly control, as did his successor Archelaus and the Romans after him.

These facts also demonstrate that another prophecy was fulfilled in the appearance of our Savior Jesus Christ. The text in Daniel specifies the exact number of weeks until the rule of Christ—I have treated the subject elsewhere[9]—and prophesies that after these weeks the anointing of Jews will cease. Clearly this was fulfilled at the time our Savior Jesus Christ was born. These preliminaries were necessary to underscore the truth of the date.

Head of Gnaeus Pompey, who conquered Jerusalem in 63 B.C. (*Glyptotek, Copenhagen*).

The Variant Genealogies of Christ

7. The Gospels of Matthew and Luke record the genealogy of Christ differently, and many suppose that they conflict with one another. Since each believer has been eager to offer uninformed guesses regarding these passages, I shall reproduce an explanation of the problem in a letter that the aforementioned Africanus wrote to Aristides on the harmony of the Gospel genealogies. After refuting the opinions of others as forced and patently false, he gives the explanation that had come to him:

> Names in the families of Israel were reckoned either according to nature or law: by nature in the case of genuine offspring; by law when another man fathered children in the name of a brother who had died childless.[10] Since no clear hope of the resurrection had as yet been given, they depicted the future promise by a mortal "resurrection" so that the name of the deceased might survive. These genealogies, then, include some who succeeded their actual fathers

---

9. In Eusebius's *Proof of the Gospel* 8.2 and *Selections from the Prophets* 3.45. Dan. 9:24–27 speaks of "seventy weeks of years" (70 x 7, or 490 years) and other such "weeks of years," which Eusebius and some scholars since have applied to Jesus' birth and ministry.

10. See Deut. 25:5–6.

and others who were children of one father but were recorded as children of another. Thus both the memories of the actual and nominal fathers were preserved. Hence neither of the Gospels is in error, since they take both nature and law into account. For the two families—one descended from Solomon and the other from Nathan—were so interconnected through the remarriage of childless widows and the "resurrections" of offspring that the same persons could correctly be deemed as children of different parents at different times—sometimes of reputed fathers, sometimes of actual. Both accounts are therefore accurate, though complicated, as they bring the line down to Joseph.

To clarify, I will explain the relationship of the families. Reckoning the generations from David through Solomon [as does Matthew 1:15-16], the third from the end is Matthan, whose son was Jacob, the father of Joseph. But if we follow Luke [3:23-37] and reckon from Nathan, the son of David, the corresponding third from the end is Melchi, whose son was Heli, the father of Joseph. It must therefore be shown how both Heli and Jacob can be fathers of Joseph, and both Matthan and Melchi, belonging to two different families, were grandfathers.

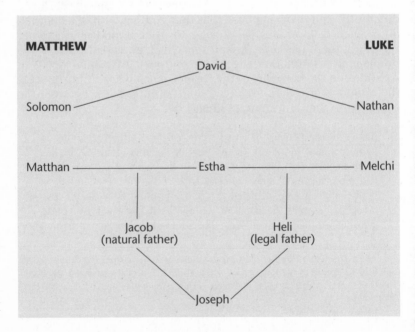

Now Matthan and Melchi, since they took the same wife, were fathers of stepbrothers, for the law permits a woman who has been divorced or widowed to marry again. Now Estha, the traditional name of the wife in question, first married Matthan (descended from Solomon) and bore him Jacob. When Matthan died, his widow married Melchi (descended from Nathan), of the same tribe but different family, and bore him Heli. Thus Jacob and Heli had the same mother, and when Heli died childless, his [half] brother Jacob married his widow and fathered Joseph by her. Joseph, then, was the natural son of Jacob but the legal son of Heli, for whom a good brother had "raised up" offspring. Matthew uses the term *begot* for physical descent, whereas Luke says, "who was, as was supposed"—note the addendum—"the son of Joseph, the son of Heli, the son of Melchi" [3:23-24]. It was impossible to express legal descent more precisely, and he never uses the term *begot* regarding such children in tracing the line back to "Adam, the son of God."

This is neither unprovable nor conjecture. The human relatives of the Savior have handed on this tradition also, either to boast or simply to give information, but in any case telling the truth. When Idumean bandits attacked the city of Ascalon in Palestine, they captured from the temple of Apollo Antipater, the child of a certain Herod, a temple servant. Because the priest was unable to pay ransom for his son, Antipater was raised as an Idumean and later befriended by the Judean high priest Hyrcanus. Sent to Pompey in Hyrcanus's behalf, he won for him [Hyrcanus] the restoration of his kingdom that had been seized by his brother Aristobulus, and so [Antipater] became overseer of Palestine. After he was treacherously assassinated, he was succeeded by his son Herod, who later was appointed king of the Jews by Antony, Augustus, and decree of the senate. His sons were Herod [Antipas] and the other tetrarchs. The Greek historians confirm this.

But the Hebrew families were still inscribed in the archives, as well as those descended from proselytes—Achion the Ammonite, Ruth the Moabitess, and mixed families who had left Egypt with them. So Herod, with no Israelite ancestry and pained by his base origins, burned the genealogical records, thinking he would appear of noble birth if no one were able to trace his bloodline from public documents. A few, however, carefully kept private records of their own, either remembering the names or finding them in copies, and took pride in preserving the memory of their aristocratic birth. Among these were the *desposyni*,[11] so called because of their relation to the Savior's family. Living in the Jewish villages of Nazareth and Cochaba, they went through the rest of the land, explaining the above genealogy of their descent and quoting from the book of daily records as much as they could. Whether or not this is true, no one could give a clearer explanation, and the Gospel record, in any case, *is* true.

At the end of this letter Africanus adds:

Matthan, Solomon's descendant, begot Jacob. When Matthan died, Melchi, Nathan's descendant, begot Heli with the same woman. Heli and Jacob thus had the same mother. When Heli died without children, Jacob raised up seed for him in fathering Joseph, his own natural son but Heli's legal son. Thus Joseph was the son of both.

This genealogy of Joseph is also virtual proof that Mary belonged to the same tribe as he, since, according to the law of Moses, it was illegal for the different tribes to intermarry. The command that partners be from the same town and clan is given so that the [family] inheritance might not be transferred from tribe to tribe.

Herod and the Infants of Bethlehem

c. 5 B.C.   **8.** Now when Christ was born, according to prophecy, at Bethlehem of Judea at the time already noted, magi from the East asked Herod where they could find the one born king of the Jews. They had seen his star, which had occasioned their long journey in their eagerness to worship the infant as God. The request greatly disturbed him [Herod]—he thought his sovereignty was in danger—and therefore he inquired among teachers of the Law where they expected the Christ to be born. When he learned of Micah's prophecy that it would be Bethlehem, he issued a single edict for the massacre of all infants two years old and under in Bethlehem and its vicinity, according to the time indicated by the magi, thinking that Jesus would surely share the same fate. The child, however, forestalled the plot by being taken to Egypt, since his parents had been forewarned by an angel. This is also reported in the sacred Gospel [of Matthew].

---

11. "Belonging to the master" in Greek, since Jesus was Lord or "Despot." In a spiritual context the Greek flavor of "despot" was not politically pejorative.

It is worth noting, in this regard, the result of Herod's crime against the Christ and the children of his age. Without any delay, the justice of God overtook him while he was still alive as prelude to what awaited him in the next world. Here it is not possible even to summarize the ways in which he darkened the reputed glories of his reign by the repulsive murder of wife, children, relatives, and friends. No tragic drama has darker shadows, as Josephus narrates at length in his histories. From the moment he plotted against our Savior and the other innocents, the scourge of God drove him to death. In Book 17 of his *Jewish Antiquities*, [Josephus] tells of his end:

Herod's illness progressively worsened as God exacted punishment for his crimes. A slow fire burned inside him, less obvious to the touch. He had an insatiable desire for food, ulcers in the intestines, terrible pain in the colon, and a clammy edema in his feet. His bladder was inflamed and his genitals gangrenous, breeding worms. His breathing was rapid and extremely offensive due to its stench, and every limb was convulsed intolerably. Wise onlookers declared that God was exacting retribution from the king for his many wicked deeds.[12]

In Book 2 of his *Jewish War*, Josephus provides a similar account:

The disease spread throughout his body with fever, an unbearable itching everywhere, continual pain in the colon, edema in the feet, inflammation of the abdomen, and gangrene in the wormy genitals. His breathing was difficult, especially if he lay down, and spasms shook each limb—a punishment, according to the diviners. Still he clung to life and planned his own treatment in hope of recovery. He crossed the Jordan and took the hot baths at Callirhoe that flow into the Dead Sea but are sweet and potable. The doctors there decided to warm his body by lowering him into a tub of hot oil, but he fainted, turning up his eyes as if dying. Noise from his attendants beating their breasts revived him, but he now gave up hope of recovery and ordered that fifty drachmas be given each of his soldiers and large sums to his officers and friends.

Returning to Jericho in extreme depression, he planned a final, monstrous crime. He assembled the most eminent men from every

---

12. *Antiquities* 17.168–70.

village in all Judea and had them locked inside the hippodrome. Then he told his sister Salome and her husband, Alexas: "I know the Jews will celebrate my death with rejoicing, but I can be mourned for the sake of others and have a splendid funeral if you do as I direct. Surround the men [in the hippodrome] with soldiers, and the moment I die, kill them all quickly, so that all Judea and every house will weep over me.". . .

Later, tortured by hunger and a convulsive cough, he tried to anticipate his fate. He took an apple and asked for a knife—he cut up apples when he ate them—and then raised his right hand to stab himself [but was prevented].[13]

4 B.C.   Josephus also relates that before he died, Herod ordered the execution of yet a third of his legitimate sons [Antipater], in addition to the two already murdered, and then died in great agony. Such was Herod's end, a just punishment for the children he murdered at Bethlehem and vicinity. After this, an angel appeared in a dream to Joseph while he was in Egypt and directed him to return to Judea with the child and his mother, declaring that those who sought the life of the little child were dead. The Evangelist continues: "But when he heard that Archelaus was ruling over Judea in place of his father Herod, he was afraid to go there. And after being warned in a dream, he went away to the district of Galilee" [Matt. 2:22].

Pilate and the Priests

9. Josephus corroborates Archelaus's succession, in accordance with Herod's will and Augustus's decision, and how, when he fell from power ten years later, his brothers Philip and the younger Herod [Antipas], together with Lysanias, continued to rule their own tetrarchies.

A.D. 26   In Book 18 of his *Antiquities,* the same author writes that Pontius Pilate was given the administration of Judea in the twelfth year of Tiberius, who had succeeded to the throne after the fifty-seven-year reign of Augustus, and that Pilate remained in office ten whole years, almost until Tiberius's death. This clearly proves that the recently published *Acts of Pilate*[14] are forgeries, since

---

13. Although Eusebius gives Book 2 of the *Jewish War* as his reference, this extract occurs in Book 1.656–60, 662 in our texts.

14. See 9.5 of this *Church History.* The *Acta* (the *Memoirs*) to which Eusebius refers were forgeries circulated at the time of the persecution under Maximin Daia (c.

they claim that the crime of the Savior's death occurred in the fourth consulship of Tiberius, which was the seventh year of his reign, a time when Pilate was not yet in charge of Judea. Josephus clearly states that it was in the *twelfth* year of his reign that Tiberius appointed Pilate procurator of Judea.[15]

10. When, according to the Evangelist [Luke], Tiberius Caesar was in the fifteenth year of his reign and Pontius Pilate in the fourth of his governorship, and Herod, Lysanias, and Philip were tetrarchs over the rest of Judea,[16] our Savior and Lord, Jesus the Christ of God—about thirty years old at the beginning [of his ministry]—came to the baptism of John and began proclaiming the Gospel.

A.D. 29

Holy Scripture states that he completed his teaching under the high priesthood of Annas and Caiaphas, thus beginning his mission under Annas and continuing to Caiaphas, a period that does not comprise four complete years. Life tenure for hereditary priests, according to the Law, was no longer the case, since Roman governors conferred the high priesthood first on one, then on another, who did not hold this office for more than one year.[17] In his *Antiquities,* Josephus records four high priests in the succession between Annas and Caiaphas:

> Valerius Gratus, having deprived Ananus [Annas] of the priesthood, appointed Ishmael the son of Phabi as high priest. Soon he removed him and named as high priest Eleazar, son of Ananus. After a year, he removed him too and transferred the high priesthood to Simon, son of Camithus. Nor did his tenure last for more than a year, and Joseph, also called Caiaphas, was his successor.[18]

---

312). The so-called *Acts of Pilate* extant today are apocryphal documents of Christian origin but just as fraudulent.

15. *Antiquities* 18.32ff., 85ff. Pilate was governor A.D. 26–36. His title was not "procurator," which is an anachronism in both Josephus and Tacitus, but "prefect," according to an inscription discovered at Caesarea in 1961.

16. Tiberius became emperor in A.D. 14, and his fifteenth year was A.D. 28–29. Eusebius inaccurately condenses Luke 3:1 here. Herod was in charge of Galilee, Lysanias of Abilene, and Philip of territories northeast of the Sea of Galilee.

17. This is incorrect. The Romans did change the high priesthood frequently, but there was no set term of office. Caiaphas, for example, was high priest for seventeen or eighteen years.

18. *Antiquities* 18.33–35.

A limestone ossuary, discovered on a slope south of the Old City of Jerusalem in 1990, is inscribed with the name of Joseph Caiaphas. Five whorl rosettes surround a center rosette inside the two great circles of this superbly carved bone chest, which most probably contained the remains of the Jewish high priest who indicted Jesus before Pontius Pilate (*Courtesy of Garo Nalbandian*).

A.D. 33   The whole period of our Savior's teaching thus was not even a full four years, since four high priests in four years from Annas to Caiaphas held the office for a year. Naturally, the Gospel named Caiaphas as high priest in the year of the Savior's passion, and so the time of Christ's teaching accords with this evidence.[19]

Our Savior and Lord called the twelve apostles shortly after the start of his preaching—of all his disciples he gave the name *apostles* to them only as a special privilege—and appointed sev-

---

19. The chronologies of Josephus and the Gospels do agree, but Eusebius's argument is faulty. In trying to interpret Luke 3:2 ("during the high priesthood of Annas and Caiaphas") as meaning the period between the two, he constructs his less-than-four-year time grid for Jesus' ministry. But this founders on the fact that Annas was dismissed by Gratus in A.D. 15. A better explanation of Luke's passage would point out the honorific nature of Annas's title as "high priest" even after leaving office, since he was the gray eminence in Jerusalem, the priestly patriarch who set a record in having five of his own sons and a son-in-law, Caiaphas, succeed to the high priesthood.

enty others whom he also sent out in advance, two by two, into every place or town where he himself planned to come.

John the Baptist and Jesus

11. Soon afterward, John the Baptist was beheaded by the younger Herod [Antipas], as we learn from the inspired Gospel [Mark 6:14–29]. Josephus confirms the Gospel narrative, mentioning Herodias by name and telling how Herod married her though she was the wife of his brother, who was still alive, and dismissed his own lawful wife, who was the daughter of King Aretas [IV] of Petra. For her sake also he put John to death and went to war with Aretas, whose daughter he had dishonored. Josephus says that the entire army of Herod was destroyed in battle as retribution for his plot against John. The same Josephus acknowledges that John was especially righteous and a baptizer, confirming the description of him in the Gospels. He also reports that Herod was stripped of his kingship because of the same Herodias and was exiled with her to   A.D. 39
Vienne, a city of Gaul. The story is found in *Antiquities,* Book 18, where he writes re garding John as follows:

> Now, to some of the Jews the destruction of Herod's army seemed to come from God as a very just recompense, a punishment for what he did to John who was called the Baptist. For Herod had executed him, though he was a good man and had exhorted the Jews to exercise virtue both in practicing justice toward one another and in piety toward God and, so doing, to join in baptism. For thus, it seemed to him, would baptismal washing be acceptable, if it were used not to gain pardon for whatever sins they committed but as a purification of the body, implying that the soul was already thoroughly cleansed by righteous conduct. When others also joined the crowds about him—for they were deeply stirred at hearing his words—Herod grew alarmed: such great influence over the people could lead to an uprising, for they seemed ready to do anything John might advise. Accordingly, Herod decided that it would be much better to strike first and get rid of him before any insurrection might develop than to get himself into trouble and be sorry not to have acted once a rebellion had begun. And so, due to Herod's suspicions, John was brought in chains to Machaerus, the fortress that we have previously mentioned, and there put to death.[20]

---

20. *Antiquities* 18.116–19.

THE PERSON AND WORK OF CHRIST

John the Baptist and Jesus

In telling this about John, he says the following concerning our Savior in the same historical work:

> About this time lived Jesus, a wise man, if indeed one ought to call him a man. For he was the achiever of extraordinary deeds and was a teacher of those who accept the truth gladly. He won over many Jews and many of the Greeks. He was the Messiah. When he was indicted by the principal men among us and Pilate condemned him to be crucified, those who had come to love him originally did not cease to do so; for he appeared to them on the third day restored to life, as the prophets of the Deity had foretold these and countless other marvelous things about him. And the tribe of Christians, so named after him, has not disappeared to this day.[21]

When a historian, himself a Hebrew, has provided in his own writing this evidence concerning John the Baptist and our Savior, what option is there but to condemn the shamelessness of those who forged the *Acts* concerning them?

The Disciples of Jesus

12. The names of the apostles are obvious to everyone from the Gospels, but no list of the seventy disciples has survived anywhere. It is said, however, that one of them was Barnabas, cited in the Acts of the Apostles and by Paul in writing to the Galatians [2:1, 9, 13]. They say that another of them was Sosthenes, who wrote with Paul to the Corinthians [1 Cor. 1:1]. Then there is the story in Clement (*Outlines*, Book 5) that the Cephas about whom Paul says, "But when Cephas came to Antioch, I opposed him to his face" [Gal. 2:11] was one of the Seventy, who had the same name as the apostle Peter.[22] Matthias also, who took Judas's place in the list of the apostles, as well as the [Justus] honored with him

---

21. *Antiquities* 18.63. This citation is of great importance because it demonstrates that this (unfortunately interpolated) version of Josephus's famous passage on Jesus read this way already in Eusebius's time. Scholars justifiably deny that Josephus, who did not convert to Christianity, ever claimed that Jesus was the Messiah who rose from the dead. Josephus's most probable original wording is in Appendix 1.

22. Clement of Alexandria (c. 155–c. 220) wrote the *Hypotyposes* (*Outlines*) as a biblical commentary. The suggestion that this Cephas was different from the apostle Peter is unfounded and merely an attempt to protect Peter from the apostolic squabble at Antioch that used to bother a few of the church fathers.

at the casting of lots [Acts 1:23], was called among the Seventy, according to tradition. They also claim that Thaddeus was one of them,[23] about whom a story has come to my attention that I shall shortly relate.

There were more disciples of the Savior than the Seventy. Paul states that after his resurrection Jesus was seen first by Cephas, then by the Twelve, and after these by more than five hundred brethren at once, some of whom, he says, had fallen asleep, but the majority were still alive at the time he wrote. Then, he says, he was seen by James, one of the alleged brothers of the Savior, and finally "by all the apostles" like Paul himself, a larger number patterned on the Twelve.

Thaddeus and the Prince of Edessa

13. Because of his miraculous powers the divinity of Christ was noised abroad everywhere, and myriads even in foreign lands remote from Judea came to him in the hope of healing from diseases of every kind. Thus, when King Abgar [V], the celebrated ruler of peoples beyond the Euphrates, was suffering terribly from an incurable illness and often heard the name of Jesus and his miracles, he sent him a request, via letter carrier, pleading for relief from his disease. Jesus did not consent to his request at the time but favored him with a personal letter, promising to send one of his disciples to cure the disease and bring salvation to him and his relatives.

The promise was soon fulfilled. After his [Jesus'] resurrection and ascension, Thomas, one of the Twelve, was divinely inspired to send Thaddeus, one of the Seventy, to Edessa as preacher and evangelist, who fulfilled all the terms of our Savior's promise. There is written evidence of this taken from the archives at Edessa, the then royal capital, which include ancient history as well as the events at Abgar's time. Here are the letters themselves, which I have extracted from the archives and translated word for word from the Syriac:

COPY OF A LETTER WRITTEN BY ABGAR THE TOPARCH
TO JESUS, SENT TO HIM AT JERUSALEM
BY THE COURIER ANANIAS

---

23. But one of the Twelve, according to Matt. 10:3 and Mark 3:18, and apparently identical with Jude.

Abgar Uchama, the Toparch, to Jesus the excellent Savior who has appeared in the region of Jerusalem, greeting.

I have heard about you and the cures you accomplish without drugs or herbs. Word has it that you make the blind see and the lame walk, that you heal lepers and cast out unclean spirits and demons, and that you cure those tortured by chronic disease and raise the dead. When I heard all these things about you, I decided that one of two things is true: either you are God and came down from heaven to do these things or you are God's Son for doing them. For this reason I am writing to beg you to take the trouble to come to me and heal my suffering. I have also heard that the Jews are murmuring against you and plot to harm you. Now, my city-state is very small but highly regarded and adequate for both of us.

(He wrote this letter when the divine light had only begun to shine on him. It is appropriate to hear also the letter that Jesus sent him by the same letter carrier. It is only a few lines long but very powerful:)[24]

THE REPLY OF JESUS TO THE TOPARCH
ABGAR BY THE COURIER ANANIAS

Blessed are you who believed in me without seeing me! For it is written that those who have seen me will not believe in me and that those who have not seen me will believe and live. Now regarding your request that I come to you, I must first complete all that I was sent to do here, and, once that is completed, must be taken up to the One who sent me. When I have been taken up, I will send one of my disciples to heal your suffering and bring life to you and yours.

The following is appended to these letters in Syriac:[25]

After the ascension of Jesus, Judas, who is also called Thomas, sent Thaddeus, one of the Seventy, to [Abgar], and he stayed with Tobias, son of Tobias. When Abgar heard that Thaddeus was healing every disease and weakness, he suspected that he was the one about whom Jesus had written. He therefore ordered Tobias to bring Thaddeus to him. So Tobias told Thaddeus, "The Toparch Abgar has instructed me

---

24. The passage in parentheses is missing in some manuscripts.

25. This addendum is somewhat condensed, since the original is incredibly redundant and obviously contrived. No factual material, however, has been surrendered.

to bring you to him so that you might heal him." Thaddeus replied, "I will go, since I have been sent to him with power."

Tobias rose early the next morning and took Thaddeus to see Abgar, surrounded by his nobility. When they arrived, Abgar saw a marvelous vision on the face of Thaddeus and bowed down to him, asking, "Are you really a disciple of Jesus, the Son of God, who wrote to me, 'I will send you one of my disciples to heal you and give you life'?"

"I was sent to you for this reason," Thaddeus replied. "If you believe in him, your prayers shall be answered in proportion to your faith."

"I believed in him so firmly that I wanted to take an army and destroy the Jews who crucified him, had I not been prevented by Roman power."

Christianity spread rapidly into the eastern Mediterranean world, the area shown in this map. Edessa, at the top right of this map, was a city in northwestern Mesopotamia near the upper bend of the Euphrates River. Eusebius reported that its ruler, Abgar, corresponded with Jesus during his public ministry.

"Our Lord has fulfilled the will of his Father," said Thaddeus. "After fulfilling it, he has been taken up to the Father."

"I too have believed in him and in his Father."

"For this reason I put my hand on you in his name."

When he did this, Abgar was immediately cured—and without drugs and herbs, just as in the healings of Jesus. Abdus, son of Abdus, fell at Thaddeus's feet and was similarly cured of his gout, while many other fellow citizens of theirs were healed. Abgar then asked Thaddeus for further information about Jesus.

Thaddeus replied: "Please assemble all your citizens tomorrow, and I will tell them about the coming of Jesus and his mission, about the Father's purpose in sending him, about his deeds and power and preaching, about his humility that made light of his divinity, and of how he was crucified and raised from the dead, descending to hades alone but ascending with a multitude to his Father."

So Abgar assembled his citizens at daybreak to hear the preaching of Thaddeus, after which he ordered that gold and silver be given him. But Thaddeus refused, asking, "If we have left behind our own property, how can we accept that of others?"

This all took place in the year 340.[26]

Let this useful and literal translation from the Syriac suffice for now.   .

---

26. The year is according to the Edessene calendar, which began in 310 B.C.; thus it is A.D. 30, three or four years too early to reflect the most accurate date for the crucifixion (A.D. 33).

EUSEBIUS ON JESUS

In Christianity's earliest history, one might have hoped for additional strategic detail on the life of Jesus to supplement the biblical record. Were there no further traditions on the childhood and ministry of Jesus, for example, that Eusebius might have recorded?

Either the traditions had been lost or Eusebius focused instead on what he deemed the most critical portion of his information on Christ: his preexistence and messiahship. Much as George Frederick Handel focused far more of his oratorio *Messiah* on Old Testament prophecy than on New Testament fulfillment, so Eusebius felt impelled to demonstrate that the Son of God was eternal and preexistent, not limited by temporal or geographical constraints. He was meeting a common objection to Christianity as a new system invented in the first century. For this reason many other early Christian authors also devoted much attention to Christ's preexistence and to Old Testament prophecies they found fulfilled in him.

Eusebius was equally concerned, however, to demonstrate the true historicity of the man Jesus. He made no appeals to blind faith but instead marshaled whatever nonbiblical sources he could find to show how well they corroborated the New Testament Gospels. Flavius Josephus was especially valuable for this purpose, as the Jewish historian has proved to be ever since.

In citing the writings of Julius Africanus regarding the divergent genealogies of Jesus, Eusebius unveils a pattern he will use throughout his history: to incorporate, with due credit, some of the most important historical sources word for word in his own record. Many crucial documents, accordingly, survive only in Eusebius, long after the original documents were lost. The problem of the genealogies also shows how ancient are many of the issues apparently just discovered by modern critics.

The story of Abgar's correspondence with Jesus, however sensational, must be regarded as apocryphal. There is no doubt that these documents were in the archives at Edessa, a city in extreme northwestern Mesopotamia near the upper bend of the Euphrates, and that Eusebius himself saw and translated them. Quite apart from other legendary aspects of the story, the spurious nature of these documents is indicated by Jesus referring to items written about him at a time when they could not yet have been written down. Eusebius was not a critical historian in the modern sense.

This narrative, however, is a romanticizing of factual material: Christianity reached Edessa early, at least by A.D. 150, and its king, probably Abgar VIII, was baptized. A church was constructed at Edessa; the Greek New Testament was translated here into Syriac, and this is also the home of the Christian scholars Tatian and Bardesanes, whom Eusebius will mention subsequently.

Each of the end commentaries in this book will conclude with a very brief overview of Roman imperial politics during the period covered in each book, since Eusebius arranged his history in segments corresponding to the reigns of the emperors ruling at the time. Book 2, for example, covers the period from Tiberius through Nero.

Unlike subsequent books of the *Church History*, Book 1 covers a vast expanse of time, from the Old Testament prophets through Jesus' birth, ministry, death, and resurrection. In chapter 5 of this first book, however, Eusebius starts to superimpose a Roman imperial time grid on his account by introducing, as did Luke, the emperor who was ruling at the time of Jesus' birth, namely, Caesar Augustus.

Augustus (27 B.C.–A.D. 14)[27] was Rome's first and probably greatest emperor. His fascinating career began in the bloody civil wars of the late Roman republic, blossomed after his victory over archrival Mark Antony, and culminated in a long era of peace and prosperity, appropriately named the *Pax Augusta*. During the forty-four years that he was head of state he reshaped the government of Rome into a form that would endure for the next three centuries. To the already sprawling empire, he added Egypt as well as all unconquered lands up to the Rhine-Danube frontier, establishing these two river systems as the natural boundaries of the Roman Empire. At home he worked harmoniously with the senate, and his vast building enterprises lent substance to his claim: "I found Rome brick and left her marble."

Less familiar than these successes and conquests is his interesting religious policy. Convinced that the public's neglect of the

---

27. Such dates following the names of emperors are their regnal years. Julius Caesar's grandnephew Octavian achieved sole power after his victory over Antony at the battle of Actium in 31 B.C. and was named Augustus by the Roman senate in 27.

Greco-Roman gods was demoralizing Roman society, he tried to stimulate a religious revival by restoring or erecting temples—eighty-two in Rome alone—and inspiring a moral renewal in society. He could never know that this would best be accomplished by a baby born in the middle of his administration at far-off Bethlehem in Judea. When Augustus died in the month named after him—August 19, A.D. 14—Jesus was a late teenager in Nazareth. His public ministry would take place under the emperor Tiberius, who is portrayed in the next chapter.

(A list of the Roman emperors, correlated with listings of the bishops of Rome, Jerusalem, Alexandria, and Antioch, is given in Appendix 2.)

Paul (left) and James the Just (right) hold the Scriptures in this early mosaic (*Martorana, Palermo*).

BOOK 2

THE APOSTLES

TIBERIUS TO NERO

As preface to the history of the church, I provided proof in the preceding book for the divinity of the saving Word and for the antiquity of our teaching and way of life, as well as details concerning [Jesus'] recent advent, the events before his passion, and the choice of his apostles. In the present book, let us now consider what followed his ascension, drawing on Holy Scripture as well as other sources that I shall quote from time to time.

The Jerusalem Apostles

1. Matthias, who had been one of the Lord's disciples, was chosen for apostleship in place of the traitor Judas. To administer the common fund, seven worthy men, led by Stephen, were appointed to the diaconate by prayer and the laying on of the apostles' hands. Stephen was the first after the Lord not only in ordination, but also in being put to death, stoned by the Lord's murderers, and so was the first to win the crown, represented in his name,[1] that was gained by the martyrs of Christ deemed worthy of victory.

James was called the brother of the Lord since he too was called Joseph's son, and Joseph Christ's father—though the Virgin was his betrothed and before they came together she was found to have conceived by the Holy Spirit, as the inspired Gospel tells us [Matt. 1:18]. This same James, whom early Christians surnamed "the Just" for his outstanding virtue, was the first to be elected to the bishop's throne of the church in Jerusalem. Clement [of Alexandria], in *Outlines*, Book 6, puts it as follows:

---

1. *Stephanos* in Greek means "crown."

Peter, James, and John, after the Savior's ascension, did not contend for the honor, because they had previously been favored by the Savior, but chose James the Just as Bishop of Jerusalem.

In Book 7 of the same work, the writer also says this about him:

> After the resurrection the Lord imparted the higher knowledge [gnosis] to James the Just, John, and Peter. They gave it to the other apostles, and the other apostles to the Seventy, one of whom was Barnabas. Now there were two Jameses: one, James the Just, who was thrown down from the parapet [of the temple] and beaten to death with a fuller's club; the other, the James who was beheaded [Acts 12:2].

Paul also mentions James the Just when he writes: "But I did not see any other apostle except James the Lord's brother" [Gal. 1:19].

At this time also, our Savior's promise to the king of the Osrhoenes was being fulfilled. Thomas was inspired to send Thaddeus to Edessa, as previously stated, and he healed Abgar by the word of Christ, amazing all the inhabitants by his wonderful miracles. He brought them to venerate the power of Christ and made them disciples of the saving doctrine. From that day to this the whole city-state of Edessa has been devoted to Christ, thus demonstrating our Savior's goodness also to them.

We return once more to the divine Scripture. Stephen's martyrdom was followed by the first and greatest persecution of the church in Jerusalem by the Jews. All the disciples, except for the Twelve, were scattered about Judea and Samaria. Some, as the divine Scripture says, traveled as far as Phoenicia, Cyprus, and Antioch, but they could not yet try to share the faith with Gentiles and proclaimed it only to Jews. At that time Paul was also still ravaging the church, entering the houses of the faithful, dragging out men and women, and committing them to prison.

Philip, however, one of those who had been ordained with Stephen to the diaconate, was among those dispersed. He went to Samaria and, filled with divine power, was the first to preach the word there. So great was the divine grace at work with him that even Simon Magus and many others were captivated by his words. Simon had gained such fame by the wizardry with which he controlled his victims that he was believed to be the Great Power of God. But even he was so overwhelmed by the wonders Philip performed through divine power that he insinuated himself [into the faith], hypocritically feigning belief in Christ even to the point of baptism. (This is still done by those who continue his foul heresy to the present day: following the practice of their progenitor, they fasten onto the church like a noxious and scabby disease, destroying all whom they succeed in smearing with the dreadful, deadly poison hidden in them. But most of these have been expelled by now, just as Simon himself paid the proper punishment once his real nature was exposed by Peter.)

While the saving message spread day by day, some providence brought from Ethiopia an officer of the queen, for that nation is still traditionally ruled by a woman. He was the first Gentile to receive the divine Word from Philip by revelation and the first to return to his native land and preach the Gospel. Through him the prophecy was actually fulfilled that states, "Ethiopia shall stretch out its hands to God" [Ps. 68:31].

Paul was appointed an apostle in addition to these, the chosen vessel neither of men nor through men but through revelation of Jesus Christ himself and God the Father who raised him from the dead. He received his call by a vision and the heavenly voice accompanying the revelation.

Tiberius Learns about Christ

2. Our Savior's extraordinary resurrection and ascension into heaven were by now famous everywhere. It was customary for provincial governors to report to the [Roman] emperor any new local movement so that he might be kept informed. Accordingly, Pilate communicated to the emperor Tiberius the story of Jesus' resurrection from the dead as already well known throughout Palestine, as well as information he had gained on his other marvelous deeds and how many believed him to be a god in rising from the dead. They say that Tiberius referred the report to the senate, which rejected it, allegedly because it had not dealt with the matter before. According to an old law, still in effect, no one could be deemed a god by the Romans unless by vote and decree of the senate, but the real reason was that the divine message did not require human ratification. In this way, the Roman council rejected the report submitted to it regarding our Savior, but Tiberius maintained his opinion and made no evil plans against the teaching of Christ.

Tertullian, a famed, distinguished expert on Roman law, has noted this in his *Defense of the Christians*, written in Latin and translated into Greek:

> There was an old decree that no one should be consecrated as a god by an emperor before he had been approved by the senate. Marcus Aemilius observed this procedure in the case of a certain idol, Alburnus. This underscores our argument that you [Romans] confer deity through human approval—if a god does not please man, he does not become god—so man must have mercy on god in your system! Tiberius then, in whose time the name *Christian* came into the world, when this doctrine was reported to him from Palestine, where it began, communicated it to the senate, plainly indicating that he favored the doctrine. The senate, however, rejected it, because it had not itself reviewed it; but Tiberius stuck to his own opinion and threatened death to any who accused the Christians.[2]

Heavenly providence had intentionally put this in his mind so that the word of the Gospel might get off to a good start and span the earth in all directions.

3. Thus the saving word started to brighten the whole world like rays of the sun. In every city and village, churches mushroomed, crowded with myriads of members. Those chained by superstition and idolatry found release through the power of Christ as well as the teaching and wonderful deeds of his followers. Rejecting demonic polytheism, they confessed the one God and Creator of the universe whom they honored with the rational worship implanted by our Savior.

Now the divine grace was being poured out also on the other nations. First Cornelius and his whole household at Palestinian Caesarea embraced Christianity through divine revelation and Peter's ministry. So did many other [Gentile] Greeks at Antioch who heard the preaching of those scattered in the persecution of Stephen's time. The church at Antioch was now flourishing and multiplying, and it was at that time and place—when many of the prophets from Jerusalem as well as Barnabas, Paul, and other brethren

---

2. Tertullian *Defense* 5. There is no record in secular sources of Tiberius's support of Christianity. That Pontius Pilate would have submitted annual *acta* or reports to his emperor that might well have included mention of Jesus is not improbable. The surviving *Acta Pilati*, however, are apocryphal, and those circulating at Eusebius's time (see 9.5) were also spurious.

were present—that the name *Christian* first appeared. One of the prophets, Agabus, predicted that there would be a famine, and Paul and Barnabas were sent to aid the brethren [in Judea].

Caligula, Philo, and Pilate

A.D. 37   **4.** After reigning about twenty-two years, Tiberius died, and the sovereignty passed to Gaius [Caligula], who at once conferred the crown on [Herod] Agrippa. He made him king of the tetrarchies of Philip and Lysanias and soon added to them the tetrarchy of Herod [Antipas]—the Herod of our Savior's passion—sentencing him and his wife Herodias to permanent exile for many offenses. Of this Josephus is also a witness.

In his [Gaius's] reign Philo grew famed as one of the greatest scholars, a Hebrew who was the equal of any of the magnates in authority in Alexandria. The quantity and quality of his studies in theology, philosophy, and the liberal arts are plain for all to see, and he surpassed all his contemporaries as an authority on Plato and Pythagoras.

5. Philo has reported in five books what happened to the Jews in the reign of Gaius: the insanity of the emperor, how he proclaimed himself a god and committed innumerable insolent deeds, the misery of the Jews in his time, Philo's mission to Rome on behalf of his compatriots in Alexandria, and how he received nothing but laughter and ridicule from Gaius in defending their ancestral laws and narrowly escaped with his life.

Josephus also relates these details in *Antiquities*, Book 18, as follows:

> When a riot took place in Alexandria between the Jews living there and the Greeks, three from each side were chosen to go as representatives to Gaius. Apion, one of the Alexandrian representatives, brought many charges against the Jews, claiming in particular that they neglected to honor Caesar and that when all Roman subjects erected altars and temples to Gaius as they did the gods, the Jews alone thought it disgraceful to honor him with statues or swear by his name. Philo—the skilled philosopher and head of the Jewish delegation, brother of Alexander the Alabarch—capably refuted the charges until Gaius cut him short, told him to leave, and became so enraged that he was clearly at the point of taking drastic measures against them. So Philo left, deeply insulted, and told his Jewish asso-

ciates to have courage: even if Gaius was furious with them he was in fact already at war with God.[3]

Thus far Josephus. Philo himself, in *The Embassy,* provides a detailed account of what he did at that time. I shall omit most of it, citing only those items that will demonstrate the calamities that quickly befell the Jews as a consequence of their crimes against Christ. He relates that in Rome at the time of Tiberius, the most influential member of the imperial court, Sejanus,[4] took steps to eradicate the entire race. Meanwhile in Judea, Pilate, under whom the crime against the Savior was committed, made an attempt on the temple in Jerusalem, contrary to the privileges accorded the Jews, and harassed them severely, **6.** while after the death of Tiberius, the emperor Gaius inflicted outrages on many, but most of all on the whole Jewish race. This may be learned from [Philo's] own words:

Now Gaius was extremely capricious toward everyone, but the Jewish race in particular. He hated them so fiercely that, beginning in Alexandria, he seized the synagogues in city after city and filled them with images and statues of himself—in granting permission to erect them, it was he who set them up—and in the Holy City he tried to transform the temple, which was still untouched and deemed inviolable, into a shrine of his own, to be called "The Temple of Jupiter Manifest, Gaius the Younger."[5]

In a second work, *On the Virtues,* the same writer tells of countless other atrocities that were inflicted on the Jews in Alexandria during the same reign. Josephus confirms this and also shows that the misfortunes that befell the whole nation began at the time of Pilate and the crimes against the Savior. In Book 2 of the *Jewish War,* he states:

Pilate, sent by Tiberius as procurator of Judea, brought into Jerusalem at night covered images of Caesar that are called standards. When day arrived this provoked a huge commotion among the Jews,

---

3. *Antiquities* 18.257–60.

4. L. Aelius Sejanus was prefect of the Praetorian Guard under Tiberius and nearly overthrew him in a coup attempt that was discovered in A.D. 31.

5. Philo *Embassy to Gaius* 43. He was designated the "younger Gaius" to differentiate him from Gaius Julius Caesar, who was also deified.

who were shocked at how their laws had been trampled upon, since they do not permit any image to be set up in the city.[6]

Now if you compare this with the account in the Gospels, you will see that it was not long before their own cry came back to haunt them, when they shouted before Pilate that they had no king but Caesar [John 19:15]. Josephus then goes on to report another disaster that befell them:

> After this [Pilate] incited another riot by spending funds from the sacred treasury known as Corban to build an aqueduct three hundred stadia long.[7] This aroused the fury of the populace, and when Pilate visited Jerusalem they surrounded him with howls of derision. But he had foreseen this uproar and had arranged that armed soldiers mingle wit h the crowd disguised in civilian clothing, with orders not to use their swords but to club those who shouted. He now signaled for this from his tribunal, and the Jews were beaten, many dying from the blows and many from being trampled to death by their compatriots as they fled. The mob, horrified at this mortal calamity, fell silent.[8]

The same writer shows that numerous other revolts broke out in Jerusalem besides this, confirming that from then on factionalism, war, and mutual plotting never ceased in the city and throughout Judea until the final scene of all: the siege under Vespasian. Such was the retribution of divine justice upon the Jews for their crimes against Christ.

7. It is also worthy of note that in the reign of Gaius, whose times I have described, Pilate himself—he of the Savior's era—is reported to have fallen into such misfortune that he was forced to become his own executioner and to punish himself with his own hand. Divine justice, it seems, did not delay his punishment for long. Those who record the Olympiads of the Greeks and the events occurring in each relate this.[9]

---

6. *Jewish War* 2.169–70.

7. Eusebius apparently averaged the two divergent figures Josephus gives for the length of this aqueduct: two hundred stadia in *Antiquities* 18.60 and four hundred stadia in *Jewish War* 2.175. The lower figure, two hundred stadia, is more likely and equals about twenty-three miles. The Greek *stadion* measured 606.75 feet.

8. *Jewish War* 2.175–77.

9. No surviving sources confirm Eusebius's claim of Pilate's suicide. Indeed, the

Claudius and Agrippa

8. Gaius had not finished four years of rule when Claudius suc- A.D. 41
ceeded him as emperor. In his time, famine afflicted the whole
world (as writers with a purpose quite different from ours have
recorded in their histories),[10] and so the prophecy of Agabus
in the Acts of the Apostles that a famine would occur all over
the world was fulfilled. Luke describes the famine at the time of
Claudius and tells how the Christians at Antioch, each according
to his ability, sent aid to those in Judea via Paul and Barnabas
[Acts 11:28–29]. He goes on to say:

9. "About that time"—clearly that of Claudius—"King Herod laid
violent hands on some who belonged to the church and killed
James the brother of John with the sword" [Acts 12:1–2]. In Book
7 of *Outlines,* Clement adds an interesting tradition regarding
James that the man who brought him into court was so moved by
his testimony that he confessed that he too was a Christian:

> So they were both taken away together, and on the way he asked James
> to forgive him. James looked at him for a moment and replied, "Peace be
> with you" and kissed him. So both were beheaded at the same time.

Then, as Scripture says, Herod [Agrippa], seeing that James's
execution pleased the Jews, arrested Peter also, put him in prison,
and would have murdered him, too, but for divine intervention:
an angel stood by him at night, and he was miraculously released
from prison and set free for the ministry of preaching.

10. Divine justice brought swift retribution to the king for his plots
against the apostles, as Acts records. He had gone to Caesarea, and
there on a feast day, adorned in magnificent royal attire, he delivered an address while standing on a dais in front of his throne.

---

earlier testimony of Origen suggests that nothing negative happened to Pilate (*Against
Celsus* 2.34). Eusebius himself ascribes this to tradition, and in his *Chronicon* he cites
"the Roman historians" rather than the Greek as his source for the same claim (J. P.
Migne, Patrologia Graeca [Paris: 1857], 19:538), demonstrating that he had trouble
documenting this.

10. Tacitus reports a famine during the reign of Claudius among the events of
A.D. 51 (*Annals* 12.43), as does Dio Cassius (60.11). Eusebius, following Acts 11:28,
exaggerates its severity.

The entire audience applauded his address as if it were delivered by a god, not a man, but the inspired Word reports that an angel of the Lord struck him instantly, and he was eaten by worms and died [Acts 12:19-23]. It is astonishing how this marvel in the divine Scripture is supported also by Josephus in *Antiquities*, Book 19, where he relates the amazing story in the following words:

> He had completed his third year as king of all Judea when he came to the city of Caesarea, formerly called Strato's Tower. There he was celebrating games in Caesar's honor, a festival for his safety that was attended by a large number of officials and other leaders in the province. On the second day of the games he put on a robe woven entirely of silver, a remarkable fabric, and entered the theater at the beginning of the day. When the silver reflected the first glint of the sun's rays it glittered so dazzlingly that those who gazed at it were terrified. His flatterers immediately shouted on all sides—though hardly for his benefit—and addressed him as a god, saying, "Be gracious! Until now we have revered you as a man, but henceforth we confess that you are of more than mortal nature." The king did not reprimand them or reject their blasphemous flattery.
>
> A moment later he looked up and saw an angel sitting above his head.[11] This he immediately perceived to be a messenger of evil as it had once been of good. He felt an instant pain in his heart and a growing agony in his stomach. Looking to his friends, he said, "I, your god, am now ordered to surrender my life, since fate has instantly disproved the lies you just uttered about me. He whom you called immortal is now being taken away to die. Fate must be accepted as God has willed it. Nor have I lived a poor life, but in a splendor that people envy."
>
> While he was saying this, the intensity of his pain grew overwhelming, so he was quickly carried into the palace, and the news spread that he would surely die shortly. According to ancestral law, the crowd sat down on sackcloth, with their wives and children, and began to pray God for the king, wailing and lamentation resounding

---

11. In *Antiquities* 19.346 Josephus states that Agrippa saw not an angel but "an owl perched on a rope over his head, and immediately interpreted it as a messenger of evil, as it had previously been of good." Agrippa had been told by a fellow prisoner on Capri that when he saw an owl, he would be released from prison—which presumably happened—but a second owl would be a harbinger of imminent death. Since Josephus terms the owl a "messenger"—*angelos* in Greek, the same term as for angel—Eusebius's failure to quote Josephus correctly is less egregious than it appears. This very rare slip on Eusebius's part has been the subject of much scholarly comment.

The reconstructed theater at Caesarea, looking northwest toward the Mediterranean. Herod Agrippa I suffered the sudden seizure preceding his death here.

everywhere. The king, lying in a room on the top floor, looked down on them as they fell prostrate and could not restrain his own tears. After being tortured by stomach pains for five days, he passed away in the seventh year of his reign at age fifty-four. He had ruled four years in the time of Gaius Caesar. He possessed the tetrarchy of Philip for three years but received also that of Herod [Antipas] in the fourth, continuing for three more years while Claudius Caesar was emperor.[12]

A.D. 44

In this and other matters, Josephus confirms the truth of the divine Scriptures in a surprising manner. If some think there is a discrepancy regarding the king's name, the date and the events show that he is the same. Either the name has been changed due to copyist's error or the same man had two names, as often happens.[13]

Josephus on Theudas

11. Again in Acts, at the examination of the apostles, Luke introduces Gamaliel as saying that Theudas raised a rebellion, claiming to be somebody, and that he was killed and his whole

---

12. *Antiquities* 19.343-51.

13. "Herod" and "Agrippa" would be a case in point.

following scattered [5:34–36]. Let us compare this with what Josephus writes about him:

> When Fadus was procurator of Judea, a certain impostor named Theudas persuaded a vast multitude to take their belongings and follow him to the river Jordan. Claiming that he was a prophet, he promised to part the river by his command and provide them an easy crossing, which deceived many. Fadus, however, did not permit them to enjoy their delusion but sent a company of cavalry against them that attacked without warning. They killed many, took many alive, captured Theudas himself, cut off his head, and brought it to Jerusalem.[14]

Just after this he also refers to the famine that took place in the time of Claudius:

> 12. At this time a great famine occurred in Judea, in which Queen Helena brought grain from Egypt at great expense and distributed it among the needy.[15]

This, too, correlates with the account in Acts, which tells how the disciples at Antioch, each according to his means, sent relief to the elders in Judea through Barnabas and Paul [11:29–30]. Splendid monuments of this Helena are pointed out in the suburbs of what is now called Aelia[16] to this day. She was said to have been queen of Adiabene.

Simon Magus and Peter

13. With faith in our Lord Jesus Christ reaching all people, the enemy of salvation planned to capture the imperial city in advance and sent Simon there, cited previously, and by assisting his sorcery took possession of many in Rome and led them astray. This is reported by Justin [Martyr], an ornament of our faith soon after

---

14. *Antiquities* 20.97–98. Since Fadus was procurator in A.D. 44–46, Gamaliel, speaking a decade earlier, could not have referred to this Theudas, a fact that Eusebius surprisingly overlooks. Critics fault Acts for inaccuracy here, while conservative scholars assume Luke was referring to an earlier Theudas.

15. *Antiquities* 20.101.

16. Hadrian renamed Jerusalem Aelia Capitolina, which sparked the Bar-Kokhba rebellion of the Jews in A.D. 132. The tomb of Queen Helena of Adiabene, a state on the upper reaches of the Tigris River, is extant in Jerusalem.

the apostles—on whom more later—who writes as follows in his
first *Defense* of our doctrines to Antoninus [Pius]:

> After the Lord's ascension, the demons presented men who claimed
> to be gods, and they not only escaped being persecuted by you but
> even became objects of worship. Simon, a Samaritan from a village
> called Gittho, worked wonders through magic in Claudius's time,
> thanks to the demons who possessed him. He was deemed a god
> at Rome and honored as a god with a statue in the river Tiber
> between the two bridges. It carries this inscription in Latin: SIMONI
> DEO SANCTO. Nearly all Samaritans and a few in other nations also
> acknowledge him as their chief deity and worship him. And a woman
> named Helen, who traveled around with him but had previously lived
> in a brothel [at Tyre], they call the First Emanation from him.[17]

This is Justin's version, and Irenaeus agrees with him in
Book 1 of his *Against Heresies,* where he collects stories about
Simon and his foul and sordid teaching that are available to any
interested. According to tradition, Simon was the original author
of all heresies. From his time down to ours, his followers, while
pretending Christianity, prostrate themselves before pictures and
images of Simon and Helen, worshiping them with incense, sacrifices, and libations. Their more secret rites are so full of frenzy,
madness, and degradation that they cannot be reported in writing or words. Whatever is more disgusting than the foulest crime
imaginable is surpassed by the utterly repulsive heresy of these
men, who, drenched in vice, make sport of wretched women.

14. Of such evil Simon was the father. Nevertheless, our Savior's
inspired apostles quickly extinguished the flames of the Evil One
before they could spread, and no conspiracy by Simon or any of
his contemporaries succeeded in those apostolic days. After the
impostor's crimes were exposed in Judea by the apostle Peter, he
quickly fled overseas from East to West so that he could live as
he wished. Arriving in Rome, he achieved such success that the
citizens erected his statue and honored him as a god. But his success was brief. Hot on his heels in the same reign of Claudius, a

---

17. The Latin inscription means "To Simon, holy god." A statue to which Justin
probably referred was found on an island in the Tiber in 1574, but it bears the
inscription SEMONI SANCO DEO, that is, "To the god Semo Sancus" (an old Sabine
deity).

gracious Providence brought to Rome the great and mighty Peter, chosen for his merits as leader of the other apostles. Like a noble captain of God, he **15.** proclaimed the Gospel of light and the Word that saves souls. With this divine Word, Simon's power was extinguished and destroyed immediately, along with the man himself.

Peter's hearers, not satisfied with a single hearing or with the unwritten teaching of the divine message, pleaded with Mark, whose Gospel we have, to leave them a written summary of the teaching given them verbally, since he was a follower of Peter. Nor did they cease until they persuaded him and so caused the writing of what is called the Gospel according to Mark. It is said that the apostle was delighted at their enthusiasm and approved the reading of the book in the churches. Clement quotes the story in *Outlines,* Book 6, and Bishop Papias of Hierapolis confirms it. He also points out that Peter mentions Mark in his first epistle and that he composed this in Rome, which they say he himself indicates when referring to the city figuratively as Babylon in the words, "Your sister church in Babylon, chosen together with you, sends you greetings; and so does my son Mark" [1 Peter 5:13].

16. Mark is said to have been the first sent to Egypt to preach the Gospel that he had also written down and the first to found churches in Alexandria itself. So great was the number of converts, both men and women, and so extraordinary their asceticism that Philo thought it appropriate to describe their conduct, gatherings, meals, and way of life.

Philo on the Egyptian Ascetics

17. Tradition claims that Philo came to Rome in the time of Claudius to converse with Peter, then preaching to the people there.[18] Nor is this improbable, since the writing to which I refer clearly contains the rules of the church still observed in our time. His very accurate description of our ascetics, moreover, shows that he not only knew but also welcomed and approved the apostolic men of his day, who were apparently of Hebrew origin. In his *On the Contemplative Life or Suppliants,* he says that they were called

---

18. This is extremely doubtful. Jerome goes even further and claims that Philo became a Christian (*Illustrious Men* 11), a claim that is unsupported by Philo's own works.

Therapeutae and their women *Therapeutrides*.[19] This name was given either because, like doctors, they cure and heal the souls of those who come to them or because of their pure and sincere service and worship of the Divine. Whether he invented this term or whether they were actually called this because the title of Christian had not yet come into general use need not detain us.

In any case, he stresses their renunciation of property, stating that when they follow [this] philosophy, they surrender their possessions to relatives, move outside the walls, and make their homes in deserts and secluded oases, well aware that association with those of different ideas is unprofitable and harmful as they emulate the ardent faith of the prophets. Similarly in Acts, the disciples sold their possessions and laid the proceeds at the apostles' feet so that it could be distributed to each according to need [4:34–35]. Philo continues:

> The race is found in many parts of the world, for that which is good should have been shared by both Greeks and foreigners. It is very strong in each of the Egyptian nomes and especially around Alexandria. The best men in each region go as colonists to the most suitable spot as if homeland for the *Therapeutae*. This district is situated on a low hill above Lake Mareotis, well suited as to security and mild climate.

He then describes the nature of their dwellings and says this about the churches in the area:

> In each house there is a sacred chamber called "a sanctuary or monastery," where they celebrate in private the mysteries of the sacred life, bringing in nothing but law and inspired oracles of prophets, hymns, and whatever augments knowledge and true religion. . . . The whole period from dawn to dusk is dedicated to spiritual discipline. They read the sacred Scriptures and interpret their ancestral philosophy allegorically, since they regard the literal sense as symbolic of a reality

---

19. "Healers." Eusebius's suggestion that these were early Christian monastics cannot be accepted, since such monasticism had not yet developed in Philo's time. These "healers" were either an example of Jewish asceticism (akin to the Essenes), or *The Contemplative Life* itself is not Philonic but was likely written by a late-third-century Christian apologist for monasticism. The latter would justify Eusebius's impression that they were Christian but expose a lapse in his critical ability. Eusebius is the first writer to mention this work.

hidden beneath the surface. They also have writings by founders of their sect that they use as models of the allegorical method.

This seems to have been said by someone who had heard their exposition of sacred Scripture. It is probable that these writings were the Gospels, the works of the apostles, and expositions of the prophets, as in the letter to the Hebrews and several other epistles of Paul. He then writes: "They not only meditate but also compose songs and hymns to God in various meters and melodies, setting them into more solemn modes."

The same book covers many other points, but it seemed necessary to select those that reflect characteristics of church life. If anyone doubts that these are unique to the evangelical life and thinks them applicable to others also, Philo adds evidence indisputable to the fair-minded:

> Having established self-control as a foundation in the soul, they build the other virtues on it. None would take food or drink until sundown, assuming that philosophy deserves daylight but bodily needs darkness. Some neglect food for three days in their great love of knowledge, while others feast so richly on wisdom that they abstain for twice that long and scarcely taste food once in six days.

Unquestionably this seems to reflect our Communion. If anyone still doubts this, let him be convinced by even clearer examples found nowhere but among Christians. Philo states that women are also members of this group, most of them elderly virgins who had remained so not from necessity, like some of the Greek priestesses, but of their own free will and the yearning to live with wisdom. Ignoring bodily pleasures, they longed not for mortal but immortal children, which only the God-loving soul can bear of itself.[20] He goes on to explain this more clearly:

> They interpret the sacred Scriptures figuratively in allegories. For the Law resembles a living being to them, with literal precepts for the body and hidden meanings for the soul. This sect was the first to concentrate on the latter, finding in the words a mirror reflecting extraordinary beauty of thought.

---

20. Eusebius implies that these quasi-nuns grew old within the church—an impossibility, since, if Philo wrote during the reign of Claudius (A.D. 41–54), Christianity was only eight to twenty-one years old at the time.

I need not include a description of their meetings, of how the men and women live separately in the same place, or of the disciplines still practiced among us, especially when we commemorate our Savior's passion by abstaining from food and spending whole nights in prayer and study of God's Word. Philo's own writings portray the parallels in the all-night vigils, disciplines, and hymns in which one man sings and others join in the refrains; how on specific days they sleep on the ground on straw and refrain from wine and meat, drinking only water and seasoning their bread with salt and mint. In addition, he describes the order of precedence of those in the ministries of the church, from the diaconate to the supremacy of the episcopate. Clearly Philo had in mind the first heralds of the Gospel teaching and apostolic customs handed down from the beginning.

Philo's Works

18. A voluminous writer and wide-ranging thinker, Philo expounded the events in Genesis through books entitled *Allegories of the Sacred Laws*. Next he dealt with the difficulties in the Scriptures, stating them and then offering solutions in books entitled *Problems and Solutions in Genesis and Exodus*. Besides these, there are special treatises on certain problems, such as:

On Agriculture	*The Three Mosaic Virtues*
On Drunkenness	*Changed Names and Why They*
What the Sober Mind Desires	*Were Changed*
and Detests	*On the Covenants, I and II*
On the Confusion of Tongues	*On Migration*
Flight and Discovery	*Life of a Wise Man*
On Assembly for Instruction	*or Unwritten Laws*
Who Inherits Divine Things?	*Giants or The Immutability of God*
The Division Between	*Moses on the Divine*
Odd and Even	*Origin of Dreams*

These are the books dealing with Genesis that have come down to us. On Exodus I know:

Problems and	*Laws according to the Ten*
Solutions, 1–5	*Commandments*
The Tabernacle	*Sacrifice: Animals and Varieties*
The Ten Commandments	*How the Law Rewards the Good*
	and Punishes the Bad

His individual writings also include:

On Providence	*Every Bad Man Is a Slave*
On the Jews	*Every Good Man Is Free*
The Statesman	*The Contemplative Life or Suppliants*
Alexander	*Interpretations of Hebrew Names*

He came to Rome in Gaius's time and later wrote about his [Gaius's] impious conduct, entitling it—with appropriate irony—*Concerning Virtues*. During Claudius's reign, he is said to have read this before the entire Roman senate, and his words were so admired that they were accorded a place in libraries.

At this time, while Paul was finishing his journey from Jerusalem via a roundabout route as far as Illyricum [Rom. 15:19], Claudius banished the Jews from Rome, and Aquila and Priscilla, with other Jews, left Rome for Asia Minor and lived there with Paul the apostle, who was strengthening churches whose foundations he had recently laid, according to Acts [18–19].

Calamities at Jerusalem under Claudius and Nero

A.D. 48   **19.** While Claudius was still emperor, so fierce a riot broke out in Jerusalem during the Feast of the Passover that thirty thousand people trampled each other to death around the exits of the temple, thus turning the feast into mourning for the whole nation and each household. Josephus goes on to say that Claudius appointed Agrippa [II], son of Agrippa, as king of the Jews and sent Felix as procurator of the whole country, including Samaria, Galilee, and Perea. Claudius himself, having ruled for thirteen years and eight A.D. 54   months, died, leaving his throne to Nero.

20. Josephus relates the following, about a priestly quarrel while Felix was procurator of Judea under Nero, in *Antiquities,* Book 20:

> A quarrel broke out between the chief priests and the priests and leaders of the Jerusalem populace. Each of them formed a band of the most brazen revolutionaries who stoned and abused each other with impunity, as if in a city without government. Such shameless audacity possessed the chief priests that they sent slaves to the threshing floors to snatch the tithes owed to the priests, so that impoverished priests could

be seen perishing of want. The violence of the factions thus completely vanquished justice.[21]

Josephus also tells of bandits in Jerusalem who murdered victims in broad daylight in the middle of the city. At festivals, in particular, they used to mingle with the crowds, stab distinguished people with concealed daggers, and then affect indignation when they had fallen, evading discovery in this way. First to be slaughtered by them was Jonathan the high priest, and after him many were murdered daily, and even worse was the fear instilled as each hourly expected death.

21. He continues:

> A worse scourge than this was inflicted on the Jews by the Egyptian false prophet, an impostor who attracted thirty thousand dupes and led them through a wilderness route to the Mount of Olives, from which he prepared to invade Jerusalem, overpower the Roman garrison, and seize supreme power. But Felix, anticipating his attack, met him with the Roman forces, supported also by the whole populace, so that when the clash occurred the Egyptian fled with a few men, and most of his followers were killed or captured.[22]

This passage, from Book 2 of the *Jewish War*, corresponds with what is noted about the Egyptian in Acts, where the military tribune at Jerusalem in the time of Felix asks Paul during the Jewish riot against him, "Then you are not the Egyptian who recently stirred up a revolt and led the four thousand assassins out into the wilderness?" [21:38]. Such were the events under Felix.

Paul Sent to Rome as Prisoner and Acquitted

22. Nero sent Festus as [Felix's] successor, and Paul was tried before him and brought as prisoner to Rome. Aristarchus went with him, whom he called his fellow prisoner in his epistles [Col. 4:10]. And at this point Luke, who wrote the Acts of the Apostles, finished his story with the statement that Paul spent two whole years in Rome in free custody, preaching without hindrance. After

---

21. *Antiquities* 20.180–81.
22. *Jewish War* 2.261–63.

defending himself [successfully], the apostle is said to have set out again on the ministry of preaching and, coming a second time to the same city, found fulfillment in martyrdom. During this imprisonment he composed the second epistle to Timothy, mentioning both his earlier defense as well as his impending fulfillment. Note his testimony on this point:

c. A.D. 66

> At my first defense no one came to my support, but all deserted me. May it not be counted against them! But the Lord stood by me and gave me strength, so that through me the message might be fully proclaimed and all the Gentiles might hear it. So I was rescued from the lion's mouth [2 Tim. 4:16-17].

He clearly shows by this that on the first occasion, so that his preaching mission might be fulfilled, he was rescued from the lion's mouth, apparently referring to Nero because of his ferocity. He does not add any such words as "He will deliver me from the lion's mouth," since he saw in the Spirit that his death was imminent. So after the words, "I was rescued from the lion's mouth" he continues: "The Lord will rescue me from every evil attack and save me for his heavenly kingdom," indicating his impending martyrdom. And this he predicts even more clearly in the same letter, saying, "I am already being poured out as a libation, and the time of my departure has come" [2 Tim. 4:6]. Now in this second epistle to Timothy, he states that only Luke was with him when he wrote and at his first defense not even he. Therefore Luke probably wrote the Acts of the Apostles at that time, having recorded events throughout the time he was with Paul. I have said this to show that Paul's martyrdom did not take place during the stay in Rome that Luke describes. Since Nero's disposition was at first milder,[23] it was likely easier for Paul's defense of the faith to be accepted, but when he [Nero] proceeded to commit reckless crimes, the apostles were attacked along with others.

The Martyrdom of Jesus' Brother James

23. When Paul appealed to Caesar and was sent to Rome by Festus, the Jews were disappointed in their hope regarding the

---

23. Up to A.D. 62—about the time of Paul's trial—it was indeed. His adviser Seneca retired that year, however, and Nero came under the baleful influence of Tigellinus.

plot they had devised against him and turned against James, the Lord's brother, to whom the bishop's throne in Jerusalem had been assigned by the apostles. This is the crime that they committed. They brought him into their midst and in front of the whole populace demanded a denial of his faith in Christ. But when he, A.D. 62 contrary to all expectation, loudly and courageously confessed before them all that our Lord and Savior Jesus Christ was the Son of God, they could not tolerate his testimony any longer, since he was universally deemed the most righteous of men because of the heights he had reached in philosophy and religion. So they killed him, using anarchy as their opportunity to seize power, because at that moment Festus had died in Judea, leaving the province without government or procurator. How James died has already been shown by a previous quotation from Clement, who says that he was thrown down from the parapet and clubbed to death. But the most accurate account of him is given by Hegesippus, who came in the generation after the apostles. He writes, in Book 5 of his *Memoirs:*

[Administration of] the church passed to James, the brother of the Lord, along with the apostles. He was called "the Just" by everyone from the Lord's time to ours, since there were many Jameses, but this one was consecrated from his mother's womb. He drank no wine or liquor and ate no meat. No razor came near his head, he did not anoint himself with oil, and took no baths. He alone was permitted to enter the sanctum, for he wore not wool but linen. He used to enter the temple alone and was often found kneeling and imploring forgiveness for the people, so that his knees became hard like a camel's from his continual kneeling in worship of God and in prayer for the people. Because of his superior righteousness he was called the Just and *Oblias*—meaning, in Greek, "Bulwark of the People" and "Righteousness"—as the prophets declare regarding him.

Representatives of the seven sects among the [Jewish] people, which I previously described (in the *Memoirs*), asked him what "the door of Jesus" meant, and he replied that he was the Savior. Because of this, some believed that Jesus was the Christ. The sects mentioned above did not believe in a resurrection or in One who is coming to reward each according to his deeds, but those who did believe did so because of James. Now, since many even of the rulers believed, there was an uproar among the Jews, scribes, and Pharisees saying that the whole populace was in danger of expecting Jesus as the Christ. So they assembled and said to James: "We call on you to restrain the

2.23

people, since they have gone astray after Jesus, believing him to be the Christ. We call on you to persuade all who come for the Passover concerning Jesus, since all of us trust you. We and the entire populace can vouch for the fact that you are righteous and take no one at face value. So do persuade the crowd not to err regarding Jesus, since we and all the people respect you. So stand on the parapet of the temple, where you can be clearly seen from that height and your words be heard by all the people with all the tribes, and Gentiles too, gathered for the Passover."

So the scribes and Pharisees made James stand on the temple parapet, and they shouted to him, "O righteous one, whom we all ought to believe, since the people are going astray after Jesus who was crucified, tell us, what does 'the door of Jesus' mean?" He replied with a loud voice, "Why do you ask me about the Son of Man? He is sitting in heaven at the right hand of the Great Power, and he will come on the clouds of heaven." Many were convinced and rejoiced at James's testimony, crying, "Hosanna to the Son of David." Then the scribes and Pharisees said to each other, "We made a bad mistake in providing such testimony to Jesus, but let us go up and throw him down so that they will be afraid and not believe him." And they cried out, "Oh, oh, even the just one has gone astray!" This fulfilled the prophecy of Isaiah: "Let us remove the just man, for he is unprofitable to us. Therefore they shall eat the fruit of their works."[24]

So they went up and threw down the righteous one. Then they said to each other, "Let us stone James the Just," and they began to stone him, since the fall had not killed him. But he turned and knelt down, saying, "I implore you, O Lord, God and Father, forgive them: they do not know what they are doing." While they were pelting him with stones, one of the priests among the sons of the Rechabites, to whom the prophet Jeremiah bore witness,[25] cried out, "Stop! What are you doing? The righteous one is praying for you." Then one of them, a laundryman, took the club that he used to beat out clothes and hit the Just on the head. Such was his martyrdom. They buried him on the spot by the temple, and his gravestone is still there by the temple. He became a true witness to both Jews and Gentiles that Jesus is the Christ.

---

24. The second sentence is from Isa. 3:10; the first, from the Wisdom of Solomon, not Isaiah.

25. Jer. 35 for the Rechabites. However, there is no evidence that this tribe, adopted into Israel, could have supplied priests. Epiphanius substitutes Simeon, son of Clopas, for the Rechabite in this episode (*Against Heresies* 78.14).

Just after this Vespasian began to besiege them.

This is the full account given by Hegesippus, which is in agreement with Clement. So extraordinary a man was James, so esteemed by all for righteousness that even the more intelligent of the Jews thought that this was why the siege of Jerusalem immediately followed his martyrdom. Indeed, Josephus did not hesitate to write:

> These things happened to the Jews as retribution for James the Just, who was a brother of Jesus who was called Christ, for the Jews killed him despite his great righteousness.[26]

Josephus also described his death in *Antiquities*, Book 20:

> When [Nero] Caesar heard of the death of Festus, he sent Albinus to Judea as governor. But the younger Ananus, who had received the high priesthood, was headstrong in temperament and bold in the extreme. He followed the sect of the Sadducees, who are cruelest of the Jews when they sit in judgment, as I have already explained. Having such a character, Ananus thought that with Festus dead and Albinus still on the way he would have the proper opportunity. Convening the judges of the Sanhedrin, he brought before them the brother of Jesus who was called the Christ, whose name was James, and certain others. He accused them of having transgressed the law and delivered them up to be stoned. But those of the city residents who were deemed the most fair-minded and who were strict in observing the Law were offended at this. Accordingly, they secretly contacted the king [Agrippa II], urging him to order Ananus to desist from any more such actions, for he had not been justified in what he had already done. Some of them even went to meet Albinus, who was on his way from Alexandria, and informed him that Ananus had no authority to convene the Sanhedrin without his consent. Convinced by these words, Albinus wrote in anger to Ananus, threatening him with punishment. And King Agrippa, because of this, deposed him from the high priesthood, in which he had ruled for three months, and replaced him with Jesus, the son of Damnaeus.[27]

---

26. This statement is not found in the extant texts of Josephus, but it is cited by Origen (*Against Celsus* 1.47), which demonstrates that Eusebius did not invent the passage. One must suspect an interpolation in the text of Josephus used by Origen and Eusebius.

27. *Antiquities* 20.197–203.

Such is the story of James, to whom is ascribed the first of the so-called General Epistles. To be sure, its authenticity is doubted, since not many of the early writers quote it, as is also the case with the epistle of Jude, which is also one of the seven called general. Still, these two letters have been used regularly, like the others, in most of the churches.

24. In the eighth year of Nero's reign, Annianus was the first after Mark the Evangelist to take charge of the parish of Alexandria.

Head of Nero, emperor A.D. 54–68, garbed as a priest (*Corinth Museum*).

The Neronian Persecution

25. Once Nero's power was firmly established, he plunged into nefarious vices and took up arms against the God of the universe. To describe his depravity is not part of the present work. Many have accurately recorded the facts about him, and from them any who wish may study his perverse and degenerate madness, which led him to destroy innumerable lives and finally to such indiscriminate murder that he did not spare even his nearest and dearest. With various sorts of deaths, he did away with his mother, brothers, and wife, as well as countless other near relatives, as if they were strangers and enemies. Despite all this, one crime still had to be added to his catalogue: he was the first of the emperors to be the declared enemy of the Deity. To this the Roman Tertullian refers as follows:

> Consult your own records: there you will find that Nero was the first to let his imperial sword rage against this sect [Christianity] when it was just arising in Rome. We boast that such a man was the originator of our pruning, for anyone who knows him can understand that nothing would have been condemned by Nero unless it were supremely good.[28]

---

28. *Defense* 5. The first line in this excerpt is translated directly from Tertullian's

So it happened that this man, the first to be announced publicly as a fighter against God, was led on to slaughter the apostles. It is related that in his reign Paul was beheaded in Rome itself and that Peter was also crucified, and the cemeteries there still called by the names of Peter and Paul confirm the record. So does a churchman named Gaius, who lived when Zephyrinus was Bishop of Rome. In a written dialogue with Proclus, the leader of the Phrygian opinion [the Montanists], Gaius says the following about the places where the sacred remains of the apostles in question are laid:

> I can point out the trophies [monuments] of the apostles. If you will go to the Vatican or the Ostian Way, you will find the trophies of those who founded this church.[29]

And that they were both martyred at the same time Bishop Dionysius of Corinth affirms in a letter written to the Romans:

> By your great counsel you have bound together what has grown from the seed that Peter and Paul sowed among Romans and Corinthians. For both of them sowed in our Corinth and instructed us together; in Italy too they taught jointly in the same place and were martyred at the same time.[30]

These citations may serve further to confirm the facts narrated.

The Beginning of the Jewish War with Rome

26. In the course of his detailed account of the catastrophe that overwhelmed the whole Jewish nation, Josephus reports that innumerable Jews of high rank were flogged with scourges and crucified in Jerusalem itself by Florus and that he was procurator of Judea when war blazed up in the twelfth year of Nero's reign. He A.D. 66 then says that throughout Syria great disturbances followed the

---

Latin, since Eusebius's translator rendered it incorrectly in Greek: "after subduing all the East, Nero was especially cruel to all in Rome." Nero never subdued the East.

29. Neither Peter nor Paul founded the church at Rome, which existed before Paul arrived (Rom. 1:8–11). Still, since both apostles were martyred very early in its history, it is understandable that they were quickly deemed honorable founders, so to speak.

30. As for Corinth, this claim is hardly supported by the New Testament, which names Paul alone as founder. That both apostles also suffered martyrdom at the same time in Rome is doubtful.

revolt of the Jews, who were mercilessly attacked in the various cities as if they were enemies. Unburied corpses filled the cities, the bodies of old men, children, and women, with nothing to cover their nakedness. The whole province was full of indescribable horror. Yet worse than the atrocities of the present were the threats of those in the future. Such is the account of Josephus, and such was the situation of the Jews.

EUSEBIUS ON THE APOSTLES

With the book of Acts as his basis, Eusebius nicely supplements the New Testament account with extrabiblical material from Josephus, Philo, Clement, Tertullian, Hegesippus, and others. His reliance on Josephus is confessed and understandable, a practice widely shared by early Christian writers and probably a reason that Josephus has survived across the centuries through recopied manuscripts when other historians were irretrievably lost. Eusebius's similar admiration for Philo underlay his overlong but unsuccessful attempt to interpret the Egyptian ascetics as early Christians, while his lengthy digression on Philo's writings shows Eusebius's fascination for literary history, a trait underlying his entire work.

Eusebius also shows himself a master at tying up any loose ends dangling from the New Testament record and possibly embroidering the ends in the process. Pilate's reports to Tiberius about Jesus and the emperor's reaction are given credence on the authority of the Western father Tertullian, and the Roman governor's ultimate suicide is presumed. (Tiberius's favorable response regarding Jesus, however, is extremely doubtful, as is the tradition of Pilate's suicide.) Whereas Simon Magus has only a cameo role in Acts 8, his subsequent career, molded by legendary accretions to the references in Justin Martyr, reach a lurid climax in Eusebius. The apostles, here and in the next chapter, are given destinations for their ministries, where known, whereas Acts focuses primarily on Paul's mission ventures.

The fates of Peter and Paul at Rome, however, rest on much firmer historical bases, and Eusebius's citation of the presbyter Gaius's comments on their "trophies" is extremely important. Similarly, the martyrdom of Jesus' half brother James, first bishop of the Jerusalem church, is reported by the sources themselves—Josephus and Hegesippus—with hardly any editorializing by Eusebius. These are highly significant addenda to the New Testament account.

The use of the Roman emperors as time grid—the chronology that structures most of the *Church History*—is modestly violated in this book, as Eusebius, who has moved the reader into Caligula's reign, reverts to Tiberius's to record imbroglios between the Jews and Pilate. This, however, is only to illustrate the historian's often-expressed theme: God's vengeance overtook the Jews for crucifying Jesus, the note on which he closes Book 2. Whether the collective guilt thus assigned has a proper theological basis is not discussed by Eusebius, an error also among other Christian writers of the time that only exacerbated the struggle between church and synagogue in the earliest centuries of church history.

Roman history in the first century A.D. is very colorful. When the great *Augustus* died in 14, eighteen or nineteen years after Jesus' birth, he was followed by four successors in the Julio-Claudian dynasty. His stepson *Tiberius* (14–37), the emperor during the public ministry of Jesus, was somewhat resentful at having been passed over earlier for emperorship, since Augustus had chosen four others to succeed himself, all of whom died before he did. Once in power, however, Tiberius proved an able administrator, and the empire prospered. But when he abandoned Rome for the island of Capri, where he spent the last ten years of his life, Tiberius's popularity suffered, also because of suspicions engendered by a conspiracy that almost toppled him in the year 31.

Tiberius appointed Pontius Pilate governor of Judea in 26 and may have read about the crucifixion of Jesus in Pilate's *acta* (official record) for the year 33. But these *acta* have been lost, and all claims about them in Eusebius's record and subsequently are spurious. After governing for ten years, Pilate was recalled to Rome, but Tiberius never heard his case, since the emperor died in March of 37, just before Pilate returned.

Tiberius's grandnephew *Gaius Caligula* (37–41) succeeded him. Caligula was an untrained prince who began acceptably but soon suffered a neurological illness that turned him into a lustful megalomaniac, who took many lives before his own was snuffed out by assassination after a mercifully brief reign. Quite probably Caligula was the worst emperor in Roman history, in terms of enormities perpetrated per month in office.

Caligula's uncle *Claudius* (41–54), the emperor during Paul's three mission journeys, succeeded him. Claudius had motor disabilities, which is why he had been passed over for Caligula, but he proved a surprisingly successful ruler. Britain was conquered in 43, while the construction of roads, aqueducts, bridges, and baths across the Roman Empire testified to his success as an administrator. His temporary expulsion of Jewish leaders from Rome resulted in Aquila and Priscilla becoming Paul's colleagues in Corinth, according to Acts 18:1-4. Claudius's poor luck with women, however, culminated when his niece Agrippina, his fourth wife, poisoned him with a bowl of tainted mushrooms so that her son might succeed.

Nero (54-68), Agrippina's offspring by a previous marriage, became the next emperor in place of Claudius's own son, Britannicus. Nero had as tutor and adviser the philosopher Seneca—brother of Gallio, the governor of Achaia who absolved Paul (Acts 18)—which may explain why the apostle appealed to Nero from his imprisonment at Caesarea. When the great fire of Rome broke out in the summer of 64 and Nero was blamed for it, he saved himself by accusing the Christians of arson and ordering their punishment. Although this persecution was local rather than empirewide, it set the deadly precedent for all persecutions to follow. In some association with this, both Peter and Paul were martyred. Two years later the great Jewish War broke out, and two years after that, Nero committed suicide, in June of 68, after a revolt by the legions and the Praetorian Guard. He was the last of the Julio-Claudians.

Book 3

MISSIONS AND PERSECUTIONS

GALBA TO TRAJAN

Apostolic Destinations and Writings

1. Such was the condition of the Jews. Meanwhile the holy apostles of our Savior were scattered across the whole world. Thomas, according to tradition, was allotted Parthia, Andrew Scythia, and John Asia, where he stayed until his death at Ephesus. Peter seems to have preached to the Jews of the Dispersion in Pontus, Galatia, Bithynia, Cappadocia, and Asia.[1] Finally he came to Rome and was crucified, head downward at his own request.[2] What need be said of Paul, who proclaimed the Gospel from Jerusalem to Illyricum and later was martyred in Rome under Nero? This is stated specifically by Origen in volume 3 of his *Commentary on Genesis*.

2. After the martyrdoms of Paul and Peter, the first to be appointed Bishop of Rome was Linus. Paul mentions him when writing to Timothy from Rome in the salutation at the end of the epistle [2 Tim. 4:21].

3. Of Peter, one epistle, named as his First, is accepted, and the early Fathers used this as undisputed in their own writings. But

---

1. Eusebius seems to have derived these locations from 1 Peter 1. The Asia referred to is not the continent but the Roman province in the western third of Asia Minor.

2. No church father mentions this prior to Origen (d. c. 254).

the so-called Second epistle [of Peter] we have not regarded as canonical, yet many have thought it useful and have studied it with the other Scriptures. However, the Acts and the Gospel bearing his name, as well as the Preaching and Revelation called his, we do not know at all among the traditional catholic writings, since no church writer either in early times or in our own has used their testimony. In the course of my narrative I will carefully indicate which of the ecclesiastical authors in each period used any of the disputed books, what they said about the canonical and accepted Scriptures, and their comments about those that are not. These, then, are the books attributed to Peter, of which I recognize only one epistle as genuine and accepted by the early Fathers.

Paul was obviously the author of the fourteen letters, but some dispute the epistle to the Hebrews in view of the Roman church's denial that it is the work of Paul, and I will relate what our predecessors have said about it at the proper time. His so-called Acts are not among the authentic books. But since the same apostle in the salutations at the end of Romans refers to a Hermas, the reputed author of *The Shepherd*, that book has also been rejected by some and therefore should not be placed among the accepted books. Others, however, have deemed it indispensable, especially for elementary education. Accordingly, it has been used in public worship, and I have found it quoted by some of the earliest writers.

4. Paul preached to the Gentiles and Peter to the circumcised in the cities and provinces cited previously. But it is not easy to determine how many in the churches they founded were zealous and able enough to become pastors except by noting the innumerable fellow workers named by Paul and Luke's listing of Paul's disciples in Acts. Timothy, for example, is said to have been the first bishop appointed to the parish in Ephesus, as was Titus to the churches of Crete.

Luke, an Antiochene by birth and a physician by profession, was long a companion of Paul and was closely associated also with the other apostles. In two divinely inspired books, the Gospel and the Acts of the Apostles, he has left us examples of the soul healing that he learned from them. The former, he states, he wrote on the basis of information he received from those who from the first were eyewitnesses and ministers of the Word. The latter he composed not from the evidence of hearing but of his own eyes. They say that Paul was actually in the habit of referring to Luke's Gospel whenever he used the phrase "According to my gospel."

Of Paul's other followers, Crescens was sent by him to Gaul [2 Tim. 4:10], and Linus, who is cited in 2 Timothy as being with Paul in Rome, was the first after Peter to be appointed Bishop of Rome, as stated previously. Clement too, who became the third Bishop of Rome, was Paul's coworker and cocombatant, as the apostle himself testifies [Phil. 4:3]. Besides these, Dionysius the Areopagite, the first convert after Paul's address to the Athenians at the Areopagus, as Luke relates in Acts [17:34], became the first Bishop of Athens, according to another Dionysius, pastor of the parish in Corinth. The chronological details of the apostles' succession will be presented in due course.

The Roman Siege of Jerusalem

A.D. 68   **5.** After Nero's rule of thirteen years, that of Galba and Otho occupied a year and a half, and then Vespasian, who had distinguished himself in the campaigns against the Jews, was proclaimed emperor while still in Judea, having been hailed as imperator by the armies there.[3] He immediately set out for Rome, entrusting to his son Titus the war against the Jews.

Now after our Savior's ascension, the Jews followed their crime against him with numerous plots against the apostles. First they stoned Stephen to death. Next James, son of Zebedee and brother of John, was beheaded. And finally James, the first to be appointed Bishop of Jerusalem, died in the way described previously, while the other apostles were driven out of Judea by numerous deadly plots. But they traveled into every land, teaching their message in the power of Christ, who had told them, "Go and make disciples of all nations in my name" [Matt. 28:19]. Meanwhile, before the war began, members of the Jerusalem church were ordered by an oracle given by revelation to those worthy of it to leave the city and settle in a city of Perea called Pella. Here they migrated from Jerusalem, as if, once holy men had deserted the royal capital of the Jews and the whole land of Judea, the judgment of God might finally fall on them for their crimes against Christ and his apostles, utterly blotting out all that wicked generation.

---

3. Nero, who died June 9, 68, was succeeded by Galba (June 68 to January 69), Otho (January to April), and Vitellius (April to December 69). Eusebius for some reason omits Vitellius, during whose reign Vespasian was proclaimed emperor at Alexandria on July 1, 69.

Those who wish may trace precisely from Josephus's history the disasters that overwhelmed the entire nation, especially how the residents of Judea were driven to the limits of suffering; how many thousands of men, women, and children died by the sword, famine, and countless other forms of death; how many famous Jewish cities endured horrors under siege; and in particular the terrors of those who fled for refuge to Jerusalem as an "impregnable fortress." They can study all the details of the entire war and how in the end the Abomination of Desolation, declared by the prophets, was set up in the very temple of God, celebrated of old, when it was utterly destroyed by fire. I must, however, point out how Josephus estimates that the people from all of Judea who at the time of the Passover thronged into Jerusalem, as if to a prison, numbered three million. It was indeed appropriate that in the very days on which they perpetrated the Savior's passion they should be shut inside a prison, as it were, and receive the destruction meted out by divine justice. Omitting their disasters by sword and other means, I shall relate only their sufferings from starvation, so that readers may learn how quickly God's punishment followed their crime against Christ.

6. Let us then take up again the fifth book of Josephus's *Jewish War* and go through the tragedy of what happened:

> For the wealthy to remain [in Jerusalem] was equally dangerous, since, under the pretext of desertion, many were killed for their money. But the madness of the rebels increased with the famine, and the terrors of both flared more fiercely each day. Since no grain could be seen anywhere, they broke into homes and ransacked them. If they found any, they tormented the occupants for claiming there was none; if not, they tortured them for having hidden it too well. The bodies of the miserable wretches were evidence enough of whether or not they had it: if sound, they were deemed to have plenty of food, while those already emaciated were passed by, for it seemed unreasonable to kill those who would soon die of starvation. Many secretly bartered their property for a measure of wheat, if they were rich, or barley, if poor. Then, shutting themselves inside the innermost interior of their houses, some ate their grain raw in extreme hunger, while others baked bread as necessity or fear dictated. No table was set: they snatched the food from the fire, uncooked, and tore it into pieces.
>
> Such pitiful sights would induce tears as the powerful plundered and the weak whimpered. Famine is truly the worst form of suffering

and decency its greatest victim. All restraint was shunned as women grabbed food from the very mouths of their husbands, children from their fathers, and—most horrid of all—mothers from their babies; and while their dearest ones were dying in their arms, they had no scruples about depriving them of the last morsel that might have kept them alive. Partisans everywhere would rob them even of such pickings, for whenever they saw a locked door, they assumed that those inside were dining and they broke down the doors, rushed in, and all but squeezed the morsels of food out of their throats. Old men were beaten for holding onto their food, and women were dragged by the hair for hiding it in their hands. They showed no pity for gray hair or infancy but picked up the babies clinging to their scraps and dashed them to the floor. To those who anticipated their coming by gulping down food they were the more savage, as if defrauded.

In their quest for food they devised dreadful methods of torture, stuffing bitter vetch into the genital passages of their victims and driving sharp stakes into their rears—torments horrible even to hear—to get people to reveal a hidden loaf or a single handful of barley. Not that the torturers were hungry—indeed, their cruelty would have been less savage had it sprung from need—but they were rather giving their madness some exercise and storing up supplies for days to come. When some crawled out at night as far as the Roman [siege] lines to gather wild herbs and grasses, thinking they had escaped the enemy, the oppressors intercepted them and seized what they were carrying. Despite all their pleading and appeals to the awful name of God to share what they had gathered at such risk, they gave them nothing at all, and those robbed were lucky not to have been killed as well.[4]

After some details, Josephus continues:

Now unable to leave the city, the Jews lost all hope of survival, and the famine became even worse, devouring house after house, family after family. The homes were filled with women and children thus destroyed, the alleys with corpses of old men. Young men and boys, swelling with hunger, haunted the marketplace like ghosts and fell dead in their tracks. The sick could not bury their relatives, while those still fit evaded the task due to the numbers of the dead and their own uncertain fate, for many fell dead while burying others, and many set out for their own graves while they were still able. There was no weeping or wailing as hunger conquered emotion, and

---

4. *Jewish War* 5.424–38.

those who were dying looked with dry eyes on those already dead. Deep silence and a lethal darkness shrouded the city.

Worse still were the brigands who broke into houses, stripped clothes from the bodies of the dead, and emerged laughing. They tried the points of their swords on the corpses and even tested the steel by running some through who were still alive. Yet those who begged for the *coup de grâce* they contemptuously left to the famine. Each of these died with eyes fixed on the temple rather than on the partisans he was leaving alive. These at first ordered the dead buried at public expense due to the intolerable stench, but later, when this proved impossible, they threw them from the walls into the valleys. When Titus, as he made his rounds, saw them full of the dead, the putrid gore oozing from the rotting bodies, he groaned, and raising his hands he called God to witness that this was not his doing.[5]

After further comments, he continues:

I cannot refrain from stating my feelings: I think that if the Romans had delayed their attack on these wicked scoundrels, the earth would have opened and swallowed the city, or a flood would have overwhelmed it or lightning destroyed it, like Sodom. For it produced a far more godless generation than those who suffered there. It was due to their madness that all the people perished.[6]

In Book 6 he writes:

The best of friends wrestled with each other for even the shadow of food. Others, mouths agape from hunger like mad dogs, staggered along, beating on the doors like drunken men and breaking into the same houses two or three times in a single hour in their hapless state. They put their teeth into everything, swallowing things even the filthiest animals would not touch. Finally they devoured even belts and shoes or gnawed at the leather they stripped from their shields. Some fed on wisps of old hay, for there were people who gathered straw and sold a tiny bunch for four Attic drachmas.[7]

But why speak of the inanimate things that hunger drove them to eat? I shall now relate something unparalleled in the annals of

---

5. *Jewish War* 5.512–19.

6. *Jewish War* 5.566.

7. The unit of silver coinage in ancient Greece, the drachma weighed 4.3 grams of silver and was a day's wage for a common laborer.

Greece or any other country, a deed horrible to tell and incredible to hear. I would gladly have omitted this tragedy lest posterity suspect me of having fabricated it, but countless witnesses of my own generation support me. There was a woman named Mary, the daughter of Eleazar, who lived beyond the Jordan in the village of Bathezor ("House of Hyssop"). She was well known for family and wealth and had fled to Jerusalem with the rest of the population, where she was trapped in the siege. The partisan chiefs seized most of the possessions she had brought from Perea, and their bodyguards plundered the rest of her property and food through daily raids. In fury, she cursed the looters, but when none of them killed her either in anger or pity, she yielded to rage and hunger. Defying nature, she took her own baby boy, whom she was suckling, and said, "Poor little mite, why do I keep you alive in war, famine, and rebellion? If we live, we're Roman slaves, but hunger will overtake slavery, and the partisans are worse than both! Come, be my food, an avenging fury to the rebels and the one story of Jewish suffering that the world must still hear." With these words she killed her son, then roasted him and ate half, hiding the rest.

At that moment the partisans arrived and, smelling the unholy aroma, threatened her with instant death if they were not given what she had prepared. She replied that she had saved a fine helping for them and uncovered the remains of her child. Overcome with horror, they were stupefied at the sight, but she said, "This child was my own and the deed is mine too. Eat, for I also have eaten. Don't be more squeamish than a woman or more tenderhearted than a mother! But if you're queasy and disapprove of my sacrifice, then, since I've eaten half, you may as well leave me the rest." They went away trembling, cowards for the first time who scarcely gave up even this food. But horror immediately filled the entire city, everyone seeing the tragedy before his own eyes and shuddering as if the crime were his own. The starving sought death and envied those who had realized it before seeing or hearing these outrageous atrocities.[8]

Jesus' Predictions

7. Such was the reward for the guilt and impiety of the Jews against the Christ of God. It is worth appending to it the infallible prediction of our Savior regarding these very things in this prophecy:

---

8. *Jewish War* 6.194–213.

Woe to those who are pregnant and to those who are nursing infants in those days! Pray that your flight may not be in winter or on a Sabbath. For at that time there will be great suffering, such as has not been seen from the beginning of the world until now, no, and never will be [Matt. 24:19-21].

In estimating the total number of lives lost, the historian [Josephus] says that 1.1 million died by famine and the sword, that the partisans and terrorists informed against each other after the city's capture and were executed, and that the tallest and handsomest of the youths were saved for the triumphal parade. Of the rest, those over seventeen were sent as prisoners to hard labor in Egypt, and even more were divided among the provinces to be killed in the theaters by sword or wild beasts. Those under seventeen were sold into slavery, and the number of these alone was ninety thousand.

This all happened in the second year of Vespasian's reign in A.D. 70 accordance with the prophecies of Christ, who foresaw them, by divine power, as if already present and wept over them. The holy Evangelist adds his [Christ's] actual words to Jerusalem herself:

If you even today would recognize the things that make for peace! But now they are hidden from your eyes. Indeed, the days will come upon you when your enemies will set up ramparts around you and surround you and hem you in on every side. They will crush you to the ground, you and your children within you [Luke 19:42-44].

On another occasion, he said:

For there will be great distress on the earth and wrath against this people; they will fall by the edge of the sword and be taken away as captives among all nations, and Jerusalem will be trampled on by the Gentiles, until the times of the Gentiles are fulfilled [Luke 21:23-24].

And again:

When you see Jerusalem surrounded by armies, then know that its desolation has come near [Luke 21:20].

Anyone comparing our Savior's words with the rest of the historian's record of the war cannot fail to be astonished or to confess the divine character of the Savior's prediction.

3.7

Statue of Vespasian, emperor 69–79 (*Uffizi, Florence*).

As to what happened to the whole nation after the Savior's passion and the mob's begging the release of the robber-murderer and the removal of the author of life, there is no need to add to the records. But it would be right to add facts that showed the kindness of a gracious Providence in delaying the destruction of the Jews for forty years after their crime against Christ. All that time, most of the apostles, including the first bishop, James himself, called the Lord's brother, were still alive, and their remaining in the city provided powerful protection for the place. For God was still patient, hoping that they might finally repent of their misdeeds and find pardon and salvation, but also sending miraculous warnings of what would happen if they failed to repent.

8. Josephus notes this in the sixth book of *The Jewish War:*

> Impostors and false prophets deluded the pitiable people, who, as if moonstruck, blind, and senseless, paid no attention to God's clear portents and warnings of the approaching desolation. A star stood over the city like a sword, and a comet that lasted for a year. Then, prior to the war, when the people had gathered for the Feast of

Unleavened Bread, on the eighth of Xanthicus[9] at 3 A.M., a light shined on the temple and the altar so brightly that it seemed to be midday, and this lasted for a half hour. To the inexperienced this seemed a good omen, but the sacred scribes gave the true interpretation. During the same feast a cow brought for sacrifice by the high priest gave birth to a lamb in the middle of the temple, and at midnight the eastern gate of the inner sanctuary opened itself—a gate of bronze fastened by iron bars and secured by long bolts so massive that twenty men were required to shut it each evening.

Not long after the feast, on the twenty-first of Artemisius,[10] a demonic apparition of incredible size was seen. It would have seemed a fairy tale had it not been attested by eyewitnesses and followed by disasters that corresponded to the omens. Before sunset there appeared in the sky over the whole land chariots and armed forces speeding through the clouds and surrounding the cities. And at the Feast of Pentecost, when the priests entered the temple at night for their usual ceremonies, they heard a disturbance, a loud crash, and then a thunderous cry, "Let us leave this place!"

Something even more alarming took place four years before the war, during a time of peace and prosperity. A common peasant, Jesus son of Ananias, came to the Feast of Tabernacles, stood in the temple courts, and suddenly shouted: "A voice from the east, a voice from the west, a voice from the four winds, a voice against Jerusalem and the temple, a voice against bridegrooms and brides, a voice against all the people!" Night and day he went through the narrow streets with this cry. Some of the prominent townspeople, enraged at these ominous words, seized the fellow and lashed him savagely. However, he uttered not a word in his own defense but persisted in shouting the same thing. The authorities, assuming correctly that the man's conduct was inspired by something supernatural, brought him before the Roman governor [Albinus]. There, though he was scourged to the bone, he uttered no plea for mercy and shed no tear, but straining his voice to the utmost, he wailed with each blow, "Woe! Woe to Jerusalem!"[11]

The same writer tells an even more remarkable story in which he claims that an oracle was found in their sacred writings

----

9. Probably April 8, 65 or 66.

10. Approximately May 21, though scholars differ. This apparition, not witnessed by Josephus and doubtless embellished in the retelling, was nevertheless rather uncritically reported by him.

11. *Jewish War* 6.288–304.

predicting that a man from their land would at that time rule the whole world, and the historian himself thought this was fulfilled in Vespasian. But he did not reign over the whole world, only that part under Roman control, and it would more justifiably be applied to Christ, to whom the Father had said, "Ask of me, and I will make the nations your heritage, and the ends of the earth your possession" [Ps. 2:8]. And it was by his holy apostles at that very time that "their voice went through all the earth and their words to the end of the world" [Ps. 19:4].

Josephus and His Writings

9. Since Josephus provided so much material for this history, it may be appropriate to tell of his origin and ancestry. He provides this information himself:

> I, Josephus, son of Matthias, am a priest of Jerusalem, who fought against the Romans in the early stages [of the war] and was an unwilling witness of the later events.[12]

He was the most famous Jew of his time not only among his fellow countrymen, but among the Romans also, so that he was honored with a statue erected in the city of Rome and the inclusion of his works in its library. He wrote the whole history of the Jews *[Jewish Antiquities]* in twenty books and the account of the war with the Romans of his own time *[The Jewish War]* in seven. The latter he published not only in Greek, but also in his native language, as he himself testifies, and also for other reasons he is worthy of credence. Two other books of his are extant, entitled *Against Apion,* in which he replies to Apion the grammarian, who had published an attack on the Jews, and to others who had tried to defame the ancestral customs of the Jewish people. In the first of these, he enumerates the canonical Scriptures forming the Old Testament, so-called, showing which of them, rooted in ancient tradition, are undisputed among the Hebrews:

10. We do not have vast numbers of discordant and conflicting books, but only twenty-two, containing the record of all of time and justly deemed divine. Of these, five are books of Moses that contain the

---

12. *Jewish War* 1.3.

Law and the tradition of human history up to his death. This period covers nearly three thousand years. From Moses' death to that of Artaxerxes, who succeeded Xerxes as King of Persia, the prophets after Moses recorded the events of their own times in thirteen books.[13] The remaining four contain hymns to God and precepts for human conduct.[14] From the time of Artaxerxes to our own the history has been recorded, but it does not merit equal credence with the rest because there has not been an unbroken succession of prophets.[15] Our actions mirror our attitude to the Scriptures, for though so much time has elapsed, no one has dared to add, subtract, or change anything in them, but it is inborn in Jews from their very birth to regard them as the ordinances of God, to live in them, and, if need be, to die for them gladly.[16]

He produced yet another work of merit on The Supremacy of Reason, which some call The Maccabaikon because it concerns the conflicts of those Hebrews cited in the so-called books of the Maccabees who fought so valiantly for the worship of God. And at the end of the twentieth book of Antiquities, Josephus announces that he had planned to write four books on Jewish belief concerning the nature of God and about why the Law permits some things and forbids others. He produced other works also, referred to in his writings.

Finally, I think it proper to cite the words that he appends to the end of Antiquities to underscore the evidence in the passages I have borrowed from him. Accusing Justus of Tiberias of false statements—he had attempted a history of the same period—and bringing many other charges against him, he adds the following:

I did not share your fear with regard to writing. I submitted my books to the emperors themselves[17] while the events were still fresh, for, since truth was paramount in my account, I expected to receive

---

13. Probably from Josh. through Job and Isa. through the prophets major and minor in groupings by number (e.g., 1 and 2 Sam. as one book) or subject matter (e.g., Ezra and Neh.), thus reducing thirty books to thirteen.

14. Pss., Prov., Eccl., and the Song.

15. Probably 1 and 2 Macc.

16. *Against Apion* 1.8.

17. Vespasian and his son and successor Titus, both of whom commanded the Roman forces in the Jewish War.

confirmation of my accuracy and was not disappointed. I also gave my history to many others, some of whom had actually taken part in the war, such as King Agrippa [II] and several of his relatives. Indeed, the emperor Titus was so concerned that from my books alone the public should derive information about these events that he wrote an order with his own hand for their publication, and King Agrippa wrote sixty-two letters attesting to their truth.[18]

He quotes from two of these letters, but let this suffice regarding Josephus and let us proceed.

Succession of Bishops

11. After the martyrdom of James and the conquest of Jerusalem that followed soon after, tradition has it that those of the apostles and disciples of the Lord who were still alive gathered from everywhere with those who were, humanly speaking, relatives of the Lord, for many of them were still alive. They all discussed together who ought to succeed James, and all unanimously decided that Symeon, son of the Clopas mentioned in the Gospels,[19] was worthy of the bishop's throne [in Jerusalem]. It is said that he was a first cousin of the Savior, for Hegesippus relates that Clopas was the brother of Joseph.

12. Hegesippus also reports that after the conquest of Jerusalem, Vespasian ordered that a search be made for all descendants of David so that no member of the royal house should be left among the Jews, which resulted in another great persecution of the Jews.

A.D. 79 **13.** When Vespasian had reigned for ten years, his son Titus succeeded him as emperor. In the second year of Titus's reign, Linus, Bishop of Rome, yielded his office to Anencletus after holding it A.D. 81 for twelve years. Titus was succeeded by his brother Domitian after reigning two years and two months.

14. Now in the fourth year of Domitian, Annianus, the first in the parish of Alexandria, died after completing twenty-two years, and Abilius succeeded him as the second.

---

18. *Vita* 65.
19. John 19:25; perhaps also Luke 24:18.

[This is an example of many such paragraphs to follow that deal with the succession of bishops. The reader would do well to hurry through these, since a complete list of bishops at Jerusalem, Antioch, Alexandria, and Rome is given in Appendix 2.]

15. In the twelfth year of the same reign, Clement succeeded Anencletus after twelve years as Bishop of Rome. In Philippians [4:3], the apostle describes him as a colleague in the words "with Clement and the rest of my coworkers, whose names are in the book of life."

Statue of Titus, emperor 79–81 (*Uffizi, Florence*).

16. In the name of the church at Rome, Clement composed one recognized epistle, long and wonderful, and sent it to the church of the Corinthians, where there had been dissension. This letter was read publicly in many churches both in days of old and in our own. That there was dissension at Corinth in Clement's day is clear from the testimony of Hegesippus.

Domitian's Persecution and Jesus' Relatives

17. With terrible cruelty, Domitian put to death without trial c. A.D. 95 great numbers of men at Rome who were distinguished by family and career, and without cause banished many other notables and confiscated their property. Finally, he showed himself Nero's successor in hostility to God. He was the second to organize a persecution against us, though his father, Vespasian, had no such evil plans.

18. Tradition has it that the apostle and evangelist John was still alive at this time and was condemned to live on the island of Patmos for his testimony to the divine Word. Writing about the number of the name given the Antichrist in Revelation [666 in 13:18], Irenaeus says this about John in Book 5 of his *Against Heresies:*

Head of Domitian, emperor 81–96
(*Glyptotek, Copenhagen*).

Had it been necessary to announce his name clearly at the present time, it would have been stated by the one who saw the revelation. For it was seen not long ago but nearly in our own time, at the end of Domitian's reign.

Indeed, the teaching of our faith glowed so brightly at that time that even writers alien to our belief cited the persecution and martyrdoms in their histories. They even indicated the precise time, stating that

A.D. 96 in the fifteenth year of Domitian, Flavia Domitilla, who was a niece of Flavius Clemens, one of the Roman consuls that year, was banished with many others to the island of Pontia for professing Christ.[20]

19. The same Domitian ordered the execution of all who were in David's line, and an old tradition alleges that some heretics accused the descendants of Jude—the brother of the Savior, humanly speaking—claiming that they were of David's family and related to Christ himself. Hegesippus reports this as follows:

20. Still surviving of the Lord's family were the grandsons of Jude, who was said to be his brother according to the flesh, and they were informed on as being descendants of David. The *evocatus*[21] brought them before Domitian Caesar, who, like Herod, was afraid of the coming of Christ. Domitian asked them if they were descended from David, and they admitted it. Then he asked them how much property and money they had, and they replied that they had only nine thousand denarii between them, half belonging to each. And this, they said, was

---

20. *Suetonius Domitian* 15 and Dio Cassius 67.14 state that Domitilla was the wife, not the niece, of Flavius Clemens. Dio adds that she was also a relative of Domitian (a niece) and that she was banished to Pandateria, not Pontia. Possibly there were two Domitillas, a common name in that clan.

21. A veteran member of the Praetorian or Urban cohorts at Rome who had served his time but continued as a volunteer.

Left: Head of Flavia Domitilla, wife of Domitian's nephew, Flavius Clemens (not his niece, as Eusebius has it). A granddaughter of Vespasian, she donated land for a Christian cemetery, but was exiled because of her conversion to Christianity (*Glytotek, Copenhagen*). *Right:* In the Catacombs of Domitilla at Rome, her name appears in the fourth line of a marble slab. In the fifth she is called the *neptis* or granddaughter of Vespasian.

not in the form of cash but the estimated value of only thirty-nine *plethra* of land,[22] from which they paid taxes and supported themselves from their own labor.

Then [Hegesippus continues], as proof of their toil, they showed him the calluses on their hands and the hardness of their bodies from incessant labor. They were asked about Christ and his kingdom—its nature, origin, and time of appearance. They replied that it was not of this world or earthly but angelic and heavenly, and that it would be established at the end of the world when he would come in glory to judge the living and the dead and reward everyone according to his deeds. At this Domitian did not condemn them but, despising them as simple sorts, let them go free and ordered that the persecution against the church cease. After their release they became leaders of the churches, both for their testimony and because they were of the Lord's family, and they lived on into Trajan's time due to the ensuing peace. Thus far Hegesippus.

---

22. About twenty acres.

Tertullian makes a similar statement about Domitian:

> A Nero in cruelty, Domitian had once tried to do the same as he, but he quickly stopped—I suppose because he had some sense— and recalled those whom he had banished.[23]

A.D. 96   After Domitian had ruled fifteen years, Nerva succeeded. By decree of the Roman senate, the honors of Domitian were annulled and those banished unjustly returned and had their property restored. At that time also, early Christian tradition relates, the apostle John, after his island exile, resumed residence at Ephesus.

Bishops

A.D. 98 **21.** After Nerva had reigned a little over a year he was succeeded by Trajan. In his first year, Abilius, after leading the church at Alexandria for thirteen years, was succeeded by Cerdo, the third in charge there after the first, Annianus. At this time Clement was still head of the Roman church, similarly the third in the list of bishops in Rome who followed Paul and Peter: Linus the first and Anencletus the second.

22. At Antioch, where Evodius had been the first bishop, Ignatius was becoming famous at this time as the second. Similarly, Symeon was second after the brother of our Savior to have charge of the church in Jerusalem.

A Narrative about John

23. At this time, the disciple whom Jesus loved—John, apostle and evangelist—still lived on in Asia [Minor] and directed the churches there, following his return from exile. That he survived this long is confirmed by two reliable and orthodox witnesses: Irenaeus and Clement of Alexandria. In Book 2 of his *Against Heresies,* Irenaeus writes:

> All the elders in Asia associated with John, the Lord's disciple, testify that John taught them the truth, for he remained with them until the time of Trajan.[24]

---

23. *Defense* 5.
24. *Against Heresies* 2.33.

He says the same in Book 3:

> Now the church at Ephesus was founded by Paul, but John remained
> there until Trajan's time, and it is a true witness of the apostolic
> tradition.[25]

In his treatise, *The Rich Man Who Is Saved,* Clement adds
this edifying narrative:

> Listen to a story that is not a story but a true account of John the
> apostle preserved in memory. After the tyrant's death, he returned
> from the island of Patmos to Ephesus and used to go, when asked, to
> the neighboring Gentile districts to appoint bishops, reconcile churches,
> or ordain someone designated by the Spirit. Arriving at a city near
> by [Smyrna], he settled disputes among the brethren and then, notic-
> ing a spirited youth of superior physique and handsome appearance,
> commended him to the appointed bishop with the words: "I leave this
> young man in your keeping, with Christ as my witness."
>
> When John returned to Ephesus, the churchman brought home
> the youth entrusted to his care, raised him, and finally baptized him.
> After this he relaxed his oversight, having put the seal of the Lord on
> him as the perfect safeguard. But some idle and dissolute youths cor-
> rupted him with lavish entertainment and then took him with them
> when they went out at night to commit robbery or worse crimes.
> Soon he joined them and, like a stallion taking the bit in mouth, he
> dashed off the straight road and down the precipice. Renouncing
> God's salvation, he went from petty offenses to major crimes and
> formed the young renegades into a gang of bandits with himself as
> chief, surpassing them all in violence and bloody cruelty.
>
> Time passed, and John paid another visit. When he had finished
> his mission, John said, "Come now, Bishop, return the deposit that
> Christ and I left in your keeping with the church as witness." At first
> the bishop was dumbfounded, thinking that he was being dunned
> for funds he had never received. But John said, "I am asking for the
> young man and his soul."
>
> "He is dead," groaned the old man, in tears.
>
> "How did he die?"
>
> "He is dead to God. He turned out vile and debauched: an out-
> law. Now he is in the mountains, not the church, with an armed gang
> of men like himself."

---

25. *Against Heresies* 3.3.

The apostle tore his clothing, beat his head, and groaned, "A fine guardian I left for our brother's soul! But get me a horse and someone to show me the way." He rode off from the church, just as he was. When he arrived at the hideout and was seized by the outlaws' sentries, he shouted, "This is what I have come for: take me to your leader!" When John approached and the young leader recognized him, he turned and fled in shame. But John ran after him as hard as he could, forgetting his age, and calling out, "Why are you running away from me, child—from your own father, unarmed and old? Pity me, child, don't fear me! I will give account to Christ for you and, if necessary, gladly suffer death and give my life for yours as the Lord suffered death for us. Stop! Believe! Christ sent me."

The young man stopped, stared at the ground, threw down his weapons, and wept bitterly. Flinging his arms around the old man, he begged forgiveness, baptized a second time with his own tears but keeping his right hand hidden.[26] John, however, assured him that he had found forgiveness for him from the Savior. He prayed, knelt down, and kissed that right hand as being cleansed through repen-

The facade of the Library of Celsus (left) and the Gate of Mithridates (right) at the ruins of ancient Ephesus, site of John's later ministry.

---

26. As unworthy of forgiveness for all the bloodshed it had caused.

tance. Then he led him back and did not leave him until—through prayer, fasting, and instruction—he had restored him to the church: a great example of true repentance and regeneration, the trophy of a visible resurrection.

I cite this extract from Clement both for its historical and edifying benefits.

John's Writings

24. Now let me indicate the undisputed writings of this apostle. His Gospel, read by all the churches under heaven, must be recognized first of all. That the early Fathers assigned it to the fourth place after the other three is understandable. Christ's inspired apostles had completely purified their lives and cultivated every virtue yet were only simple men in speech. Bold in the power of the Savior, they had neither the ability nor the desire to present the Master's teachings with rhetorical skills but relied only on the Spirit of God working through them. Thus they proclaimed the kingdom of heaven to all the world and gave little thought to writing books. Paul, for example, who outdid all others in argumentation and intellect, wrote only very short epistles and yet had countless ineffable things to say, caught up as he was in the vision of the third heaven and hearing unutterable words [2 Cor. 12:2].

The other students of our Savior had similar experiences—the twelve apostles, the seventy disciples, and countless others in addition. Yet of all those who had been with the Lord, only Matthew and John have left us their memoirs, and tradition has it that they did so of necessity. Matthew at first preached to Hebrews, and when he planned to go to others also, he wrote his Gospel in his own native language for those he was leaving, his writing filling the gap left by his departure. Mark and Luke had already published their Gospels, but John, it is said, had used only the spoken word until he finally took to writing for the following reason. The three written Gospels in general circulation also came into John's hands. He welcomed them, it is said, and affirmed their accuracy, but noted that the narrative lacked only the account of what Christ had done at the beginning of his mission.

And this is true. The three Evangelists recorded what the Savior did for only one year following the imprisonment of John the Baptist, and they indicated this at the beginning of their narratives. After the forty-day fast and the temptation that followed, Matthew fixes the time clearly in the words, "When Jesus heard that John had been arrested, he withdrew to Galilee" [Matt. 4:12]. Similarly, Mark says, "After John was arrested, Jesus came to Galilee" [Mark 1:14]. Luke, too, makes a similar comment before relating Jesus' deeds in stating that Herod added one more crime to his record by "shutting up John in prison" [Luke 3:19–20].

They say, then, that for this reason John was urged to record in his own Gospel the Savior's deeds during the period passed over in silence by the earlier Evangelists—that is, the events before the Baptist's imprisonment. This is indicated in his words, "Jesus did this, the first of his signs" [2:11], and later, amid his report of Jesus' doings, in mentioning the Baptist as still baptizing at Aenon near Salim, which he makes even clearer in adding, "John, of course, had not yet been thrown into prison" [3:24].

Thus John records what Christ did before the Baptist's imprisonment, while the other three tell of events following. Once this is understood, the Gospels no longer seem to disagree, since John covers Christ's early deeds and the others his later.[27] John probably omitted the genealogy of our Savior as a man since it had already been written by Matthew and Luke and began with the proclamation of his divinity, because the divine Spirit had reserved this for him as one superior to them.

Let this suffice regarding the composition of John's Gospel, and the provenance of Mark's has already been explained. In his preface Luke explains the origin of his work: since many others had somewhat hastily tried to write an account of things for which he was fully informed, he felt obliged to free us from the dubious efforts of the others by providing an accurate account based on his association with Paul and conversation with the other apostles.

Of John's writings, in addition to the Gospel, the first of his epistles has been accepted as authentic both in past and present, but the other two are disputed. As to the Revelation, opinions are evenly divided. Early writers will be cited subsequently on all these issues.

Canonical and Noncanonical Writings

25. At this point it may be appropriate to list the New Testament writings already referred to. The holy quartet of the Gospels are first, followed by the Acts of the Apostles. Next are Paul's epistles, 1 John, and 1 Peter. The Revelation of John may be added, the arguments regarding which I shall discuss at the proper time.

---

27. A faulty explanation. See commentary at the end of this chapter.

These are the recognized books. Those that are disputed yet known to most are the epistles called James, Jude, 2 Peter, and the so-named 2 and 3 John, the work of the Evangelist or of someone else with the same name.

Among the spurious books are the Acts of Paul, the Shepherd [of Hermas], the Revelation of Peter, the alleged epistle of Barnabas, the so-called Teachings of the Apostles *[Didache]*, as well as the Revelation of John, if appropriate here: some reject it, others accept it, as stated before. In addition, some have included the Gospel of the Hebrews in the list, for which those Hebrews who have accepted Christ have a special fondness. These would all be classified with the disputed books, those not canonical yet familiar to most church writers, which I have listed separately in order to distinguish them from those writings that are true, genuine, and accepted in the tradition of the church.

Writings published by heretics under the names of the apostles, such as the Gospels of Peter, Thomas, Matthias, and others, or the Acts of Andrew, John, and other apostles have never been cited by any in the succession of church writers. The type of phraseology used contrasts with apostolic style, and the opinions and thrusts of their contents are so dissonant from true orthodoxy that they show themselves to be forgeries of heretics. Accordingly, they ought not be reckoned even among the spurious books but discarded as impious and absurd.

Menander the Charlatan

26. Let us now continue the history. Menander succeeded Simon Magus, a second tool of the Devil as evil as his predecessor. He too was a Samaritan who, having risen to the same heights of sorcery as his master, reveled in still more miraculous pretensions. He claimed to be the savior who had been sent from above for the salvation of men from invisible eons and taught that no one—not even the angels who made the world—could survive unless rescued through his magic skills and baptism. Such would gain eternal immortality in this present life, no longer mortal but destined to remain here forever and ageless. The writings of Irenaeus record this, while Justin, too, appends to his account of Simon the following:

> A certain Menander, who was also a Samaritan from the village of Caparattea, became a disciple of Simon and was similarly driven by

demons. He appeared in Antioch and deluded many by magical arts. He even persuaded his followers that they would not die, and there are still some of his devotees who believe this.[28]

Certainly it was through the Devil's urging that such impostors usurped the name of Christian to defame the great mystery of religion by magic and to destroy the church's teaching on the immortality of the soul and the resurrection of the dead. But those who termed these men "saviors" fell from the true hope.

The Ebionites, Cerinthus, and Nicolaus

27. Others whom the wicked demon could not shake from God's plan in Christ he made his own through a different trap. These the first Christians named Ebionites—appropriately, in view of their poor and mean opinions about Christ.[29] They regarded him [Christ] as a plain, ordinary man, born of intercourse between a man and Mary, who gained righteousness through character growth. They observed every detail of the Law and did not think that they would be saved by faith in Christ alone and a corresponding life.

Others, however, had the same name but escaped the absurd folly of the aforementioned. They did not deny that the Lord was born of a virgin and the Holy Spirit but nevertheless shared their failu re to confess his preexistence as God the Word and Wisdom. Thus equally impious, they too were zealous in observing the Law literally and thought that the letters of the apostle [Paul] ought to be rejected totally, calling him an apostate from the Law. They used only the so-called Gospel of the Hebrews and accorded the others little respect. Like the former, they observed the Sabbath and the whole Jewish ceremonial, but on the Lord's Days they celebrated rites like ours in commemoration of the Savior's resurrection. Because of these practices, then, they have been dubbed *Ebionites*, a name indicating the poverty of their intelligence, since the term means "poor" in Hebrew.

28. Tradition tells us that at this time Cerinthus founded another heresy. Gaius, whose words I quoted earlier, writes this about him in the *Dialogue* attributed to him:

---

28. Justin Martyr *Defense* 1.26.

29. The term *Ebionite* was derived from the Hebrew term for "the poor."

Moreover, Cerinthus, through revelations supposedly penned by a great apostle, offers us false tales of wonders allegedly shown to him by angels. After the resurrection, he says, the kingdom of Christ will be on earth, and humanity living at Jerusalem will again be enslaved to lusts and pleasure. He is the enemy of the Scriptures of God and, in his anxiety to deceive, claims that the marriage festivities will last a thousand years.

Dionysius too, who was Bishop of Alexandria in my own time, comments from ancient tradition on the Revelation of John in Book 2 of his *Promises* and then refers to Cerinthus in the following words:

> Cerinthus was founder of the Cerinthian heresy named for him, since he wished to add an authoritative note to his creation. He taught that Christ's kingdom would be on earth, and, being in love with his own body and thoroughly sensual, he dreamed up a paradise for his own lusts, full of endless gluttony in eating, drinking, and marrying, or in the euphemisms for these: festivals, sacrifices, and immolation of victims.

Thus far Dionysius. In Book 1 of his *Against Heresies*, Irenaeus cited some of his [Cerinthus's] more disgusting errors and in Book 3 records a memorable incident. According to Polycarp, he states, the apostle John one day went into a bathhouse to take a bath, but when he found Cerinthus inside he leaped out of the place and ran for the door, since he could not endure to be under the same roof. He urged his companions to do the same, crying, "Let's get out of here lest the place fall in: Cerinthus, the enemy of the truth, is inside!"

29. At this time the heresy of the Nicolaitans existed for a short time, mentioned in the Revelation of John [2:15]. They laid claim to Nicolaus, one of the deacons who, with Stephen, was appointed by the apostles to care for the poor [Acts 6:5]. In his *Miscellanies*, Book 6, Clement of Alexandria offers this account of him:

> This man had a beautiful young wife, they say, but when the apostles accused him of jealousy, after the Savior's ascension, he brought her forward and said that anyone who wished could have her. This gesture, they say, resulted from the command, "Treat the flesh with contempt." What was done and said with simplicity and not perversion became unrestrained promiscuity among members of this heresy. But I have learned that Nicolaus had no relations with any other woman than his wife and that his daughters reached old age in virginity and that his

son remained chaste. Accordingly, his bringing the wife whom he loved jealously into the midst of the apostles was the renunciation of passion, and it was control of the pleasures he had sought that prompted the rule, "Treat the flesh with contempt." Obeying the Savior's command, he did not wish to serve two masters: Pleasure and the Lord. They also say that Matthias taught this: fight against the flesh; never yield to pleasure, but nourish the soul through faith and knowledge.[30]

So much, then, for attempts against the truth made at this time, which were extinguished completely in less time than it takes to tell.

Apostles Who Married

30. In rebuttal to those who rejected marriage, Clement goes on to list those apostles who married:

Or will they reject even the apostles? For Peter and Philip had children, and Philip gave his daughters in marriage, while Paul himself does not hesitate in one of his letters to address his wife,[31] whom he did not take around with him in order to facilitate his ministry.[32]

To quote another interesting narrative from Clement on this theme, from Book 7 of his *Miscellanies:*

They say that when the blessed Peter saw his wife led away to death, he rejoiced that her call had come and that she was returning home. He called out to her by name in encouragement and comfort, "Remember the Lord!" Such was the marriage of the blessed and their perfect affection.[33]

The Deaths of John and Philip

31. When and how Peter and Paul died and where their bodies were laid I have already related. The time of John's death has also been mentioned, and the place where his remains lie is shown

---

30. *Miscellanies* 3.4.25–26.

31. In Phil. 4:3, the Greek *suzuge* (literally "yokefellow") can be translated either "wife" or "comrade." Whether Paul married is not known.

32. 1 Cor. 9:5. Clement's citation: *Miscellanies* 3.6.52ff.

33. *Miscellanies* 7.11.63–64.

in a letter from Polycrates, Bishop of Ephesus, to Victor, Bishop of Rome. In it he refers to John, Philip the apostle, and Philip's daughters as follows:

> Great luminaries sleep in Asia who shall rise again on the last day at the Lord's advent, when he shall come with glory from heaven and call back all his saints—such as Philip, one of the twelve apostles, who sleeps at Hierapolis, with two of his aged, virgin daughters, while a third daughter lived in the Holy Spirit and rests in Ephesus. There is also John, who leaned on the Lord's breast and who became a priest wearing the miter, a martyr, and a teacher; he too sleeps in Ephesus.

In the *Dialogue* of Gaius, mentioned earlier, Proclus, with whom he was disputing, speaks similarly about the deaths of Philip and his daughters:

> After him the four daughters of Philip, who were prophetesses, were at Hierapolis in Asia. Their grave is there and so is their father's.

In Acts, Luke mentions Philip's daughters as then living with their father at Caesarea in Judea and accorded the gift of prophecy:

> We left and came to Caesarea; and we went into the house of Philip the evangelist, one of the seven, and stayed with him. He had four unmarried daughters who had the gift of prophecy.[34]

These are the facts regarding the apostles and their times, as I know them, as well as their sacred writings, the books disputed though used in many churches, and those altogether fictitious. Let us now resume the narrative.

The Martyrdom of Symeon, Bishop of Jerusalem

32. After Nero and Domitian, under the emperor [Trajan] whose times I am now describing, tradition tells of sporadic persecution against us in some cities as a result of popular riots. In the course of it, Symeon, son of Clopas, the second Bishop of Jerusalem, as

---

34. Acts 21:8-9. Clearly there is a confusion in these citations between Philip the apostle and Philip the deacon.

stated earlier, ended his life in martyrdom. This is on the authority of Hegesippus, who, writing about certain heretics, goes on to describe how they accused Symeon and how, after many days of varied tortures for being a Christian—to the astonishment of the judge and his assessors—he suffered an end like that of the Lord. It is better, however, to listen to the historian himself:

> Some of these heretics accused Symeon,[35] the son of Clopas, of being descended from David and a Christian, and so he suffered martyrdom at age 120, when Trajan was emperor and Atticus was consular governor.[36]

The same writer says that his accusers were also arrested for being members of the Judean royal house when such were being hunted. And one may reasonably conclude that Symeon both saw and heard the Lord, in view of the length of his life and reference in the Gospels to Mary, wife of Clopas whose son he was, as previously noted.

The same writer says that other descendants of one of the Savior's brothers named Jude lived on into the same reign after declaring their faith in Christ before Domitian, as recorded earlier. He writes:

> Therefore they came and presided over every church as witnesses and members of the Lord's family, and since there was total peace in every church they survived until the reign of Trajan, when the son of the Lord's uncle, the aforesaid Symeon,[37] son of Clopas, was similarly accused by heretical sectarians on the same charge before Atticus, the provincial governor. He was tortured for many days in giving his witness, so that all, even the governor, were astounded at how he endured it all at 120 years of age; and he was sentenced to crucifixion.

Hegesippus goes on to say that until then the church had remained a virgin, pure and uncorrupted, and any who might have tried to defile her lurked in obscure darkness. But when the sacred band of the apostles and the generation of those who heard the divine wisdom with their own ears passed on, then godless

---

35. Here spelled "Simon" in the Greek text of Eusebius.

36. In his *Chronicle* Eusebius places Symeon's martyrdom in the ninth or tenth year of Trajan (107 or 108). Atticus is not datable.

37. Here also spelled "Simon" in the Greek text.

Bust of Trajan, emperor 98–117 (*Uffizi, Florence*).

error began through the deceit of false teachers who, now that the apostles were gone, tried to counter the truth by proclaiming falsely the knowledge *[gnosis]* so-called.

Trajan Halts Hunting of Christians

33. So great was the persecution[38] against us in many places that Pliny the Younger, one of the most distinguished governors, was alarmed at the number of martyrs, which he reported to the emperor. In the same letter he mentioned that they did nothing evil or illegal: they merely rose at dawn to sing to Christ as if a god, and they forbade adultery, murder, and similar crimes and in every way conformed to the law. In response Trajan issued an edict that Christians were not to be hunted out but were to be punished if they were identified. While this meant that the threat of imminent persecution was curbed to some extent, opportunities remained to those who wished to injure us. Sometimes the common people, sometimes the authorities, devised plots against us, so that even with no open persecution, periodic attacks broke

c. 112

---

38. The adjacent date and all such marginal dates henceforth are A.D.

out in scattered provinces, and many of the faithful endured martyrdom in various forms. This information derives from the Latin Defense of Tertullian, cited earlier, which translates as follows:

> Seeking us out was also forbidden, for Pliny the Younger, governor of the province [Bithynia], after condemning certain Christians and reducing their rank, was alarmed at their number. Not knowing what to do in the future, he wrote the emperor Trajan that he found nothing wicked in their behavior, other than their unwillingness to worship idols. He further informed him that the Christians rose at dawn, sang hymns to Christ as a god, and upheld their teachings by forbidding murder, adultery, fraud, robbery, and the like. In response Trajan sent a rescript that Christians were not to be hunted out but were to be punished if found.[39]

Succession of Bishops

34. In the third year of Trajan's reign, Clement turned over the ministry of the bishops of Rome to Evarestus and departed this life, having supervised the teaching of the divine Word for nine years.

35. When Symeon had found fulfillment [in martyrdom] in the manner already described, a certain Jew named Justus, one of the vast number of the circumcision who believed in Christ by that time, succeeded to the bishop's throne of Jerusalem.

Ignatius of Antioch

c. 110
36. Celebrated at that time in Asia was a companion of the apostles, Polycarp, who had been appointed Bishop of Smyrna by the eyewitnesses and ministers of the Lord. Distinguished contemporaries of his were Papias, Bishop of Hierapolis, and Ignatius, still a famed name as second after Peter to succeed to the bishopric of Antioch. Tradition has it that he [Ignatius] was sent from Syria to Rome and became food for wild animals because of his witness to Christ. He was brought through Asia under the strictest guard, strengthening the Christian community by speech and encouragement in every city where he stayed. He warned them in particular

---

39. *Defense* 2. The letter that Pliny wrote and Trajan's response have survived intact. Although the letters are more detailed than the summaries provided by Tertullian and Eusebius, the latter faithfully reported the gist of their contents.

to be on guard against the heresies that were then first beginning to spring up, urging them to hold fast to the apostolic tradition, which he thought necessary to put in writing for safety's sake. Thus, while he was in Smyrna where Polycarp was, he wrote one letter to the church at Ephesus, referring to their pastor Onesimus; another to the church at Magnesia on the Meander, in which he refers to Bishop Damas; and another to the church at Tralles, then under the rule of Polybius, as he states. He also wrote to the church at Rome, requesting in it that they not deprive him of his longed-for hope by asking that he be released from martyrdom. To quote short passages from these letters:

> From Syria to Rome, I am fighting with wild animals on land and sea night and day, chained to ten leopards—a troop of soldiers—whom kindness makes even worse. Their shameful deeds increase my discipleship, but this does not justify me. May I benefit from those wild beasts that are ready for me, and I pray that they are prompt. I will coax them to devour me quickly, not as with some whom they have been afraid to touch. If they are unwilling, I will force them to do it. Pardon me, but I know what is best for me: now I am starting to be a disciple. May I envy nothing seen or unseen in gaining Jesus Christ. Let fire and cross, struggles with beasts, tearing bones apart, mangling of limbs, crushing of my whole body, and tortures of the Devil come upon me, if only I may attain to Jesus Christ![40]

This he wrote from Smyrna. Later in his journey he wrote the Christians at Philadelphia from Troas, as well as the church at Smyrna, especially Polycarp, the head of the church. Knowing that Polycarp was an apostolic man, he commended to him the flock at Antioch like a true shepherd, asking his earnest care for it. In his letter to Smyrna he quotes an unknown source regarding Christ:

> I know and believe that even after the Resurrection he was in the flesh. When he came to Peter and his companions he said to them, "Take hold, touch me and see that I am not a bodiless spirit." And they touched him at once and believed.[41]

Irenaeus knew of his martyrdom and quotes from his letters:

---

40. Ignatius *Romans* 5.

41. Ignatius *Smyrneans* 3. The scene is obviously based on Luke 24:39, but the Greek is different, and Luke does not report Jesus being touched.

As one of ours said when condemned to the beasts as martyr for God: "I am the wheat of God, to be ground by the teeth of the beasts that I may be found pure bread."[42]

Polycarp also mentions these things in his letter to the Philippians:

> I urge all of you to practice the obedience and endurance you saw not only in the blessed Ignatius, Rufus, and Zosimus, but also in others among you and in Paul himself and the other apostles, who did not run in vain but in faith and righteousness, who are in the place they deserve at the side of the Lord whose suffering they shared. For they did not love this present world but him who died for us and was raised by God on our behalf. . . . You and Ignatius both wrote me that if anyone was going to Syria he should take your letters also. I will do so either personally or by sending a representative in our behalf. With this letter I enclose the epistles Ignatius sent us, as requested, as well as others I have. You will greatly benefit from them, for they offer faith, patience, and edification.[43]

Such is the material regarding Ignatius. Hero succeeded him as Bishop of Antioch.

Evangelist Missionaries

37. Among the illustrious of that time was Quadratus, who, according to tradition, had a prophetic gift like that of Philip's daughters. Many others besides them were famed members of the first rank in apostolic succession, eager disciples of great men, who built everywhere on the foundations of churches laid by the apostles, sowing the saving seed through the whole [known] world. Many of them, smitten by the divine Word, first fulfilled the Savior's command by distributing their property to the needy. Then, leaving their homes, they took up the work of evangelists, eager to preach the message of faith to those who had never heard it and to provide them the inspired Gospels in writing. As soon as they had laid the foundations of the faith in some foreign place, they appointed others as pastors to tend those newly brought in and then set off again to other lands and peoples. The grace and cooperation of God assisted them, for even at that date many miraculous wonders of the divine

---

42. Irenaeus *Against Heresies* 5.28, quoting Ignatius *Romans* 4.
43. Polycarp *Philippians* 10.13.

Spirit worked through them, so that whole crowds eagerly embraced worship of the universal Creator at the first hearing.

It is impossible to give the names and numbers of all who first succeeded the apostles and became pastors or evangelists in churches throughout the world. Therefore I have recorded by name only those whose tradition of apostolic teaching still survives to our time in their writings.

The Writings of Clement

38. Such writings, of course, include the letters of Ignatius, already listed, and the epistle of Clement, recognized by all, which he wrote in the name of the church at Rome to the Corinthians. In this he reflects many thoughts from the epistle to the Hebrews and indeed makes verbal quotations from it—proving clearly that it was not of recent origin—and for this reason too it has seemed natural to include it among other writings of the apostle. For Paul had written to the Hebrews in their native language, and some say that the evangelist Luke, others that this same Clement translated the writing. The truth of the latter shows in the similar phraseology of Clement and Hebrews and the lack of any great difference in thought in the two works.

A second epistle is also ascribed to Clement, but it was not well known like the first, and I do not even know if the early Fathers used it. Recently other long and wordy treatises have been claimed as Clement's, with [alleged] dialogues between Peter and Apion,[44] but there is no mention of them whatever by early writers, nor do they preserve the purity of apostolic orthodoxy.

The Writings of Papias

39. So much for the recognized writings of Clement, Ignatius, and Polycarp. Of Papias, five books are extant, entitled *The Sayings of the Lord Interpreted.* These are mentioned also by Irenaeus as his only works:

> To these things also Papias—who was an ancient writer, heard John, and was a companion of Polycarp—bears written witness in the fourth of his books, for he composed five.[45]

---

44. Probably the so-called *Clementine Homilies*, which are early didactic novels.
45. *Against Heresies* 5.33.

So says Irenaeus. But Papias himself, in his preface, by no means claims that he had been a hearer and an eyewitness of the holy apostles but says that he had learned the basics of the faith from those who had known them:

> Along with the interpretations, I shall not hesitate to add all that I ever learned and carefully remembered from the elders,[46] for I am sure of its truth. Unlike most, I did not delight in those who say much but in those who teach the truth; not in those who recite the commandments of others but in those who repeated the commandments given by the Lord. And whenever anyone came who had been a follower of the elders, I asked about their words: what Andrew or Peter had said, or Philip or Thomas or James or John or Matthew or any other of the Lord's disciples, and what Aristion and the presbyter John, disciples of the Lord, were still saying. For I did not think that information from books would help me as much as the word of a living, surviving voice.

It should be noted that twice Papias includes the name of John, the first listed with Peter, James, Matthew, and the other apostles; the second in another nonapostolic group, putting Aristion first and clearly calling John a presbyter. This confirms the truth of the story that two men in Asia had the same name and that there are two tombs at Ephesus, each called John's to this day. This is important, for it is likely that the second saw the Revelation bearing the name of John—unless anyone prefer the first. Papias thus admits that he learned the words of the apostles from their followers but says that he personally heard Aristion and John the presbyter. He often quotes them by name and includes their traditions in his writings.

Papias also reports certain miraculous incidents and other matters that apparently reached him by tradition. That Philip the apostle lived at Hierapolis with his daughters has already been mentioned, but it must now be told how Papias, who knew them, heard a wonderful story from Philip's daughters. He tells of the resurrection of a corpse in his own lifetime[47] and of another miracle, involving Justus, surnamed Barsabas, who drank poison but by the Lord's grace suffered no harm. This is the Justus whom the

---

46. The Greek *presbyteroi* translates either "elders" or "presbyters." I have used the former in much of the text but "John the Presbyter" in the material that follows, since he is usually styled thus.

47. The wife of Manaen (Acts 13:1), according to Papias.

Major centers of early Christianity cited in the New Testament and Eusebius. In the first three centuries, Asia Minor contained the greatest number of Christians in the world, a number drastically reduced in modern Turkey due to the rise of Islam.

holy apostles nominated along with Matthias after the Savior's ascension to replace, by casting lots, the traitor Judas. According to Acts [1:23], "So they proposed two, Joseph called Barsabas, who was known as Justus, and Matthias."

Papias supplies other stories that reached him by word of mouth, along with some strange parables and unknown teachings of the Savior, as well as other more legendary accounts. Among them, he says that after the resurrection of the dead there will be a thousand-year period when the kingdom of Christ will be established on this earth in material form. I suppose that he got these notions by misunderstanding the apostolic accounts, not realizing that they had used mystic and symbolic language. For he was a man of very limited intelligence, as is clear from his books. Due to him, however, many church writers after him held the same opinion, relying on his early date: Irenaeus, for example, and any others who adopted the same views.

Papias also quotes other interpretations of the Lord's sayings given by Aristion, mentioned above, or John the presbyter. Regarding Mark, the writer of the Gospel, he states:

The Presbyter used to say this also: "Mark became Peter's interpreter and wrote down accurately, but not in order, all that he remembered of the things said and done by the Lord. For he had not heard the Lord or been one of his followers, but later, as I said, a follower of Peter. Peter used to teach as the occasion demanded, without giving systematic arrangement to the Lord's sayings, so that Mark did not err in writing down some things just as he recalled them. For he had one overriding purpose: to omit nothing that he had heard and to make no false statements in his account."

Such is Papias's reference to Mark. Of Matthew he had this to say:

Matthew compiled the sayings [*logia* of Christ] in the Hebrew language,[48] and each interpreted them as best he could.

Papias also used evidence from 1 John and 1 Peter and provides another story about a woman falsely accused before the Lord of many sins, which is contained in the Gospel of the Hebrews. Let this suffice.

---

48. Probably Aramaic is intended, just as in the New Testament.

EUSEBIUS'S SOURCES

That Eusebius was in the habit of quoting source after source is by now patent, and some scholars have faulted him for stringing together long citations with very little historiography of his own. Were he a modern historian, this critique would be justified, particularly in Book 3—the present chapter. But several things might be said in his behalf. Subsequently, when Eusebius records events closer to his own day, he does this less, and when he deals with contemporary material as in the Great Persecution after 303, he reports as an eyewitness and has less need of prior sources.

At it happened, however, it is most fortunate that Eusebius did quote his sources extensively, since many of them have been lost and would not have survived, even in fragments, had Eusebius not incorporated them into his history. This is not true for Josephus, whom we have virtually intact, or for some of the works of the two Clements, Ignatius, Polycarp, Justin, Irenaeus, or Tertullian. But it is true for the important testimony of Papias, Quadratus, Melito, Hegesippus, Rhodo, Apollinarius, and other early authors, as well as for important edicts and documents that would otherwise have been lost.

Contemporary readers may recoil at Eusebius's repeated references to God's punishing the Jews with the destruction of Jerusalem for their "crime against Christ." Unfortunately, this opinion was rather typical of early Christian polemic in the struggle between church and synagogue, and Eusebius is more restrained in this respect than some other writers of his day. If many of the early Christian writers were anti-Judaic, it is equally true that many early Jewish writers were anti-Christian, and Jews in some localities helped incite persecution against the Christians. This, of course, is not to defend excesses and intolerance on either side.

Eusebius's concern to ferret out information on the fate of the apostles and early church fathers nicely mirrors modern interests in doing the same, and he is not uncritical in his judgments. While appreciating Papias's tangency with early apostolic tradition, for example, he does not hide his disdain for Papias's chiliastic notions. Similarly, he vents his doubts about disputed books in the canon while trying to be fair to those who deemed them canonical.

His attempt to explain why John differs from the Synoptic Gospels as to the length of Jesus' ministry—namely, that John covers Jesus' public ministry before the imprisonment of John the Baptist, whereas the Synoptics focus on what happened afterward—is only fractionally true and untenable as a full explanation. This is a strange lapse on the part of Eusebius, who usually is more careful in his biblical interpretation.

Terms that Eusebius uses early in his history (e.g., the "Bishop of Rome" or "of Antioch," the "bishopric of Jerusalem," the "diocese at Alexandria") are largely anachronistic and reflect later stages in the development of church hierarchy closer to Eusebius's own day. Clement of Rome, for example, was hardly bishop in the later sense but rather a presbyter in charge of communicating concerns of the Roman church to believers in Corinth.

This book in Eusebius's *Church History* is particularly valuable for tracing the formation of the New Testament canon. As is clear in these pages, the canon was not arrived at through any decisions of an early ecumenical council. Rather, it was the use of the various New Testament writings at various centers of early Christendom that determined eventual canonicity. Eusebius will have much more to say about the development of the canon.

In Roman history at this time, Nero was toppled by the Roman governor of Spain, *Galba* (68–69), followed in quick succession by *Otho* (69), *Vitellius* (69), and *Vespasian* (69–79), giving rise to the phrase "the year of the four emperors." Vespasian, Roman commander of the Jewish War until he was called to the purple, was founder of the Flavian dynasty, and he brought order, respect, and economy back into Roman government. A no-nonsense sort with a good sense of humor, Vespasian was a bald sixty-year-old at his accession, toughened from service on many Roman frontiers and loved by the army. Astute in mathematics, he was able to balance the books and even find new revenues from such inventions of his as the pay toilet (called *vespasiani* in Rome to this day). His public works included the great Flavian Amphitheater (Colosseum) at Rome, which he did not intend for Christian persecution, since neither he nor his son Titus resumed Nero's policy of suppression.

Titus (79–81), whom Vespasian had left in charge of the Jewish War, conquered Jerusalem in 70. He became a very popular emperor upon the death of his father. Titus had a love affair with the Jewish princess Bernice, sister of Agrippa II (Acts 25), but subsequently left her for political reasons. Early in his administration Mount Vesuvius erupted, inundating Herculaneum and Pompeii, and his too-brief reign was terminated by a mortal fever in 81.

His brother *Domitian* (81–96), who succeeded Titus, was an inferior autocrat who seems to have instigated the second Roman persecution of Christians. This one affected also the Roman nobility—Domitian's relatives Clemens and Domitilla were among the victims—and it must have involved the East as well, since Eusebius tells of the apostle John's exile to Patmos. The first letter of Clement (c. 95) may well reflect this persecution, which did not continue beyond Domitian's assassination in 96 and the end of the Flavian dynasty.

Then followed the so-called five good emperors, from 96 to 180, four of whom chose as successors not sons (they had none) but the most worthy subordinates they could find. *Nerva* (96–98) was a clever old jurist who was deferent to the senate and good for Rome. He adopted as son and successor *Trajan* (98–117), whose conquests in Dacia and Mesopotamia expanded the boundaries of the Roman Empire to their greatest extent. Trajan's moderate policy vis-à-vis the Christians surfaced in his celebrated correspondence with Pliny, governor of Bithynia (c. 112), in which the emperor advised him not to seek out the Christians, even if the law had to take its course in the case of those properly indicted. Still, Bishop Ignatius of Antioch was arrested and martyred (probably c. 110) in Rome under his administration.

Book 4

BISHOPS, WRITINGS, AND MARTYRDOMS

TRAJAN TO MARCUS AURELIUS

1. About the twelfth year of Trajan's reign, the Bishop of Alexandria [Cerdo] departed this life, and Primus succeeded him, the fourth from the apostles. At Rome, meanwhile, when Evarestus had completed his eighth year, Alexander became bishop, the fifth successor to Peter and Paul.

Jewish Revolts

2. While our Savior's teaching and the church were flourishing and growing day by day, the tragedy of the Jews was nearing its climax. In the emperor's eighteenth year, another Jewish rebellion broke out that destroyed vast numbers of them. In Alexandria, the rest of Egypt, and especially in Cyrene, they rushed into rioting against their Greek fellow citizens, and, augmenting the insurrection in the following year, they started a full-scale war while Lupus was governor of all Egypt. In the first clash they defeated the Greeks, who fled to Alexandria where they captured or killed the city's Jews. Though losing their help, the Jews of Cyrene continued plundering the districts of Egypt under their leader Lucuas.[1]

The emperor sent Marcius Turbo against them with sea and land forces, including cavalry. He waged a relentless war against them, killing vast numbers of Jews in many battles, not only those in Cyrene, but also those from Egypt who had rallied behind Lucuas their leader. Suspecting that Jews in Mesopotamia would

---

1. Dio Cassius (68.32) names him Andreas.

also attack people there, the emperor ordered Lusius Quietus to clean them out of the province. He organized his forces and slaughtered great numbers there, for which the emperor appointed him governor of Judea. The Greek authors who wrote histories of the same period have recorded the events similarly.[2]

Hadrian, Quadratus, and Aristides

3. When Trajan had ruled for nineteen and a half years, Aelius 117 Hadrian succeeded to the throne. To him Quadratus addressed a defense of our faith, because certain wicked men were trying to get our people into trouble. Many of the brethren still have copies of this work, as I do myself, a clear proof of the author's intellect and apostolic orthodoxy. The following reveals his early date:

> Our Savior's deeds were always there to see, for they were true: those who were cured or those who rose from the dead were seen not only when they were cured or raised but were constantly there to see, not only while the Savior was living among us, but also for some time after his departure. Some of them, in fact, survived right up to our own time.

A man of faith and devoted to our religion, Aristides has also, like Quadratus, left us a defense of the faith addressed to Hadrian. Many still preserve copies of his work also, even to the present day.[3]

Bishops at Rome, Alexandria, and Jerusalem

4. In the third year of the same reign, Alexander, Bishop of Rome, died after finishing the tenth year of his ministry; his successor was Xystus. About the same time, in the diocese of Alexandria Justus succeeded Primus, who died in the twelfth year of his rule.

5. I have failed to find any written record of the dates of the bishops in Jerusalem—tradition says they were very short-lived—

---

2. Dio Cassius and Orosius.

3. Although Quadratus, the earliest known Christian apologist, is preserved only in the preceding fragment from Eusebius, Aristides' *Apology*, also thought lost, was discovered in Syriac form by J. Rendel Harris in 1889 at Mount Sinai. Many scholars think the treatise was addressed not to Hadrian but to his successor, Antoninus Pius.

Statue of Hadrian, emperor 117–138
(*Uffizi, Florence*).

but I have documentary evidence that there were fifteen up to Hadrian's siege of the Jews. All were said to have been Hebrews in origin who had accepted the knowledge of Christ and so were deemed worthy of the episcopal office. For the church there consisted entirely of Hebrew Christians from the apostles down to the Roman siege following the second Jewish revolt. Since bishops of the circumcision then ceased, this is the time to give their names from the beginning. First was James, called the Lord's brother, and after him Symeon was the second. Third was Justus, fourth Zaccheus, fifth Tobias, sixth Benjamin, seventh John, eighth Matthias, ninth Philip, tenth Seneca, eleventh Justus, twelfth Levi, thirteenth Ephres, fourteenth Joseph, and fifteenth and last, Judas. These were the bishops of Jerusalem in that period, all of the circumcision.

In Hadrian's twelfth year, Xystus, Bishop of Rome for ten years, was succeeded by Telesphorus, the seventh from the apostles. One year and some months later, Eumenes succeeded his predecessor of eleven years in the diocese of Alexandria.

The Bar-Kokhba Revolt

132–135   **6.** When the Jewish rebellion again grew formidable, Rufus, the governor of Judea, received military assistance from the emperor and moved against their madness with no mercy. He destroyed thousands of men, women, and children, and—under the laws of war—confiscated their lands. The Jews at the time were led by a certain Bar-Kokhba, which means "star,"[4] a murderous bandit who, on

---

4. Literally, "son of a star" in Aramaic. The star was a messianic symbol among the Jews (see Num. 24:17; Matt. 2:2–12). After his defeat he was called *Bar-Koziba*, "son of a liar."

the strength of his name, claimed to be a luminary come down from heaven to shed light on those in misery, as if they were slaves.

In Hadrian's eighteenth year, the war reached its climax at Betthera, a strongly fortified little town not far from Jerusalem. After a long siege, hunger and thirst drove the rebels to destruction, and the instigator of their madness paid the penalty he deserved. Hadrian then commanded that the whole [Jewish] nation be forbidden to set foot anywhere near Jerusalem, so it could not even be seen from a distance. Aristo of Pella tells the story.[5] Then, with the city divested of the Jewish race and its inhabitants destroyed, it was colonized by foreigners, and the Roman city that later arose changed its name to Aelia, in honor of the reigning emperor, Aelius Hadrian. Since the church there was now composed of Gentiles, the first bishop after those of the circumcision was Mark.

The Gnostics

7. Like brilliant lights the churches were now illuminating the world, and faith in our Lord Jesus Christ was flourishing everywhere when the Devil, who hates what is good, true, and saving, turned all his weapons against the church. Previously he had attacked her from the outside through persecutions, but now that he was prevented, he resorted to internal tactics, using wicked impostors as corrupt agents of destruction, assuming the name of our religion to destroy every believer they could ensnare while deflecting unbelievers from the path that leads to salvation.

From Menander, previously mentioned as successor to Simon [Magus], issued a serpentine power with two mouths and twin heads that established two heretical leaders: Saturninus, an Antiochene by birth, and Basilides of Alexandria, who founded schools of detestable heresy in Syria and in Egypt. Saturninus largely taught the same false doctrines as Menander, as Irenaeus makes clear, but Basilides, under the pretense of secret mysteries, stretched fantasy to the infinite in devising monstrous myths. Among the many churchmen fighting for the truth and apostolic beliefs, some also put into writing for their successors' benefit methods of defense against these heresies.

Of these, I have a very powerful refutation of Basilides from the pen of Agrippa Castor, a famous author of that time. Exposing his deception, he says that Basilides compiled twenty-four books

---

5. His writings are not extant.

on the Gospel and that he named as his own prophets Bar-Cabbas and Bar-Coph and other imaginaries, inventing outlandish names for them to impress the gullible. He taught that there was no harm in eating things offered to idols or in freely denying the faith in times of persecution. Like Pythagoras, he directed those who came to him to keep silent for five years. Castor writes similar items about Basilides, magnificently refuting his heresy.

Irenaeus also writes that Carpocrates was a contemporary of these, the father of another heresy called that of the Gnostics. Unlike Basilides, who claimed to transmit Simon's magic secretly, they did so openly, flaunting their spells and sorcery, dreams and seances. They teach that those who intend to become initiates in their mysteries (or rather, obscenities) must perform all the vilest deeds, for in no other way can they elude the "cosmic rulers." By using such ministers, the demon made slaves of pitiful dupes and brought discredit on the divine Word among unbelievers, since scandal tainted the whole Christian community. It was primarily because of this that a wicked and blasphemous suspicion regarding us circulated among the heathen of that day: that we practiced incest with mothers and sisters and partook of wicked food.[6]

But this success was brief, for the truth reasserted itself and gleamed more brightly as time went on. Though one new heresy after another was invented, the earlier ones continually fragmented and disappeared. But the universal and only true church, remaining ever the same, continued to grow in greatness, shedding on Greeks and non-Greeks alike the free, sober, and pure light of the divine teaching for conduct and thought. The passage of time, then, squelched the defamations against our teaching so that it stands alone, victorious and supreme, and no one today dares to resume the vile slanders of past enemies against our faith.

Church Writers of the Period

At that time, however, Truth again deployed more champions for herself who did battle against the godless heresies in both oral and written form.

8. Among these, Hegesippus was famed, whom I have often quoted regarding the apostolic age. In five books, written in the simplest

---

6. A popular calumny against Christians of the time was that they killed and ate small children.

style, he provided the authentic tradition of the apostolic preaching. In writing about those who made idols he indicates when he flourished:

> They erected cenotaphs and temples to them and still do. Among them was Antinous, a slave of Hadrian Caesar, in whose memory the Antinoian Games are held. He was my contemporary. Hadrian even built a city named after him and appointed prophets [for his cult].[7]

At the same time also, Justin, a lover of the true philosophy, was still studying Greek learning. He too indicates this period in his *Defense* to Antoninus [Pius] in the words:

> At this point I think it not out of place to mention Antinous of our own day. All were intimidated into worshiping him as a god, though everyone knew who he was and where he came from.[8]

And in telling of the war against the Jews, Justin remarks:

> In the recent Jewish war, Bar-Kokhba, the leader of the Jewish rebellion, ordered Christians alone to be punished severely if they did not deny Jesus as the Messiah and blaspheme him.[9]

In the same book he shows that his conversion from Greek philosophy to true religion did not happen irrationally but from cool deliberation:

> While reveling in Plato's teaching, I myself heard the Christians abused, but when I saw that they were not afraid of death or anything dreadful, it occurred to me that they could not possibly be living in wickedness as libertines. For how could a hedonist or a voluptuary who enjoyed devouring human flesh greet the death that would deprive him of the objects of his lusts? Would he not instead try to prolong his present life by all means and elude the authorities rather than surrender himself to certain death?[10]

---

7. Antinous, from Bithynia, was Hadrian's homosexual lover who drowned in the Nile in 130. Hadrian built the city of Antinoöpolis in his honor.

8. *Defense* 1.29.

9. *Defense* 1.31.

10. *Defense* 2.12.

Justin also tells how Hadrian received an appeal in behalf of the Christians from Serennius Granianus, a distinguished governor, who wrote that it was not right to put them to death without a trial to appease popular clamor, and that he sent a rescript to Minucius Fundanus, proconsul of Asia, ordering him to try no one unless he were charged and prosecuted in a reasonable manner. Justin appends a copy of the letter in the original Latin, with the following as preface [written to Antoninus Pius]:

> Though I might have requested that you order trials to be held on the basis of a letter from the great and glorious Caesar Hadrian, your father, I prefer to plead justice rather than Hadrian's command. But I also append a copy of Hadrian's letter, that you may know I am speaking the truth in this matter. Here it is.

The writer appends the Latin rescript itself, but I have translated it into Greek as well as I can:

c. 125   9.   To Minucius Fundanus. I received a letter written to me by your predecessor, the illustrious Serennius Granianus. I think the matter should not remain uninvestigated lest people be harassed and informers be aided in their mischief. If, then, the provincials can establish so clear a case against the Christians as to plead it before a legal tribunal, let them use this procedure only and not be moved by mere petitions or howling. It is much more appropriate, if anyone should wish to prosecute, that you decide the matter. If, then, anyone indicts them and proves their acting illegally, you should judge them according to the seriousness of the offense. But, by Hercules, if anyone launches such proceedings as a false informer [for financial gain], investigate thoroughly and see that you make the punishment fit the crime.[11]

Such were the terms of Hadrian's rescript.

Bishops and Heretics

138   **10.**   After twenty-one years, Hadrian paid nature's debt, and Antoninus Pius received Roman sovereignty. In his first year, Telesphorus departed this life in the eleventh year of his minis-

---

11. *Defense* 1.68.

try, and Hyginus became Bishop of Rome. Irenaeus reports that Telesphorus died nobly in martyrdom. He also states that while Hyginus was bishop, Valentinus, founder of a heresy of his own, and Cerdo, who introduced the Marcionite error, were both prominent in Rome. He writes:

> **11.** Valentinus came to Rome in the time of Hyginus, flourished under Pius, and survived until Anicetus. Cerdo, before Marcion's time, in the days of the ninth bishop, Hyginus, also joined the Roman church and confessed his faith. But then he went on in this way: sometimes he taught in secret, sometimes publicly, and another time he was convicted of false teaching and expelled from the Christian community.[12]

This comes from Book 3 of *Against Heresies*. In Book 1 he says the following about Cerdo:

> A certain Cerdo, influenced by the followers of Simon, had settled in Rome in the time of Hyginus, who held ninth place in the succession from the apostles. He taught that the God proclaimed by the Law and the Prophets was not the Father of our Lord Jesus Christ, for the latter was known, the other unknown; the former also was just, but the other was gracious. Marcion of Pontus succeeded him and expanded his teaching with unblushing blasphemy.[13]

Irenaeus skillfully exposed the boundless depths of error in Valentinus's system and the wickedness in which he lurked like a reptile. He also tells of a Marcus, their contemporary, a master of the magical arts, and of his senseless initiations and disgusting mysteries:

> Some of them arrange a bridal chamber and celebrate a mystery with invocations on their initiates, claiming that what they are doing is a spiritual marriage patterned on those above. Others take them to water and baptize them with the invocation, "Into the name of the unknown Father of the universe, into Truth the Mother of all things, into him who descended into Jesus." Others invoke Hebrew words in order to astonish initiates even more.[14]

---

12. *Against Heresies* 3.4.
13. *Against Heresies* 1.14.
14. *Against Heresies* 1.14.

After four years as Bishop of Rome, Hyginus died, and Pius succeeded. At Alexandria, Mark was appointed when Eumenes had completed thirteen years, and when Mark rested from the ministry after a decade, Celadion took it over. In Rome, Pius passed away in the fifteenth year of his ministry and Anicetus presided there. In his time Hegesippus states that he settled in Rome and remained there until the episcopate of Eleutherus.

In their time Justin was at the height of his career. In the garb of a philosopher he served as ambassador of the divine Word and fought for the faith through his writings. He wrote a treatise against Marcion and says that the heretic was alive and notorious at the time he was writing:

> A certain Marcion of Pontus is still teaching that there is another god greater than the Creator. All over the world, aided by demons, he has caused many to blaspheme in denying that the Maker of the universe is the Father of Christ and declaring that there is another greater than he. But all these are called Christians, as I said before, just as the term *philosopher* is common to all such, even though their doctrines vary. . . . I have written a book in answer to all heresies that have appeared, which I will give to any who wish to study it.[15]

Justin Martyr and Antoninus Pius

The same Justin, after having contended with much success against the Greeks, addressed a *Defense* of the faith to the emperor Antoninus Pius and to the senate of Rome, where he was living. In it he explains who he was and where he came from:

> **12.** To the Emperor Titus Aelius Hadrian Antoninus Pius, Caesar Augustus, and to Verissimus, his son the philosopher, and to Lucius, son by nature of the philosopher-emperor, and by adoption of Pius, a lover of knowledge, and to the sacred senate and all the people of Rome, on behalf of all in every race who are unjustly hated and abused, I, Justin, being one of their number, son of Priscus and grandson of Bacchius, of Flavia Neapolis in Syria Palestine, have composed this address and petition.[16]

---

15. *Defense* 1.26.

16. *Defense* 1.1. Flavia Neapolis is the present Nablus in the Palestinian West Bank. That Justin was born in Samaria, adjacent to Galilee and Judea, adds considerable authority to his biblical references.

Head of Antoninus Pius, emperor 138–161 (*Louvre, Paris*).

The same emperor, petitioned by other Christians in Asia who were suffering all kinds of abuse from the local population, sent the following decree to the Council of Asia:[17]

13. The Emperor Caesar Marcus Aurelius Antoninus Augustus, Armenius, pontifex maximus, holding tribunician power for the fifteenth time, consul the third time, to the Council of Asia, greeting. I know that the gods are also concerned that such men as these should not go undetected, for they would be far more likely to punish those who will not worship them than you are. But you hound them into trouble by accusing them of atheism and thereby add to their resolve to choose apparent death rather than life for the sake of their own god. They, then, become the conquerors when they sacrifice their lives rather than obey your commands. As to the earthquakes that happened—and are happening—you lose heart whenever they occur and provide a painful comparison between our character and theirs. They repose greater trust in their god,

161

---

17. This provincial council, with representatives from the cities of western Asia Minor, originally met in the temple to Augustus and Rome at Pergamum. Later it met at Ephesus, Sardis, Smyrna, and elsewhere.

whereas you neglect yours and the worship of the Immortal. But when the Christians worship him you harass and persecute them to death. On behalf of such people many of the former provincial governors wrote our divine father, and he replied that they were not to be troubled unless they appeared to be plotting against the Roman government. Many have reported about them to me also, and I have replied in accordance with my father's opinion. But if anyone persists in taking action against one of these people [as a Christian], the accused shall be acquitted of the charge even if it is clear that he is one, and the accuser shall be liable to penalty. Published at Ephesus in the Council of Asia.

Melito, the distinguished Bishop of Sardis at that time, corroborates these matters, as is apparent from what he says in his *Defense* of our faith that he sent to the emperor Verus.[18]

Polycarp of Smyrna

14. While Anicetus was head of the Roman church, Irenaeus relates, Polycarp was still alive and came to Rome to discuss with Anicetus some problem regarding the date of Easter [literally, Passover]. The same writer tells another story about Polycarp that must be included here:

From Book 3 of Irenaeus's Against Heresies

Polycarp not only was instructed by apostles and conversed with many who had seen the Lord, but also was appointed by apostles in Asia as Bishop of Smyrna. I also saw him in my childhood, for he lived a long time and passed away in extreme old age in glorious martyrdom. He continually taught the things he had learned from the apostles, the traditions of the church that alone are true. These facts are confirmed by all the churches of Asia and the successors

---

18. How Melito confirms this is unknown. Some scholars consider the edict of Antoninus Pius as spurious—not invented by Eusebius but uncritically used by him from unknown sources. There is indeed an overtone of Christian apologetic in some of the phrases. Others deem it a genuine, though interpolated, document. In any case, Antoninus Pius's apparently favorable attitude toward the Christians hardly seems consistent with the death of some prominent Christian martyrs under his administration.

of Polycarp to this day, and he is a much more reliable witness to the truth than Valentinus, Marcion, and all other errorists. In the time of Anicetus, he visited Rome and converted many among these heretics to the church of God, proclaiming that the one and only truth he had received from the apostles was that transmitted by the church. And there are those who heard him tell how John, the Lord's disciple, went to take a bath at Ephesus, but, seeing Cerinthus inside, he rushed out of the bathhouse without bathing, crying, "Let's get out of here lest the place fall in: Cerinthus, the enemy of the truth, is inside!" Polycarp himself, when Marcion once met him and asked, "Don't you recognize me?" replied, "I do indeed: I recognize the firstborn of Satan!" So careful were the apostles and their disciples not even to converse with any mutilators of the truth, as Paul also said, "After a first and second admonition, have nothing more to do with anyone who causes divisions, since you know that such a person is perverted and sinful, being self-condemned" [Titus 3:10–11]. There is also a most powerful letter Polycarp wrote to the Philippians, from which those who wish and care for their salvation may learn about the nature of his faith and preaching.[19]

Thus Irenaeus. Polycarp, in his letter to the Philippians, mentioned above and still extant, has included some quotations from the First Epistle of Peter.

Antoninus Pius, after reigning twenty-two years, was succeeded by his son Marcus Aurelius Verus (also called Antoninus), along with his brother Lucius [Verus].[20] **15.** At this time Asia was again disrupted by great persecution, and Polycarp found fulfillment in martyrdom.[21] An account of his end is still extant and ought to be included in these pages, a document from the church over which he presided to neighboring communities: **161**

19. *Against Heresies* 3.3.

20. Antoninus Pius died March 7, 161. Marcus Aurelius and Lucius Verus, as they are usually named, were two adopted sons. Their joint rule was suspended when Verus died in 169.

21. The date of Polycarp's death is disputed. Although Eusebius places it during the reign of Marcus Aurelius (specifically, his seventh year or 167/8 in the *Chronicle*), evidence in the *Martyrdom of Polycarp* suggests that it occurred in 156 during the reign of Antoninus, a dating favored by most scholars.

Statue of Marcus Aurelius, emperor
161–180 (*Louvre, Paris*).

The church of God at Smyrna to the church of God at Philomelium[22] and to all gatherings of the holy catholic church everywhere. Mercy, peace, and love from God the Father of our Lord Jesus Christ be yours in large measure. We are writing to you, brethren, to tell about the martyrs and the blessed Polycarp, whose martyrdom put an end to the persecution.

They first relate what happened to the other martyrs, describing the fortitude they showed when tortured, amazing the spectators. Sometimes the scourges tore into their innermost veins and arteries, revealing their entrails and organs. At other times they were stretched across pointed seashells and sharp spikes and finally were fed to wild animals.

They say that the noble Germanicus overcame the natural fear of death by the grace of God. Even when the proconsul tried to dissuade him, pleading that he spare himself as still in the very flower of his youth, he did not hesitate to drag the beast to himself, nearly forcing and goading it, the sooner to be free of their unjust, wicked life. At his glorious death, the whole crowd was so amazed at the bravery of the God-loving martyr and at the courage of Christians in general that they began to shout together, "Kill the atheists! Get Polycarp!" When a great uproar greeted this cry, a certain Quintus, newly arrived from Phrygia, seeing the animals and the impending tortures, broke down and surrendered his salvation. He and others rushed to the tribunal too hastily but were convicted nevertheless, a proof of their irreligious folly.

The wonderful Polycarp, however, was undisturbed at the news and had a fixed determination to stay in the city [Smyrna]. But when his friends pleaded with him to escape, he was persuaded to go to a farm not far from the city, where he stayed with

---

22. A city near Antioch in Pisidia. This letter is usually called the *Martyrdom of Polycarp*.

a few others and prayed to the Lord night and day that peace be granted the churches throughout the world, as was his custom. Three nights before his capture, while at prayer, he saw in a vision the pillow under his head suddenly burst into flame and burn up, which he interpreted to his friends as foretelling that for Christ's sake he would give up his life by fire. Since those hunting him were relentless, the love of the brethren obliged him to move on to another farm. Soon the pursuers arrived and arrested two of the servants there, one of whom, under torture, showed them to Polycarp's quarters. It was night, and they found him lying in an upper bedroom. He could have moved to another house, but he had refused, saying, "God's will be done." When he heard that they had come, he went down and talked with them in such a cheerful, serene manner that they were astounded in view of his old age and confident air and wondered why there was such anxiety to arrest an old man of such character. He ordered that a table be set for them and invited them to dine with gusto, asking only for a single hour to pray undisturbed. This granted, he stood up and prayed, filled with the grace of the Lord, to the astonishment of those present, many of whom grew distressed that so dignified and godlike a man was going to his death.

The letter *[Martyrdom of Polycarp]* continues as follows:

Finally he finished his prayer, after remembering all with whom he **156** had ever come into contact—small or great, famous or obscure—and the whole catholic church throughout the world. When the hour for departure had come, they set him on a donkey and led him into the city on a great Sabbath.[23] Herod, the chief of police, and his father Nicetes met him and transferred him to their carriage. Sitting beside him, they tried to persuade him: "What harm is there in saying 'Lord Caesar' and sacrificing—and so be saved?" At first he did not answer them, but when they persisted, he said, "I will not do what you advise." Threats now replaced persuasion, and they ejected him so quickly that he scraped his shin in getting down from the carriage. But he walked on briskly to the stadium, as if nothing had happened. There the noise was so great that no one could be heard.

When Polycarp entered the stadium, a voice from heaven said, "Be strong and play the man, Polycarp!" No one saw the speaker, but

---

23. A "great Sabbath" occurred when Saturday coincided with a festival in the Jewish calendar. Since there is good reason to accept the traditional date of Polycarp's death as February 23, the day here referred to was probably the Feast of Purim.

Roman colonnade along the agora at Smyrna, where Polycarp was bishop prior to his martyrdom there. Smyrna, today's Izmir, received unqualified praise among the seven churches addressed in the book of Revelation (1:11, 2:8ff.).

many of our people who were there heard the voice. As word spread that Polycarp had been arrested, there was a tremendous roar. When he approached, the proconsul asked him if he were Polycarp, and after he admitted it he tried to dissuade him, saying, "Respect your years! Swear by Caesar's fortune! Recant and say, 'Away with the atheists!'" But Polycarp swept his hand across the crowd, sighed, looked up to heaven, and cried, "Away with the atheists!" But the governor pressed him, "Take the oath and I will set you free. Curse Christ!" But Polycarp replied, "For eighty-six years I have been his servant, and he has never done me wrong. How can I blaspheme my King who saved me?" But when he persisted, "Swear by Caesar's fortune," he replied, "If you suppose that I could do this, pretending not to know who I am, listen carefully: I am a Christian. And if you wish to learn the teachings of Christianity, choose a day and you will hear them." The proconsul replied, "Persuade the people!" Polycarp responded, "*You* would be worthy of such a discussion, for we have been taught to render appropriate honor to rulers and authorities ordained by God if it does not compromise us. As for the people, I do not feel a defense is appropriate." Said the proconsul, "I have wild beasts. I'll throw you

to them if you don't change your mind!" "Call them," he replied, "for
we cannot change our mind from better to worse. But to change from
cruelty to justice is excellent." Again he countered, "If you disregard
the beasts, I'll have you consumed by fire unless you repent!" But Polycarp declared, "You threaten a fire that burns for a time and is quickly
extinguished. Yet a fire that you know nothing about awaits the wicked
in the judgment to come and in eternal punishment. But what are you
waiting for? Do what you will."

As he said these and many other things, he was filled with
courage and joy, and his features with such grace that they did
not pale with alarm at what was said to him. The proconsul was
astounded and sent his herald into the center of the stadium to
announce three times: "Polycarp has confessed that he is a Christian!" At this, the whole multitude of Gentiles and Jews living
in Smyrna boiled with anger and shouted at the tops of their
lungs, "This is the teacher of Asia, the father of the Christians, the
destroyer of our gods, who teaches many not to offer sacrifice or
worship!" They then demanded that Philip the Asiarch let a lion
loose on Polycarp. But he said that this would be illegal, since he
had closed the sports. Then a general shout arose that Polycarp
should be burned alive. Indeed, the vision of the burning pillow
had to be fulfilled, and, turning to the faithful with him, he said,
prophetically, "I must be burned alive."

In less time than it takes to tell, the crowd gathered logs and
faggots from the workshops and baths—as usual, the Jews in particular. When the pyre was ready, he took off all his clothes, loosened his
belt, and tried to take off his shoes though he was unused to doing
this because the faithful had vied with each other for this privilege.
As they were going to nail him to the grid for the fire, he said, "Let
me be, for he who enables me to endure the flames will also enable
me to remain in them unmoved, even without nails." So they bound
him without nailing, hands behind his back, like a noble ram from a
great flock, as a whole burnt offering acceptable to almighty God.

He prayed: "O Father of your beloved Son, Jesus Christ, through
whom we know you, I bless you for this day and hour, that I may,
with the martyrs, share in the cup of Christ for the resurrection to
eternal life of both soul and body in the immortality of the Holy
Spirit. May I be received among them today as a rich and acceptable
sacrifice, according to your divine fulfillment. For this reason I praise
you for everything, I bless and glorify you through the eternal high
priest, Jesus Christ, your beloved Son, through whom be glory to you
and the Holy Spirit, both now and in the ages to come. Amen."

When he had finished, the fire was lit and a great flame blazed up, and we who were privileged to witness it saw something marvelous. The fire assumed the shape of a room, like a billowing ship's sail that surrounded the martyr's body inside it, not like burning flesh but like gold and silver being refined in a furnace. We also smelled a pleasant fragrance like the scent of incense or other costly spices. Finally the lawless mob, seeing that his body could not be consumed by fire, ordered an executioner to slash him with a sword. When he did so, blood gushed out and quenched the fire, and the entire crowd was amazed at the difference between unbelievers and the elect. Indeed he was one of the elect, the most wonderful apostolic and prophetic teacher of our time, bishop of the catholic church in Smyrna. For every word that he uttered was and will be fulfilled.

But when the Evil One saw the greatness of his martyrdom and his blameless life, he saw to it that we could not even take away his poor body, as many desired to do. He prompted Nicetes, the father of Herod and brother of Alce, to ask the governor not to give us his body "lest they abandon the one crucified and start worshiping this man." This idea came from pressure by the Jews, who watched when we were going to take him from the fire, not realizing that we can never abandon Christ to worship anyone else. Him we worship as the Son of God, but the martyrs we love as disciples and imitators of the Lord. When, then, the centurion saw that the Jews were making trouble, he put [the body] into their midst and burned it, as was their custom. Later we gathered up his bones, more precious than jewels and finer than gold, and laid them where appropriate. There, if possible, we will assemble in gladness and joy to celebrate the anniversary of his martyrdom, both in memory of those who have already contended and for the training of those who will do so. Such is the account of the blessed Polycarp. Including those from Philadelphia, he was the twelfth martyr in Smyrna, but he alone is particularly remembered and spoken of by all, even by the heathen.

And so ended the life of the marvelous and apostolic Polycarp, according to the letter of the Christians in Smyrna. The same document records other martyrdoms that took place in Smyrna at the same time. Among them, Metrodorus, apparently an elder in the Marcionite error, was put to death by fire. Pionius, a famous martyr who was bold in his defense of the faith before the people and the authorities, brought correction and comfort to those who had wilted in persecution and encouragement to those who visited him in prison before he was tortured, nailed, and burned to death—the details included in my collection of early martyrdoms.[24] There are also memoirs of others martyred in the city of Pergamum in Asia—Carpus, Papylas, and a woman, Agathonice—who found glorious fulfillment after many noble confessions of faith.

Justin the Martyr

16. In their time, Justin, whom I mentioned earlier, after presenting to the rulers named [Antoninus Pius and his sons] a second book in defense of our doctrines, was adorned with divine martyrdom. The philosopher Crescens, who worked to make his life and conduct justify his designation as a Cynic, instigated the plot against him, for Justin had repeatedly defeated him in debate before an audience. This martyrdom the preeminent philosopher clearly foretold as imminent in these words from the *Defense:*

c. 165

> I also expect to be plotted against and clamped in the stocks by one of those I have named or perhaps by Crescens, that lover not of wisdom but of bragging. He does not merit the name *philosopher,* seeing that he publicly decries what he does not understand, claiming that the Christians are impious atheists in order to win the favor and pleasure of many who are deluded. For if he attacks us without studying Christ's teachings, he is utterly depraved and worse than the simpleminded, who usually avoid discussing subjects they know nothing about. Or if he has studied them and failed to comprehend their greatness, or if he does so comprehend but is low enough to act shamefully to avoid suspicion, he is all the more base and ignoble in yielding to ignorance and fear. I want you to know that in asking him questions of this kind, I learned—even proved—that he really knows nothing. To show that I speak the truth, in case you have not learned of our exchanges, I am ready to discuss the questions again in your presence, a task worthy of an emperor. But if you are already aware of my questions and his answers, it is surely obvious to you that he knows nothing of what we believe. Or, if he does know, he dares not say so because of the audience and, as I said before, proves to be a lover not of wisdom but of repute. He does not even honor Socrates' esteemed precept.[25]

---

24. Pionius was indeed martyred at Smyrna, but on the anniversary of Polycarp's martyrdom a century later. Evidently Eusebius included him here thematically rather than chronologically.

25. *Defense* 2.8. Socrates' precept, quoted by Justin, was "A man must not be honored above the truth" (Plato *Republic* 10.595). Eusebius failed to copy it in his text.

So says Justin. And that he was indeed ensnared by Crescens and found his fulfillment, according to his own prophecy, is told by Tatian—a man distinguished in Greek learning and memorable for his writings—in his work, *Against the Greeks:* "The wonderful Justin rightly declared that these people are like outlaws." Then, he continues:

> Crescens, who made his den in the great city, surpassed all in pederasty and love of money. He advised others to despise death but feared it so much himself that he conspired to inflict it on Justin as a great evil, since Justin convicted the philosophers of gluttony and hypocrisy simply by proclaiming the truth.[26]

Such was the cause of Justin's martyrdom.

Martyrs Named by Justin

17. Before his own ordeal, Justin mentions in his first *Defense* others who were martyred before him:

> A woman living with a depraved husband was at first as depraved as he. But when she learned Christ's teaching she reformed and tried to induce her husband to do the same, warning him of eternal punishment. But he remained as dissolute as ever and his conduct broke up their marriage, for his wife thought it wrong to continue sharing a bed with a man who sampled every sort of unnatural and immoral pleasure. Her family, however, implored her not to divorce him, in the hope that he would change. But when her husband went to Alexandria and she learned that his conduct was even worse, she gave him a writ of divorce to avoid involvement in his abominable ways.
>
> Her "noble" husband should have been delighted that she had abandoned the former drunken bacchanals and varieties of vice she had engaged in with servants and domestics and that she wished him to do the same. Instead, since she had left him against his will, he accused her of being a Christian. She in turn filed a petition with you, as emperor, requesting that she first be allowed to settle her affairs and then answer the accusation. This you granted.
>
> Her former husband was now unable to attack her, so he turned against a certain Ptolemy, who had taught her Christian doctrine and had been punished by Urbicius. He had a centurion friend arrest

---

26. *Against the Greeks* 18.19.

Ptolemy and ask him one question only: Was he a Christian? When Ptolemy, a lover of truth, confessed that he was, the centurion tortured him in prison for a long time. Finally, the man was brought before Urbicius and asked, as before: Was he a Christian? He confessed it. When Urbicius ordered his execution, a certain Lucius, also a Christian, protested the unreasonable verdict, saying, "Why punish this man, who is not an adulterer, fornicator, murderer, thief, robber, or offender in any way, but merely confesses the name Christian? Your verdict, Urbicius, is unworthy of Emperor Pius, of Caesar's philosopher son, or of the sacred senate." Urbicius merely replied, "You seem to be a Christian yourself, Lucius." And when Lucius answered, "I certainly am," he ordered his execution also. Lucius expressed his thanks, for he was being removed, he said, from such wicked despots and going to God, the gracious Father and King. Then a third man also came forward and was sentenced to the same punishment.[27]

To this Justin appropriately added the words I quoted earlier, "I also expect to be plotted against by one of those named."

Justin's Writings

18. Justin has left us many helpful treatises, the work of a cultured intellect trained in theology, of which I recommend the following as useful to students:

A Defense of Our Faith, addressed to Antoninus Pius, his sons, and the Roman senate;

A Second Defense of Our Faith, to his successor Antoninus Verus [Marcus Aurelius], whose period I am discussing here;

Against the Greeks, a lengthy discussion of issues debated by both Christian and Greek philosophers, as well as a discourse on demons;

A Refutation, another reply to the Greeks;

The Sovereignty of God, drawn from both the Scriptures and Greek works;

Songs for the Harp;

On the Soul, reflecting his opinions and those of the Greek philosophers.

He also composed a dialogue against the Jews, held at Ephesus: the *Dialogue Against Trypho,* one of the most distinguished Hebrews of the day. In this he tells how God's grace guided him

---

27. *Defense* 2.2.

to faith after philosophical studies and zealous inquiry into the truth. Describing how Jews plotted against the teaching of Christ, he indicts Trypho similarly:

> Not only did you fail to repent of your evil deeds, but also you chose selected men at that time and sent them from Jerusalem to all parts of the world, saying that a godless sect of Christians had arisen and adding the charges that all who do not know us lodge against us, so that you are guilty of injustice not only against yourselves, but the whole of humanity.[28]

He also writes that even up to his own day prophetic gifts brightened the church and cites the Revelation of John, stating that it was the work of the apostle. He also quotes some passages from the Prophets, demonstrating, against Trypho, that the Jews had cut them out of the Scriptures. Many works of his are extant and were quoted also by earlier writers. In Book 4 of *Against Heresies*, Irenaeus writes:

> Justin said it well in his treatise against Marcion that he would not have believed the Lord himself if he had preached another god than the Creator.[29]

And in Book 5 of the same work:

> Justin put it well: before the Lord's coming, Satan dared not blaspheme God, since he did not yet know his condemnation.[30]

These items should encourage students to study his writings carefully, and such are the facts about him.

Bishops and Hegesippus

19. When this reign [Marcus Aurelius's] was in its eighth year, Soter succeeded Anicetus as Bishop of Rome, who was eleven years in office, and when Celadion had presided over the see of Alexandria for fourteen years, **20.** Agrippinus succeeded. In the church of Antioch,

---

28. *Dialogue* 17.

29. *Against Heresies* 4.11.

30. *Against Heresies* 5.26.

the famed Theophilus was the sixth from the apostles. The fourth had been Cornelius, appointed after Hero, and Eros the fifth.

21. Among those flourishing in the church at this time were Hegesippus, whom we met earlier, Bishop Dionysius of Corinth, Bishop Pinytus of Crete, Philip, Apollinarius, Melito, Musanus, Modestus, and above all Irenaeus. Their orthodoxy and ardor for the apostolic tradition have reached us in written form.

22. Hegesippus has left a full record of his beliefs in five books that have come down to us. In them he tells of traveling to Rome and finding the same doctrine among all the bishops there. After some comments about Clement's Letter to the Corinthians, he writes:

> The Corinthian church remained in the true doctrine until Primus became bishop. I conversed with the Corinthians on my voyage to Rome, and we were refreshed by the true doctrine. After arriving in Rome I compiled the succession down to Anicetus, whose deacon was Eleutherus. Anicetus was succeeded by Soter and he by Eleutherus. In each succession and in every city, preaching corresponds with the Law, the Prophets, and the Lord.

The same writer also describes the origins of the heresies of his time:

> After James the Just had suffered martyrdom like the Lord and for the same reason, Symeon, the son of his [James's] uncle Clopas, was appointed bishop, recommended by all as the Lord's cousin. They used to call the church a virgin because she had not yet been seduced by profanities. But Thebouthis, because he had not been made bishop, began to defile her by means of the seven heresies to which he belonged. Among these were Simon and his Simonians, Cleobius and his Cleobians, Dositheus and the Dositheans, Gorthaeus and the Gorathenes, and the Masbotheans. From these derive the Menandrianists, Marcionites, Carpocratians, Valentinians, Basilidians, and Saturnilians, each injecting their own opinion in their own peculiar way. From these come the false Christs, the false prophets, and the false apostles, who shatter the unity of the church by their poisonous teachings against God and his Christ.

Hegesippus also describes the sects that once existed among the Jews:

Various opinions among the circumcision, the children of Israel, against the tribe of Judah and the Messiah included: the Essenes, Galileans, Hemerobaptists, Masbotheans, Samaritans, Sadducees, and Pharisees.

He wrote much else, some of which I have already quoted, and cites the Gospel of the Hebrews, the Syriac Gospel, and especially works of Hebrew language and oral tradition, showing that he was a Hebrew convert. Not only he, but Irenaeus too and all early writers used to call Solomon's Proverbs "the All-Virtuous Wisdom." He also says that some of the so-called Apocrypha were fabricated by certain heretics of his own day. But now I must move on to another writer.

Bishop Dionysius of Corinth

23. As Bishop of Corinth, Dionysius gave inspired service not only to those under him, but also those distant, especially through the general epistles he wrote for the churches. Among these, the letter to the Spartans is orthodox instruction in peace and unity, while the one to the Athenians is a call to faith and to life in accord with the Gospel—for disdaining which he censures them as all but apostates from the Word, since Publius, their bishop, was martyred in the persecution of the time. He relates that after this martyrdom Quadratus was appointed their bishop and that through his fervor they were reunited and their faith revived. He also states that Dionysius the Areopagite, who was converted by the apostle Paul, as reported in Acts [17:34], was the first to be appointed Bishop of Athens. Another extant epistle of his to the Nicomedians contests Marcion's heresy, in defense of the truth. He also wrote to the church at Gortyna and elsewhere on Crete, congratulating Philip, their bishop, on the courage of the church there but warning him to guard against the heretics.

In a letter to the church at Amastris and those in Pontus, he says that Bacchylides and Elpistus had urged him to write, and he then expounds the divine Scripture and refers to their bishop, Palmas, by name. He discusses marriage and celibacy at length and directs that those who return after moral or heretical lapse should be welcomed back.

Another on the list is an epistle to the Cnossians, in which he urges Pinytus, the bishop, not to make celibacy compulsory for the brethren but to remember the weakness of many. To this Pinytus replied that he admired Dionysius but urged him to provide more

Looking south along the Lechaion Road at the ruins of ancient Corinth, which Paul visited on his second mission journey and where Dionysius was later bishop. The Jewish synagogue where Paul preached and the *macellum* or meat market were both located along this street. The city's citadel, the Acrocorinth, looms in the background.

solid food in a more advanced letter, so that they might not be fed on milky words and be treated as children even in old age. In this letter Pinytus's orthodoxy, compassion, learning, and theological perception are well reflected.

A letter of Dionysius to Bishop Soter and the Romans is also extant, in which he acclaims the custom of the Romans, observed down to the persecution of our own times:

> It has been your custom from the beginning to show kindness to all Christians and to send contributions to churches in every city, reliev-ing the distress of those in need at some places or in the mines. This, your ancestral Roman custom, Bishop Soter not only has maintained, but also increased by generously sharing bounty among the saints and encouraging brethren coming to Rome with inspired, paternal words.

In the same letter he refers to Clement's *Letter to the Corinthians,* showing that it had been customary to read it in the church from the beginning:

4.23   141

We read your letter today, the Lord's Day, and shall continue to read it frequently for our admonition, as we do with the earlier letter Clement wrote on your behalf.

The same writer says the following about the fabrication of his own letters:

> When the brethren asked me to write letters, I wrote them, but the apostles of the Devil have filled them with weeds, omitting some things and adding others. But grief awaits them. No wonder, then, that some have distorted even the word of the Lord when they have schemed against writings so inferior.

Besides these, there is extant a letter of Dionyius to Chrysophora, a most faithful believer, in which he supplies her with appropriate spiritual food. Such are the facts about Dionysius.

Bishop Theophilus of Antioch

24. Three elementary treatises addressed to Autolycus are extant from Theophilus, the previously mentioned Bishop of Antioch, and another, entitled *Against the Heresy of Hermogenes,* in which he quotes the Revelation of John. Heretics of the time were active as ever in corrupting the pure seed of apostolic teaching like so many weeds, and the pastors of the churches everywhere drove them off like wild beasts from Christ's sheep by warning the brethren and exposing the heretics through oral inquiry and refutation of their opinions in written treatises. That Theophilus joined in the campaign against them is clear from his admirable work against Marcion, which has been preserved. His successor as Bishop of Antioch was Maximin, the seventh from the apostles.

Philip, Modestus, and Melito of Sardis

25. Philip, whom we know from Dionysius's letter as Bishop of Gortyna, also wrote an admirable treatise against Marcion, as did Irenaeus and Modestus, who excelled in exposing the man's errors.

26. As contemporaries with them, Bishop Melito of Sardis and Bishop Apollinarius of Hierapolis were at the height of their fame, and each addressed defenses of the faith to the Roman emperor of the time [Marcus Aurelius]. Of their works, the following have come to our attention:

By Melito:

Concerning Easter [Passover],	*Soul and Body*
Books 1 and 2	*Baptism, Truth, Faith*
On Christian Life and	*The Birth of Christ*
the Prophets	*A Book of Prophecy*
The Church	*Hospitality*
The Lord's Day	*The Key*
The Faith of Man	*The Devil*
Creation	*The Revelation of John*
The Obedience of Faith	*God Incarnate*
The Senses	*To Antoninus*

At the beginning of *Concerning Easter*,[31] he indicates the time of its composition:

This was written when Servillius Paulus was proconsul of Asia and Sagaris was martyred, and there was a great argument at Laodicea over the Easter festival that fell due at that time.

Clement of Alexandria quotes this work in his own *Concerning Easter*, which he says he wrote in consequence of Melito's. And in his petition addressed to the emperor, Melito states that we were treated at his time as follows:

Never before has it happened as now that a body of religious people are being persecuted by new decrees throughout Asia. Shameless informers lusting after the property of others have taken advantage of the decrees to plunder night and day those who are innocent. . . . And if this is done by your command, fine: a just king would never have an unjust policy, and we gladly bear the honor of such a death. But we make this one request: first learn the truth about the authors of such discord and then judge whether they are worthy of punishment and death or of acquittal and immunity. But if this new decree—which would not be proper even against foreign

---

31. Here and elsewhere, the Greek *pascha*—paschal festival or Passover—is translated as "Easter" (for benefit of modern readers), a term used only later in church history.

BISHOPS, WRITINGS, AND MARTYRDOMS   Philip, Modestus, and Melito of Sardis

enemies—does not stem from you, we appeal to you all the more not
to abandon us to pillaging by a mob.

He then continues:

> Our philosophy first sprang up in a foreign land, but it reached
> full flower among your people in the great reign of your ances-
> tor Augustus and became a portent of good for your empire, for
> Roman power grew splendid from then on. Happily, you are now his
> successor and shall remain so, along with your son [Commodus],
> if you protect the philosophy that began with Augustus and grew
> with the empire. Your ancestors respected it along with the other
> cults, and the greatest proof that our belief was for the good at the
> time when the empire began so nobly is this fact: since the reign
> of Augustus, no disaster has overtaken the empire but rather every-
> thing splendid and glorious, the answer to every prayer. Of all the
> emperors, the only ones ever persuaded by evil advisers to slander
> our teaching were Nero and Domitian, and from them stemmed
> the unreasonable practice of falsely accusing the Christians. But
> their ignorance was corrected by your pious fathers, who regularly
> reprimanded in writing all who dared to take new measures against
> us. Your grandfather Hadrian, for example, wrote letters to many,
> and especially to the proconsul Fundanus, governor of Asia. And
> while you were associated with your father [Antoninus Pius] in
> the government of the world, he wrote to the cities that no new
> measures were to be taken against us. Among these are letters
> to Larissa, Thessalonica, Athens, and to all the Greeks. Since you
> have the same opinion on this matter as they did, though with far
> more human sympathy and philosophic wisdom, we are convinced
> that you will do all that we request of you.

This passage is taken from the treatise cited. In his *Extracts*,
the same author begins in his preface with a list of the recognized
writings of the Old Testament, which must be cited here:

> Melito to Onesimus his brother, greeting. In your fervor for the Word
> you have often wanted extracts from the Law and the Prophets
> regarding the Savior and all of our faith, as well as the accurate
> facts about the ancient books, especially their number and order. I
> was eager to do this for you, knowing your fervor for the faith, the
> Word, and your eternal salvation. So when I visited the East and
> reached the place where all these things were proclaimed and done,

144   4.26

I gained accurate information about the Old Testament books that I send you herewith:

> Five books of Moses: Genesis, Exodus, Numbers,
>   Leviticus, Deuteronomy
> Joshua (son of Nun), Judges, Ruth
> Kings (four books), Chronicles (two books)
> The Psalms of David
> The Proverbs (Wisdom) of Solomon, Ecclesiastes,
>   Song of Songs, Job
> The Prophets: Isaiah, Jeremiah, the Twelve in a single
>   book, Daniel, Ezekiel, Ezra.

I have taken extracts from these and compiled them in six books.

Apollinarius, Musanus, Tatian

27. Thus far Melito. Many writings of Apollinarius have been preserved, of which the following have reached us: An address to the emperor named above [Marcus Aurelius]; *Against the Greeks* (five books); *On Truth* (two books); *Against the Jews* (two books); and his writings against the Phrygian heresy, an innovation beginning to sprout, with Montanus and his false prophetesses already starting their descent into error.[32]

28. Musanus, mentioned previously, wrote a very admirable treatise, still extant, to some Christians who had fallen away to the heresy of the so-called Encratites, which was then just beginning to sprout and give life to its bizarre and corrupting false doctrine.

29. Word has it that Tatian was the author of this error, whom I quoted previously regarding the wonderful Justin, whose disciple he was. Irenaeus states this in his *Against Heresies*, Book 1:

> Stemming from Saturninus and Marcion, the so-called Encratites preached celibacy, annulling the original creation of God and tacitly condemning him who made male and female for the generation of humanity. They also abstained from what they called "animate" things, in ingratitude to God who made all things, and deny the salvation of the first created man. This innovation they made recently

---

32. Eusebius discusses Montanus in detail in the next book, 5.14–19.

when a certain Tatian first introduced this blasphemy. He had been a student of Justin, and as long as he was with him he offered nothing like this, but, after Justin's martyrdom, he left the church and grew inflated at the idea of becoming a teacher and superior to others. He taught his own brand of doctrine, spinning stories of invisible eons, like the followers of Valentinus, and condemning marriage as depravity and fornication, as did Marcion and Saturninus. He devised arguments of his own in denying salvation to Adam.[33]

This Irenaeus wrote at that time. But a little later a man named Severus augmented this heresy, for which reason its members have been called Severians after him. They use the Law, the Prophets, and the Gospels—though interpreting them in their own way—but they blaspheme the apostle Paul, rejecting his epistles and even the Acts of the Apostles. Their former leader Tatian somehow produced a combination of the Gospels and called it the *Diatessaron*,[34] which is still extant in some places. They say that he dared to alter some of the apostle's words as if correcting their style. He has left a great number of writings, of which the most famous is *Against the Greeks*, in which he discusses primitive history and shows that Moses and the Hebrew prophets preceded all those touted among the Greeks. This also seems to be the best and most helpful of his writings.

Bardesanes the Syrian

30. In the same reign heresies flourished in Mesopotamia, and Bardesanes, a very able Syriac linguist, wrote dialogues against the Marcionites and other leaders of various doctrines, as well as many other works. Those who knew him as a powerful defender of the Word translated his dialogues from Syriac into Greek. Among them is his very effective dialogue with Antoninus, *Concerning Fate*, and many other works he wrote because of the persecution of that time. At first he had been a Valentinian, but later he rejected this school and refuted many of its fantasies, thinking that he had become orthodox. In fact, however, he did not entirely wipe away the filth of his old heresy.

At this time also, Soter, Bishop of Rome, died.

---

33. *Against Heresies* 1.26.

34. A Greek musical term meaning "harmony of four parts." This is the first known harmony of the four Gospels.

DEFENDERS AND DEFAMERS
OF THE FAITH

This book of the *Church History* offers remarkable source material on the dual campaign the second-generation Fathers had to wage in trying to repair church-state relationships externally while counteracting multiform heresy internally. It was a two-front warfare pursued boldly by an inspired few who did not scruple to address their defenses of Christianity to no less than the Roman emperors themselves. Known as the early apologists (from the Greek *apologia* or "defense"), intellectuals such as Quadratus, Aristides, Justin, and Melito—at great personal risk—reminded emperors of how their predecessors had modified the previous governmental policy of hunting out Christians, even as they remind us that the Christian persecutions were not one long, all-inclusive, empirewide horror story but a selective torture that was localized and an on-and-off proposition.

It was the Christian leadership that suffered most at this time, perhaps as visible symbols for the rest: an Ignatius of Antioch, a Polycarp of Smyrna, a Justin Martyr. The dauntless determination of Ignatius and the serene nobility of Polycarp in the face of a horrifying death have always illuminated these apostolic Fathers, and Eusebius did well to quote his sources regarding them directly.

Those who accused the Christians were not the emperors, as in the first century, but a local individual or group, a provincial governor, or, as we shall see, the pagan priesthood. Eusebius chose his sources well in this segment, letting the *ipsissima verba* of the imperial decrees and the commentaries of the various apologists speak for themselves.

Meanwhile, within the church (or related to it), heresy had blossomed and subdivided into sects, and sects within sects, boasting a myriad names. Gnosticism alone was a crazy quilt of recondite teachings that thrived in the syncretistic climate of the Roman Empire. Such errorist teachings never ceased to inflame church writers of this period—or Eusebius after them—and their rule for countering such was to invoke variations of Irenaeus's argument that the teachings publicly expounded among the churches in apostolic tradition guaranteed orthodoxy, rather than the hidden notions of Gnosticism or the extravagant claims of Montanism.

The schools of heresy seemed to run for several generations of increasingly disparate error before foundering. Eusebius, however, failed to mention one important benefit to the church from such heretical challenges: it forced Christian thinkers to agree on an authoritative canon of Scripture and a unifying tradition of its interpretation and compelled them to teach and express church doctrines with greater precision and a deepened theology.

Four of the five good emperors ruled during the period covered by Book 4 of the *Church History*. It begins in the later reign of *Trajan* (98–117) and the Second Jewish War that broke out in Egypt, Cyrene, and Mesopotamia (115–117), which he subdued just before his death, from a stroke, at Cilicia.

Hadrian (117–138), his adopted son and successor, was a tall, cultured, imposing figure who decided to grow a beard and thereby set a new style for many subsequent emperors. He put down the Third Jewish War (the Bar-Kokhba Revolt, 132–135), which ended with the exclusion of Jews from Jerusalem and its rebuilding as a Gentile city named Aelia Capitolina. Hadrian's rescript to Fundanus, governor of Asia (c. 125), continued Trajan's moderate policy regarding the Christians: their religion was illegal but they were not to be sought out via illegal methods. To him Quadratus addressed the earliest Christian apology. Stressing consolidation instead of conquest, Hadrian pulled back from some of the frontiers conquered by Trajan but maintained a strong defense of the empire through walls and fortresses. He traveled much, introduced needed reforms, and tried to emulate Rome's first emperor, calling himself Hadrianus Augustus. A painful illness felled him in 138.

Hadrian's adopted son and successor, *Antoninus Pius* (138–161), pursued a reign characterized by peace, prosperity, and progress through public works and social welfare. Aristides addressed his *Apology* to this emperor and with good reason, since Antoninus was an attractive personality, said to possess every known virtue, as symbolized by his Latin epithet *Pius*, which means "dutiful, upright, virtuous." Yet during his administration, though not at his instigation, the aged Polycarp, Bishop of Smyrna, was martyred at the stadium in Smyrna (contra Eusebius, who places it under the next emperor).

Marcus Aurelius (161–180), the adopted son and successor of Antoninus, shared the rule with *Lucius Verus* until the latter's death in 169. Noble in character and a Stoic philosopher who wrote the famed *Meditations,* Marcus Aurelius spent much of his administration doing what he liked least: commanding his forces on the Danube frontier, since the Germans were growing restless along the boundaries of the empire. Despite his Stoicism, he did not legitimize or grant toleration to Christianity, and the great apologist Justin was martyred at Rome (c. 165), while Melito of Sardis petitioned him against persecutions in the East.

Book 5

WESTERN HEROES,
EASTERN HERETICS

MARCUS AURELIUS TO SEPTIMIUS SEVERUS

177 Soter, Bishop of Rome, departed this life in his eighth year. He was succeeded by Eleutherus, twelfth from the apostles, in the seventeenth year of the emperor Antoninus Verus [Marcus Aurelius]. At this time the persecution against us at various places flared up again more fiercely, and mob violence in the cities led countless martyrs to their glory, to judge from events in one province. Since the entire record has been written down and included in our *Collection on Martyrs,* I will merely excerpt what is relevant to the present work. Other historians have limited their coverage to recording victories in war, the exploits of commanders, and the heroics of soldiers stained with the blood of the thousands they have slaughtered for the sake of country, family, and property. My account, instead, will make indelible the wars fought for the peace of the soul and the men who battled courageously in such wars for truth rather than country, piety rather than family. It is the contests of the courageous athletes of piety, their endurance in victories over satanic opponents, and the crowns they won at the end that it will make eternally famed.

Martyrs in Gaul

1. Gaul was the country that served as the stadium for these events. Its capital cities were Lyons and Vienne, through both of which the river Rhone flows broadly. The leading churches there

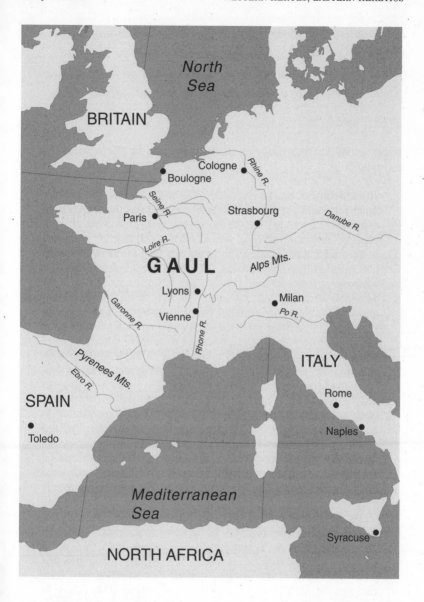

Gaul, today's France, was the site of terrible persecutions of Christians at Lyons and Vienne under Marcus Aurelius. Remains of the victims were thrown into the Rhone River by the pagan persecutors.

sent a document about the martyrs to the churches in Asia Minor, from which I quote:

> The servants of Christ at Vienne and Lyons in Gaul to our brothers in Asia and Phrygia who share the same faith and hope of salvation as we: Peace, grace, and glory from God the Father and Christ Jesus our Lord.

After other introductory remarks, they begin their narrative as follows:

> The intensity of the pressure here, the awful rage of the heathen against the saints, and the sufferings of the blessed martyrs are beyond description or writing. For the Adversary, in a foretaste of his own imminent advent, attacked us with all his might. He used every means to train his followers against the servants of God, so that we were not only excluded from homes, baths, and marketplaces, but were even forbidden to appear anywhere. But the grace of God rescued the weak by deploying the strong, pillars of men who drew on themselves the full attack of the Enemy and endured every punishment as they hurried to Christ, proving that the sufferings of this present time are not worthy to be compared with the glory that shall be revealed in us.[1]
>
> First they endured the full abuse of the mob: the howling, beating, dragging, plundering, imprisonment, stoning, and all that a furious rabble does against its hated enemies. Then they were dragged into the marketplace and indicted by the tribune and the city authorities, and when they confessed [Christ] they were imprisoned to await the governor's arrival. When they were brought before him and treated cruelly, Vettius Epagathus intervened, who had observed all the Lord's commandments so meticulously that, despite his youth, his reputation equaled that of the elder Zacharias.[2] Filled with love to God and neighbor and brimming with anger at the unreasonable judgment against us, he asked for permission to speak in our defense and show that we were neither atheistic nor impious. Those around the tribunal howled him down, as he was a man of status, and the governor rejected his reasonable request, asking only, "Are you a Christian?" In the clearest manner, Vettius replied that he was and joined the ranks of the martyrs himself. He was called the "Comforter of the Christians," but he had the Comforter [Holy Spirit] in

---

1. The final clause restates Rom. 8:18.
2. The father of John the Baptist (Luke 1:5–6).

Top: One end of the Amphitheater of the Three Gauls at Lyons, where the terrible Gallic persecutions described by Eusebius took place.

Bottom: A wooden post marks the spot where the ancient torture stake once stood (*both photographs: Paul Kreiss, Joy Mason, Jon Weidler*).

himself, as evidenced in the love by which he laid down his own life for the defense of the brethren as a true disciple of Christ.

The rest were then divided, and the first martyrs clearly and eagerly made their confession of martyrdom. Others, however, did not seem ready. Having failed in training, they were not equal to the struggle, and ten of them proved stillborn, causing us much grief and restraining the enthusiasm of those not yet arrested. Despite their agonies, however, they remained with the martyrs and did not desert them. At that point we were all tormented by uncertainty about their confession, not fearing the impending punishment but afraid lest anyone fall away.

Day after day, those who were worthy continued to be arrested, so that all the most effective members of the two churches were collected. Some of our heathen servants were also arrested, since the governor had decreed that we should all be prosecuted. Ensnared by Satan and in dread of the torments they saw the saints suffering, they falsely accused us—prompted by the soldiers—of Thyestean feasts and Oedipean intercourse,[3] as well as things we should not even speak or think about. When these rumors spread, people turned against us like beasts, and even those who had previously shown moderation as relatives raged against us, fulfilling the Lord's statement, "An hour is coming when those who kill you will think that by doing so they are offering worship to God" [John 16:2]. Then, finally, the holy martyrs endured sufferings beyond all description as Satan tried to wring blasphemy even from them.

The full fury of the mob, the governor, and the soldiers fell on Sanctus, the deacon from Vienne; on Maturus, a novice but a heroic contender; on Attalus, who had always been a pillar among the Christians in Pergamum; and on Blandina, through whom Christ proved that what men think lowly God deems worthy of great glory. When we were all afraid, and her mistress was herself facing martyrdom and distressed lest she through bodily weakness be unable even to make confession [of Christ], Blandina was filled with such power that those who tortured her from morning to night grew exhausted and admitted that they were beaten, for they had nothing left to do to her. They were astounded that she was still alive, since her whole body was smashed and lacerated, and they claimed that any one of the tortures was enough to end life, let alone a succession of them augmented. But the blessed woman, like a noble athlete, gained in strength while confessing the faith and found comfort for her sufferings by saying, "I am a Christian, and nothing wicked happens among us."

---

3. Cannibalism and incest. In Greek mythology, Thyestes had unknowingly eaten his own children, and Oedipus had unintentionally married his own mother.

Sanctus too endured all cruelty with superhuman courage. Although the wicked applied persistent tortures to wring something wrong from him, he resisted with such tenacity that he did not even tell them his own name, race, city of origin, or whether he was slave or free but replied to every question, in Latin, "I am a Christian." Therefore the governor and the torturers were eager to master him, and, when all else failed, they finally pressed red-hot plates of brass against the most tender parts of his body. These were burning, but he remained steadfast in his confession, refreshed by the water of life that flows from Christ. His body was a witness to his torment: it was all one wound, mangled and shorn of human shape, but Christ, suffering in that body, vanquished the Adversary and showed that there is nothing to fear where the Father's love is and nothing to wound where Christ's glory is.

After some days, the wicked again applied the same tortures to the martyr, assuming they would subdue him now that his body was swollen and inflamed—he could not stand even the touch of a hand—or that his dying from torture would terrify the rest. But nothing of the sort happened: beyond all belief, his body was straightened by these new tortures and regained its former appearance and the use of his limbs. Through the grace of Christ, then, his second bout on the rack became not torment but cure.

Biblis too, one of those who had denied [Christ], the Devil brought to torment by forcing her (presumed fragile and broken) to say evil things about us, assuming he had already devoured her and hoping to damn her through blasphemy as well. But she recovered on the rack and awakened from a deep sleep, as it were, reminded through the temporal punishment of the eternal in hell, and she contradicted the blasphemers: "How could such people eat children when they are not even permitted to eat the blood of irrational animals?" From then on she confessed that she was a Christian and joined the ranks of the martyrs.

When the tyrant's tortures had been overcome by Christ through the perseverance of the blessed saints, the Devil thought up other devices: imprisonment in filth and darkness, stretching feet in stocks to the fifth hole, and other atrocities that angry jailers, full of the Devil, inflict on prisoners. Thus, many of them were strangled in prison, while others were tortured so cruelly that it seemed impossible for them to survive, yet they did so, deprived of human help but strengthened by the Lord to encourage the rest. But the young, recently arrested and unaccustomed to torture, could not endure confinement and died in prison.

The blessed Pothinus, Bishop of Lyons, was more than ninety years old and physically weak. He could scarcely breathe but was fortified by his fervor for martyrdom. He was dragged before the tribunal by soldiers, accompanied by local authorities, and with the populace howling at him as if he were Christ himself. But he gave a noble witness. When the governor asked him, "Who is the god of the Christians?" he replied, "If you are worthy, you will know." Then he was dragged about mercilessly, pummeled by hands and feet that showed no respect for his age, while those at a distance hurled whatever was at hand at him, all imagining that they were avenging their gods. He was thrown into prison, barely breathing, and died two days later.

Then a great dispensation of God occurred, and the measureless mercy of Jesus was revealed in a rare manner but not beyond the skill of Christ. Those who had denied him at the first arrests were imprisoned with the others, despite their denial, whereas those who confessed what they were imprisoned as Christians, with no additional charges, while the others were also charged as foul murderers and punished doubly. For the burden of the former was lightened by the hope of the promises of Christ, but the latter were tormented by their consciences, as was obvious from the look on their faces. The faithful emerged with a joyful smile, glory, and grace, wearing their chains as ornaments and perfumed with the sweet aroma of Christ, so that some thought they had used worldly cosmetics. The others were depressed, humbled, and wretched, ridiculed by the heathen as miserable cowards. They were accused of murder and had lost the glorious and life-giving name. This sight firmed up the rest: those who were arrested confessed their faith without hesitation and ignored the Devil's promptings. . . .

After this, the martyrdoms occurred in all varieties, like so many shapes and colors of flowers woven into one crown to offer the Father. Maturus, Sanctus, Blandina, and Attalus were taken to the beasts in a special public exhibition. Maturus and Sanctus were again subjected to every torture in the amphitheater as if they had not suffered previously. Again they ran the gauntlet of whips, the mauling by beasts, and whatever the crazed mob demanded, and finally the iron chair, which roasted their bodies and clothed them with the stench. Not even then did their tormenters cease, but in mounting frenzy they tried to overpower the martyrs' resistance. Yet they got nothing more from Sanctus than the confession of faith he had made from the beginning.

After their long ordeal, they were finally sacrificed, having served as substitutes for the various gladiatorial contests all day long. Blandina, however, was hung on a stake and offered as food to wild beasts that were let loose. She appeared to be hanging in the shape of a cross, and her constant prayers greatly inspired her fellow victims, who saw the One who was crucified in the form of their sister, to convince all who suffer for Christ that they have eternal fellowship with the living God. When none of the animals would touch her, she was taken down from the post and returned to the jail, to be reserved for another ordeal so that her victory might encourage the brethren. Small, weak, and despised, she had put on the great, invincible champion: Christ.

The throng loudly demanded Attalus, since he was well known. He entered as a ready contender with a clear conscience, well trained in Christian discipline and a constant witness to the truth. He was led around the amphitheater with a placard carried before him, on which was written, in Latin, "This is Attalus, the Christian." The people were frenzied in fury against him, but when the governor learned that he was a Roman, he ordered him returned to jail with others about whom he had written the emperor and was awaiting a reply.

Their time of respite was not fruitless. The mercy of Christ was revealed through their endurance, and through the living the dead were being restored, martyrs conferring grace on those who had failed martyrdom. Through them a majority of those who had lapsed were reborn, learned to confess Christ, and went to the tribunal to be interrogated by the governor again. For Caesar [Marcus Aurelius] had written that they should be tortured to death but that if any recanted they should be set free. At the beginning of a local festival, attended by a vast number of heathen, the governor led them to the tribunal, making a spectacle of the blessed men for the throng. Examining them again, he beheaded all who seemed to possess Roman citizenship and sent the rest to the beasts. Christ was greatly glorified by those who had earlier denied him but now confessed, contrary to the expectation of the heathen. For they were examined individually with the intention of releasing them, but they confessed and joined the ranks of the martyrs. There were also outsiders who had never had a trace of faith or fear of God and blasphemed the Way[4] by their conduct–sons of perdition–but all the rest were added to the church.

While they, too, were being examined, Alexander, a Phrygian by birth and a physician by profession, who had lived in Gaul for many years and was well known for his love of God and boldness in discourse, stood by the tribunal and by gestures urged them to

---

4. One of the earliest names for Christianity, according to Acts 9:2. The group here castigated so judgmentally could well have included borderline believers too frightened to recant their recantation.

confess Christ. It seemed to those standing around the tribunal that he was in birth pangs. But the crowd, angry that the deniers were once again confessors, shouted that Alexander was the one responsible. The governor summoned him and asked him who he was. When he replied, "A Christian," he [the governor] was enraged and condemned him to the beasts.

The next day he [Alexander] entered the amphitheater with Attalus, whom the governor, to please the mob, was giving back to the beasts. After enduring all the devices of torture, they were finally sacrificed. Alexander uttered not a sound, communicating with God in his heart, while Attalus, when roasting in the iron chair with the stench rising from his body, told the crowd, in Latin: "Look! Eating men is what you are doing! We neither eat people nor commit any crimes!" When asked God's name, he replied, "God doesn't have a name as a human does."

In addition to all this, on the last day of the games Blandina was again brought in, with Ponticus, a lad of about fifteen. Each day they had been led in to watch the torturing and were urged to swear by the idols. Furious at their steadfast refusal, they showed no sympathy for the boy's youth or respect for the woman but subjected them to every torture. Ponticus was heartened by his sister in Christ and bravely endured each horror until he gave up his spirit. Last of all, the blessed Blandina, like a noble mother who had comforted her children and sent them on triumphantly to the king, rejoiced at her own departure as if invited to a wedding feast. After the whips, the beasts, and the gridiron, she was finally put into a net and thrown to a bull. Indifferent to circumstances through faith in Christ, she was tossed by the animal for some time before being sacrificed. The heathen admitted that never before had a woman suffered so much so long.

Not even this was enough to satisfy their maniacal cruelty. Goaded on [by Satan], they threw to the dogs those who had been strangled in jail, watching day and night that we did not tend to them. Then they threw out the remains left by the beasts and the fire, torn and charred, while a military guard watched the heads and the trunks of the rest for many days, denying them burial. Some gnashed their teeth at them; others laughed and jeered, glorifying their idols for punishing their foes. The more moderate, with little sympathy, taunted, "Where is their god?" and "What did they get out of their religion, which they preferred to their own lives?" We, however, greatly grieved at not being able to bury the bodies. . . .

After they were exposed and insulted for six days, the martyrs' bodies were burned to ash and swept by the wicked into the Rhone, which flows nearby, so that not even a trace of them would still appear on earth. They did this as if to conquer God and defeat their rebirth so that, as they said, "they might not have any hope of resurrection, because of which they have introduced a strange new cult, ignored torture, and gone joyfully to death. Now let's see if they will rise again and if their god will save them."

Rehabilitating the Lapsed

2. This is what happened to the Christian churches under the emperor mentioned, from which one may infer what took place in other provinces. Further statements from the same document should be added, in which the gentle compassion of the martyrs cited above is described:

> They were so eager to imitate Christ that for all their glory in witnessing not once or twice but many times and returning from the beasts covered with burns, scars, and wounds, they neither announced themselves as martyrs nor allowed us to address them by that name, sharply rebuking any who tried. For they gladly yielded the title of martyr to Christ, the true Martyr and Firstborn from the dead, and they reminded us of martyrs who had already passed away: "They are martyrs indeed who were taken up as soon as they had confessed Christ; we are merely humble confessors." They pleaded with their brothers in tears to pray for their fulfillment, proving the power of martyrdom by their actions but refusing the title through fear of God. . . .
>
> They defended all and accused none. They prayed for those who tortured them, as did Stephen: "Lord, do not hold this sin against them" [Acts 7:60]. If he prayed for those stoning him, how much more for the brethren?
>
> Their greatest struggle was this, that the beast be choked into disgorging those whom he had thought to have swallowed.[5] They did not boast over the fallen but shed tears in their behalf to the Father, praying for life, and he gave it to them. This they shared among their neighbors before departing victoriously to God, leaving behind them joy, peace, concord, and love.

Let this quotation suffice regarding the love of those blessed ones for their brothers who had fallen from grace, in view of

---

5. That is, that the Devil surrender those who had at first lapsed from the faith.

the inhuman and merciless character of those who later acted so cruelly to the members of Christ.[6]

The Revelation to Attalus the Martyr

3. The same account of these martyrs includes yet another memorable story. A certain Alcibiades, who lived a very austere life among them, refused everything but bread and water. But after his first contest in the amphitheater, it was revealed to Attalus that Alcibiades was not doing well in failing to use what God had created and offering offense to others. Alcibiades was persuaded and started to eat everything freely and gave thanks to God.

Just at this time in Phrygia, Montanus, Alcibiades,[7] Theodotus, and their followers began to gain fame for prophecy, since many other miraculous gifts of God, still occurring in various churches, led many to assume that they were also prophets. When dissension about them developed, the brothers in Gaul again offered their own careful and orthodox judgment on the issue, attaching letters from the martyrs fulfilled among them, letters composed while they were still in prison to their brothers in Asia and Phrygia as well as to Eleutherus, then Bishop of Rome, as ambassadors of peace in the churches.

The Martyrs Commend Irenaeus

4. The same martyrs warmly commended Irenaeus, already a presbyter at Lyons, to the Bishop of Rome just mentioned, in the words:

> Once more and always, Father Eleutherus, greetings in God. We have entrusted this letter to our brother and companion Irenaeus to bring to you. We beg you to hold him in high regard as one zealous for the covenant of Christ. For if we had thought that rank could confer righteousness on anyone, we would first have recommended him as a presbyter of the church, which he is in fact.

Need I transcribe the list of martyrs in the document previously mentioned, some fulfilled through decapitation, some thrown

---

6. The Novatians and Eusebius's own contemporaries, the Donatists. See 6.43–46.

7. A different Alcibiades.

as food for wild beasts, others who fell asleep in jail, and the number of the confessors still surviving at the time? Whoever wishes may easily read the complete letter included in my *Collection on Martyrs,* as I said before. Such were the events that took place under Antoninus [Marcus Aurelius].

Christian Prayers Bring Rain

5. Word has it that when his brother, Marcus Aurelius Caesar,[8] was battling the Germans and Sarmatians, he was in difficulty because his men were extremely thirsty. But the soldiers of the Melitene Legion[9] knelt on the ground (our custom in praying) in a faith that has sustained them from that time to this in struggles with their enemies, and turned to God in supplication. Amazed at the sight, the enemy was even more amazed at the lightning that drove them to flight and destruction, while rain fell on the army that had prayed to the Divinity, refreshing all who were on the point of dying from thirst.

This story is told also by writers outside our faith who have recorded the times of these emperors and also by our own. The pagan authors have recorded the astonishing phenomenon, though without acknowledging it as the result of Christian prayers,[10] but our own writers, as lovers of truth, have described the episode in a simple, straightforward manner. Apollinarius, for example, states that from then on, the legion whose prayers induced the miracle received an appropriate name from the emperor and was called, in Latin, "the Thundering Legion."[11] And in his Latin *Defense of the Faith,* addressed to the senate, which I quoted earlier, Tertullian

---

8. Unfortunately, Eusebius is sometimes confused by the Antonines. Thus far he has referred to Marcus Aurelius as Antoninus (to be distinguished from his adoptive father, the emperor Antoninus Pius). Here, however, he wrongly implies that the Antoninus just mentioned is instead Lucius Verus (co-emperor with Marcus Aurelius until Verus's death in 169). But the emperor involved in this episode continues to be Marcus Aurelius.

9. Melitene, called Malatya today, is in eastern Cappadocia, then a stronghold of Christianity.

10. Dio Cassius attributes the wonder to Arnuphis, an Egyptian magician (71.8), while on his coins Marcus Aurelius himself has Jupiter attacking the Germans with thunderbolts.

11. The legion XII *Fulminata* ("the Thundering Twelfth") had been sent by Titus to guard a crossing of the Euphrates at Melitene in Cappadocia already in 70, the error being that of Apollinarius rather than Eusebius.

confirmed the story with further proof. He said that the letters of Marcus, the wisest of the emperors, were still extant in which he testified that when his army in Germany was on the verge of ruin for lack of water, it was saved by the prayers of the Christians and that the emperor threatened death to any who tried to accuse us. Tertullian continues:

> What sort of laws are these that wicked, unjust, and cruel men apply against us alone? Vespasian did not enforce them, although he conquered the Jews. Trajan partially observed them but forbade that Christians be sought out. Hadrian, though curious about everything mysterious, never ratified them, nor Pius, as he is called.[12]

Everyone is welcome to his own opinion on these matters. I must pass on to further events.

The Bishops of Rome

177   When Pothinus had found fulfillment with the martyrs of Gaul at age ninety, Irenaeus became Bishop of Lyons. We have been told that in his early youth he had listened to Polycarp. In Book 3 of his *Against Heresies,* he lists the succession of bishops at Rome down to Eleutherus, the period I am now relating, in which Irenaeus also wrote:

6. When the blessed apostles had founded and built the church, they conferred the episcopal office on Linus, who is mentioned by Paul in his letter to Timothy [2 Tim. 4:21]. Anencletus succeeded him and Clement after him, in the third place after the apostles. He had seen the blessed apostles and conversed with them, their teaching still ringing in his ears. Nor was he the only one: many were still alive at that time who had been taught by the apostles. In Clement's day, no little dispute broke out among the Christians at Corinth, and the Roman church sent a strong letter to the Corinthians uniting them in peace, renewing their faith, and passing on the tradition they had recently received from the apostles. . . .

Evarestus succeeded Clement, Alexander Evarestus, and then Xystus was appointed, sixth from the apostles. Telesphorus followed him, who was also gloriously martyred, next Hyginus, then Pius, and Anicetus after him. Soter succeeded Anicetus, and now, in the

---

12. *Defense* 5.

twelfth place from the apostles, Eleutherus is bishop. The apostolic tradition in the church and the preaching of the truth have reached us in the same order and teaching.[13]

Miraculous Powers Continue

7. Irenaeus relates these facts in five books entitled *Refutation and Overthrow of Knowledge Falsely So-Called,* in the second book of which he shows that displays of divine and miraculous power had continued in some churches down to his own time:

> But they[14] fall far short of raising the dead, as the Lord and his apostles did through prayer and as [happens] among Christians due to great need when the whole local church has implored God with fasting and prayer, and the spirit of the deceased has returned and he has been restored through the prayers of the saints. . . .[15]
>
> But if they claim that the Lord has done these things in appearance only, I will show them from the prophetic writings that all these things had been foretold about him and that they really happened and that he alone is the Son of God. His true disciples, in turn, having received grace from him, use it in his name to benefit others according to the gift each has received from him. Some truly expel demons, so that those cleansed of evil spirits believe and join the church. Others have foreknowledge of the future, visions, and prophetic speech. Still others heal the sick by the laying on of hands and restore them to health. And even the dead have been raised, as I said, and lived on with us for many years. It is not possible to number the gifts that the church throughout the world has received from God in the name of Jesus Christ, who was crucified under Pontius Pilate, and uses daily for the benefit of the heathen, deceiving none and profiting from none. Having freely received from God, it freely ministers.[16]

Elsewhere the same author writes:

> We hear also of many brothers in the church who have prophetic gifts and speak through the Spirit in all kinds of tongues, surfacing

---

13. *Against Heresies* 3.3.

14. The followers of Simon and Carpocrates.

15. *Against Heresies* 2.31. Such astonishing claims seem to cease after the second century.

16. *Against Heresies* 2.32.

people's hidden thoughts for the common good and explaining the mysteries of God.[17]

Thus a variety of gifts continued among those worthy until the time of which I speak.

Irenaeus on Holy Scripture

8. At the beginning of this work I promised to quote the traditions of early elders and church historians regarding the canonical Scriptures. One of these was Irenaeus, who writes as follows concerning the holy Gospels:

> Matthew composed a written Gospel for the Hebrews in their own language, while Peter and Paul were preaching the gospel in Rome and founding the church there. After their deaths, Mark too, the disciple and interpreter of Peter, handed on to us in writing the things proclaimed by Peter. Luke, the follower of Paul, wrote down in a book the Gospel preached by him. Then John, the disciple of the Lord who had rested on his breast, produced a Gospel while living at Ephesus in Asia.[18]

These statements Irenaeus made in Book 3 of the cited work. In Book 5 he says this about the Revelation of John and the number in Antichrist's name:[19]

> This number is found in all the good, ancient copies and confirmed by those who saw John face-to-face, and reason tells us that the number of the Beast's name appears according to Greek enumeration by the letters in it. . . . I won't run the risk of making a positive statement about the name of the Antichrist. If it were necessary for his name to be announced plainly at present, it would have been declared by him who saw the revelation. For it was not seen long ago but nearly in my own generation, at the close of Domitian's reign.[20]

---

17. *Against Heresies* 5.6.

18. *Against Heresies* 3.1.

19. The number of the "beast," according to Rev. 13:18, is 666. Letters of the alphabet were used as numbers in Greek, and 666 was understood to refer to Nero or Domitian in the early church.

20. *Against Heresies* 5.30.

He also mentions 1 John, deriving many quotations from it, and similarly 1 Peter. And he not only knew, but also accepted *The Shepherd:* "Well did Scripture say, 'First of all believe that God is one, who created and fit all things together, etc.'"[21] He quoted loosely, too, from the Wisdom of Solomon: "The vision of God confers incorruption, and incorruption brings us near to God."[22]

He also cites an unnamed apostolic presbyter on Scripture and frequently quotes the writings of Justin Martyr and Ignatius, promising to refute Marcion on the basis of his own works. Regarding the Septuagint, he writes as follows:

> So God became man, and the Lord himself saved us, giving us the sign of the Virgin, but not as claimed by some in our day who venture to translate the text: "Behold, a young woman shall conceive and bear a son," as rendered by the Jewish proselytes Theodotion of Ephesus and Aquila of Pontus, whom the Ebionites follow and contend that he was Joseph's child. . . .
>
> Before the Romans established their rule, while the Macedonians still possessed Asia, Ptolemy the son of Lagus,[23] eager to adorn the library he had founded at Alexandria with all the finest writings from everywhere, asked the people of Jerusalem to have their Scriptures translated into Greek. Still subject to the Macedonians at the time, they sent him seventy elders, the most competent they had in the Scriptures and in both languages, thus fulfilling God's purpose. Fearing that they might conspire to conceal in their translation the true meaning of the Scriptures, Ptolemy separated them from each other and ordered them all to write the same translation of all of the books. When they reconvened before Ptolemy and compared their separate versions, God was glorified and the Scriptures recognized as truly divine, for they all said the same things in the same words and phrases from beginning to end, so that even the heathen who were present knew that the Scriptures had been translated by the inspiration of God. That God accomplished this is not surprising, for when the Scriptures were destroyed in the captivity by Nebuchadnezzar and the Jews returned to their land after seventy years, then at the time of Artaxerxes, king of Persia, he inspired Ezra, the priest of

---

21. *Against Heresies* 4.34.

22. *Against Heresies* 4.63.

23. Ptolemy I, usually called Soter, was the father of Ptolemy II Philadelphus, to whom this passage refers.

the tribe of Levi, to restore all the words of the prophets of old, as well as the Law given by Moses.[24]

Thus far Irenaeus.

Pantaenus of Alexandria

180 **9.** When Antoninus [Marcus Aurelius] had ruled for nineteen years, Commodus received the sovereignty. In his first year, Julian was appointed Bishop of Alexandria, Agrippinus having completed twelve years in ministry.

10. At that time Pantaenus, a man famed for his learning, was in charge of a school of believers in Alexandria. This academy has lasted into our own time, and I have heard that it is supervised by men of high intellect and spiritual zeal, but Pantaenus was one of the most distinguished teachers and Stoic philosophers of his day. He was so enthusiastic for the divine Word, they say, that he was sent to preach the Gospel of Christ to people in the East and went as far as India. He found that the Gospel of Matthew had preceded him there among some who had come to know Christ. Bartholomew, one of the apostles, had preached to them and had left them Matthew's account in Hebrew letters, which was preserved until that time. After many achievements, Pantaenus finally became head of the school at Alexandria, where he revealed the treasures of divine doctrine in both oral and written form.

Clement of Alexandria

11. In his time Clement, who had the same name as the pupil of the apostles and former head of the Roman church, was prominent in Alexandria for his study of Holy Scripture. In his *Outlines* he mentions Pantaenus by name as his teacher, and he seems to allude to him in Book 1 of the *Miscellanies*. He speaks as follows regarding the more distinguished members of the apostolic succession that he had joined:

---

24. *Against Heresies* 3.24. This tradition is not biblical, and the whole point of introducing the Septuagint into this argument regarding Isa. 7:14 is that the Septuagint translates the Hebrew as *parthenos* in Greek or "virgin" rather than "young woman," which Eusebius should surely have explained.

This is not a writing designed to impress but notes preserved for my old age, a treatment for forgetfulness and merely a sketch of those clear and vital words that I was privileged to hear and of blessed and truly extraordinary men. Of these, one, the Ionian, was in Greece, a second in south Italy, a third in Lebanon, a fourth from Egypt. Others were in the East, one an Assyrian, another, in Palestine, of Hebrew origin. When I met the last—who was first in competence—by hunting him out of his haunt in Egypt, I found rest. These men preserved the authentic tradition of the blessed teaching directly from Peter, James, John, and Paul, the holy apostles, son receiving it from father (but few were like their fathers). By the grace of God, they have come down to me, to deposit those ancestral and apostolic seeds.[25]

Bishops of Jerusalem

12. In their time, Narcissus was bishop of the church in Jerusalem, who is still widely famed, fifteenth in the succession after the siege of the Jews under Hadrian. From then on the church there was composed of Gentiles in place of Jewish Christians, and the first Gentile bishop was Mark, as noted earlier. After him the local record shows Cassian as bishop, Publius after him, then Maximus, Julian, Gaius, Symmachus, another Gaius, another Julian, Capito, Valens, Dolichian, and finally Narcissus, thirtieth from the apostles in regular succession.[26]

Rhodo versus Marcion

13. At the same time Rhodo, an Asiatic, was a student of Tatian at Rome who composed various books, in particular one aimed at the heresy of Marcion. He reports that it split into dissident groups in his era, and, describing the schismatics, he refutes the false teachings concocted by each of them:

Accordingly, they no longer agree with one another but hold irreconcilable opinions. One of their herd is Apelles, held in awe for his way of life and old age. He concedes that there is one Source of being but says that prophecies stem from a hostile spirit, trusting the

---

25. *Miscellanies* 1.1.11.

26. Eusebius states that Narcissus was fifteenth but lists only thirteen names here. In his *Chronicle* the names Maximus II and Antoninus follow Capito.

utterances of a possessed girl named Philoumene. Others, such as the captain himself, Marcion, introduce two Sources, as do Potitus and Basilicus, who followed the wolf of Pontus in failing to discover the division of things[27] and turning to a simple solution in announcing two Sources, baldly and without proof. Still others plunged into even worse error, presuming not only two but even three Natures. Their leader is Syneros, according to members of his school.

The same writer [Rhodo] also says that he conversed with Apelles:

When the old man Apelles was in discussion with us, his many false statements were evident, so he claimed that it was not necessary to argue about doctrine but that each should maintain his own beliefs: those who placed their hope in the Crucified would be saved, if they continued in good works. As I said before, the most obscure aspect of his teachings concerned God, for he asserted a single Source, as in our doctrine.

After defining all of Apelles's doctrine, Rhodo continues:

When I said to him, "What is your proof for a single Source? Please explain," he replied that prophecies were inconsistent, false, and contradicted themselves, and as for a single Source, he said that he did not know it but merely inclined to that opinion. Then when I pressed him to speak the truth, he swore that he was doing so in claiming he did not know how the uncreated God is one but that he believed it. I laughed in condemning him, because he called himself a teacher yet did not know how to confirm what he taught.

Speaking to Kallistio in the same work, Rhodo says that he was once a disciple of Tatian at Rome and that Tatian had authored a book on *Problems,* in which he recorded what was unclear and obscure in the divine Scriptures, to which Rhodo himself promised to provide answers. An essay of his on the *Hexaemeron*[28] is also extant. As for Apelles, he uttered innumerable impieties against Mosaic law and blasphemed the divine words in many treatises in his efforts to refute and destroy them, or so he thought.

---

27. Marcion came from Sinope in Pontus. The "division of things [into good and evil]" refers to his failure to find an answer to the problem of evil.

28. *The Six Days [of Creation].*

False Prophets and Schism

14. The enemy of God's church left no plot against humankind untried and raised a fresh harvest of heresies to harm the church. Some of these sectarians slithered like poisonous reptiles over Asia and Phrygia, boasting that Montanus was the Paraclete and that his female followers Priscilla and Maximilla were his prophetesses.

15. Others flourished at Rome, led by a defrocked presbyter, Florinus, as well as a similarly disgraced Blastus. They lured many away from the church into their own opinions, each trying to distort the truth in his own way.

Montanus and the Phrygian Heresy

16. Against the so-called Phrygian heresy, the Power that champions the truth raised up a strong, invincible weapon at Hierapolis in Apollinarius, previously mentioned, and many other scholars of the time, who have left us ample sources for writing the history. One of them, at the beginning of his treatise against these heretics, says that he had also debated orally with them and writes this preface:

> For a long time, my dear Avircius Marcellus, you have urged me to write a treatise against the sect named after Miltiades,[29] but I have been rather reluctant until now, not from inability to refute error and affirm truth but from concern that some might think I was adding to the words of the New Testament of the Gospel, which no one living according to it can add to or subtract from. But I came to Ancyra in Galatia and found that the local church was torn apart by this new craze—not prophecy, as they regard it, but rather false prophecy, as I will prove. As much as I could, I spoke in the church for days on end about these people and disputed their arguments, the Lord helping me. The church rejoiced and was reinforced in the truth, but our opponents were defeated for the time being. So the local presbyters asked me to leave them a summary of what I had said against the adversaries of truth when Zoticus of Otrous, our fellow presbyter, was also present. Though I did not do so, I promised to write from here, the Lord willing, and send it to them promptly.

---

29. A leader of the Montanists in Pentapolis on the Black Sea.

After similar comments, he goes on to report the cause of this heresy as follows:

> Their recent heretical schism started while Gratus was proconsul of Syria. At the village of Ardabau in Phrygian Mysia, a recent convert named Montanus, whose limitless ambition was tinder for the Adversary, became obsessed and, in his frenzy, fell into a trance. He began raving, chattering, and speaking nonsense, prophesying contrary to church tradition and custom from the beginning. Of those who heard his bastard utterances, some were angry, considering him possessed by a demon and a spirit of error in disturbing the populace. They censured him and tried to stop his babble, recalling the Lord's distinction and his warning to guard against false prophets. Others, however, as if elated by the Holy Spirit and a gift of prophecy—and not a little conceited—forgot the Lord's distinction and welcomed a spirit that harmed and deluded the mind, misleading people so deceived by it that it could not now be silenced. By some art or evil artifice, the Devil ruined the disobedient and, inflaming minds already dead to true faith, raised up two others—women[30] whom he infused with the spurious spirit so that they babbled madly, abnormally, and grotesquely, like Montanus. That spirit swelled the heads of the affected with wild promises or sometimes, in order to appear critical, condemned them, but few of the Phrygians were deceived. The believers in Asia met many times in many places to investigate the recent utterances, pronounced them sacrilegious, and rejected the heresy. And when the arrogant spirit of false prophecy instructed them to blaspheme the entire church across the world in general, then at last [the Montanists] were excommunicated and ejected from the church.

After this opening account, he continues to refute their error throughout his work. In Book 2 he says this about their end:

> Since they called us "prophet killers" because we did not receive their babbling prophets (whom, they say, the Lord promised to send), let them answer us before God. Was any one of those whose talking started with Montanus and the women ever persecuted by Jews or killed by the wicked? Not one. Was any arrested and crucified for the Name? No indeed. Was any one of the women ever scourged in Jewish

---

30. Maximilla and Prisca or Priscilla. Phrygia was the center of the ecstatic cult of Cybele, and Montanus, according to one tradition, had been a priest of Cybele.

synagogues or stoned? Never anywhere. Montanus and Maximilla are said to have died a different death, a mind-destroying spirit driving each to a separate suicide, like the traitor Judas. Similarly, according to common report, Theodotus—that amazing fellow, the first adminis- trator, so to speak, of their "prophecy"—was once raised up to heaven but in a trance committed himself to the spirit of deception and plummeted to the ground, dying miserably. That, at any rate, is what they claim happened. Since, however, we did not see them ourselves, Montanus, Theodotus, and the woman mentioned may or may not have died in this way.

Further on he says that the holy bishops of the time tried to argue with the spirit that was in Maximilla but were prevented by others who were clearly cooperating with the spirit:

The spirit that speaks through Maximilla, according to Asterius Orba- nus, should not say, "I am driven off like a wolf from the sheep. I am not a wolf, I am word and spirit and power." But let the power of the spirit be proven before those who were present to test and dialogue with the spirit as it spoke—distinguished men and bishops: Zoticus from the village of Cumane and Julian from Apamea, who were muzzled by Themiso and his party so that the false spirit that deceived the people could not be refuted.

After refuting the false prophecies of Maximilla, he indicates the time at which he was writing and also exposes her false pre- dictions of future wars and revolutions:

Is it not already obvious that this is another lie? It is now over thirteen years since the woman died, and neither local nor general war has broken out in the world but rather continuing peace by the mercy of God, even for Christians.[31]

This is from Book 2. From Book 3, I will also give a brief quote in which he replies to those [Montanists] who boasted that they had had many martyrs:

When all their arguments have been refuted and they have nothing to reply, they try to take refuge in the martyrs, claiming that they have

---

31. No major wars occurred in the reign of Commodus (180–192) or the earliest years of Septimius Severus (to approximately 197).

many as proof of what is allegedly their prophetic spirit. What could be farther from the truth! Some of the other heresies have countless martyrs, but we do not accept them for that reason or admit that they have the truth. The Marcionites (so-called after the heresy of Marcion) claim innumerable martyrs for Christ, but Christ himself they do not truly confess. . . . Therefore, whenever church members called to martyrdom for the true faith meet any of the so-called martyrs of the Phrygian heresy, they separate from them and have nothing to do with them until their own fulfillment, since they will not recognize the spirit in Montanus and the women. That this is true and that it happened in our time in Apamea on the Meander is clear from the case of those martyred with Gaius and Alexander of Eumenia.

Miltiades versus the Montanists

17. In this work he also cites Miltiades as an author who had written a treatise against this heresy too. After quoting some of their sayings, he continues: "This summarizes what I found in a writing of theirs attacking the work of our brother Miltiades[32] in which he shows that a prophet need not speak ecstatically." Further on, he gives a list of those who were prophets in the New Testament and includes a certain Ammia and Quadratus:

But the pseudoprophet speaks in ecstasy, without shame or fear. He begins with intentional ignorance but ends in unintentional madness. They cannot show that any prophet, either in the Old or New Testament, was inspired in this way—not Agabus or Judas or Silas or Philip's daughters, or Ammia in Philadelphia or Quadratus, or any others who do not belong to them. . . . For if the Montanist women succeeded Quadratus and Ammia in the prophetic gift, let them tell who among them succeeded the followers of Montanus and the women, for the prophetic gift should continue in the whole church until the final coming, according to the apostle. But they can point to no one, seeing that this is the fourteenth year since the death of Maximilla.

The Miltiades to whom he refers has also left us memorials of his zeal for the divine Word in the treatises that he wrote against

---

32. Eusebius's text has "Alcibiades" here rather than "Miltiades." Most scholars assume that Eusebius intended the latter. Since both were names also of famed Greek generals, the error is likely.

the Gentiles and against the Jews, as well as a *Defense* of his philosophy addressed to the secular rulers.

Apollonius versus the Montanists

18. When the Phrygian heresy was still flourishing in Phrygia
itself, a church writer named Apollonius wrote a refutation, proving their "prophecies" false and exposing the lifestyle of the heresiarchs. Listen to his very words about Montanus:

> His own deeds and teachings show the character of this new teacher.
> He is the one who taught the annulment of marriage, who prescribed
> fasting, who renamed the little Phrygian towns Pepuza and Tymion as
> Jerusalem so people everywhere would gather there, who appointed
> agents to collect money and gifts under the name of "offerings,"
> and who salaried those preaching his message in order that it might
> advance through gluttony.

Thus he says about Montanus. A little farther on he says this
about his prophetesses:

> We have therefore shown that these first prophetesses left their hus-
> bands from the time that they were filled with the spirit. What a lie,
> then, for them to call Priscilla a virgin!

Then he continues:

> Doesn't all Scripture forbid a prophet from accepting gifts and
> money? So when I see that a prophetess has received gold, silver,
> and expensive clothing, how can I fail to condemn her?

Farther on, he says the following about one of their confessors:

> The covetous Themiso failed to hold high the standard of confes-
> sion but exchanged imprisonment for great wealth. Although this
> should have humbled him, he boasted of martyrdom and, imitating
> the apostle, he dared to write a "general epistle" to those with bet-
> ter faith than his and to contend [for truth] with empty words while
> blaspheming the Lord, the apostles, and the holy church.

Again, he writes this about another of those they honor as
martyrs:

As an example, let the prophetess tell us about Alexander, who calls himself a martyr, who is revered by many, and with whom she dines. We need not mention his robberies and the other crimes for which he has been punished, for they are on file in the records office. Who forgives whose sins? Does the prophet forgive the martyr's robberies or the martyr forgive the prophet's greed? The Lord said, "Take neither gold nor silver nor two coats,"[33] but these do just the opposite in acquiring these forbidden things. Their prophets and martyrs so-called rake it in not only from the rich, but also from the poor, the orphans, and the widows. If they have the courage, let them stop and discuss the issue so that, if convicted, they may at least refrain from future transgressions, for "the tree is known by its fruit" [Matt. 12:33], and the fruits of these prophets must be tested.

As for Alexander, he was tried by Aemilius Frontinus, the proconsul at Ephesus, not because of the Name but for his brazen robberies and a record of convictions. Then he deceived the faithful by a false appeal to the name of the Lord and won his release, but his own diocese would not receive him because he was a robber. Those who wish to learn his story may consult the public archives of Asia. The prophet who lived with him for many years knows nothing about him, but I have exposed him and the character of the "prophet" as well. I can do the same in the case of many others: let them stand for exposure, if they dare.

In another part of the book he says this about their vaunted "prophets":

If they deny that their prophets have received gifts, let them admit that if convicted, they are not prophets, and I can supply countless proofs of this. But the fruits of a prophet must be tested. Tell me, does a prophet dye his hair? Pencil his eyelids? Does he love accents? Does he gamble and shoot dice? Lend money? Let them declare whether these things are right or not, and I will show that they have been going on in their midst.

In the same book Apollonius says that it was forty years from the time that Montanus undertook his fake prophesying to the time when he was writing. He also says that when Maximilla was pretending to prophesy in Pepuza, Zoticus tried to thwart the spirit inside her but was prevented by her supporters. He

---

33. A condensation of Matt. 10:9–10.

also mentions a certain Thraseas[34] as among the martyrs of that time. Moreover, he says, on the basis of tradition, that the Savior ordered his apostles not to leave Jerusalem for twelve years. He also cites the Revelation of John and tells how by divine power a dead man was raised at Ephesus by John himself. In other passages too, he demonstrated the error of this heresy in a powerful manner. Thus far Apollonius.

Serapion versus the Montanists

19. Serapion, who is said to have been Bishop of Antioch at this time after Maximin, has mentioned the works of Apollinarius against this heresy also. He refers to him in his own letter to Caricus and Pontius, in which he also refutes the same heresy, and adds:

> So that you may know that the so-called new prophecy of this false organization is detested by the whole brotherhood across the world, I am sending you the writings of Claudius Apollinarius, Bishop of Hierapolis in Asia, of blessed memory.

In this letter of Serapion the signatures of various bishops are preserved, one of whom signed himself: "I, Aurelius Quirinius, a martyr, pray for your welfare." Another, as follows:

> I, Aelius Publius Julius, Bishop of Debeltum, a colony in Thrace. As God in heaven lives, the blessed Sotas in Anchialus wanted to drive the demon out of Priscilla, but the hypocrites would not let him.

The signatures of a number of other bishops who shared their opinion are also preserved in this document.

Irenaeus and the Roman Schismatics

20. Against those who were distorting the sound institutions of the church at Rome, Irenaeus wrote various letters. One he addressed to Blastus, *On Schism,* another to Florinus, *On the Sole Sovereignty* or *God Is Not the Author of Evil,* an opinion Florinus seemed to be defending. And when the latter was enmeshed by the Valentinian delusion, Irenaeus composed *The Ogdoad,*[35] in which

---

34. Bishop of Eumenia, who will be mentioned in 5.24.
35. "On the Number Eight," since some Gnostics portrayed God as eightfold.

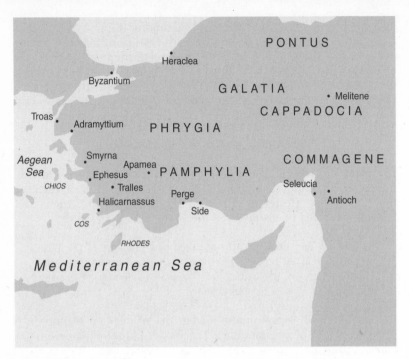

Asia Minor, where Montanism ("the Phrygian heresy") originated in the latter half of the second century. From its center in Phrygia at the western center of what is today Turkey, Montanism spread as far west as Carthage where it won a strategic convert in Tertullian. The followers of Montanus were excommunicated by the bishops of Asia Minor under the leadership of Apollinarius (c. 177), but the movement continued until Justinian proscribed it in the sixth century. The Phrygian Montanists then locked themselves inside their churches and set fire to them.

he also shows that he himself was in the apostolic succession. At the end of this work I find a very graceful note of his that I cannot resist including:

> If you copy this little book, I adjure you by the Lord Jesus Christ and by his glorious advent when he comes to judge the living and the dead that you compare your transcript and carefully correct it from this copy and that you also include this solemn charge in your copy.

May these words remind us of the scrupulous accuracy of those truly saintly men of yore. In the letter to Florinus mentioned above, Irenaeus again refers to his association with Polycarp:

These opinions, Florinus, do not reflect sound judgment—to put it mildly. These opinions are discordant with the church and consign those who share them to the greatest wickedness. Not even heretics outside the church ever dared to proclaim these opinions. Those before us who were presbyters who accompanied the apostles did not hand on to you opinions like these. When I was still a boy I saw you in Lower Asia with Polycarp, when you had high status at the imperial court and wanted to gain his favor. I remember events from those days more clearly than those that happened recently—what we learn in childhood adheres to the mind and grows with it—so that I can even picture the place where the blessed Polycarp sat and conversed, his comings and goings, his character, his personal appearance, his discourses to the crowds, and how he reported his discussions with John and others who had seen the Lord. He recalled their very words, what they reported about the Lord and his miracles and his teaching—things that Polycarp had heard directly from eyewitnesses of the Word of life and reported in full harmony with Scripture. I listened eagerly to these things at that time and, through God's mercy, noted them not on paper but in my heart. By God's grace I continually reflect on them, and, as God is my witness, if that blessed, apostolic presbyter had heard any of these opinions he would have stopped his ears and cried out, characteristically, "O good God, to what times have you preserved me that I should have to endure this?" He would have fled from wherever he was sitting or standing upon hearing such words. This is clear from the letters he sent either to neighboring churches to reinforce them or to some of the brethren to advise and exhort them.

The Martyrdom of Apollonius

21. During this same period in the reign of Commodus our circumstances improved, and by God's grace, peace came to the churches throughout the world. The word of salvation began to incline every race toward the devout worship of the God of the universe, including whole households and relatives of many at Rome who were distinguished by wealth or family. The demon who hates the good and envies by nature found this unendurable, and once again he stripped for battle and invented various devices to destroy us. At Rome, he haled Apollonius into court, a man acclaimed among the faithful of the time for his learning and philosophy, having prompted one of his servants to accuse him. But the wretch brought the case at the wrong time, for by imperial decree informers on such matters were not allowed to live. They broke his legs immediately by sentence of the judge, Perennius. But God's most beloved martyr, when the judge pleaded with him to defend himself before the senate, made a most eloquent defense of the faith before them all and found fulfillment in beheading—as if by decree of the senate, for an ancient law still prevailed that there could be no other verdict in the case of those brought to court who refused to change their opinions. The actual words of Apollonius in response to Perennius's interrogation and in his defense before the senate can be found in the record I compiled on the early martyrs.

The Succession of Bishops

189   **22.** In the tenth year of Commodus's reign, Victor succeeded Eleutherus after his thirteen years as bishop [of Rome]. In the same year, when Julian had completed his tenth year, Demetrius was appointed Bishop of Alexandria, and concurrently the famous Serapion, already mentioned, was Bishop of Antioch as eighth from the apostles. Theophilus ruled Caesarea in Palestine, and Narcissus, previously mentioned, was still in charge of the Jerusalem diocese. Other contemporaries include Bacchyllus, Bishop of Corinth, and Polycrates, Bishop of Ephesus. While there were many others prominent at this time, I have listed only those whose orthodoxy is preserved for us in writing.

The Controversy over Easter

23. At that time, no small controversy erupted because all of the Asian dioceses thought the Savior's paschal festival should be observed, according to ancient tradition, on the fourteenth day of the moon, on which the Jews had been commanded to sacrifice the lamb. On that day it was necessary to finish the fast, no matter what day of the week it might be. In churches throughout the rest of the world, however, it was not customary to celebrate in this way, since, according to apostolic tradition, they maintained the view that still prevails: the fast ends only on the day of our Savior's resurrection [Sunday].[36] Synods and conferences of bishops were held on this

---

36. Hence the dispute turned on the Asiatic use of an absolute date—the fourteenth of the Jewish New Year lunar month of Nisan, according to Ex. 12:6 (on whatever day of the week this occurred)—and an absolute day favored by the rest of Christendom, namely, Sunday.

issue, and all were of one opinion in formulating a decree for the church through letters everywhere that the mystery of the Lord's resurrection from the dead should be celebrated on no other day than Sunday, and only on that day should we observe the end of the paschal fast. Still extant is a letter from those who attended a conference in Palestine, with Bishop Theophilus of Caesarea and Bishop Narcissus of Jerusalem presiding, as well as from those who attended a similar conclave at Rome on the same issue, under Victor as bishop. There are others from the bishops of Pontus, over whom Palmas presided as the senior; from Gaul, over which Irenaeus presided; from Osrhoene and the cities there; from Bacchyllus, Bishop of Corinth, and many more who expressed the same, unified opinion and gave the same vote.

24. The bishops in Asia, however, who insisted on the custom handed down to them long ago, were led by Polycrates, whose letter to Victor and the Roman church explains the tradition he had received as follows:

> Thus we keep the day precisely, without addition or subtraction. Great luminaries sleep in Asia who shall rise again on the last day at the Lord's advent, when he shall come with glory from heaven and call back all his saints—such as Philip, one of the twelve apostles, who sleeps at Hierapolis with two of his aged, virgin daughters, while a third daughter lived in the Holy Spirit and rests in Ephesus. There is also John, who leaned on the Lord's breast and who became a priest wearing the miter, a martyr, and a teacher; he too sleeps in Ephesus. Then there is Polycarp at Smyrna, bishop and martyr, and Thraseas, bishop and martyr from Eumenia, who also sleeps at Smyrna.
>
> Need I speak of Sagaris, bishop and martyr, who sleeps at Laodicea, or the blessed Papirius, or Melito the eunuch, who lived entirely in the Holy Spirit and lies in Sardis, awaiting the call from heaven when he will rise from the dead? All these kept the fourteenth day of the month as the start of the paschal festival with no deviation and in accord with the Gospel. And I, too, Polycrates, the least of all of you, live according to the tradition of my relatives, some of whom I have followed. Seven of them were bishops and I am the eighth, and my relatives have always kept the day when the people discarded the leaven. Therefore, my brothers, I who have lived sixty-five years in the Lord and conferred with brethren from all parts of the world and have studied all of Holy Scripture, am not afraid of threats, for men better than I have said, "We must obey God rather than men" [Acts 5:29].

As for the bishops who were with him when he wrote and shared his opinion, he says:

> And I could name the bishops who are with me and whom I summoned at your request, but if I write their names, there will be many. Although they see my frailty, they approve this letter, knowing that my hair is not gray in vain but that I have always lived in Christ Jesus.

At this Victor, who presided at Rome, immediately tried to cut off from the common unity as heterodox all the Asian dioceses, along with neighboring churches, and pilloried them in letters announcing the absolute excommunication of all the brethren there. But not all the bishops were pleased by this, and they requested instead that he pursue the cause of peace, unity, and love toward his neighbors. Their words, sharply reprimanding Victor, are still extant. Among them was Irenaeus, who wrote in the name of the Christians he supervised in Gaul. While maintaining that the mystery of the Lord's resurrection be celebrated only on the Lord's Day, he nevertheless urges Victor not to excommunicate entire churches of God for following ancient tradition. Then he goes on:

> For the dispute is not only about the day but also the practice of the fast. Some think that they ought to fast for one day, others for two, others even more, and some count forty day-night hours in their "day."[37] Such variation in observance did not begin in our own day but much earlier in the time of our predecessors, who seem to have disregarded accuracy for simplicity in establishing future practice. Nevertheless, they all lived in peace with each other, as do we, and the disagreement in the fast affirms our agreement in the faith.

He adds to this a historical narrative that I may appropriately quote:

> Among these also were the presbyters before Soter who headed the church over which you now preside—I mean Anicetus, Pius, Telespho-

---

37. Forty hours marked the traditional interval between Jesus' death at 3 P.M. on Good Friday and his resurrection—at 7 A.M. in this calculation—on Sunday. Whether this gave rise to the Lenten period of forty days' fasting before Easter or, more probably, in congruence to Jesus' forty-day fast in the wilderness, is still debated.

rus, and Xystus. They themselves did not observe it,[38] nor their follow-ers, yet they lived in peace with those who arrived from dioceses that did, even though to observe it was more offensive to those who did not. No one was ever rebuffed for this reason, but the presbyters before you who did not observe it sent the Eucharist to those from dioceses that did. And when the blessed Polycarp visited Rome in Anicetus's time, though they had minor disagreements also on other matters, they made peace immediately, having no wish to quarrel on this point. Anicetus could not persuade Polycarp not to observe it, since he had always done so with John, our Lord's disciple, and the other apostles whom he knew. Nor did Polycarp persuade Anicetus to observe it, who said that he was bound to the practice of the presbyters before him. Neverthe-less, they communed with each other, and in church Anicetus yielded the consecration of the Eucharist to Polycarp, obviously out of respect. They parted from each other in peace, and peace in the whole church was maintained both by those who observed and those who did not.

Irenaeus, whose character suited his name[39] as a peacemaker, negotiated such issues for the peace of the church. He wrote not only to Victor, but also to many other heads of churches in dis-cussing the question.

25. The Palestinian bishops referred to above, Narcissus and Theophilus, along with Bishop Cassius of Tyre, Clarus of Ptolemais, and those assembled with them, wrote at length about the paschal tradition they had received from apostolic succession and con-cluded with the following:

Try to send copies of our letter to every diocese so that we may not shirk our responsibility to those who easily deceive their own souls. We point out to you that in Alexandria also they celebrate on the same day as we, for we exchange letters to insure that we observe the holy day at the same time.

The Works of Irenaeus and His Contemporaries

26. Besides the letters and works of Irenaeus already cited, a concise and very convincing treatise of his against the Greeks

---

38. The fast, according to those in Asia who observed it on Nisan 14, sometimes called the Quartodecimans.

39. Irenaeus means "peaceful" in Greek.

is extant, entitled *Concerning Knowledge*. Another, dedicated to a Christian named Marcian, is the *Demonstration of Apostolic Preaching,* as well as a little book of various addresses in which he quotes from the epistle to the Hebrews and the Wisdom of Solomon, so-called. These are the works of Irenaeus of which I know.

192/193   When Commodus died after a reign of thirteen years, Pertinax was emperor for not quite six months, and then [Septimius] Severus took office.

27. Many works by churchmen of that time are still widely preserved, and I have read them myself. These include Heraclitus's *On the Apostle;* Maximus on the problem much debated by the heretics, *The Origin of Evil,* and *The Creation of Matter;* Candidus on the *Hexameron;* Apion on the same subject; Sextus on *The Resurrection;* a treatise by Arabianus; and many others whose dates and history are unknown. Finally, there are many other orthodox writings, as is clear from their interpretations of the divine Scripture, but the authors are unnamed and unknown.

The Heresy of Artemon and Theodotus

28. A treatise by one of these against Artemon's heresy, which Paul of Samosata has tried to renew in my own time, applies to the historical period under discussion. He refutes this heresy, which asserts that the Savior was merely human, as a recent innovation, since those who introduced it tried to make it respectable by claiming it as ancient. After many other arguments against their blasphemous falsehood, the treatise continues:

> They claim that all their predecessors and the apostles themselves taught what they do and that the true teaching was preserved until the time of Victor, the thirteenth Bishop of Rome after Peter, but that the truth has been perverted from the time of his successor, Zephyrinus. Their claims might be credible if the divine Scriptures were not opposed to them. And Christian writers before Victor also defended the truth against both the pagans and the heretics of their own day—I mean the works of Justin, Miltiades, Tatian, Clement, and many more, in all of which Christ is treated as God. For who does not know the books of Irenaeus, Melito, and the others who proclaim Christ as God and man or all the earliest psalms and hymns that sing of Christ as the Word of God and regard him as God? When the

church's understanding has been proclaimed for so many years, how then is it possible that Victor's predecessors can have preached as these people claim? Are they not ashamed of slandering Victor in this way when they know well enough that he excommunicated Theodotus the shoemaker, the father of this God-denying apostasy, when he first said that Christ was merely human? If Victor's attitude toward them was as their blasphemy teaches, how could he have ejected Theodotus who invented this heresy?

Such were the events in Victor's time. When he had held office for ten years, Zephyrinus succeeded him, around the ninth year of Severus's reign. The author of the book on the heresy mentioned above adds another incident that occurred in Zephyrinus's time:

An event occurred in my time that I think would have served as warning to the men of Sodom had it happened there. A confessor named Natalius was led astray by Asclepiodotus and a second Theodotus, a banker. Both were disciples of Theodotus the shoemaker, who was the first to be excommunicated by Victor for this way of thinking, or rather, of not thinking. They persuaded Natalius to be named bishop of this heresy, with a salary of 150 denarii a month. After joining them, he was often warned by the Lord in visions, for our merciful God and Lord did not want one who had been witness to his own sufferings to die outside the church. After paying scant attention to the visions, for he was ensnared by his fame among them and the greed that ruins so many, he was finally whipped all night by holy angels and suffered considerably. In the morning he put on sackcloth and ashes and hurried in tears to prostrate himself before Bishop Zephyrinus, rolling at the feet of both clergy and laity. Although he begged for mercy and showed the stripes he had received, he was readmitted into communion only after much reluctance.

To this I would add another citation on the same persons by the same author:

They have not been afraid to corrupt divine Scriptures, they have rescinded the rule of ancient faith, they have not known Christ, they ignore Scripture but search for a logic to support their atheism. If anyone challenges them with a passage from Scripture, they examine it to see if it can be turned into a conjunctive or disjunctive syllogism. Abandoning the holy Scripture of God, they study "geometry" [earth measurement], for they are from the earth and speak of the earth and do not know the One who comes from above. Some of them study the geometry of Euclid and revere Aristotle and Theophrastus, and some virtually worship Galen. In using the arts of unbelievers for their heresy, they corrupt the simple faith of the Scriptures and claim to have corrected them.

That I am not slandering them anyone will learn who compares their writings, which are in great discord, for those of Asclepiades do not agree with those of Theodotus. Many manuscripts are available because their disciples zealously made copies of their "corrected"—though really corrupted—texts. Nor do these agree with the texts of Hermophilus, while those of Apolloniades are not even consistent among themselves, earlier copies differing greatly from later ones subjected to a second corruption. This sinful impudence can hardly have been unknown to the copyists, who either do not believe the Scriptures were inspired by the Holy Spirit and are unbelievers or deem themselves wiser than the Holy Spirit and are possessed. They cannot deny their crime: the copies are in their own handwriting, they did not receive the Scriptures in this condition from their teachers, and they cannot produce originals from which they made their copies. Some have even found it unnecessary to emend the text but have simply rejected the Law and the Prophets, using a wicked, godless teaching to plunge into the lowest depths of destruction.

Let this suffice for these matters.

CHRISTIAN AGONIES
AND ARGUMENTS

There is a stronger Western focus in this book of the *Church History* than in any other, due to Eusebius's understandable detail on the ghastly persecution at Lyons in what is today France. It is commonly assumed that the early Christians were martyred mostly at Rome, but this is far from the case. Within the Roman Empire, fewer Christians were persecuted in Rome and Italy than in the North African provinces—Egypt in particular—as well as Palestine, Syria, and Asia Minor. As for Gaul, the grisly scenes in the amphitheater at Lyons were equaled only by the horrors in the stadium at Alexandria. Today it is difficult even to imagine the bestial inhumanity involved in these human demolition derbies, which prominently included even valiant women and children. But any society that could delight in gladiatorial combats, mock naval battles that drew genuine blood, and prisoners fighting wild animals with their bare hands would have found such (to them) strange cultists as the Christians fair game for civic entertainment.

It is also widely assumed that most early Christian martyrs faced death heroically rather than surrendering their faith. Not only would this hardly have been possible realistically, due to human weakness, but Eusebius rather honestly shows us otherwise. In view of his predilection to record the "glory story" of how the embattled church won eventual triumph, his mention of those who were terrified enough to abandon their faith in the face of torment and death is both credible and commendable. However, the number of those who were indeed faithful unto death and their genuinely heroic courage in the jaws of horror is as astonishing today as it was then. In view of this, Eusebius can perhaps be forgiven for his cloyingly repetitive phrases for martyrdom, such as "he was fulfilled," "she won her triumph," or "he gained the victor's crown."

During the many decades when the church was not under general persecution, her spread and success were tempered by internal challenges. As Eusebius will relate in Book 6, there were the rigorist schismatics at Rome who wanted to exclude from the church those who had lapsed from the faith under duress. Book

5 discussed "the Phrygian heresy" of the Montanists, who clearly were the extreme chiliastic charismatics of their day, indulging in ecstatic glossolalia. As these pages demonstrate, most of today's conservative-liberal polarizations, theological extremes, and even heresies within (and beyond) Christendom were adumbrated eighteen centuries ago. Millennialists and amillennialists, charismatics and noncharismatics characterize churches now as they did then.

In 1952, a debate raged over the new *Revised Standard Version* of the Bible, which translated Isaiah 7:14: "Behold, a young woman [rather than "virgin," as in the KJV] shall conceive and bear a son, and shall call his name Immanuel." Clearly that debate is merely eighteen hundred years old. As for outright heresy, Gnosticism is reflected in current ultrafeminist theologies that advocate the worship of Sophia alongside or in place of God. Even the second-century dispute over the proper date to celebrate Easter still divides the Christian East and West. Some things never change.

In Roman imperial history, the last three or four years of *Marcus Aurelius's* administration witnessed the terrible Gallic persecutions at Vienne and Lugdunum (Lyons) in 177, which open Book 5, as well as at Scillium in Africa (c. 180). These were local, not empirewide, and were instigated by angry mobs at these locations. Still, this emperor had not prevented Justin's martyrdom at Rome itself, and when the governor of Gaul asked him for a ruling regarding the Christians there, Marcus Aurelius replied in language similar to Trajan's: those who recanted were to be set free, but those who persisted were to be condemned to the beasts or, if they were Roman citizens, beheaded. Marcus Aurelius was otherwise preoccupied with the Danube frontier, as well as a plague that had infected the empire and probably caused his own death at Vindobona (Vienna) in 180.

Commodus (180–192), the worthless son of Marcus Aurelius, seems to have been a degenerate and a slave of pleasure, even though Eusebius admits that in his reign "our circumstances improved, and by God's grace, peace came to the churches throughout the world" (5.21). His hedonism and lunacy likely distracted the emperor, who was finally strangled to death by his wrestling coach on the last day of 192.

Auctioning off the imperial throne, the Praetorian Guard installed, then murdered *Pertinax* and after him *Didius Julianus*, both in 193. The legions of the Danube now declared for their commander, *Septimius Severus* (193–211), who founded the Severan dynasty. Born at Leptis Magna in North Africa (near Tripoli), the well-educated Severus improved conditions in the provinces and curbed the Praetorian Guard. His fiscal, legal, and military reforms reinforced the state. Eusebius concludes Book 5 around the ninth year of Severus's reign (c. 202).

Bust of Septimius Severus, emperor 193–211 (*Louvre, Paris*).

BOOK 6

ORIGEN AND ATROCITIES AT ALEXANDRIA

SEPTIMIUS SEVERUS TO DECIUS

c. 203 **1.** When [Septimius] Severus was inciting persecution against the churches, champions of piety achieved glorious martyrdoms everywhere, but particularly at Alexandria. There, as if to a huge stadium, God's champions were led from the whole of Egypt and the Thebaid and in enduring every sort of torture and death were wreathed with the crowns dedicated to God. Among them was Leonides, known as the father of Origen, who was beheaded, leaving behind his young son, a lad very attuned to the divine Word from early age. **2.** His life story would fill a whole book. Here, however, I shall condense as much as possible, presenting facts drawn from his letters and the recollections of his surviving friends.

Origen's Youth

Origen's story ought to be told right from his cradle. In the tenth year of Severus, when Laetus was governor of Egypt and Demetrius had just received the episcopate there after Julian, the flames of persecution became a fierce blaze and countless numbers received the crown of martyrdom. Such a passion for martyrdom possessed Origen, boy though he was, that he wanted to court danger and plunge into the conflict. In fact, he came within a hair's breadth of ending his days, had not divine providence acted through his mother for the good of humankind. First she tried words, pleading with him to spare a mother's feelings, but

6.1

when he learned that his father had been thrown into prison, he was filled with a craving for martyrdom. Seeing that he was more determined than ever, she hid all his clothes and so forced him to stay at home. With an intensity beyond his years that could not be silenced, he sent his father a letter urging martyrdom, in which he advised, "Don't change your mind on our account!"

This first example of Origen's boyish acumen and devotion to God reflects his firm foundation in the faith, based on study of the divine Scriptures from early childhood. His father had insisted that he not devote time to the usual curriculum until he had mastered sacred studies each day through memorization and repetition. Not at all disinclined, the boy studied excessively and was not satisfied to read the sacred words in a simple and literal sense but sought something more, and even at that age looked for deeper interpretations, worrying his father with questions regarding the inner meaning of inspired Scripture. His father would pretend to scold him, advising that he not search beyond his years or for any meaning other than the obvious, but in private he rejoiced and thanked God that he had thought him worthy of being the father of such a son. It is said that he often stood over the sleeping boy and kissed his breast in reverence, as if it enshrined a divine spirit, counting himself blessed in his promising offspring.

But when his father was fulfilled in martyrdom, he was left destitute, with his mother and six younger brothers, when he was not quite seventeen. His father's property was confiscated for the imperial treasury, leaving the family without the necessities of life. But through divine aid, he was received into the home of a very wealthy and distinguished lady who, however, was devoted to one of the noted heretics in Alexandria at the time. The lady kept him [the heretic] at her house as her adopted son—he was an Antiochene by birth—and accorded him special favor. Even though young Origen could not help associating with him, he gave clear proofs of his own orthodoxy in the faith. Crowds of heretics—our own people too—gathered to hear Paul (for that was his name), attracted by his rhetoric, yet Origen could never be persuaded to join him in prayer, keeping the rule of the church from boyhood and loathing (Origen's own word) all heretical teachings. His father had fostered his progress in secular studies, and after his [father's] death he pursued the humanities with such enthusiasm that soon he enjoyed a high standard of living despite his youth.

3. While he applied himself to teaching, since there were no catechetical instructors at Alexandria—they had all fled the threat of persecution—some of the pagans approached him to hear the Word of God. The first of these was Plutarch, whose noble life was adorned with martyrdom. The second was Heraclas, Plutarch's brother, a notable example of the disciplined, philosophic life, who became Bishop of Alexandria after Demetrius. Origen was in his eighteenth year when he became head of the catechetical school[1] and came into prominence during the persecutions under Aquila, governor of Alexandria, for his eager assistance to all the holy martyrs, known and unknown. For he was with them not only in prison or in court, right up to the final sentence, but even when they were being led away to their death he courageously approached them and kissed them boldly. Often a surrounding heathen mob came close to stoning him, but for the divine right hand arranging his extraordinary escape.

This same heavenly grace protected him again and again on other occasions when plots targeted him for his fearless enthusiasm for the Word of Christ. So great was the unbelievers' war against him that soldiers were posted around his house because of the number of those he was instructing in the sacred faith. Day by day the persecution aimed at him blazed hotter so that there was no longer any room for him in the city. He moved from house to house, pressured on all sides in reprisal for his many converts, since his conduct reflected his most genuine philosophy in amazing fashion. His deeds matched his words and his words his deeds, as the saying goes, which explains why, under God, he led so many to share his enthusiasm.

Demetrius, prelate of the church, had entrusted the catechetical school to him alone, but when still more pupils flocked to him, he [Origen] decided that teaching literature did not accord with theological study, so he broke off lecturing on literature as a useless hindrance to sacred studies. Then, so that he might not be dependent on the assistance of others, he disposed of all the volumes of ancient literature he had so cherished, satisfied if the purchaser paid him four obols a day.

For many years he continued living the philosophic life, dismissing all stimuli to youthful lusts and disciplining himself with arduous tasks by day but spending most of the night studying the divine Scriptures. Sometimes he fasted, at other times he restricted the time for sleep, which he took on the floor—never

---

1. The equivalent of a middle school in which both secular and religious instruction took place.

in bed. Above all, he felt that he had to keep the Savior's sayings urging us not to own two coats or wear shoes or worry about the future. By enduring cold, nakedness, and extreme poverty, he astonished his concerned followers, who begged him to share their possessions. Yet he did not bend: for many years he is said to have walked shoeless, to have refrained from wine and all but the most necessary food, so that he actually risked his health.

By demonstrating the philosophic life in this manner, he inspired a large number of his students to similar enthusiasm, so that he even won over some unbelieving pagans, scholars, and philosophers, who believed the divine Word, were conspicuous in the present persecution, and were even arrested and fulfilled in martyrdom.

Student Martyrs

4. The first of these was Plutarch, whom I mentioned earlier. As he [Plutarch] was led to his death, Origen accompanied him to the very end and again was almost killed by his fellow citizens as being responsible for his death, but once again he was saved by the will of God. The second of Origen's students to be martyred was Serenus, who proved his faith through fire. Heraclides, from the same school, was the third martyr, and Hero was the fourth, the former still a catechumen, the latter recently baptized. Both were beheaded. In addition to these, a fifth member of the same school was proclaimed a champion of piety: another Serenus who, after enduring great torture, was decapitated. Among the women, Herais, still under instruction for baptism, received instead "the baptism of fire," as Origen himself puts it, and so ended her life.

5. Seventh was Basilides, who led the famous Potamiaena to execution. Praises of this woman resound to this day among her people. Because her beauty of mind and body was in full flower, she had to struggle continually with lovers in defense of her chastity and virginity, which were above reproach. After suffering tortures too terrible to describe, she and her mother, Marcella, were fulfilled by fire. It is said that Aquila, the judge, inflicted horrible tortures over her whole body and finally threatened to hand her over to the gladiators for ravishing. When asked what her decision was, she thought briefly and gave a reply that offended their religion. Instantly she was sentenced, and a soldier named Basilides led her off to execution. But as the crowd tried to harass and insult her with obscenities, he pushed them back and drove them off, showing

Founded by Alexander the Great, the city of Alexandria was the capital of Egypt and its chief seaport throughout the period covered by Eusebius's history. The city was built on a lateral strip of land separating Lake Mareotis from the Mediterranean. A mole leading out to the island of Pharos divided its waterfront into eastern and western harbors. The hippodrome or race course in the lower center of the map witnessed many gruesome persecutions of Christians.

extreme pity and kindness to her. She accepted his sympathy and encouraged him, promising to ask her Lord for him after her departure and before long she would repay him for all he had done in her behalf. Having said this, she endured her end nobly when boiling tar was poured slowly, drop by drop, over various parts of her body from head to toe. Such was the contest won by this splendid girl.

Not long afterward, one of his fellow soldiers asked Basilides, for some reason, to take an oath, but he maintained that swearing was absolutely forbidden to him as a Christian, confessing it openly. At first they thought he was joking, but when he continued to affirm it, they brought him before the judge, who sent him to prison when he confirmed his beliefs. His brothers in God visited him and asked the reason for this sudden, incredible inclination, and he is reported to have said that three days after her martyrdom, Potamiaena appeared to him at night, wreathed his head with a crown, and said that she had prayed the Lord for him, had obtained her request, and before long would take him to herself. At this the brethren conferred on him the seal of the Lord [in baptism], and the next day he gave a noble testimony for the Lord and was beheaded. They say that many others at Alexandria suddenly came to Christ at this time because Potamiaena appeared to them in dreams and invited them.

Clement of Alexandria and Jude

6. Pantaenus was succeeded by Clement, who directed the school at Alexandria long enough to have Origen as a pupil. When he wrote his *Miscellanies,* he prepared a chronological table in Volume 1, keying his dates to the death of Commodus as base.[2] It is clear, then, that he wrote the work under [Septimius] Severus, the period presently described.

7. At this time also, Jude, another author, composed a treatise on the seventy weeks in the book of Daniel, closing his account in the tenth year of the reign of Severus. He also believed that the much-discussed arrival of the Antichrist was near—so greatly did the persecution of that time unhinge the minds of many.

Origen's Orchiectomy

8. While Origen was teaching in Alexandria at this time, he did something that gave proof enough of his young and immature mind but also of his faith and self-control. He took the saying, "There are those who have made themselves eunuchs for the kingdom

---

2. December 31, 192. *Miscellanies* 1.21.

of heaven's sake" [Matt. 19:12] in too literal and absurd a sense, and he was eager to fulfill the Savior's words and also to forestall all slander on the part of unbelievers (for, despite his youth, he held forth on religious matters before women as well as men). So he quickly carried out the Savior's words, trying to do so unnoticed by most of his students. But however much he wished it, he could not possibly hide such a deed. Demetrius learned of it later, since he presided over the community there. He was astonished at Origen's rash act but approved the genuine enthusiasm of his faith, told him to take heart, and urged that he apply himself more fervently than ever to the work of instruction.

Such was his attitude at the time. Not long afterward, however, when he saw Origen prosperous, great, and esteemed by all, he was overcome by human weakness and tried to portray the deed as outrageous to bishops across the world—just when the bishops of Caesarea and Jerusalem, the most distinguished in Palestine, considered him worthy of the highest honor and ordained him as presbyter. Against this universal fame, then, Demetrius, with no other reason to charge him, maligned him savagely for what he had done long ago as a boy and had the audacity to include those who raised him to the presbyterate in his accusations.

This happened a short time later. At the time under consideration, Origen was busy with sacred instruction in Alexandria to all who came to him by night or day, giving all his time unstintingly to sacred studies and his students.

Bishops Narcissus and Alexander

When Severus had ruled for eighteen years, he was succeeded
211 by his son Antoninus [Caracalla]. At this time Alexander—one of those who manfully confessed the faith during persecution and were preserved by God's providence—was thought worthy of the Jerusalem episcopate, as related earlier. His predecessor Narcissus was still alive.[3]

9. Among the reported wonders performed by Narcissus, as handed down by brethren of the community in succession, is the following. Once, during the great all-night vigil of Easter, the congregation was deeply disturbed when the deacons ran out of oil. At this, Narcissus told those tending the lamps to draw water and bring it to him.

---

3. See 6.10–11.

This done, he prayed over the water and had them pour it into the lamps with absolute faith in the Lord. When they did this, against all reason but by divine power its nature was changed from water into oil. From then on until the present, many of the brethren there have preserved a little of it as proof of that wonder.

Here is another interesting story about him. Certain contemptible wretches, jealous of his energy and conscientiousness and afraid that they would be put on trial for their evil deeds, tried to forestall this by devising a plot and spreading vile slander against him. Then, to convince their hearers, they propped up their charges with oaths. One swore: "[If this isn't true], let me be destroyed by fire!" Another: "Let my body be ravaged by a terrible disease!" A third: "May I go blind!" But, swear as they might, none of the faithful paid any attention to them, since Narcissus's integrity and virtuous lifestyle were known to all. Still, he could not tolerate their odious allegations, and besides he had long opted for the philosophic life; so he departed from the church community and spent many years hiding in deserts and remote haunts. The great eye of Justice, however, was not passive at these events but quickly brought down on those godless perjurers the very curses with which they had bound themselves. The first was

Bust of Caracalla, emperor 211–217 (*Louvre, Paris*).

burned to death, with all his family, when nothing more than a small spark happened to set ablaze the house in which he was staying. The body of the second was covered from head to toe with the very disease he had prescribed as penalty, while the third, seeing the fate of the other two and fearing God's judgment, publicly confessed his part in the plot. In his remorse, however, he shed so many endless tears that both his eyes were ruined. Such was the penalty these men paid for their lies.

10. Since Narcissus had gone and no one knew where he was, the heads of the neighboring churches appointed another bishop, named Dius. After a short time, he was succeeded by Germanion and he by Gordius. In his time Narcissus appeared out of nowhere, as if restored to life, and was again called by the brethren to preside, for all admired him even more for his philosophic life and especially for the judgment by which God avenged him.

11. When he had reached so advanced an age that he could no longer perform the ministry, the previously mentioned Alexander,[4] then bishop of another community, was called by the providence of God to a joint ministry with Narcissus through a nocturnal revelation. Responding, as if to an oracle, he traveled from his episcopate in Cappadocia to Jerusalem in order to worship there and view the [sacred] sites. The people there welcomed him cordially and would not let him return, for their devout had also received a revelation at night that they were to go outside the gates and welcome the man God had already selected as their bishop. Having done this, they compelled him to remain, with the common consent of the neighboring bishops. Alexander himself, in a letter to the Antinoites[5] that I still have, mentions Narcissus as sharing the episcopate with him, using these words at the close of the letter:

> Narcissus, who held the office of bishop before me here and is now, at age 116, my associate in public worship, greets you, and urges you to be of one mind, as do I.

Serapion of Antioch

When Serapion entered into rest, he was succeeded as Bishop of Antioch by Asclepiades, who confessed [his Lord] courageously in the persecution. Alexander mentions his appointment also in a letter to the Antiochenes:

> Alexander, a servant and prisoner of Jesus Christ, to the blessed church of Antioch, greetings in the Lord. He made my chains light and easy to bear when I learned at the time of my imprisonment that by divine providence Asclepiades, whose great faith makes him most qualified, had been entrusted with the episcopate of your holy church at Antioch.

---

4. See 6.8.

5. Those living in Antinoöpolis on the Nile, a city founded by Hadrian in honor of his favorite, Antinous, who had drowned there.

This letter was delivered by Clement [of Alexandria], as is shown at the close:

> I send you this letter, dear brothers, by the hand of Clement the blessed presbyter, of whom you have already heard and will now get to know. Through the Master's providence, he both strengthened and increased our church during his presence here.

12. While it is probable that other writings of Serapion are extant, I have only those addressed to Domnus, who lapsed from the faith during persecution to Jewish will worship, and those to the churchmen Pontius and Caricus, as well as letters to other people and a treatise *Concerning the So-Called Gospel of Peter.* He wrote this to refute the falsehoods in it, which seduced some in the community at Rhossus into heterodox teachings. A passage from this work will illustrate his attitude toward the book:

> We, dear brothers, receive both Peter and the other apostles as Christ, but writings falsely attributed to them we reject, knowing that such were not handed down to us. When I visited you, I presumed that all of you adhered to the true faith, so instead of going through the "gospel" alleged by them to be Peter's, I said: "If this is the only thing that seems to engender quibbling notions among you, then read it." But since I now learn that they are ensnared in some heresy, I will strive to visit you again, so expect me soon, brothers. Macrian's heresy was obvious to me, though he contradicted himself in not knowing what he was saying. Others have studied this "gospel," namely, the successors of those who produced it, whom we call Docetists,[6] for the ideas reflect their teaching. I have gone through the book and conclude that most of it accords with the genuine teaching of the Savior, but some [spurious] addenda are appended below for your benefit.

Clement of Alexandria

13. Of Clement's writings, I have all eight books of the *Miscellanies*, which he entitled *Titus Flavius Clement's Miscellanies on the Knowledge of the True Philosophy.* There are another eight volumes of his *Outlines,* in which he names Pantaenus as his

---

6. From the Greek *dokein,* "to seem," the term was applied to those who claimed the Son of God seemed to have a physical nature but did not in reality.

teacher and explains his interpretations of Scripture as well as the traditional. He also wrote an *Exhortation to the Greeks,* three books entitled *Paedagogus, The Rich Man Who Finds Salvation,* a treatise on *The Paschal Festival,* discourses *On Fasting* and *On Slander,* the *Exhortation to Endurance* or *For the Newly Baptized,* and a book entitled the *Ecclesiastical Canon* or *Against the Judaizers,* which he dedicated to Alexander, the bishop previously mentioned.

In the *Miscellanies* he has produced a patchwork of the divine Scripture and anything he deemed useful from Greek writings. He mentions opinions of Greeks and non-Greeks alike and even corrects the false views of the heresiarchs while including a large historical context, to give us a work of great erudition. He also adds the precepts of the philosophers to this mixture, more than justifying the work's title, *Miscellanies.* He has also included evidence from the disputed writings: the Wisdom of Solomon, the Wisdom of Jesus the Son of Sirach, the epistle to the Hebrews, and those of Barnabas, Clement, and Jude. He mentions Tatian's *Against the Greeks* and Cassian, who also wrote a chronology, as well as Philo, Aristobulus, Josephus, Demetrius, and Eupolemus, Jewish writers whose works show that Moses and the Jewish race had more ancient origins than the Greeks. In Book 1 of this work he claims that he was almost a successor of the apostles. In it he also promises to write a commentary on Genesis.

In his book *On the Paschal Festival,* he states that friends insisted that he put down in writing the traditions he had heard from the elders of old for the benefit of later generations. He mentions Melito, Irenaeus, and others, whose statements he has cited.

14. In the *Outlines* he has given brief explanations of all the canonical Scriptures, including even the disputed writings, that is, the epistle of Jude and the other catholic epistles, the epistle of Barnabas, and the so-called Revelation of Peter. The epistle to the Hebrews he attributes to Paul but says that it was written in Hebrew for Hebrews and then carefully translated by Luke for the Greeks. Therefore the translation has the same style and color as Acts. [The prefatory] "Paul, an apostle" was naturally omitted, as Clement says:

> In writing to Hebrews prejudiced against him and suspicious of him, he wisely did not offend them at the start by adding his name. . . .

As the blessed presbyter[7] used to say, since the Lord, the apostle of the Almighty, was sent to the Hebrews, Paul, who was sent to the Gentiles, modestly avoids styling himself an apostle to the Hebrews both in deference to the Lord and because, as apostle to the Gentiles, he was outside his turf in writing the Hebrews.

In the same books, Clement has included a tradition of the earliest elders regarding the order of the Gospels, namely, that those with the genealogies were written first and that Mark originated as follows. When, by the Spirit, Peter had publicly proclaimed the Gospel in Rome, his many hearers urged Mark, as one who had followed him for years and remembered what was said, to put it all in writing. This he did and gave copies to all who asked. When Peter learned of it, he neither objected nor promoted it. Last of all, John, aware that the external details had been recorded in the Gospels, was urged by his disciples and divinely moved by the Spirit to compose a spiritual Gospel.

In a letter to Origen, Alexander, mentioned earlier,[8] refers to Clement as well as Pantaenus as follows:

> It is God's will that the friendship we inherited from our forefathers should remain inviolate and grow warmer and more enduring. For we know well those fathers who preceded us and whom we shall join before long: Pantaenus, my truly blessed master, and holy Clement, my master and helper, and others like them. Through them I came to know you, best in all things and my master and brother.

Origen's Scholarship on Scripture

When Zephyrinus was head of the Roman church, Adamantius (this also was Origen's name) states that he visited Rome "to see the most ancient church of the Romans." After a brief time there, he returned to Alexandria and enthusiastically resumed his teaching, Bishop Dionysius urging, even pleading with him to continue helping the brethren in this task. **15.** But he had no chance to study theology in depth or to examine and translate the sacred writings, with group after group of students thronging his lecture hall from morning to night and giving him no time to breathe. So

---

7. Probably Pantaenus, first head of the catechetical school in Alexandria and teacher of Clement.

8. See 6.8, 10–11.

he divided them up, selecting Heraclas from among his students, a man of theological fervor skilled also in secular philosophy, and shared the teaching task with him. He was assigned the introductory lessons for beginners, while the advanced students were reserved for himself.

16. So painstaking was Origen's analysis of the divine books that he even mastered Hebrew and obtained a text in the original Hebrew still circulating among the Jews. He also sought out other translations of the sacred writings besides the Septuagint, and in addition to the common versions—those of Aquila, Symmachus, and Theodotion—he discovered others that had been long lost and brought them to light. Since he had no idea who wrote them, he merely stated that he had found one at Nicopolis near Actium and the other at a similar place. In his *Hexapla*[9] of the Psalms, after the four familiar editions he placed a fifth, sixth, and seventh translation next to them. He noted that one of these was found in a jar at Jericho during the reign of Antoninus [Caracalla], the son of Severus. All these he included in one volume, placing them in adjacent parallel columns next to the Hebrew text, producing the *Hexapla*, as it is called. He put the versions of Aquila, Symmachus, and Theodotion alongside the Septuagint in a separate work, the *Tetrapla*.

17. Of these translators, Symmachus was an Ebionite. Followers of this heresy claim that Christ was the son of Joseph and Mary and regard him as only a man. They insist that the Law should be observed in a more Jewish manner, as previously mentioned.[10] Commentaries of Symmachus are still extant in which, by opposing Matthew's Gospel, he seems to share this heresy. Origen states that he received these and other interpretations of Scripture by Symmachus from a certain Juliana, who was given the books by Symmachus himself.

Origen and Heretics

18. At this time Ambrose, who followed the heresy of Valentinus, was refuted by the truth as set forth by Origen, and, so illuminated,

---

9. So named because it was arranged in six columns in the following order: Hebrew, a Greek transliteration of the Hebrew, as well as the versions of Aquila, Symmachus, the Septuagint, and Theodotion.

10. See 3.27.

he accepted the orthodox doctrines of the church. Since Origen was famous everywhere, many of the educated came to test his skill in sacred literature. Numerous heretics and a number of the most prominent philosophers paid close attention to him also, learning not only theology but—in the case of gifted students—secular philosophy as well. He taught them geometry, arithmetic, and other introductory subjects and then led them on to the different philosophic systems, discussing and criticizing each, with the result that even the Greeks deemed him a great philosopher. He also urged the less gifted to take up elementary subjects as useful tools for studying the Scriptures, for the same reason that he himself found secular and philosophic studies of prime importance.

Opinions on Origen

19. Witnesses to his success in this respect are contemporary Greek philosophers who mention him frequently in their treatises. Sometimes they dedicated their works to him or submitted them to him for a critique. Then there is Porphyry,[11] who settled in Sicily in my own day and in attacking us tried to slander Holy Scripture and its interpreters. Since he could not raise any gross charge against our doctrine, he turned, for lack of arguments, to derision and slandered its interpreters, Origen in particular. He says that he knew him as a young man and tries to malign him but unknowingly commends him in the process. He tells the truth when he must, lies when he thinks he can get away with it. Sometimes he accuses him as a Christian, at others he describes his commitment to philosophic studies. Hear his actual words:

> In trying to find an explanation for the absurdities of Jewish Scriptures rather than giving them up, some have resorted to interpretations that cannot be harmonized with those Scriptures, offering not a defense of the bizarre original so much as pompous flattery for the interpreters. They boast that the perfectly clear statements of Moses are "enigmas," exalting them as oracles full of hidden mysteries and bewitching the critical skill by their vanity. . . . This ridiculous methodology must be attributed to a man whom I met when I was still rather young, who had—and has—a great reputation due to the writings he has left behind him. I mean Origen, who is famous among teachers of this

---

11. Neoplatonist philosopher (232–c. 305) who wrote fifteen books attacking Christianity and was answered by Eusebius himself.

sort of learning. He was a student of Ammonius,[12] the most celebrated philosopher of our time. As to a wide range of knowledge, he owed much to his master, but as to the proper way to live, he took the opposite course. For Ammonius was raised a Christian by his parents, but when he began to study philosophy, he quickly turned around to a law-abiding way of life. Origen, however, a Greek educated in Greek thought, plunged headlong into foreign foolhardiness, immersed in which he hawked himself and his academic skills. His way of life was Christian and against the law, but in his views on external affairs and the Deity he played the Greek, putting a Greek spin on foreign fables. For he was always associating with Plato and was familiar with the works of Numenius, Cronius, Apollophanes, Longinus, Moderatus, Nicomachus, and the prominent Pythagoreans. He also used the books of Chaeremon the Stoic and Cornutus, where he learned the allegorical [method of] interpretation, as utilized in the Greek mysteries, and applied it to the Jewish Scriptures.

Such were Porphyry's statements in the third book of his treatise against the Christians. While he tells the truth about Origen's teaching and erudition, he obviously lies—the opponent of Christianity will do anything—when he says that he came over from the Greeks and that Ammonius lapsed from a life of reverence to God into paganism. For Origen held firmly to the Christianity his parents had taught him, as previously noted, and the inspired philosophy of Ammonius remained pure and unaltered to the very end of his life.[13] To this his famed writings, still extant, bear witness, as, for example, *The Harmony of Moses and Jesus* and all the other works in the possession of connoisseurs.

Let this prove the error of Origen's slanderer and his own great mastery of Greek learning, about which he writes the following in defense against those who faulted his zeal:

When I was fully engrossed in the Word, reports spread about my skills, attracting both heretics and those familiar with Greek learning, especially philosophy. So I thought I would probe the opinions of

---

12. Ammonius Saccas (c. 175–242), an Alexandrian philosopher who taught Plotinus, both of whom are deemed founders of Neoplatonism. Ammonius intentionally left no writings.

13. Eusebius is either mistaken here—Ammonius Saccas was not a Christian later in life—or he may be referring to another Ammonius Saccas who was a Christian, in view of the work cited.

the heretics as well as the philosophers' claims to speak the truth. In this regard I followed the example of Pantaenus, an expert in these matters who helped many before me, and also Heraclas, now presbyter in Alexandria, who had been with a teacher of philosophy for five years before I started attending his lectures. Because of him, he exchanged normal dress for a philosopher's cloak, which he maintains to this day, while he dedicates himself to Greek literature.

At this time, while he was living in Alexandria, one of the military delivered letters from the ruler of Arabia to Bishop Demetrius and to the governor of Egypt, asking them to send Origen to confer with him as soon as possible. He visited Arabia indeed, accomplished his mission, and returned to Alexandria. Some time later violence broke out in the city,[14] so he left Alexandria in secret, went to Palestine, and settled at Caesarea. There the bishops asked him to give public lectures in the church on the Holy Scriptures, even though he had not yet been ordained as presbyter. This is evident in what bishops Alexander of Jerusalem and Theoctistus of Caesarea wrote regarding Demetrius, in their own defense:

> In his letter he stated that it was unprecedented and unheard-of for laymen to preach in the presence of bishops—which clearly is not true. Wherever people are qualified to assist brother [clergy], they are invited by the bishops to preach to the people, as, for example, Euelpis in Laranda by Neon, Paulinus in Iconium by Celsus, and Theodore in Synnada by Atticus—our blessed brother bishops. In other places this probably happens also, without our knowing it.

Such was the honor accorded Origen while he was still young, not only by his own countrymen, but even by bishops in a foreign land. But when Demetrius sent a letter recalling him, deacons of the church urged his quick return, [and] he came back and resumed his work with typical enthusiasm.

Writers, Bishops, Emperors

20. During this period flourished many learned churchmen whose correspondence still survives and is easily accessible in the library at Aelia[15] established by Alexander, who had charge of the church

---

14. Probably Caracalla's massacre of the Alexandrians in 215.
15. Jerusalem; see 4.6.

there. It was here that I myself was able to gather the material for this book.

Of these churchmen, Beryllus, Bishop of the Arabians at Bostra, has left us letters as well as admirable compositions, as has Hippolytus, who also administered another church somewhere. I also have a dialogue that Gaius, a very learned man, published at Rome in Zephyrinus's time in response to Proclus, the champion of the Phrygian heresy. In this, while bridling the impudence of his opponents in devising new scriptures, he mentions only thirteen epistles of the holy apostle [Paul], not including that to the Hebrews with the rest, for even to this day some at Rome do not consider it the apostle's.

21. When Antoninus [Caracalla] had reigned for seven years and 217 six months, he was succeeded by Macrinus. After he had reigned a year, another Antoninus [Elagabalus] received the government of Rome. In his first year Zephyrinus, Bishop of Rome, departed this life after an eighteen-year ministry. Callistus followed him for five years, then left his office to Urban.

222   After this, Alexander [Severus] succeeded as emperor, Antoninus having held office for only four years. Now, too, Philetus succeeded Asclepiades in the church of Antioch.

The emperor's mother, [Julia] Mamaea, was a most religious woman, and when Origen's fame had spread far enough to reach her ears, she was determined to get an interview with him and test his universally esteemed theological prowess. She was staying in Antioch at the time and sent a military escort to bring him to her. He visited with her for some time, showing her many things that redounded to the glory of the Lord and the virtue of the divine teaching. Then he hurried back to his customary duties.

22. During this same period Hippolytus, besides many other works, wrote *The Paschal Festival,* a chronology offering a sixteen-year cycle of dates for the Passover [Easter], using the first year of the emperor Alexander [Severus] as base. Of his other writings, the following have come into my hands: *The Hexameron,*[16] *What Followed the Hexameron, Against Marcion, The Song, Ezekiel in Parts, The Paschal Festival,* and *Against All Heresies.* Many others can probably be found elsewhere.

---

16. Greek for "the six days" [of creation].

Origen's Commentaries at Alexandria

23. At this time Origen began working on his *Commentaries on Holy Scripture,* prompted by Ambrose, who not only urged him on, but also provided him lavishly with all the necessities. When he dictated, more than seven shorthand writers were available to spell each other at intervals and as many copyists, as well as girls skilled in penmanship—all generously supplied by Ambrose. His great enthusiasm for theology was the most powerful stimulus to Origen's composing the *Commentaries.*

Meanwhile, Pontian succeeded Urban, Bishop of Rome for eight years, and Zebennus Philetus at Antioch. In their time Origen traveled to Greece via Palestine, due to an urgency in church affairs, and at Caesarea he was ordained presbyter by the bishops there. This made him a center of controversy, for which the decisions of the church authorities on the matter, as well as his other theological attainments upon reaching his prime, require separate treatment, which I have provided in my *Defense of Origen,* Book 2.

Bust of Julia Mamaea, mother of Alexander Severus, who conferred with Origen while she was in Antioch (*Capitoline Museum, Rome*).

24. In the sixth book of his *Commentary on John,* he remarks that he composed the first five while still at Alexandria, but of the whole work only twenty-two books have come to my attention. And in the ninth of twelve books in his *Commentary on Genesis* he shows that he wrote not only the first eight at Alexandria, but also his *Commentary on Psalms 1–25,* as well as that on *Lamentations,* of which I have five books. In these he mentions also his *On the Resurrection,* a work in two books. Moreover, he wrote his *First Principles* before leaving Alexandria and authored ten books of *Miscellanies* in the same city during the reign of Alexander, as he himself notes in the preface.

25. In commenting on Psalm 1, he supplied a list of books in the Old Testament as follows:

There are twenty-two canonical books, according to Hebrew tradition, the same as the number of letters in their alphabet. They are these:

Genesis (as we call it, but *Bresith* by the Hebrews, from the opening word for "In the beginning")

Exodus (*Ouele smoth,* that is, "These are the names")

Leviticus (*Ouikkra,* "And he called")

Numbers (*Ammes phekodeim*[17])

Deuteronomy (Elle addebareim, "These are the words")

Jesus son of Nave (*Joshua ben nun*)

Judges-Ruth (*Sophetim,*[18] one book among the Hebrews)

Kings 1 and 2 (*Samuel,* "The called of God," one book with them)

Kings 3 and 4 (*Quammelch David,* "The kingdom of David," one book)

Chronicles 1 and 2 (*Dabre iamin,* "Words of days," one book)

Esdras 1 and 2 (*Ezra,* "Helper," one book)

Book of Psalms (*Sphar thellim*)

Proverbs of Solomon (*Meloth*)

Ecclesiastes (*Koelth*)

Song of Songs (not "Songs of songs," as some suppose: *Sir assirim*)

Isaiah (*Iessia*)

Jeremias, Lamentations, and The Letter (*Jeremiah,* one book)

Daniel (*Daniel*)

Ezekiel (*Ezekiel*)

Job (*Job*)

Esther (*Esther*)

Apart from the list is Maccabees (*Sar beth sabanai el*)

Early in his *Commentary on Matthew,* in defending the canon of the church, he testifies that he knows only four Gospels:

I learned by tradition that the four Gospels alone are unquestionable in the church of God. First to be written was by Matthew, who was once a tax collector but later an apostle of Jesus Christ, who

---

17. "Of the mustered men," a translation not supplied by Eusebius.
18. "Judges" in Hebrew.

published it in Hebrew for Jewish believers. The second was by Mark, who wrote it following Peter's directives, whom Peter also acknowledged as his son in his epistle: "The church in Babylon greets you . . . and so does my son Mark" [1 Peter 5:13]. The third is by Luke, who wrote the Gospel praised by Paul for Gentile believers. After them all came John's.

In Book 5 of his *Commentary on John,* Origen says this about the epistles of the apostles:

Paul, the minister of the new covenant who proclaimed the Gospel from Jerusalem to Illyricum, did not write to all the churches he had taught, and even to those to which he did write he sent only a few lines. And Peter, on whom Christ's church is built, left one authentic epistle and possibly a second, which is doubted. Need I say anything about John, who leaned on Jesus' breast? He left one Gospel, while claiming he could write so many that the world itself could not contain them [John 21:25]. He also wrote the Revelation but was ordered not to write the words of the seven thunders [Rev. 10:3-4]. He has left an epistle too, of very few lines, and perhaps a second and third, though these are disputed, and both together do not contain a hundred lines.

In his *Homilies on the Epistle to the Hebrews,* he comments as follows:

The diction in Hebrews does not have the rough quality the apostle himself admitted having [2 Cor. 11:6], and its syntax is better Greek. The content of the epistle is excellent, however, and not inferior to the authentic writings of the apostle. . . . If I were to venture my own opinion, I would say that the thoughts are the apostle's but the style and construction reflect someone who recalled the apostle's teachings and interpreted them. If any church, then, regards this epistle as Paul's, it should be commended, since men of old had good reason to hand it down as his. But who wrote the epistle only God knows. Traditions reaching us claim it was either Clement, Bishop of Rome, or Luke, who wrote the Gospel and the Acts.

Origen and the Bishops

26. In the tenth year of Alexander's reign, Origen moved from   **232** Alexandria to Caesarea, leaving to Heraclas the catechetical school.

Not long afterward, Demetrius, Bishop of Alexandria, died after forty-three years in office. He was followed by Heraclas.

27. At this time Firmilian, Bishop of Caesarea in Cappadocia, held Origen in such esteem that he would invite him to assist the churches in his region or travel to Judea himself to spend some time with him in order to improve his own theology. Similarly, Alexander, head of the Jerusalem church, and Theoctistus of Caesarea continued regarding him as their only teacher and left to him the task of interpreting the divine Scriptures and other aspects of church instruction.

Persecution under Maximinus Thracian

28. After reigning thirteen years, the Roman emperor Alexander
235 [Severus] died and was succeeded by Maximinus [the Thracian]. Hostile to the house of Alexander, since it consisted for the most part of believers, he started a persecution and ordered only the leaders of the church to be put to death as being responsible for the teaching of the Gospel. It was then that Origen wrote his *On Martyrdom*, dedicating the treatise to Ambrose and Protoctetus, a presbyter at Caesarea, both of whom endured extraordinary suffering in the persecution but confessed the faith nobly throughout Maximinus's reign of only three years. Origen noted this time frame in his *Commentary on John*, section 22.

Fabian and the Dove

238 **29.** Gordian succeeded Maximinus as Roman emperor, and Pontian, Bishop of Rome for six years, was followed by Anteros and then, after a month, by Fabian. It is said that Fabian had come with others from the country to visit Rome and came into office through a miracle of divine grace. When the brethren had all assembled to elect a successor to Anteros, many distinguished men were in the thoughts of most, but no one had Fabian in mind, who was present. But suddenly, they say, a dove flew down from above and perched on his head, as when the Holy Spirit in the form of a dove descended on the Savior. At this, as if by divine inspiration, the whole assembly shouted with unanimous enthusiasm, "He is worthy!" and without further ado they took him and placed him on the bishop's throne.

About this time Zebennus, Bishop of Antioch, departed this life, and Babylas succeeded. And in Alexandria, where Heraclas had followed Demetrius, one of Origen's students, Dionysus, next directed the catechetical school.

Origen's Other Students

30. While Origen was teaching at Caesarea, many students, both local and from many foreign countries, studied under him. The most distinguished among these were Theodore—who was none other than the acclaimed bishop of my own day, Gregory[19]—and his brother Athenodore. Both were strongly engrossed in Greek and Roman studies, but Origen instilled in them a love of philosophy and convinced them to exchange their previous passion for theological study. They continued with him for five years and made such progress in theology that while both were still young they were elected bishops of the churches in Pontus.

Julius Africanus

31. At this time [Julius] Africanus, author of the books called *Cesti*,[20] was another prominent writer. A letter that he wrote to Origen is extant in which he suggests that the story of Susanna in the book of Daniel is spurious. Origen sent a full reply. A five-volume *Chronography* of his is also at hand, a work of great accuracy. In it he says that he journeyed to Alexandria because of the great fame of Heraclas, who, after outstanding scholarship in philosophy and secular studies, had become bishop, as previously stated. Another of his extant letters, addressed to Aristides, deals with the presumed inconsistency between Matthew and Luke regarding Christ's genealogy. In it he clearly shows the harmony of the Evangelists, which I included in Book 1 of the present work.

Origen's Commentaries at Caesarea

32. Meanwhile, Origen was writing his *Commentary on Isaiah* as well as that on *Ezekiel.* Of the former, thirty tomes on the third section of Isaiah have come to hand, up to the vision of the beasts in the desert [Isa. 30:6]; of Ezekiel, twenty-five, the only ones he

---

19. He was generally known as Gregory Thaumaturgus ("miracle worker"), though Eusebius does not use that epithet. He died c. 270, when Eusebius was a young boy. Further detail on Gregory follows in 7.14, 28.

20. "Embroidered girdles," indicating the miscellaneous character of the work.

wrote. During a visit to Athens, he finished the *Commentary on Ezekiel,* as well as five books on the *Song of Songs,* and then, returning to Caesarea, he completed that task at ten volumes in all. But this is not the place to list all his works, which would be a project in itself. I have already included such a catalog in my *Life of Pamphilus,* the holy martyr of my own day, in which I quoted the list of Origen's works and of other church writers in his library, to show his enthusiasm for theology.

The Error of Beryllus

33. Beryllus, the previously mentioned Bishop of Bostra in Arabia, perverted church doctrine by introducing opinions alien to the faith, daring to claim that our Savior and Lord did not preexist before residing among men and had no divinity of his own apart from the Father's indwelling. A large number of bishops therefore questioned and debated with him until Origen and several others were invited into the discussion. After conversing with the man to learn his ideas, Origen corrected what was unorthodox and through reason restored him to his previous sound convictions. Records of Beryllus and the synod he occasioned still survive, which contain Origen's questions, the discussions at Bostra, and all that took place. There are many other traditions about Origen, but the most important information may be gathered from the *Defense of Origen* that the holy martyr Pamphilus and I wrote jointly in response to the fault-finding of critics.

Philip: A Christian Emperor?

244   **34.** After six years as Roman emperor, Gordion died, and Philip [the Arab] succeeded him. Word has it that he was a Christian and wanted to join with believers in the prayers of the church on the day of the last Easter vigil. But the prelate of the time would not let him enter until he confessed publicly and joined those who were judged sinful and were occupying the place [in church] for penitents. Otherwise, had he not done so, he would never have been received due to the many charges against him. It is said that he readily obeyed, showing by his actions how genuinely and piously disposed he was toward the fear of God.[21]

---

21. Philip's relation to Christianity is discussed in the commentary following this chapter.

35. In Philip's third year, Heraclas departed this life after presiding for sixteen years over the churches in Alexandria. Dionysius assumed office as bishop.

Mature Writings of Origen

36. As the faith grew and our doctrine was widely and boldly proclaimed, it is said that Origen, now over sixty, finally allowed his lectures to be recorded by shorthand writers, though he had never before permitted this. During this period he wrote eight treatises to refute the attack on us by Celsus the Epicurean, entitled *The True Word,*[22] as well as twenty-five tomes of his *Commentary on Matthew,* and his *Commentary on the Twelve [Minor] Prophets,* of which I have only twenty-five. A letter of his to the emperor Philip himself is extant, another to his [Philip's] wife, Severa, and various other letters. I have collected as many of these as possible from random sources and stored more than a hundred of them in separate roll cases to prevent their being dispersed again. Regarding his orthodoxy, he

Bust of Philip the Arab, emperor 244–249 (*Vatican Museum*).

also wrote to Bishop Fabian of Rome and to the heads of many other churches. This is all explained in Book 6 of my *Defense of Origen.*

Arab Error, Helkesaite Heresy

37. In Arabia, again, a doctrine wide of the truth was introduced claiming that the human soul dies and decays along with our bodies

---

22. Or *The True Discourse* or *Doctrine.* (*Logos* is one of the most elastic terms in Greek.) Origen's response to this important, earliest known pagan polemic against Christianity is usually titled *Contra Celsum,* and it is from this that most of Celsus's work can be reconstructed. Although Eusebius calls Celsus an Epicurean, he was most probably a Platonist.

at death, but will return to life with them at the resurrection. When a large synod was then convened, Origen was again invited. He opened a public debate on the issue in question and presented so strong a case that he changed the views of those who had previously been led astray.

38. Also at that time, another corrupt concept originated in the Helkesaite heresy, which no sooner began than it was terminated. In a public address on Psalm 82, Origen refers to it as follows:

> Recently, a man has proudly championed a godless and impious opinion, that of the so-called Helkesaites, which has clashed with the churches. I shall present their error for your benefit so it will not seduce you. It rejects portions of every book in Scripture, using every part of the Old Testament and the Gospels but rejecting the apostle [Paul] entirely. It says that to deny [the truth] does not matter and that a sensible person under duress will deny it with his mouth but not his heart. They also produce a book they claim fell from heaven, and anyone who hears it read and believes will receive forgiveness of sins—a forgiveness other than that won for us by Christ Jesus.

The Persecution under Decius

249   **39.** After a reign of seven years Philip was succeeded by Decius. Because of his hostility to Philip, he began a persecution against the churches, in which Fabian found fulfillment in martyrdom at Rome and was succeeded by Cornelius as bishop.

In Palestine, Bishop Alexander of Jerusalem again appeared in the governor's court at Caesarea, boldly confessed his faith a second time, and was imprisoned, though crowned with the hoary locks of ripe old age. After his glorious witness he fell asleep in prison, and Mazabanes was named his successor in the bishopric of Jerusalem. And when at Antioch Babylas departed this life in prison as did Alexander, Fabius became head of the church there.

In this persecution the evil demon attacked Origen, in particular, with all the weapons in his arsenal, making him endure chains and torture for the Word of Christ as he lay in irons in the depths of his dungeon. Day after day his legs were stretched apart four paces in the stocks, but he courageously endured threats of fire and every other torment devised by his enemies. The way it all ended when the judge tried valiantly to avoid sentencing him to death and his final messages to us, so full of help for those in need of solace, all is recorded truthfully and in detail in his own numerous letters.[23]

Bishop Dionysius' Deliverance in Egypt

40. What happened to Dionysius is cited in his letter against Germanus, in which he refers to himself as follows:

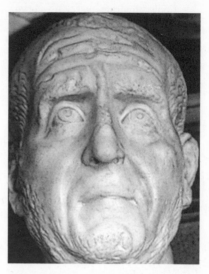

Bust of Decius, emperor 249–251, who launched a systematic persecution of the Christians (*Capitoline Museum, Rome*).

> I speak also before God, and he knows if I lie: I did not make my escape on my own initiative or apart from God. Even before that, when the persecution under Decius was announced, Sabinus immediately sent a *frumentarius*[24] to hunt me out, and for four days I awaited him at my house. Although he went about searching every place where he thought I was hiding–roads, rivers, fields–he was struck with blindness and did not find the house. He never thought that I, his target, would be staying at home! After four days, when God ordered me to leave and miraculously made this possible, many of the brethren, the boys, and I set out together. That this was the deed of divine providence is shown by what followed, when we perhaps proved helpful to some.

After further remarks, he tells what happened to him after the flight:

> About sunset we were captured by soldiers and brought to Taposiris, but Timothy providentially happened to be absent and was not

---

23. Origen survived imprisonment but died several years later from the effects of his torture and was buried at Tyre (c. 254).

24. Aurelius Appius Sabinus was prefect of Egypt in 249-250. The *frumentarii* were provincial centurions who had both commissary and police responsibilities. Bishop Germanus accused Dionysius of cowardice for escaping persecution, see 7.11.

caught. Later he arrived to find the house empty but for servants guarding it and learned that we had been taken captive. . . . Now let God's wondrous mercy be shown. As Timothy fled, one of the villagers met him and asked the reason for his haste. He had been on his way to attend a wedding feast, an all-night affair in that area, and when he learned the truth, he informed the guests reclining at the table. They all arose en masse, came running as fast as they could, and broke in on us with such a shout that the soldiers guarding us fled instantly. When they came upon us, lying on bare mattresses, I at first thought they were robbers come for plunder and stayed in bed. Naked except for my linen shirt, I offered them the rest of my clothes lying near by. But they told me to get up and flee. Then I realized why they had come and begged them to let us alone and leave or, if they wanted to confer a favor, to anticipate my captors by cutting off my head themselves. While I was shouting this, they pulled me up by force, as my companions know, but I struggled back onto the ground. Then they grabbed my hands and feet and dragged me outside, followed by those who witnessed all this: Gaius, Faustus, Peter, and Paul, who picked me up and carried me out of the village, set me on a donkey bareback, and led me away.

Such is Dionysius's account regarding himself.

The Martyrs of Alexandria

41. In a letter to Bishop Fabius of Antioch, he gives the following account of those who suffered martyrdom at Alexandria under Decius:

The persecution against us did not begin with the imperial edict but preceded it by a whole year. Whoever was the prophet and creator of evils for this city stirred up the heathen masses against us, fanning the flames of their superstition until they were convinced that thirsting for our blood was the only true form of religion.

First they seized an old man named Metras and ordered him to blaspheme. When he refused, they beat him with clubs, stabbed his face and eyes with pointed reeds, took him to the suburbs, and stoned him to death. Then they led a believer named Quinta to the temple of idols and tried to make her worship. When she turned away in disgust, they tied her feet and dragged her across the city over the rough pavement, beating her while she was being bruised by the big stones, and stoned her to death at the same place. Then they all rushed in a group to the houses of the godly and attacked, plundered, and looted their own neighbors, stealing the more valuable possessions and burning the cheaper, wooden items in the streets, making the city look as if it had been overwhelmed by enemies. The brethren gradually yielded and cheerfully endured the plundering of their possessions, and I do not know of anyone who has denied the Lord, with one possible exception.

They also seized that wonderful old virgin Apollonia, knocked out all her teeth, built a pyre in front of the city, and threatened to burn her alive if she failed to join in their blasphemies. She asked for a brief respite, and when they released her she eagerly jumped into the fire and was burned to death. Serapion they arrested in his own home. They broke all his limbs through severe torture and threw him down head first from the upper floor.

No road, no highway, no alley could we use either by night or day: everywhere there was shouting that whoever did not join in the chorus of blasphemy must be dragged off and burned. This state of affairs continued long and intense, but discord and civil war overtook these wretched men, turning on themselves the fury they had aimed at us. For a brief period we could breathe again, since they had no time to vent their fury against us, but soon came news of the change from the reign that had been kinder to us,[25] and the threat of punishment filled us with foreboding. The edict arrived indeed, almost like that predicted by our Lord in his fearful words: "so as to lead astray, if possible, even the elect" [Matt. 24:24]. All cringed in terror. Some of the better known immediately came forward through fear, others in public positions did so for professional reasons, and still others were dragged out by bystanders. Called up by name, they approached the unclean, unholy sacrifices, some pale and trembling as if they were not going to do sacrifice but be sacrificed as victims to the idols, evoking mockery from the surrounding crowd, and it was obvious that they were total cowards, afraid to die and afraid to sacrifice. Others, however, ran to the altars eagerly, as if to show that they had never been Christians. Concerning these the Lord had truly predicted that they would be saved only with difficulty.[26] Of the rest, some followed one or another of these groups, while others fled. Some were captured and imprisoned, of whom some, after long incarceration, renounced their faith even before coming into court, while others endured torture for a while before giving in.

---

25. The reign of Philip the Arab.
26. Alluding to Matt. 19:23.

The firm and blessed pillars of the Lord, however, strengthened by him and receiving power and endurance in proportion to their vigorous faith, proved magnificent martyrs of his kingdom. Among these the first was Julian, who could not stand or walk because of gout. He was carried into court by two others, one of whom immediately denied [the faith]. The other, Cronion by name but surnamed Eunus, confessed the Lord, as did the old man Julian himself. They were put on camels and beaten as they were taken through the whole city, which is vast as you know, and finally burned in quicklime before the populace. A soldier who stood by as they were led off protested the insults of the mob, which responded in rage. Besas, that gallant warrior of God, was brought to trial and, having fought heroically in the great war of faith, was beheaded. Another man, a Libyan by race, true both to his name Macar and to the "Blesseds,"[27] resisted all efforts of the judge to make him deny [the faith] and so was burned alive. After these, Epimachus and Alexander, after enduring long imprisonment and endless agony from scrapers and whips, were also destroyed in quicklime.

With them were four women. Ammonarion, a holy virgin, though tortured long and savagely by the judge for making it clear beforehand that she would never utter the things he ordered her to say, was faithful to her promise and was led away. The others included Mercuria, an elegant old woman, and Dionysia, mother of many children but just as devoted to the Lord. When the governor was embarrassed at torturing them without results and being defeated by women, they were put to death by the sword without further tortures. These Ammonarion, champion for them all, had taken on herself.

Hero, Ater, and Isidore, Egyptians, and with them a lad of about fifteen named Dioscorus were informed against. [The judge] first tried to induce the lad through words, as an easy mark, then to force him through tortures, as one who would easily break down. But Dioscorus neither obeyed nor gave in. The others he tore in pieces savagely, and when they survived they were also consigned to the flames. Dioscorus, however, bore up so well in public and gave such wise answers to questions in private that he let him go, saying that he allowed him a period to reconsider because of his youth.

Nemesion, another Egyptian, was falsely accused of associating with robbers. After clearing himself of that absurd charge before the centurion, he was denounced as a Christian and brought before the

---

27. "Blessed" in Greek is *makar*, which in its plural form is the first word of each of the Beatitudes (Matt. 5:3-11).

governor in chains. With flagrant injustice he ordered twice as many tortures and floggings inflicted on him as on the robbers and burned him between them, honoring him with a similarity to Christ.

A band of soldiers, Ammon, Zeno, Ptolemy, and Ingenuus, as well as an old man, Theophilus, were standing before the court. When a man on trial as a Christian was at the point of denying [Christ], they ground their teeth, glared, and gestured at him. While all turned toward them but before anyone could seize them, they ran to the prisoner's dock and said that they were Christians. The governor and his assessors were frightened, while the accused were courageous in facing their future sufferings. Proud of their witness, they marched out of the court in triumph.

42. Many others in the cities and villages were torn to pieces by the heathen. Let one example suffice. Ischyrion was an agent of one of the rulers, who ordered him to sacrifice. When he refused, he insulted him, and when he stood by his refusal he heaped abuse on him. When he still persisted, he took a large stick, skewered it through his vital organs, and killed him.

Need I speak of the multitudes who wandered across deserts and mountains, dying from hunger, thirst, cold, disease, robbers, and wild beasts? The survivors honor those chosen to be victors. As one example, Chaeremon, the very aged Bishop of Nilopolis, fled with his wife to the mountains of Arabia. He never returned, and despite a thorough search, the brethren found neither them nor their remains. Many were enslaved by the barbaric Saracens in that area, some of whom were ransomed at great cost, others never to this day. . . .

And so even the divine martyrs among us, who now are Christ's assessors and share his authority, have taken up the cause of their fallen brethren accused of sacrificing. Their conversion and repentance they judged acceptable to him who has no pleasure in the death of the sinner but rather his repentance. So they received and readmitted them to the congregation as "bystanders," according them fellowship in prayers and feasts. What then is your advice in this matter, brothers? What should we do? Shall we share their opinion and deal mercifully with those they pitied? Or shall we regard their decision as unjust and overturn their practice?

The Heresy of Novatian

43. Dionysius's raising the issue of those who had proven weak in the time of persecution was most appropriate, since Novatus

[Novatian],[28] a presbyter of the Roman church, had contempt for them: they no longer had any hope of salvation, not even if they did everything demanded in a genuine confession and conversion. He became leader of a new sect whose members pridefully called themselves "the Pure." In response, a large synod convened at Rome attended by sixty bishops and an even greater number of presbyters and deacons, while in the provinces the local clergy separately considered what was to be done. It was decreed unanimously that Novatus, his companions in arrogance, and all who supported his hatred and inhumanity to the brethren should be considered outside the church, but that those brothers who had fallen should be treated and restored with the medicine of repentance.

I have a letter at hand from Bishop Cornelius of Rome to Bishop Fabius of Antioch, giving a report on the Roman synod and the decisions reached by the others in Italy, Africa, and the adjacent regions; and another, in Latin, from Cyprian and his associates in Africa, clearly agreeing that those who had suffered in trial should be helped and that it was appropriate for the leader of the heresy to be excommunicated from the catholic church, as well as all who erred with him. Attached to these was another letter of Cornelius on the resolutions of the synod and also a third on the conduct of Novatus, from which I will quote. In portraying for Fabius the character of Novatus, Cornelius writes:

> You should know that for a long time this wonderful fellow has been seeking the office of bishop, hiding his insane folly with the claim that the confessors supported him in the beginning. Maximus, one of our presbyters, and Urban—both of whom twice gained highest renown in confessing the faith—as well as Sidonius and Celerinus, whose faith fortified his bodily weakness to endure torture of every kind and so has triumphed over the Adversary—these men watched him. Detecting his duplicity, perjury, and falsehoods, his unsociability and wolflike "friendship," they returned to the holy church. And all the dirty tricks that he had hidden they exposed in the presence of some bishops and many presbyters and laymen, weeping in repentance over their brief exit from the church under the influence of this treacherous and malicious beast. . . .

---

28. So named by most Greek writers but called, doubtless correctly, Novatianus by the Latins. He founded the Novatianist sect. There was indeed a Novatus, a different man who was a presbyter at Carthage, who agreed with the Novatianists.

What an extraordinary transformation came over him a short time later, dear brother! This wondrous person who swore terrible oaths never to seek the office of bishop suddenly appears as a bishop *ex machina*. For this champion of church dogma, in trying to wrench away the episcopate not conferred on him from above, chose two associates who had renounced their own salvation and sent them to a remote part of Italy to deceive three uneducated and simple-minded bishops there. He urged that they come quickly to Rome in order to join other bishops in mediating the dissension that had developed. When they arrived, they were too gullible to deal with the stratagems of scoundrels and were detained by men as disruptive as himself, who got them drunk. At the tenth hour,[29] when they were sick with the effects, he forced them to make him a bishop through a sham and invalid laying on of hands. Shortly afterward one of the bishops returned to the church, tearfully confessing his error. We readmitted him as a layman, since all the laity present interceded in his behalf. As for the other two, we replaced them with successors.

This "champion of the gospel," then, did not know that there can be only one bishop in a catholic church, in which, as he certainly knew well enough, there are forty-six presbyters, seven deacons, seven subdeacons, forty-two acolytes, fifty-two exorcists, readers, and doorkeepers, and more than fifteen hundred widows and people in distress—all supported by the Master's grace and love. Yet not even this great and necessary number, which is growing by God's providence, nor the countless laity were able to turn him from such insanity and recall him to the church. . . .

Why did he aspire to the episcopate? Was it because he had been brought up in the church and had fought dangerous conflicts on her behalf? Not at all. It was Satan who prodded him into the faith as he entered and possessed him for a considerable time. While the exorcists were trying to cure him, he fell gravely ill, and since he was thought to be at the point of death, he received a baptism by affusion[30] as he lay in bed—if indeed it can be said that such a man received it. Upon recovery, he did not receive the other ministrations of the church or sealing by the bishop. Failing these, how could he receive the Holy Spirit? . . .

At the time of persecution, through cowardice and love of life he denied that he was a presbyter. When the deacons urged him to come out of the room in which he had shut himself in order to help

---

29. About 4 P.M.
30. By pouring water rather than immersion.

his brothers who were in danger, as a presbyter should, he left in a rage, declaring that he did not wish to be a presbyter any longer, since he was in love with a different philosophy. . . .

This wondrous fellow deserted the church of God in which he had been consecrated a presbyter through the favor of the bishop. All the clergy and many of the laity objected that one who had been baptized in bed by affusion, due to illness, could not be ordained to an order, so the bishop asked permission only to ordain this man.

Then he adds something else, the worst of the man's transgressions:

When he has made the offerings and is distributing [the Sacrament] to each, he places it [into their hands], then encloses those hands in his own and does not let go until the unfortunate people utter the following oath instead of the blessing: "I swear by the blood and the body of our Lord Jesus Christ never to forsake you and turn to Cornelius." And the miserable man does not taste until he first calls down a curse on himself, and, instead of saying "Amen" as he receives the bread, he says, "I will not go back to Cornelius." . . .

Now, however, he is abandoned and desolate as the brethren desert him day by day and return to the church. Moses too, the blessed martyr who recently gave a marvelous testimony among us, while still alive saw his mad arrogance and broke off all fellowship with him and with the five presbyters who like him had cut themselves off from the church.

At the close of the letter he listed the bishops meeting at Rome who condemned the stupidity of Novatus, giving both their names and their locations. Those not at Rome but who concurred in writing with the decision of those just mentioned are also named, as well as the cities from which they wrote. All this is what Cornelius wrote to inform Fabius, Bishop of Antioch.

Dionysius on Repentance

44. When this same Fabius was inclining slightly toward the [Novatianist] schism, Dionysius of Alexandria wrote him much regarding repentance and described the ordeals of recent martyrs in Alexandria. He included the following astonishing account:

Among us was an old believer named Serapion who lived blamelessly for most of his life but who lapsed in the trial. He pleaded again and again [for forgiveness], but no one listened: he had sacrificed. He fell sick and was unconscious for three days, but on the fourth he rallied and called his grandson to his bedside. "How long, child, do you intend to keep me alive?" he asked. "Let me go quickly. Go and get one of the presbyters." After this he again became speechless. The boy ran to get the presbyter, but it was night and he was ill and could not come. Since, however, I had issued instructions that the dying should be absolved if they so desired—especially if they had previously sought this—so that they might depart in hope, he gave the little boy a portion of the Eucharist, telling him to soak it and let it fall drop by drop into the old man's mouth. As the boy returned, Serapion again revived and said, "Is that you, child? The presbyter could not come, but you must quickly do as he told you, and let me depart." The boy soaked [the bread] and dripped it into his mouth, and when he had swallowed a little he died. Was he not clearly kept alive until he gained release, and, his sin blotted out, he could be recognized for all his good deeds?

Other Letters of Dionysius

45. Now let us see the sort of letter Dionysius wrote to Novatus when he was disturbing the Roman brotherhood. Novatus had blamed his defection and schism on coercion by some of the brethren:

> Dionysius to brother Novatian, greeting. If you were led on unwillingly, as you claim, then you can prove it by retreating willingly. One should endure anything rather than split the church of God, and martyrdom to avert schism I think more glorious than that to avoid idolatry. For in the case of the latter one is martyred for the sake of his own single soul, but in the former for the sake of the whole church. If you were able even now to persuade or compel the brethren into unanimity, your recovery would be greater than your fall, which would be disregarded in praise for the former. But if they will not listen and you are powerless, by all means save your own soul. I pray that you may fare well and hold fast to the peace of the Lord.

46. He also wrote the Egyptians a letter *On Repentance*, in which he expressed his views on those who had fallen, citing degrees of guilt. He sent a personal letter, still extant, on the same subject to Bishop Colon of Hermopolis, and another, admonishing his own flock at Alexandria. Other surviving letters include the one written to Origen on martyrdom. To the Christians of Laodicea, whose bishop was Thelymidres, and to those of Armenia, whose bishop was Meruzanes, he also wrote concerning repentance. In addition to all these, he wrote to Cornelius of Rome after receiving his letter against Novatus. In this he indicated that he had been invited by Bishop Helenus of Tarsus in Cilicia and others with him—Firmilian in Cappadocia and Theoctistus in Palestine—to attend the synod at Antioch, where some were trying to strengthen the schism of Novatus. He learned that Fabius had fallen asleep, he further wrote, and that Demetrian had been appointed Bishop of Antioch in his place. Referring also to the Bishop of Jerusalem, he wrote: "Alexander, that wonderful man, was put in prison but has now entered into blessed rest."

Next to this is another extant letter from Dionysius to the Romans, delivered by Hippolytus. To them he wrote another letter, *On Peace,* and a third, *On Repentance,* and still another to the confessors there while they were still supporting the opinions of Novatus. After their return to the church they received two more. He wrote many others as well, leaving a colorful reward to those who still study his writings to this day.

A lion prepares to attack a group of praying Christians in the Roman arena, which is lined with martyrs tied to stakes, some of whom are already ablaze, in *The Christian Martyrs' Last Prayer* by Jean-Léon Gérôme, 1883 (*The Walters Art Gallery, Baltimore*).

EUSEBIUS'S HORIZONS

In Book 6, Eusebius's longest, he focuses on Origen with far more detail than he devotes to anyone else in his history. The reasons are not hard to find. Aside from the great theological respect he paid to one of the finest minds in the first three centuries of Christendom, he and his adored preceptor Pamphilus could not bear to see their master under doctrinal attack and so composed a *Defense of Origen,* which extended also to the *Church History*. Moreover, as Bishop of Caesarea, Eusebius was something of a geographical successor to an Origen who spent his later career at Caesarea, partially assembling the great library from which Eusebius subsequently drew so much of his material, as he indicates.

That Eusebius favors the Eastern rather than Western Mediterranean world in his history, Greek rather than Latin Christendom, is obvious. Although he quoted Tertullian in previous books, he says very little about him or other Latin church fathers. Apparently he knew nothing of the martyrdoms of Perpetua and Felicitas and their companions in the amphitheater at Carthage in 203. To be sure, he cites the apostolic martyrs and the succession of bishops at Rome, and devotes much attention to the persecution at Lyons in Gaul and the Novatian heresy in Italy. His history is also framed around the reigns of Roman emperors. But the most frequent horizons in these pages are Egypt, Palestine, Syria, and Asia Minor, areas most familiar to Eusebius. The East also saw the worst persecutions by far in the entire empire, with Egypt the very worst. Sadly, the "theoretical" East was also home to the greatest thinkers and theologians in the early history of the church, although Tertullian, the later Augustine, and others in the "practical" West would surely contribute their share to church doctrine and thought.

Was *Septimius Severus* (193–211) responsible for the widespread pockets of severe persecution that broke out sporadically in his later administration, where Book 6 begins? Eusebius clearly thought so, by his opening words: "When Severus was inciting persecution against the churches." Strangely, many historians doubt this, and their coverage of his administration often fails to mention his attitude toward the Christians. But another ancient author, Aelius Spartianus, claims, in his *Augustan History,* that

Severus "forbade conversion to Judaism under heavy penalties and laid down a similar penalty in the case of the Christians also" (*Severus* 17.1). Prime instigators of persecution at this time continued to be local mobs, and perhaps Severus was responding to reports of such outbreaks in language stronger than that of a Trajan or a Marcus Aurelius. After a campaign against the Scots, he died at York in Britain in 211.

Caracalla (211–217), Severus's son and successor, ended a fierce rivalry with his brother Geta by stabbing him to death in their mother's arms. The rest of his rule was more statesman-like. He conferred Roman citizenship on all free inhabitants of the empire and tried to make peace with Rome's chronic eastern enemy, Parthia. Ruins of the colossal baths he constructed along the end of the Appian Way at Rome are used for opera performances to the present day. During a campaign in the east, Caracalla was assassinated by the praetorian prefect Macrinus.

Macrinus (217–218) tried to legitimize his usurpation by winning military glory against the Parthians. Instead, they defeated him, after which he was captured and killed by troops loyal to the Severan dynasty, which was now restored.

Heliogabalus (218–222), rumored to be the natural son of Caracalla (in fact, his second cousin), had been high priest of Elagabal, the Syrian sun god, and the young teenager now arrived in Rome wearing silk, a pearl necklace, and rouged cheeks. A grotesquely colorful sort on the model of Caligula, he tried to make Elagabal supreme at Rome, but his idiotic, depraved conduct and surrender to total debauchery led his grandmother and aunt to arrange his assassination while he was hiding in a latrine.

Alexander Severus (222–235), his cousin and successor, brought sobriety back to Roman government. He consulted the senate, reduced taxes, increased public works, and established a universal primary school system throughout the empire. Moreover, ever since Septimius Severus, a period of peace seems to have descended on Christendom. In his contribution to the *Augustan History*, Lampridius states that under Alexander Severus "Christians were allowed to exist" (*Severus Alexander* 22.4). Eusebius writes that his religious mother, Julia Mamaea, invited Origen to Antioch for an interview (6.21) and even that the emperor's house "consisted for the most part of believers" (6.28), surely an exaggeration. While he was on the German frontier, however, Alexander's legions mutinied and murdered both him and his mother, terminating the Severan dynasty in 235.

This also marked the beginning of a horrendous period for the Roman Empire, which was torn by a half century of civil war. In the years between 235 and 284 (Diocletian's accession) there were twenty emperors, many of whom reigned only months before being assassinated. Following is the usual list:

Maximinus Thracian 235–238	Gallus 251–253	Tacitus 275–276
Gordian I and II 238	Aemilianus 253	Florianus 276
Balbinus and Pupienus 238	Valerian 253–260	Probus 276–282
Gordian III 238–244	Gallienus 253–268	Carus 282–283
Philip the Arab 244–249	Claudius II 268–270	Carinus 283–285
Decius 249–251	Aurelian 270–275	Numerian 283–284

Yet even this listing is misleading, since it includes only those twenty emperors recognized by the senate, most of whom had rivals backed by strong armies, who often controlled a good part of the empire. In all, well over fifty or sixty claimed to be emperor during this period. Obviously, to provide even minibiographies for this bewildering list will no longer do, but several will be selected under whom important developments took place regarding Christianity. Eusebius's Book 6 concludes with two of them.

Philip the Arab (244–249) was a sheik from Jordan who became praetorian prefect and led a successful mutiny against Gordian III. Not only had he married a Christian wife, Otacilia Severa, but, it will be recalled, Eusebius made the remarkable claim: "Word has it that he was a Christian and wanted to join with believers in the prayers of the church" (6.34). If this is true, then Philip, not Constantine, would be the first Christian emperor. But it is quite doubtful that Philip converted. Eusebius's phrase "Word has it" or "There is reason to believe" adds a note of caution, and, with Rome celebrating her thousandth anniversary under his administration, disruptions would surely have erupted had the emperor made his Christianity public. With Islam still almost four hundred years in the future, however, Arabs of that day could and did convert to Christianity, and since the next emperor persecuted the churches "through hatred of Philip," according to Eusebius, we can at very least predicate a benign attitude toward Christendom on the part of Philip. He was killed near Verona in 249, trying to put down a rebellion led by Decius.

Decius (249–251) introduced a drastic change in Roman policy vis-à-vis the Christians. What had thus far been sporadic, local persecutions of the church now became a systematic, empirewide enterprise in which Decius sought to arrest Christians city by city, ward by ward, block by block, and house by house in an imperially authorized dragnet. Sharing with other pagans the idea that Christians were responsible for the turmoil in the empire, he felt that only a return to the traditional gods and the emperor cult would revive Rome. His edict ordered all citizens to perform an act of worship in the presence of commissioners—often no more than throwing a pinch of incense into a votive lamp burning in front of the emperor's bust—after which they would receive a certificate (*libellus*) that they had sacrificed. Prison, slavery, and death awaited those who refused.

Christians responded in four ways. Some fled or hid in the catacombs and elsewhere. Others, who broke under pressure and "sacrificed," were called *lapsi,* "the fallen." Still others, who had friends in the government and had certificates written out for them even though they had never sacrificed, were called *libellatici,* "certificaters." And the incredibly brave faithful who refused to sacrifice were called "confessors" while in prison but martyrs, "witnesses," after their tortures and deaths.

This is the political background for the horrors in Alexandria and Caesarea portrayed by Eusebius. Only Decius's brief reign and fortuitous death on the field of battle prevented his drastic scheme from being accomplished to any great extent.

Christian symbols scratched inside the Catacombs of St. Sebastian at Rome. (*Left to right:*) the anchor—symbolizing hope and assurance; the fish—a Greek acrostic for "Jesus Christ is Son of God and Savior"; and the *Chi-Rho* symbol—a superimposing of the first two letters for "Christ" in Greek.

BOOK 7

DIONYSIUS AND DISSENT

GALLUS TO DIOCLETIAN

In writing Book 7 of the *Church History*, the letters of Dionysius, the great Bishop of Alexandria, will again assist me in my task. I will begin my record with these as a starting point.

The Folly of Gallus

1. When Decius had reigned for less than two years, he and his sons were killed and Gallus succeeded him. It was at this time that Origen died, at age sixty-nine.[1] In writing to Hermammon, Dionysius says this about Gallus:

> Gallus failed to note Decius's mistake or avoid that which caused his fall, and he stumbled over the same stone with his eyes open. When his reign was prospering and matters going to his liking, he expelled the holy men who were praying God for his peace and health. In banishing them, then, he also banished their prayers on his behalf.

Rebaptism of Former Heretics; Sabellianism

2. In the city of Rome, when Cornelius was bishop for about three years, Lucius was chosen as his successor, but after serving less than eight months he died, passing the office on to Stephen. To

251

---

1. Decius was killed in 251. Origen died c. 254 in the reign of Valerian.

him Dionysius wrote the first of his letters on baptism, a considerable controversy having arisen as to whether it was necessary to cleanse through [re]baptism those who turned away from heresy of any kind. In such cases, an old custom prevailed that only prayer and the laying on of hands sufficed. **3.** But Cyprian, pastor of the see of Carthage, was the first of his day to insist that they be readmitted only after purification through baptism. Stephen, however, thought it wrong to make any innovation contrary to the tradition established from the beginning and was very angry.

4. So Dionysius wrote him a lengthy letter on this issue, at the close of which he showed that, with the persecution abated, the churches everywhere had rejected the innovation of Novatus and resumed peace among themselves. He wrote as follows:

> **5.** All the formerly divided churches in the East and beyond, my brother, are now reunited, and all their prelates are of one mind, overjoyed at the surprising arrival of peace: Demetrian at Antioch, Theoctistus at Caesarea, Mazabanes at Aelia, Marinus at Tyre (since Alexander fell asleep), Heliodorus at Laodicea (since Thelymidres entered his rest), Helenus at Tarsus and all the churches of Cilicia, Firmilian and all Cappadocia. I name only the more prominent bishops to avoid making my letter too long and tedious. Still, the whole of Syria and Arabia, which you continually help and to which you have written, as well as Mesopotamia, Pontus, and Bithynia—in a word, everyone rejoices everywhere, praising God for the concord and brotherly love.

When Stephen had fulfilled his ministry for two years, Xystus [II] succeeded him. To him Dionysius wrote a second letter on baptism, indicating the views held by Stephen and the other bishops, and speaking of Stephen as follows:

> He had written earlier regarding Helenus, Firmilian, and all those from Cilicia, Cappadocia, and Galatia and all adjacent provinces that he would not have fellowship with them in the future because they rebaptized heretics. Consider how serious a matter this is. The largest synods of bishops have passed resolutions that those come over from heresies are first instructed, then washed and purified again from the filth of the old leaven. So I wrote him in appeal on all these matters. . . . I also wrote to my beloved fellow presbyters Dionysius and Philemon, who had previously shared Stephen's opinion and wrote me in that regard.

6. In the same letter he refers to the Sabellian heretics[2] as numerous in his day:

> The doctrine now emanating from Ptolemais in the Pentapolis is impious, a blatant blasphemy against almighty God, Father of our Lord Jesus Christ; utter unbelief in his only begotten Son, the first-born of all creation, the Word made man; and indifference to the Holy Spirit. When first documents and then brethren ready to debate the issue came at me from both sides, I wrote letters as best I could, with God's help, dealing with the question in a rather didactic manner. I am sending you copies of them.

Dionysius on Other Heretics

7. In his third letter on baptism, Dionysius writes the following to the Roman presbyter Philemon:

> I myself have read the writings and teachings of the heretics, polluting my soul for a while with their abominable notions, though deriving this benefit: I was able to refute them for myself and loathe them even more. Indeed, one of the brethren, a presbyter, tried to dissuade me from wallowing in the mire of their wickedness lest I harm my own soul. He was right, but a vision from God strengthened me and a voice commanded: "Read everything that comes to hand, since you are able to test everything, which is why you came to faith." I accepted the vision, since it accorded with the apostolic precept addressed to those who are stronger: "Be skilled money changers."[3]

Then, commenting on all the heresies, he goes on to say:

> This is the rule and practice I myself received from our blessed pope[4] Heraclas. Those who abandoned the heresies, while still deemed

---

2. Sabellius, who was condemned at Rome by Callistus (c. 220), taught that Father, Son, and Holy Spirit were merely names for the various modes by which the one God revealed himself in his deeds. They were also called Modalistic Monarchians and Patripassians ("the Father suffered").

3. Quoted widely by the Fathers, this *agraphon* may have been said by Jesus or Paul.

4. In using the term *pope* (Greek and Latin *papa*) for his predecessor, Dionysius provides the earliest known instance in which the Bishop of Alexandria is referred to as pope.

members of the congregation though charged with learning from heterodox teachers, he expelled from the church and turned a deaf ear
to all their pleas until they publicly declared all that they had heard
from their adversaries. Then he readmitted them without requiring
that they be rebaptized, for they had previously received the holy
[baptism] from him.

After a lengthy discussion of the question, he adds:

The Africans did not introduce this practice. Long before, in the days
of my predecessor bishops, the most populous churches and synods, Iconium, Synnada, and many other places adopted this course.
I would not dare overturn their decisions and plunge them into
strife and controversy. "You must not move your neighbor's boundary
marker, set up by former generations" [Deut. 19:14].

The fourth of his letters on baptism was written to Dionysius
of Rome, who had then been ordained presbyter and would shortly
become bishop. In it Dionysius of Alexandria pays tribute to his
learning and admirable character while saying this of Novatus:

8. I resent Novatian for good reason: he has split the church, seduced
brethren into profanity and blasphemy, introduced impious teachings
about God, and falsely slanders our most merciful Lord Jesus Christ
as being merciless. In addition to all this, he sets holy baptism aside,
overturns the faith and confession that precede it, and completely
banishes the Holy Spirit, when there was some hope of his remaining
or even returning.

9. His fifth letter was written to Xystus [II], Bishop of Rome, in
which he raises many charges against the heretics and reports
this incident:

Truly, my brother, I need your advice regarding a problem I am facing, for fear I may be mistaken. A faithful member of the congregation before my election, and, I think, before the appointment of the
blessed Heraclas, attended a recent baptism at which he listened to
the questions and answers. He then came to me in tears, fell at my
feet, and confessed that the baptism he had received from the heretics was not like ours, since it was full of profanity and blasphemy.
He was now cut to the heart, he said, and dared not even raise his
eyes to God after beginning with such unholy words and deeds. He

begged, then, to receive this pure cleansing, acceptance, and grace [of rebaptism]. This I dared not do, saying that his long fellowship with us was enough. He had heard the eucharistic prayers and joined in the Amen; he had stood beside the table and received the holy food in his hands, partaking of the body and blood of our Lord for a long time. So I could not dare to rebuild him from the beginning. I urged him to take courage and partake of the holy things with firm faith and assured hope. But he continues mourning and shudders to approach the table, and, though invited, he can scarcely join the "bystanders" at the prayers.

In addition to the letters mentioned above, he and his diocese wrote another on baptism to Xystus and the church at Rome, in which he discusses the subject at great length. Yet another of his letters to Dionysius at Rome is extant, dealing with Lucian.

The Persecution of Valerian

10. When Gallus and his associates had ruled for less than two years, they were removed in favor of Valerian and his son Gallienus. From his letter to Hermammon, Dionysius gives the following description: 253

> In Revelation, John says: "He was given a mouth uttering great things and blasphemy, and he was given authority for forty-two months."[5] Both aspects of Valerian are astonishing. His earlier conduct was mild and friendly to God's people: no emperor before him was so kindly disposed toward them, not even those said to have been Christians, as he clearly was in receiving them in close friendship at the start. Indeed he filled his whole palace with godly people, making it a church of God. But the teacher and leader of the assembly of Egyptian magicians [Macrian] persuaded him to persecute and kill pure and holy men as rivals who impeded his own disgusting incantations. (For they were and are able to scatter the wicked demons simply by their word and breath.) He also encouraged him to perform unholy rites, abominable tricks, and ill-omened sacrifices, such as cutting the throats of boys and tearing out the vital organs of newborn babies, as if shredding God's handiwork would bring them happiness. . . .
>
> When Macrian was manager of the imperial accounts, he showed neither a logical nor a catholic mind. Now he has fallen

---

5. In Rev. 13:5 this quotation refers to "the beast."

under the prophetic curse, "Woe to those who prophesy from their heart and do not see the whole."[6] For he did not understand the universality of Providence or the judgment of him who is before, through, and over all. Therefore he has become an enemy of his catholic church, estranged from God's mercy, and banished himself as far as possible from his own salvation, proving the truth of his name.[7] . . . Coaxed by him into this course, Valerian was subjected to insults and abuse, as was said to Isaiah, "These have chosen their own ways, and in their abominations they take delight. I will choose their mockings and repay them for their sins" [Isa. 66:3–4].

Mad to become emperor but unable to adorn his crippled body with the imperial robes,[8] [Macrian] put forward his two sons, who therefore inherited their father's sins, fulfilling the prophecy, "Visiting the father's sins on the children until the third or fourth generation of those who hate me" [Ex. 20:5]. In loading his own evil, though failed, ambitions onto the heads of his sons, he wiped off on them his own wickedness and hatred of God.

11. With regard to the persecution that raged fiercely in his day, what Dionysius and his associates endured due to their devotion to God is evident in his lengthy writing against Germanus, a bishop in his day who was trying to defame him:

I risk folly and stupidity in being forced to report God's wonderful kindness to me, but since "it is good to keep the secret of a king but glorious to reveal the works of God,"[9] I will respond to Germanus's attack. I appeared before Aemilianus[10] not alone but followed by my fellow presbyter Maximus and the deacons Faustus, Eusebius, and Chaeremon, as well as one of the brethren from Rome. Aemilianus did not open with the words "Do not hold assemblies," for that would have been useless for one who was going to the root of the matter. Instead he ordered me to abandon my Christianity, assuming that if I were to change the rest would follow me. But I replied in effect, "We must obey God rather than men" [Acts 5:29], that I worship the only God and no other, and would never cease to be a Christian. At that

---

6. The Septuagint version of Ezek. 13:3.

7. *Makros* is "far off" in Greek. This paragraph also plays on the term *catholic*.

8. Macrian was lame.

9. Tob. 12:7.

10. The deputy prefect of Egypt in 258.

he ordered us to leave for a village near the desert, called Cephro. But let me quote from the official record:

When Dionysius, Faustus, Maximus, Marcellus, and Chaeremon were brought into court, Aemilianus, the deputy governor, said: "I told you of the generosity our lords [Valerian and Gallienus] have shown you: the opportunity of freedom if you do what is natural and worship the gods that preserve their rule but forget those that are unnatural. What do you say to this? I doubt that you will be ungrateful for their kindness, since they advise you for your own good."

Dionysius: Not all men worship all gods but each those whom he regards as such. We worship the one God and Creator of all things, who entrusted the empire to his most beloved Augusti, Valerian and Gallienus, and we pray to him continually that their rule will remain unshaken.

Aemilianus, the acting governor: Who prevents you from worshiping this god too—if he is a god—along with the natural gods? You were commanded to worship gods, and gods known to all.

Dionysius: We worship no one else.

Aemilianus: I see that you are both ungrateful and insensitive to the indulgence of our Augusti. Therefore you shall not remain in this city but leave for a place called Cephro in Libya, a spot I selected by command of our Augusti. Under no circumstances will you or any others be permitted to hold assemblies or enter the so-called cemeteries.[11] If anyone fails to go to the place designated or is found at any meeting, he will endanger himself, for you will be observed. Be gone, then, to the place appointed.

Even though I was sick, he rushed me off without granting a single day's grace. What time did I then have for holding or not holding an assembly? . . . Still, we did not refrain from assembling with the Lord openly, but I tried all the harder to convene those in the city [Alexandria] as if I were with them—"absent in body but present in spirit" [1 Cor. 5:3]. At Cephro a large church formed, some following us from the city, others joining us from the rest of Egypt. And there God opened to us a door for the Word [Col. 4:3]. At first we were persecuted and stoned, but then some of the heathen abandoned their idols and turned to God. Through us the Word was sown among them for the first time, and it seems that for this God exiled us to them and returned us when we had finished our mission.

---

11. *Koimeterion* in Greek means "sleeping place," a term used only by Christians, who often assembled at the graves of martyrs.

Aemilianus planned to move us to what he thought rougher and more Libyan-like places, so he ordered the [scattered Christians] to stream together to the Mareotian district, assigning villages to the various groups. He situated us closer to the highway, so that we would be the first to be arrested. Apparently he was arranging it so that we would all be easy to catch whenever he decided to seize us. As for me, when I was told to leave for Cephro, I had no idea of its location and had barely heard the name before. Still, I set out in a good mood and caused no trouble. But when I was ordered to move on to the Colluthion district, I was vexed and very angry. While these places were better known to me, I learned that there were no brethren or reputable people there, where, moreover, robbers raided travelers. But I took courage when the brethren reminded me that it was nearer [Alexandria] and that while Cephro brought us much association with brethren from Egypt so that our congregation drew from a wide area, we were now closer to our nearest and dearest. They would come and stay the night, and, as in the outer suburbs, there would be local assemblies. And so it happened.

After further remarks about his exploits, he resumes as follows:

Germanus, to be sure, prides himself on many confessions of faith and many things he has had to endure—all the items he can list in my own case: sentences, confiscations, proscriptions, plundering of possessions, loss of privileges, disdain for worldly glory and praise; or the reverse from governor and council: threats, shouts, dangers, persecutions, exile, anguish, and afflictions of every kind—all of which happened to me under Decius and Sabinus and are still happening under Aemilianus. But where did Germanus appear? What was said about him? But I must abandon the utter folly into which I am falling because of Germanus, so I will omit further detail for brethren who know about it already.

In a letter to Domitius and Didymus, he again mentions events in the persecution:

It is unnecessary to name our people, since they are numerous and unknown to you. Only know that men and women, boys and patriarchs, girls and old ladies, soldiers and civilians, every race and every age, some suffering scourging and fire, others the sword—all conquered in the struggle and have received their crowns. For others, a long time was not enough to render them acceptable to the

Lord, as, apparently, in my own case thus far. I have been delayed until that suitable time known to him who said: "At an acceptable time I have listened to you, and on a day of salvation I have helped you" [2 Cor. 6:2; Isa. 49:8]. Now, since you inquire about us, you have heard, of course, that when we were being taken away as prisoners by a centurion and magistrates with their soldiers and servants—Gaius, Faustus, Peter, Paul, and I—a band from Mareotis dragged us off by force when we refused to follow them. And now only Gaius, Peter, and I, bereft of the other brethren, have been confined in a lonely, parched spot in Libya, three days' journey from Paraetonium. . . .

In the city, the presbyters Maximus, Dioscorus, Demetrius, and Lucius have gone underground to visit the brethren in secret. The better known Faustinus and Aquila are wandering about Egypt. Deacons who survived those who died on the island are Faustus, Eusebius, and Chaeremon—the Eusebius whom God empowered to aid the confessors who were in prison and to perform the risky task of laying out the bodies of the blessed martyrs. For even now the governor continues to put to a cruel death some who are brought before him, while others he tortures to pieces or lets languish in prison, denying any visitors and ready to catch any. But through the perseverance of the brethren, God gives respite to those who are hard pressed.

It should be noted that Eusebius, the deacon, was soon appointed Bishop of Laodicea in Syria, while the presbyter Maximus succeeded Dionysius himself at Alexandria. At the end of a long life, however, Faustus, who nobly confessed the faith, like Dionysius, was fulfilled in martyrdom by beheading during the persecution of our own day.

Martyrdoms at Caesarea

12. During Valerian's persecution, three prominent confessors of Christ at Caesarea in Palestine were also crowned with martyrdom by becoming food for wild beasts: Priscus, Malchus, and Alexander. It is said that these men, who were living in the country, at first charged themselves with indifference and sloth: instead of hurrying to gain the martyr's crown, they scorned the prizes then available. But when they had discussed it, they set out for Caesarea, appeared before the judge, and met the end previously described. They claim that, besides these, a woman in the same city endured a similar ordeal, but she belonged to Marcion's sect.

Gallienus Ends the Persecution

260 **13.** Not long afterward, however, Valerian was enslaved by the barbarians.[12] His son, now sole emperor, ruled more prudently and immediately ended the persecution against us by an edict with these words:

> The Emperor Caesar Publius Licinius Gallienus Pius Felix Augustus to Dionysius, Pinnas, Demetrius, and the other bishops. I have commanded that the benefit of my bounty be proclaimed throughout the world. They [non-Christians] must leave all places of [Christian] worship, and therefore you may also use the provisions of this decree against any who would trouble you. This, your freedom of action, has long been granted by me, and therefore Aurelius Quirinius, my chief minister, will enforce this ordinance of mine.

This was translated from the Latin for greater clarity. Another ordinance exists by the same emperor addressed to other bishops, permitting them to recover the sites of cemeteries, as they are called.

14. At that time, Xystus [II] still ruled the Roman church; Demetrian, following Fabius, the church at Antioch; Firmilian at Caesarea in Cappadocia; and Gregory and his brother Athenodore, students of Origen, the churches of Pontus. At Caesarea in Palestine, on the death of Theoctistus, Domnus became bishop, who lasted only a short time and was succeeded by Theotecnus, our contemporary. He also came from Origen's school. And at Jerusalem, when Mazabanes had gone to his rest, Hymenaeus occupied his throne, the man distinguished for many years in my own day.

Marinus and Astyrius at Caesarea

15. Churches everywhere enjoyed peace in their time. At Caesarea in Palestine, however, Marinus, honored with high rank in the army and also prominent through birth and wealth, was beheaded for his witness to Christ in the following way. A mark of honor among the Romans is the vine switch, and those who win it become centurions. A post became vacant, and in the order of seniority Marinus was next in line. But when he was on the point of receiv-

---

12. The Persian Shapur I invaded Antioch and took Valerian prisoner in 260.

ing the honor, another stepped up to the tribunal and stated that Marinus was disqualified by long-established laws from sharing any Roman rank since he was a Christian and did not sacrifice to the emperors, and so the office fell to himself. Achaeus, the judge, first asked what opinions Marinus held, and when he saw that he steadfastly confessed his Christianity, he granted him three hours to reconsider.

When he left the court, Theotecnus, the local bishop, took him by the hand and led him to the church. Once inside, he placed him in front of the altar, and, raising his cloak, he pointed to the sword at his side. Then he brought the book of the divine Gospels, placed it before him, and asked him to choose which of the two he preferred.

Without hesitation, he put out his right hand and took the divine book. "Hold fast then," Theotecnus told him, "hold fast to God. With his strength may you obtain what you have chosen. Go in peace." Just as he was returning, a herald announced that the time had expired and summoned him to the court. Standing before the judge, he showed still greater fervor for the faith. He was immediately led off to execution and so found fulfillment.

16. There [at Caesarea], Astyrius is also remembered for his God-pleasing boldness. A member of the Roman senate and favored by emperors, he was well known for his birth and affluence. He was present when the martyr was fulfilled, and, shouldering the remains, he placed them on a splendid, costly robe and gave them an expensive—and fitting—burial. Many other stories about this man are told by his friends who have survived to my own time, such as the following miraculous episode.

17. At Caesarea Philippi, which the Phoenicians call Paneas, on the slopes of a mountain called Paneion, springs are shown that are the source of the Jordan. Into these a victim is hurled at a certain festival, they say, and it disappears miraculously through the demon's power—a phenomenon deemed a marvel by observers. One day Astyrius was there while this was taking place, and when he saw the crowd's amazement at the affair he pitied their deception, and, looking up to heaven, he asked God through Christ to squelch the demon who was deceiving the people and to stop the deception. After he had prayed, it is said, the sacrifice suddenly floated to the surface of the springs. Thus their miracle ceased, and no marvel ever took place there again.

The Statue of Jesus

18. Since I have mentioned this city, I should not omit a story that should be recorded also for those who follow us. The woman with a hemorrhage who was cured by our Savior, as we learn from the holy Gospels [Mark 5:24–34], came from here, they claim. Her house was pointed out in the city, and amazing memorials of the Savior's benefit to her were still there. On a high stone [base] at the gates of her home stood a bronze statue of a woman on bent knee, stretching out her hands like a suppliant. Opposite to this was another of the same material, a standing figure of a man clothed in a handsome double cloak and reaching his hand out to the woman. Near his feet on the monument grew an exotic herb that climbed up to the hem of the bronze double cloak and served as an antidote for diseases of every kind. This statue, they said, resembled the features of Jesus and was still extant in my own time: I saw it with my own eyes when I stayed in the city.[13] It is not surprising that those Gentiles, who long ago were benefited by our Savior, should have made these things, since I have examined likenesses of his apostles also—Peter and Paul—and in fact of Christ himself preserved in color portrait paintings. And this is to be expected, since ancient Gentiles customarily honored them as saviors in this unreserved fashion.

The Throne of Bishop James

19. The throne of James—the first to receive the episcopacy of the Jerusalem church from the Savior and the apostles and who was called a brother of Christ, as the divine books show—has been preserved to this day. The brethren in succession there show by the honor they accord it the reverence in which the holy men, beloved by God, were and still are held by those of old and of our own time.

Strife and Plague in Alexandria

20. In addition to letters already cited, Dionysius also composed the "festival letters," in which he writes solemnly regarding the pas-

---

13. The eastern emperor Maximin Daia destroyed this statue shortly after 305, according to Eusebius's *General Elementary Introduction* (J. P. Migne, *Patrologia Graeca* [Paris: 1857], 24.541). But the later historians Sozomen (*Church History* 5.21) and Philostorgius (*Church History* 7.3) claim it was Julian the Apostate. While either emperor would be a worthy fit, the priority goes to Eusebius.

chal feast [Easter]. One of these is addressed to Flavius, another to Domitius and Didymus, in which he gives a rule based on an eight-year cycle, proving that Easter should not be celebrated at any other time than after the vernal equinox. Besides these, he penned another letter to fellow presbyters in Alexandria and to others—all while the persecution was still going on.

21. When peace was virtually established, he returned to Alexandria. But when faction fighting again erupted there, it was impossible for him to maintain oversight over all the brethren in the city, divided as they were into two hostile camps. So at Easter he communicated with them by letter from Alexandria as if he were in a foreign country. After this he wrote another festival letter to Hierax, a bishop in Egypt, in which he speaks of the Alexandrian factionalism as follows:

> It is not surprising that I find it difficult to communicate even by letter since I cannot converse or meditate even with myself. Surely I must write the brethren who are of the same household, church, and mind with me, but there seems no way to get such letters through. It would be easier to go not merely to a foreign country but from East to West than to pass from Alexandria to Alexandria. The street that runs through the center of the city is harder to travel than the great trackless desert Israel crossed for two generations! Our harbors mirror the sea that divided for them to drown the Egyptians, for the murders that occur in them resemble the Red Sea. And the river [Nile] that flows past the city at one time appeared drier than Israel's desert, but at another it overflowed both roads and fields, threatening a deluge as in the days of Noah. And it is always polluted with blood, murders, and drownings, as when it turned to blood and stank for Pharaoh at Moses' hand. Such are the vile exhalations wafted from land, sea, rivers, and the harbor mists that it is the discharges from corpses rotting down to their component elements that form the dew. Yet people are puzzled as to the source of the constant epidemics, the serious diseases, and the variety of deaths, or why this immense city is depopulated.[14] Formerly, those aged forty to seventy outnumbered those now fourteen to eighty, according to those registered for the public food ration, and those who look the youngest are now regarded as equal in age to the oldest of long ago.

---

14. In 250 plague broke out, infecting the Roman Empire for the next fifteen years.

Yet despite the diminishing of the human race, they show no concern as its extinction approaches.

22. Later, when epidemic followed war and the festival was at hand, he again wrote the brethren regarding the calamity:

This is hardly a time for celebration. Alas! All is lamentation and mourning for those dead and dying day by day. As was written of the Egyptian firstborn so also now: there is not a house without one dead, and would that it were only one!

Many terrible things happened to us also before this. At first we were driven out, persecuted, and killed, but we kept our festival even then, and every spot where we were molested became for us a place to celebrate, whether field, desert, ship, inn, or prison. But the brightest festival of all was kept by the fulfilled martyrs, who feasted in heaven. After that, war and famine befell us and the heathen as well. We alone had to endure the injuries they inflicted, though we benefited from what they suffered at each other's hands, and once again we found our joy in the peace of Christ, given only to us. But after the shortest breathing space, disease struck us, which was more terrifying to them than any terror, "the only thing of all that proved worse than what was anticipated," as one of their own historians declared.[15] To us, however, it was not that but a discipline and testing no less than other trials, for we did not escape it, even if it struck the heathen more heavily. . . .

Most of our brethren showed love and loyalty in not sparing themselves while helping one another, tending to the sick with no thought of danger and gladly departing this life with them after becoming infected with their disease. Many who nursed others to health died themselves, thus transferring their death to themselves. The best of our own brothers lost their lives in this way—some presbyters, deacons, and laymen—a form of death based on strong faith and piety that seems in every way equal to martyrdom. They would also take up the bodies of the saints, close their eyes, shut their mouths, and carry them on their shoulders. They would embrace them, wash and dress them in burial clothes, and soon receive the same services themselves.

The heathen were the exact opposite. They pushed away those with the first signs of the disease and fled from their dearest. They even threw them half dead into the roads and treated unburied

---

15. Thucydides *Peloponnesian War* 2.64, in describing the plague of Athens.

corpses like refuse in hopes of avoiding the plague of death, which, for all their efforts, was difficult to escape.

After this letter, when peace was restored in the city, he again sent a festival letter to the brethren in Egypt, and others followed this. A letter of his on the Sabbath and another on training are also extant.

The Success of Gallienus

In a letter to Hermammon and the brethren in Egypt, he tells much about the wickedness of Decius and his successors and mentions the peace under Gallienus:

> **23.** After goading one of his emperors and attacking the other, he[16] suddenly disappeared altogether with his whole family, and Gallienus was proclaimed and recognized by all. He was both an old and a new emperor: he was before them and came after them. Just as the sun's rays are blocked by a cloud only to reappear after it has moved on or dissolved, so Gallienus is just as he was before while Macrian, after trying to appropriate the imperial power of Gallienus, is no more. And the monarchy, having purged its former wickedness, now flourishes everywhere.

Following this, he also indicates the time when he wrote this:

> In looking at the lengths of the various reigns, I notice that the wicked [emperors], once famous, have quickly been forgotten, while he who has more reverence and love for God is now finishing a ninth year, in which we may indeed keep the festival.

The Schism of Nepos

24. In addition to all these letters, he composed two treatises, *On Promises,* occasioned by Nepos, a bishop in Egypt, who taught that the promises made to the saints in the divine Scriptures should be interpreted in a more Jewish fashion and that there would be a sort of millennium of bodily indulgence on this earth. Thinking to support his peculiar opinion from the Revelation of John, he wrote

---

16. Macrian, who urged Valerian to persecute Christians and tried to replace Gallienus. He and his son were later killed in battle.

a book on the subject, *Refutation of the Allegorists.*[17] Dionysius
answered him in the books, *On Promises,* in the first of which he
explains his own opinion regarding the doctrine and in the second
deals with the Revelation of John, referring to Nepos as follows:

> They rely strongly on a treatise of Nepos as indisputable proof that
> Christ's kingdom will be on earth. Now in general I endorse and
> love Nepos for his faith and industry, his study of Scripture, and
> his splendid hymnody, which still heartens the brethren, and I fully
> respect the man, especially now that he has gone to his rest. But
> truth is paramount, and one must honor what is correct and criticize
> what appears unsound. If [Nepos] were now present and airing his
> opinions orally, not writing but conversation would suffice—questions
> and answers to persuade our opponents. But a book has been pub-
> lished that some find convincing, while certain teachers, disregard-
> ing Scripture, make lofty claims for this treatise as if it were some
> great and hidden mystery. They do not let our simpler brethren have
> high and noble thoughts about the glorious epiphany of our Lord or
> about our own resurrection from the dead, when we shall be like
> him, but persuade them to hope in the kingdom of God for what is
> petty, mortal, and like the present. Thus we have no option but to
> debate our brother Nepos as if he were present. . . .
>
> When I arrived at Arsinoe, where, as you know, this teaching
> had long been prevalent and caused schisms and separations of
> whole churches, I convened a meeting of the presbyters and teach-
> ers of the village congregations (and any brethren who wished) and
> urged them to air the issue in public. When they brought me this
> book as some invincible fortress, I sat with them for three days in a
> row, from morning until night, criticizing what had been written. In
> so doing I was greatly impressed by the soundness, sincerity, logic,
> and intelligence of the brethren as we discussed methodically and
> with restraint the difficulties and points of agreement. We refused to
> cling blindly to prior opinions or avoid problems but tried our utmost
> to grapple with the issues and master them. Nor were we ashamed
> to alter our opinions, if convinced, but honestly and trusting in God,
> we accepted whatever was proven by Holy Scriptures. In the end,
> Coracion, the originator of this teaching, in the presence of all the
> brethren agreed and promised us that he would no longer adhere to
> it, debate it, mention it, or teach it, since he was convinced by the

---

17. That is, those who opposed, like Dionysius, a literal interpretation of
Revelation.

counterarguments. As to the rest, some rejoiced at the conference and the concord achieved.

The Revelation of John

25. Further on, he says this about the Revelation of John:

> Some of our predecessors rejected the book altogether, criticizing it chapter by chapter as unintelligible, illogical, and its title false. They say it is neither John's nor a "revelation" in any sense, since it is veiled by its thick curtain of incomprehensibility, and its author was neither an apostle nor saint nor even church member but Cerinthus, the one who founded the "Cerinthian" sect and wanted to attach to his own forgery a name that commanded respect. They say that he taught this doctrine: Christ's kingdom would be on earth and would offer the desires of his dreams: endless gluttony and sexual indulgence at banquets, bacchanals, and wedding feasts or (what he thought more respectable names) festivals, sacrifices, and immolations.
>
>   I, however, would not dare reject the book, since many brethren hold it in esteem, but since my intellect cannot judge it properly, I hold that its interpretation is a wondrous mystery. I do not understand it, but I suspect that the words have a deeper meaning. Putting more reliance on faith than on reason, I have concluded that they are too high for my comprehension. I do not reject what I have failed to understand but am rather puzzled that I failed to understand.

After examining all of Revelation and proving that it cannot be understood in the literal sense, he continues:

> On completing his prophecy, the prophet blesses those who observe it, including himself: "Blessed is the one who keeps the words of the prophecy in this book, and I, John, who heard and saw these things" [Rev. 22:7–8]. That, therefore, he was named John and that this book is by a John—some holy, inspired writer—I will not deny. But I do not agree that he was the apostle, the son of Zebedee, the brother of James, who wrote the Gospel according to John and the general epistle. From the character of each and on the style and format of [Revelation], I conclude that the author is not the same. For the Evangelist nowhere names himself in either the Gospel or Epistle in either the first or third person, whereas the author of Revelation announces himself at the very beginning: "The revelation of Jesus

Christ, which he . . . sent by his angel to his servant John" [Rev.
1:1-2]. Then he writes a letter: "John to the seven churches in Asia:
grace to you and peace" [Rev. 1:4]. Yet the Evangelist did not write
his name even at the beginning of the general epistle but started
with the mystery of the divine revelation: "What was from the beginning, what we have heard, what we have seen with our eyes" [1 John
1:1]. Not even in the second or third extant epistles of John, even
if they are short, is John named: he is merely the nameless "presbyter." Yet this writer was not satisfied to give his name once and
continue his account but names himself again: 'I, John, your brother
and partner . . . was in the island called Patmos' [Rev. 1:9]. Even at
the close he says: "Blessed is the man who keeps the words of the
prophecy in this book, and I, John, who saw and heard these things"
[Rev. 22:7-8].

That the writer was John is credible, but which John? He does
not say, as in the Gospel, that he was the disciple loved by the Lord,
the one who leaned on his breast, the brother of James, the eye- and
earwitness of the Lord. Had he wished to identify himself he would
surely have used one of these epithets. But he uses none of them,
merely referring to himself as our brother, partner, a witness of Jesus,
and blessed with revelations. Many have taken the name John in love
and admiration for the apostle, much as Paul and Peter are common
names for children of believers. In Acts there is another John whose
surname was Mark, whom Barnabas and Paul took with them. Was he
the writer? Hardly. For he did not go into Asia with them, as Scripture
says: "Having set sail from Paphos, Paul and his companions came to
Perga in Pamphylia; but John left them and returned to Jerusalem"
[Acts 13:13]. I think there was another John in Asia, since it is said
that there were two tombs of a "John" in Ephesus.

The concepts, words, and syntax show two different writers. There
is full harmony between the Gospel and Epistle, and they begin alike.
The one says: "In the beginning was the Word"; the other, "That which
was from the beginning." The one says: "And the Word became flesh
and lived among us." The other, the same in slightly different words:
"What we have heard, seen, and touched . . . concerning the Word of
life, the life was manifested." This prelude aims at those who denied
our Lord's coming in the flesh. The careful reader will find [words and
phrases] common to both: the life, the light, turning from darkness,
truth, grace, joy, the flesh and blood of the Lord, judgment, forgiveness of sins, God's love for us, the commandment to love one another,
keeping all the commandments, convicting the world, the Devil, the
Antichrist, the promise of the Holy Spirit, the adoption of the sons of

God, faith, and the Father and the Son throughout. In sum, the Gospel and the Epistle have the same characteristics.

But Revelation is completely different from these writings and has hardly a syllable in common with them, so to speak. Nor does the Epistle or Gospel contain any concept of the Revelation, whereas Paul in his epistles hints at revelations, which he did not record.

The style, too, shows the difference. The Gospel and Epistle are written not only in errorless Greek but also with high literary skill in diction, logic, and syntax. Not a barbarous term, solecism, or vulgarity occurs, for their author apparently possessed, by the Lord's grace, the gift of knowledge and the gift of speech. I will not deny that the other saw revelations and received prophecy, but his style and use of Greek is inaccurate, and he uses barbarous idioms and occasional solecisms. There is no need to cite these now, since I have not said this in derision—not at all—but only to prove the dissimilarity of the writings.

Letters of Dionysius

26. Besides these, there are many other letters of Dionysius, as, for example, those to Ammon, Bishop of Bernice, against Sabellius, and those to Telesphorus, Euphranor, Ammon again, and Euporus. He also wrote four treatises on the same subject to his namesake at Rome. I have many other letters and books of his, such as those on nature addressed to his boy Timothy, and one on temptations, dedicated to Euphranor. In writing to Basilides, Bishop of Pentapolis, among other letters, he says that he had written a commentary on the beginning of Ecclesiastes. So much for Dionysius. Let us move on to our own generation.

Paul of Samosata

27. When Xystus [II] had charge of the Roman church for eleven years,[18] he was succeeded by Dionysius, namesake of the Bishop of Alexandria. Then, too, when Demetrian departed this life at Antioch, Paul of Samosata received the episcopate. Since he held a low view of Christ, contrary to the church's teaching, regarding him as an ordinary man, Dionysius of Alexandria was invited to attend the synod.[19] Excusing himself because of age and weakness,

---

18. Eleven *months*, in fact. Xystus II was bishop from September 257 to August 258.

19. At Antioch, which opened the inquiry into Paul's teaching.

however, he postponed his attendance and sent a letter on the issue in question. But other pastors hurried to Antioch from all directions to deal with this destroyer of Christ's flock.

The Synod of Antioch

28. The most distinguished among these were Firmilian, Bishop of Caesarea in Cappadocia; the brothers Gregory and Athenodore, pastors in Pontus; Helenus, [Bishop] of Tarsus; Nicomas of Iconium, Hymenaeus of Jerusalem, Theotecnus of neighboring Caesarea, and Maximus, who was leading the brethren at Bostra with distinction. Many more assembled at Antioch for this purpose, as well as presbyters and deacons, but these are the most eminent. During the arguments and questions raised at their many sessions, the Samosatene and his party tried to hide or disguise his heterodoxy, while the others tried their best to uncover and display his heretical blasphemy against Christ.

264   At that time, in the twelfth year of Gallienus, Dionysius died, having presided as Bishop of Alexandria for seventeen years.
268 Maximus was his successor. And after fifteen years as emperor, Gallienus was succeeded by Claudius [Gothicus], who conferred
270 the government on Aurelian after his second year.

Paul's Excommunication

29. During his reign, a final synod with a very large number of bishops was held, and the leader of the heresy at Antioch was exposed, condemned for heterodoxy, and excommunicated from the catholic church throughout the world. The person most responsible for unmasking him was Malchion, the learned head of a school of Greek rhetoric at Antioch and a presbyter of that community by reason of his absolute faith in Christ. He had his debates with Paul taken down in shorthand, which are extant to this day, and he alone was able to expose that crafty deceiver.

30. The assembled pastors then unanimously drafted a single letter to Bishop Dionysius of Rome and Maximus of Alexandria and sent it to all the provinces. In it they recounted their zealous efforts, the perverse heterodoxy of Paul, their debates with him, and a summary of his life and conduct, as follows:

To our beloved brothers in the Lord, Dionysius, Maximus, and to all our colleague bishops, presbyters, and deacons throughout the world and to the whole catholic church—Helenus, Hymenaeus, Theophilus, Theotecnus, Maximus, Proclus, Nicomas, Aelian, Paul, Bolanus, Protogenes, Hierax, Eutychius, Theodore, Malchion, Lucius, and all our members—greeting. . . .

We invited even the more distant bishops to come and cure this deadly teaching, as, for example, Dionysius of Alexandria and Firmilian of Cappadocia, both of blessed memory. The former wrote to the whole community at Antioch—not to the leader of the heresy, deeming him unworthy of personal correspondence. We enclose a copy. Firmilian, however, even came twice and condemned Paul's novel notions, as we and many others witnessed. But when Paul promised to change, he adjourned [the proceedings], hoping that the matter would be settled without any offense to the Word—though he was duped by one who denied his God, his Lord, and the faith he had previously held. Firmilian was again at the point of crossing over to Antioch—now wise to the God-denying evil of this man—and had gotten as far as Tarsus. But while we convened and awaited his arrival, he reached life's end.

They go on to describe [Paul's] manner of life:

Since he has abandoned the canon and turned to false and bastard doctrines, we need not judge the conduct of one outside the church. Previously penniless, neither having received a livelihood from his forebears nor acquiring one by skill or occupation, he now possesses immense wealth through lawless deeds, plundering churches, and blackmailing the brethren. Depriving the injured of their rights, he promises to help them—for cash—only to break his word, and he makes easy money from those enmeshed in lawsuits who wish to buy relief from those harassing them, presuming that godliness means gain. Overambitious and arrogant, he adorns himself with worldly honors and wants to be called *ducenarius*[20] rather than bishop and struts about the marketplaces, reading or dictating letters as he strides in public surrounded by a large bodyguard. As a result, the faith is discredited and loathed due to his bloated conceit and pride.

This charlatan puts on a show in church assemblies to dazzle the simple souls as he sits on the dais and lofty throne he designed for himself—how inappropriate for a disciple of Christ!—or in the

---

20. A procurator with a large salary of 200,000 sesterces a year.

secretum[21] he devised in imitation of the rulers of this world. He slaps his thigh and stamps on the dais. Some fail to applaud or wave their handkerchiefs as in a theater or shout and jump up as do the disorderly men and women who are his partisans, listening instead in orderly reverence, as in God's house. These he scorns and insults. Against interpreters of the Word who have departed this life he makes vulgar attacks in public, while boasting of himself as if he were a sophist or mountebank rather than bishop.

All hymns to our Lord Jesus Christ he has banned as recent compositions, yet he instructs women to sing hymns to himself in the middle of the church on the great day of Easter, which one would shudder to hear! Such is the fare that he also permits fawning bishops and presbyters of neighboring districts and towns to include in their sermons. He will not confess that the Son of God descended from heaven (which will be documented shortly in many of the attached notes, especially where he says that Jesus Christ is "from below"), yet those who sing hymns and praises to him claim that their impious teacher is an angel descended from heaven. Nor does he prevent this, but in his arrogance he is even present when such things are said.

And what about his "spiritual brides," as the Antiochenes style them, and those of his presbyters and deacons? He joins them in concealing this and their other incurable sins so that, indebted to him, they are too frightened to charge him with his crimes in word and deed. He has even made them rich, thus insuring their loyalty and admiration. However, we know, beloved, that the bishop and the whole priesthood should set an example of all good works to the people, even as we are aware of how many have fallen in procuring "spiritual brides" for themselves, while others are suspected of doing so. Even if we concede that [Paul] does nothing licentious, he should at least have avoided the suspicion arising from such practices lest he lead someone astray in imitating him. How could he reprove someone or advise him not to consort any longer with a woman lest he slip, as it is written, when he has already dismissed one and now has two young and pretty ones living with him, whom he takes with him everywhere, in a life of luxury and excess? Although all groan and weep at this in secret, they are so afraid of his tyranny and power that they dare not accuse him. Yet, as we said before, a man could be held accountable for these things if only he had a catholic mind as one of our number. But for one who caricatured the mystery

---

21. The private chamber of a judge or a magistrate.

and paraded in the execrable heresy of Artemas[22]—why should we not name his father?—from such we feel no obligation to require a reckoning. . . .

Since he opposed God and refused to yield, we were compelled to excommunicate him and appoint another bishop for the catholic church in his place. By the providence of God, we feel certain, [we chose] Domnus, the son of the blessed Demetrian who once presided over the same community with distinction. He is adorned with all the excellent qualities required in a bishop, and we inform you [of his appointment] so that you may write him and receive letters [establishing] communion with him. But let this fellow write to Artemas, and let his party hold communion with him.

When Paul had lost his orthodoxy as well as his episcopate, Domnus assumed the ministry at Antioch, as stated. But Paul categorically refused to surrender possession of the church building, so an appeal was made to the emperor Aurelian, who rendered a very just decision in the matter: he ordered the building assigned to those with whom the bishops of the religion in Italy and Rome should correspond in writing. Accordingly, the man in question was ejected from the church in the most humiliating fashion by secular authority.

Such was Aurelian's disposition toward us at the time. But as his reign went on his attitude changed, and he was now pressured by certain advisers to institute a persecution against us, which provoked much comment everywhere. But just as he was almost at the point of signing the decrees against us, divine justice seized his hands, so to speak, to frustrate his plan—clear evidence that the rulers of this life would never find it easy to attack the churches of Christ, unless the hand that champions us allowed this as a divine judgment to punish and reform us at chosen times. In any case, when Aurelian had ruled for six years he was succeeded **276** by Probus,[23] who reigned for about as long and was followed by Carus and his sons Carinus and Numerian. When they, in turn, lasted less than three years, the government fell to Diocletian and those he brought in. Under them the persecution and destruction **284** of churches in my own day occurred. Shortly before this, Bishop Dionysius of Rome, after nine years, was succeeded by Felix.

---

22. In 5.28 Eusebius calls him Artemon.

23. Tacitus and Florianus ruled briefly between Aurelian and Probus, from 275–276.

The Manichean Heresy

31. Then, too, the maniac whose name [Mani] is reflected in his demon-possessed heresy, was arming himself with mental delusion, since Satan, God's adversary, had put him forward for the destruction of many. A barbarian in lifestyle, as his speech and manners revealed, and demonic and manic by nature, he acted accordingly in trying to pose as Christ. At one time he proclaimed himself the Paraclete—the Holy Spirit himself—conceited crackbrain that he was; at another he chose twelve disciples, as did Christ, to be associates in his newfangled notions. Stitching together false and godless doctrines he had collected from countless, long-extinct heresies, he infected our world with a deadly poison imported from Persia. From him derived the unholy name of Manichean, still in common use. Such, then, was the basis for this so-called knowledge.

Contemporary Churchmen

32. Felix, head of the Roman church for five years, was followed by Eutychian. He lasted less than ten months, and Gaius, my contemporary, succeeded him for almost fifteen years. His successor was Marcellinus, who has fallen victim to persecution.

At Antioch, in their time, the episcopate passed from Domnus to Timaeus, whom my contemporary Cyril followed. During his time I came to know Dorotheus, a learned presbyter at Antioch. In his theological fervor, he mastered Hebrew so thoroughly that he could read and understand the Hebrew Scriptures and was also familiar with the liberal arts and Greek elementary education. He was, however, a eunuch by nature from his very birth. The emperor himself, regarding this as a kind of miracle, extended his friendship and appointed him director of the purple dye works at Tyre. I heard him give a cogent exposition of the Scriptures in church.

After Cyril, Tyrannus became Bishop of Antioch, and in his day the attack on the churches reached its climax.

At Laodicea, Eusebius, a native of Alexandria, followed Socrates as bishop. The reason for his move was the Paul affair, for which he had come to Syria, where eager theologians prevented his return home. He was one of the finest examples of piety among us, as is evident from previously quoted statements of Dionysius. Anatolius was his successor, one good man following another. Also an Alexandrian by birth, he ranked in first place among our most distinguished contemporaries for his learning, secular studies, and philosophy, reaching the summit in arithmetic, geometry, astronomy and other sciences, logic, physics, and rhetoric. For this reason the citizens there asked him to establish the School of the Aristotelian Tradition at Alexandria. His countless exploits during the siege of Pirucheum[24] at Alexandria are recorded—an extraordinary privilege among officials. I shall cite only one of these.

When the besieged ran out of wheat so that hunger was now worse than the enemy without, [Anatolius] devised the following scheme. The other part of the city, fighting on the Roman side, was not besieged. Eusebius, who had not yet gone to Syria, was here and had won so high a reputation that it reached even the Roman general. When Anatolius apprised him of those dying of hunger in the siege, he asked the Roman commander for a great favor: a grant of immunity to deserters from the enemy. Learning that this was approved, Anatolius convened a council of the Alexandrians and first asked that they extend the right hand of friendship to the Romans. When they got angry at this proposal, he replied, "I don't think you would say no if we allowed those who are useless to us—old men and women and young children—to leave. Why keep these people with us who are at the point of death? Why let the maimed and crippled starve to death when we ought to ration the wheat for the men and youths defending the city?"

With such arguments he persuaded the assembly. All those not required for the army were permitted to leave, and he was able to save almost all of the besieged. He arranged that those belonging to the church were first to escape and then the rest of the city whatever their age, not merely those specified in the vote but a great number of others pretending to be so. Disguised in women's dress, they left the gates by night, according to his plan, and hurried to the Roman army. There Eusebius welcomed them, and like a father and a doctor he gave the siege victims tender care. Such were the two pastors that successively served the church at Laodicea: by divine providence they left Alexandria after the war to come there. Anatolius did not write a great number of works but enough have reached us to reveal his great eloquence and learning. In these he offers his opinions on the Easter festival in particular, from which I quote:

---

24. Or Bruchium, the Greek sector of Alexandria.

FROM THE CANONS OF ANATOLIUS
ON THE EASTER FESTIVAL

In the beginning of the nineteen-year cycle, it has the new moon of
the first month in the first year–26 Phamenoth according to the Egyptians, 22 Dystrus according to the Macedonians, or, as the Romans
would say, 11 before the Kalends of April [March 21]. On this day, the
sun is already through the fourth day of the first sign of the zodiac.
This first of the twelve signs is equinoctial: the beginning of months
and starting point of the planetary course. The preceding twelfth
sign, however, is the last of the months and the end of the planetary
circuit. Therefore those who place the first month in it and calculate
the Paschal fourteenth day accordingly make an extraordinary error.
(This is not my own claim, but a fact known to Jews even before
Christ and carefully observed by them, as witness Philo, Josephus,
Musaeus, and the two Agathobuli, famed as teachers of Aristobulus
the Great. He was one of the Seventy who translated the Hebrew
Scriptures for Ptolemy Philadelphus and his father and dedicated to
them commentaries on the Mosaic law.)

In dealing with problems regarding the Exodus, these writers
say that all should sacrifice the Passover after the vernal equinox
in the middle of the first month and that this occurs when the sun
passes through the first sign of the solar (or zodiacal) cycle. Aristobulus adds that not only the sun but also the moon should be passing
through an equinoctial sign. There are two such signs, one in spring
and one in autumn, diametrically opposite each other, and the day
of the Passover is the fourteenth of the month after sunset, so the
moon will be diametrically opposed to the sun as in the case of full
moons. Hence the sun will be in the sign of the vernal equinox and
the moon necessarily in the autumnal. I know many of their other
arguments by which they show that the festival of the Passover and
Unleavened Bread should always occur after the equinox. But I shall
not require such proofs from those for whom the veil on the law of
Moses has been removed in order to behold Christ, as in a mirror.
That the first month among the Hebrews straddles the equinox is
shown also in the book of Enoch.[25]

[Anatolius] has also left us an *Introduction to Arithmetic*
in ten parts, as well as studies in divinity. Bishop Theotecnus
of Caesarea in Palestine first consecrated him as bishop, intending him as his own successor after death, and indeed they both

---

25. 1 Enoch 72:6, 9ff.; cf. Jude 14.

presided over the same church for a short time. But he was summoned to the synod at Antioch that dealt with Paul, and while passing through Laodicea he was retained by the brethren there, Eusebius having fallen asleep.

Leaders in Laodicea, Caesarea, Jerusalem, and Alexandria

When Anatolius also departed this life, Stephen became bishop there, the last before the persecution. While he was widely respected for his knowledge of philosophy and secular learning, he was not equally devoted to the divine faith, as the persecution proved, exposing him as more of a cowardly hypocrite than a true philosopher. But the church and her activities were not to be ruined because of him; they were rescued by one whom God himself chose as bishop of that community: Theodotus, whose deeds proved the truth of his name.[26] While he had reached the first rank in the science of healing the body, he was second to none in the healing of souls, due to his kindness, sincerity, and genuine sympathy for all who sought his aid. He also devoted much effort to the study of divinity.

At Caesarea in Palestine, Theotecnus, after a vigorous episcopate, was succeeded by Agapius, who also worked hard for his people's welfare and cared generously for the poor. In his time I came to know Pamphilus, a most eloquent man and genuine philosopher who became presbyter of that community. To portray his background and character would be too great an undertaking, but the details of his life, the school that he founded, his ordeals and confessions of faith during persecution, and his ultimate crown of martyrdom I have covered separately in a special work devoted to him. He was surely the most admirable man in that city.

Two of my rarest contemporaries were Pierius, presbyter at Alexandria, and Meletius, bishop of the churches in Pontus. The former had been famed for his life of total poverty and his philosophical learning. He plumbed the depths of theology and was skilled in his sermonizing. Meletius (the educated used to call him *Mellifluous*, the honey of Attica) was a universal scholar. Extraordinarily gifted in oratory, unrivaled in erudition, and the most skilled in all branches of literature—as you would conclude from meeting him once—he was also distinguished for virtue.

---

26. Theodotus means "God-given" in Greek.

During the persecution, I noted that he was hunted all over Palestine for seven years.

In the church at Jerusalem, Zabdas followed Hymenaeus as bishop. After a short time he fell asleep, and Hermo, last of the bishops up to the persecution of my day, succeeded to the apostolic throne preserved there to this day.

At Alexandria, Maximus, bishop for eighteen years after Dionysius, was followed by Theonas. In his time Achillas became presbyter along with Priscus and was much admired. The school of the sacred faith had been entrusted to him, since he had shown extraordinary ability as a philosopher and a character congruent with the Gospel. When Theonas had given his best efforts for nineteen years, Peter succeeded as Bishop of Alexandria, and he was also esteemed for twelve years. He guided the church for less than three years before the persecution and spent the rest of his life in severe discipline and obvious care for the good of the churches. As a result, he was beheaded in the ninth year of the persecution, and thus adorned with the crown of martyrdom.

In these books I have completed the subject of the successions from our Savior's birth to the destruction of our places of worship, an account that covers 305 years. Now, for the information of those who come after us, I shall record the nature and extent of the ordeals in my own day on the part of those who fought so manfully for the true faith.

DIONYSIUS OF ALEXANDRIA

Much of the material in this chapter comes from the letters of Bishop Dionysius of Alexandria, often called Dionysius the Great, whom Eusebius greatly admired and to whom he devotes the second most space in his *Church History*. As will be recalled, these letters covered everything from the question of rebaptism for penitent heretics to the Easter controversy. They were written in a climate of an on-again, off-again persecution in Egypt, where civil discord was exacerbated by a horrendous epidemic that swept Alexandria, claiming far more victims than religious repression. Dionysius appears as a bishop—in the true sense of shepherd—with a large heart and liberal attitude toward penitents.

To be sure, Eusebius borrows too many vast sections of Dionysius's correspondence for use in his history by today's standards of historiography, but he is not guilty of plagiarism, since he always attributes the authorship of his citations. And were it not for Eusebius's borrowing, we would not have such important primary sources today, since most of Dionysius's surviving documents have been preserved only through Eusebius and Athanasius.

Dionysius's letters show the church life of his day in fascinating detail. He was also a good, critical scholar, as is evident from his lucid discussion of the authorship of Revelation. Until his time, the final book of the New Testament had generally been thought the work of John the apostle, but Dionysius convincingly ascribes it to another John in Asia Minor, which is the majority view among New Testament scholars today, and for the very reasons advanced by Dionysius.

Book 7 also describes two material items of maximum interest: the statue of Jesus at Caesarea Philippi and the bishop's throne of his half brother James in Jerusalem. Mention of the former and of paintings of the apostles is especially significant, since the second commandment against worshiping engraved images of any kind fairly ruined art among the Jews, whereas Christian Gentiles did not feel similarly restricted with regard to images, provided they were not worshiped. Accordingly, the bronze statue of Jesus could indeed have been fashioned in a Gentile center like Caesarea Philippi, and Eusebius claims to have seen it himself. This will also explain why all statues or busts of human beings in this book are of Gentiles (especially the emperors) and none of Jews.

The perversion of the bishop's office in the case of Paul of Samosata only continues the sad succession of those churchmen corrupt either in morals or doctrine (or usually both), whose progenitor seems to have been Simon Magus. Novatian had proved another glaring example, and Paul was in a lineage that surfaces today among several of the fallen television apostles.

In the Roman political arena, the rest of the ephemeral "army emperors" are covered in Book 7. *Gallus* (251–253) maintained some pressure on Christendom by exiling certain leaders. Eusebius quotes Bishop Dionysius's statement that Gallus "expelled the holy men who were praying God for his peace and health. In banishing them, then, he also banished their prayers on his behalf" (7.1). Among these was Bishop Cornelius of Rome, but there is no evidence that Gallus resumed a general persecution of the church. Both he and his successor *Aemilianus* (253) were assassinated by legionary mutineers.

Valerian (253–260) and his son *Gallienus* (253–268) became co-emperors, administering the eastern and western halves of the Roman Empire respectively. Their joint rule was riddled with crises: Germanic and Gothic tribes were penetrating Rome's Rhine-Danube frontier as at no time previously; in the Near East, a revived Persia under Shapur I was moving into Syria; pirates were infesting Mediterranean sea lanes and bandits the highways. As if all this were not enough, a plague broke out in Egypt and spread across the empire for the next fifteen years. Dionysius's letters vividly tell of the natural disasters at Alexandria, but in a short time people were dying at the rate of five thousand a day at Rome also.

Valerian proved to be a poor general against the Persians and in June 260 was even captured by them, the first time a Roman emperor had ever been taken prisoner. A rock relief near Persepolis still shows him kneeling in chains before a victorious Shapur on horseback, and he died shortly thereafter in shameful captivity. Christians, however, were hardly grieving. Earlier, Valerian, who had been friendly to the church, reversed course and renewed its persecution with a vengeance. Eusebius describes the magician Macrian's nefarious role in seducing Valerian into quasi-devil worship, and again it was church leaders who became special targets, such as Bishop Xystus of Rome and Cyprian of Carthage.

Gallienus, who assumed sole control of the empire after his father's death, fared much better against Rome's enemies in both East and West. He reformed the legions and improved their battle strategy, but he was also a man of intelligence and culture, very much resembling Hadrian. His wife, the empress Salonina, was a Christian, and Gallienus himself, though no convert, reversed his father's policy of persecution and published an edict of toleration—the first such in Roman history—ordering restoration of all church property, which Eusebius quotes in 7.13.

After fifteen successful years—a record at this time of turmoil—Gallienus was treacherously assassinated by his Illyrian staff officers, who installed one of their own as emperor: *Claudius II* (268–270). Named "Gothicus" for his victory over the Goths, Claudius died two years later of the plague.

Aurelian (270–275), another Illyrian, took his place. He halted the Germanic invasions in Italy, though he did surrender Dacia to the Goths, and captured Zenobia, queen of a rebellious Palmyra. Having restored the Rhine-Danube frontier, he stabilized the economy and tried to curb inflation. He also built the famous Aurelian Wall around Rome, which was twelve miles long and twenty feet high, sections of which still stand today. As for his religious policy, he championed Sol Invictus, the Unconquered Sun, as supreme god of the universe, but was sufficiently tolerant of Christianity that the church could appeal to him against Paul of Samosata and receive a favorable decision. Later, however, Aurelian changed policy and planned a renewed persecution of Christians but was assassinated in a plot forged by his secretary.

A string of transitory emperors, seated but soon murdered, followed: *Tacitus* (275–276), chosen by the senate, and the rest Illyrians chosen by the army: *Florianus* (276), *Probus* (276–282), *Carus* (282–283), *Carinus* (283–285), and *Numerian* (283–284).

A final Illyrian, *Diocletian* (284–305), became one of the ablest emperors of the third century, the man who put an end to the Roman civil wars. So far as the church was concerned, however, he was also one of the most devastating, as we shall see.

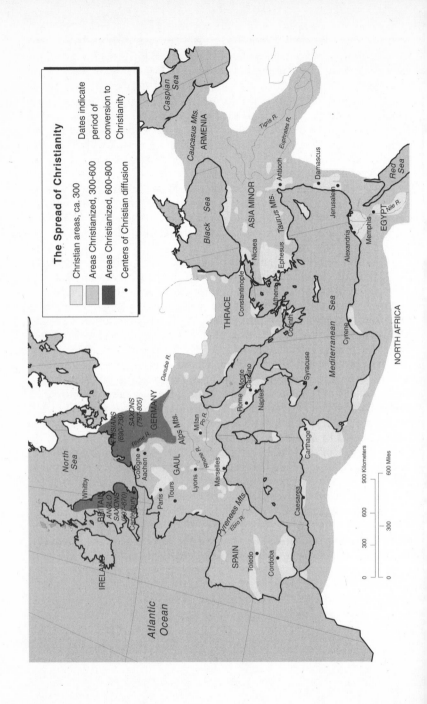

The Spread of Christianity

Dates indicate period of conversion to Christianity

- Christian areas, ca. 300
- Areas Christianized, 300–600
- Areas Christianized, 600–800
- Centers of Christian diffusion

Caspian Sea

Caucasus Mts.

ARMENIA

Tigris R.

Euphrates R.

Black Sea

ASIA MINOR

Taurus Mts.

Antioch

Damascus

Red Sea

Nicaea

Ephesus

Jerusalem

Constantinople

Athens

Memphis

EGYPT

Nile R.

THRACE

Corinth

Alexandria

Mediterranean Sea

Cyrene

NORTH AFRICA

Danube R.

Syracuse

Rome Monte Cassino

Milan

Napies

Po R.

Alps Mts.

FRISIANS (690–739)

SAXONS (772–805)

GERMANY

Rhine R.

Cologne

Aachen

GAUL

Lyons

Rhone R.

Marseilles

Carthage

North Sea

Whitby

BRITAIN

ANGLO-SAXONS (597–670)

Canterbury

Paris

Tours

Caesarea

IRELAND

Pyrenees Mts.

Ebro R.

SPAIN

Toledo

Cordoba

Atlantic Ocean

0   300   600   900 Kilometers

0   300   600 Miles

BOOK 8

THE GREAT PERSECUTION

DIOCLETIAN TO GALERIUS

Having covered the succession from the apostles in seven books, it is most important for future generations that I deal carefully in the eighth with the events of my own time.

The Growth of Christianity

1. Before the persecution of my day, the message given through Christ to the world of reverence to God was accorded honor and freedom by all men, Greeks and non-Greeks alike. Rulers granted our people favors and even permitted them to govern provinces, while freeing them from the agonizing issue of [pagan] sacrifice. In the imperial palaces, emperors allowed members of their own households—wives, children, and servants—to practice the faith openly, according men like the loyal Dorotheus and the celebrated Gorgonius higher favor than their fellow servants or even officers. All governors honored the church leaders, mass meetings gathered in every city, and congregations worshiped in new, spacious churches that replaced the old. This all progressed day by day, the divine hand protecting its people from jealousy or plot so long as they were worthy.

But greater freedom brought with it arrogance and sloth. We began envying and attacking one another, making war on ourselves with weapons formed from words. Church leaders attacked church leaders and laymen formed factions against laymen, while unspeakable hypocrisy and pretense reached their evil limit. Finally, while the assemblies were still crowded, divine judgment, with its accustomed mercy, gradually started to intervene, and the persecution began with our brothers in the army. In our blindness, however, we made no effort to propitiate the Deity but, like atheists, assumed that our affairs went unnoticed, and we went from one wickedness to another. Those who were supposed to be pastors, unrestrained by the fear of God, quarreled bitterly with one another and only added to the strife, threats, jealousy, and hate, frantically claiming the tyrannical power they craved. Then it was that the Lord in his anger humiliated his daughter Zion, in the words of Jeremiah, and threw down from heaven the glory of Israel [Lam. 2:1-2]. And, as foretold in the Psalms, he renounced the covenant with his servant and profaned to the ground his sanctuary—through the destruction of churches—exalting the right hand of his servant's enemies, not assisting him in battle, and covering him with shame.[1]

The Destruction of Churches

2. All this was fulfilled in my time, when I saw with my own eyes the houses of worship demolished to their foundations, the inspired and sacred Scriptures committed to flames in the middle of the public squares, and the pastors of the churches hiding shamefully in one place or another, or arrested and held up to ridicule by their enemies. But I will neither describe their wretched misfortunes nor record their quarrels and inhumanity to each other prior to the persecution, only enough to justify the divine judgment. I will say nothing even about those who made utter shipwreck of their salvation in the persecution and of their own free will hurled themselves into the depths of the sea. Instead, I shall include in my history only those things from which

A head of Diocletian, emperor 284–305, which was discovered at Nicomedia, where he located his capital (*Archaeological Museum, Istanbul*).

---

1. Eusebius freely adapts Ps. 89:39-45 here, which I have condensed.

first we ourselves and then later generations may benefit. We proceed, then, to describe briefly the sacred ordeals of the martyrs of the divine Word.

In March of the nineteenth year of Diocletian's reign, when   303
the festival of the Savior's passion [Easter] was approaching, an imperial edict was announced everywhere ordering that the churches be demolished and the Scriptures destroyed by fire. Any [Christians] who held high places would lose them, while those in households would be imprisoned if they continued to profess Christianity. Such was the first decree against us. Soon, however, other edicts appeared ordering that the presidents of the churches everywhere be thrown into prison and then forced by every sort of device to offer sacrifice.

Ordeals and Martyrs

3. Then, then it was that many church leaders endured terrible torments heroically, while countless others succumbed to the first assault, cowardice having numbed their souls. As to the rest, each was subjected to a series of various tortures: one was scourged mercilessly, another racked and scraped to death. People emerged from the ordeal in different ways: one man would be shoved at the loathsome, unholy sacrifices and dismissed as if he had sacrificed when he had not; another who came nowhere near any such abomination but was said to have sacrificed would leave in silence at the falsehood. Still another, half dead, would be discarded as a corpse, while a man who had sacrificed willingly was nevertheless dragged a long distance by his feet. One man would shout at the top of his voice that he had not sacrificed and never would, while yet another would proclaim that he was a Christian and glory in the Savior's name. These were silenced by a large band of soldiers, who struck them on the mouth and battered their faces. The overriding goal of the enemies of godliness was to appear to have accomplished their purpose.

Such methods, however, failed against the holy martyrs. How could I adequately describe them? **4.** Countless numbers of them showed a marvelous enthusiasm for worshiping the God of the universe not only when the persecution against us broke out, but long before, when we had peace. During the period after [the emperors] Decius and Valerian, he who received the authority[2]

---

2. Possibly Satan but probably Galerius, a fanatic pagan who became Diocletian's

had made secret attempts against the churches but was now, as it were, waking up from the deepest sleep. First he struck at those in the camps, thinking that if he won there the rest would be easily defeated. Now large numbers of soldiers were glad to become civilians so as not to renounce their reverence for the Creator. The commander-in-chief, whoever he was,[3] first began persecuting the soldiers by sorting them out and letting them choose either to conform and retain their rank or to disobey the edict and be stripped of it. A great many soldiers of Christ's kingdom unhesitatingly chose to confess him rather than hold onto their apparent glory and prosperity. Of these, a few here and there were already receiving not only loss of honor, but even death in exchange for their loyal devotion, for as yet the instigator of the plot was risking bloodshed only rarely, apparently fearing the number of believers and hesitating to make war on all of them at once. But once he had readied himself, words are inadequate to describe the number or the nobility of God's martyrs, as witnessed by people in every city and region.

The First Martyrs in Asia Minor

5. When the edict against the churches was published at Nicomedia and posted in a public place, a distinguished man[4] was so moved by his burning faith that he seized it and tore it to pieces—this despite the presence in the same city of two emperors [Diocletian and Galerius]. But he was only the first of those who so distinguished themselves at that time, suffering the consequences of such a daring act with a cheerful confidence to his very last breath.

6. Among all who have been praised for virtue and courage among Greeks and non-Greeks alike, none was more outstanding than Dorotheus and the imperial servants like him. This group had been highly honored by their masters, who treated them with no less affection than their own children. But they regarded suffering and

---

Caesar or vice emperor of the East in 293 and induced him to begin persecuting the Christians.

3. Venturius, as Eusebius wrote in his *Chronicle*.

4. Euethius, who was martyred at Nicomedia on February 24, 303, the day on which the edict was issued.

death in its many forms as greater riches than worldly fame and luxury. Let one example illustrate what happened to the rest.

Under the aforementioned rulers, a certain man was brought into a public place and ordered to sacrifice. When he refused, he was hoisted up naked and lashed with whips until he should give in. Since even this failed to bend him, they mixed salt with vinegar and poured it over the lacerations of his body where the bones were already protruding. When he scorned these agonies too, a lit brazier was applied, and the rest of his body was roasted by the fire as if meat for eating—not all at once, lest he find too quick a release, but little by little. Still he clung immovably to his purpose and expired triumphantly in the middle of his tortures. Such was the martyrdom of one of the imperial servants who was truly worthy of his name: Peter.

The martyrdoms of the others were in no way inferior, but space limitations in this book permit my recording only that Dorotheus and Gorgonius, along with many others in the imperial household, after a series of ordeals departed this life by strangling.

At that time Anthimus, who presided over the church at Nicomedia, bore witness to Christ and was beheaded. A large number of martyrs followed him, because a fire broke out in the palace at Nicomedia—I don't know why—and a false rumor spread that our people were responsible. Whole families and groups were butchered with the sword by imperial command, while others were fulfilled by fire, men and women leaping on the pyre with divine enthusiasm. Executioners bound many others and threw them into the sea from boats. As for the imperial servants already buried with appropriate honors, their bodies were dug up and thrown into the sea also, under the absurd notion that otherwise in their very graves they would be worshiped as gods!

Such were the events in Nicomedia at the beginning of the persecution. But when, soon afterward, attempts were made in Melitene and Syria to overthrow the empire,[5] an imperial decree ordered that church leaders everywhere be chained and imprisoned, resulting in a spectacle beyond description. Countless numbers were incarcerated everywhere. Prisons prepared for murderers and grave robbers were now filled with bishops, presbyters and deacons, readers and exorcists, so that there was no longer any room for criminals.

---

5. Melitene was capital of the Roman province of Armenia Minor. This attempted revolt is not recorded elsewhere.

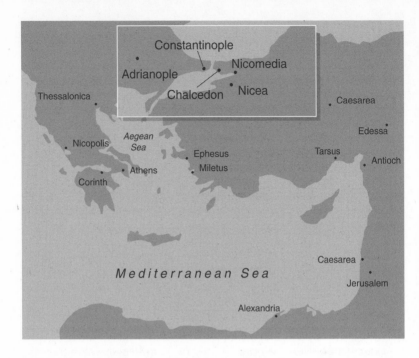

The Roman emperor Diocletian established a capital for the eastern half of the empire at Nicomedia, which today is the Turkish city of Izmit, located fifty-four miles east-southeast of Istanbul. The Great Persecution of Christians began here in March of 303. Southwest of Nicomedia at Nicea, Constantine convened the great council that in 325 formulated the Nicene Creed. Chalcedon was the site of another great church council in 451 that affirmed the divine and human natures of Christ.

The first decree was followed by others, according to which those imprisoned were to be set free if they sacrificed but mutilated by constant torture if they refused. Now, again, how could one number the host of martyrs in each province, especially those in Africa, Mauretania, the Theban area, and Egypt? From Egypt at this time some went off to other cities and provinces, where they distinguished themselves in martyrdom.

Martyrs in Phoenicia

7. We know those who were luminaries in Palestine and those at Tyre in Phoenicia. Who, seeing them, was not astounded at the countless lashes and perseverance displayed by these superb champions of godliness; at the contests with man-eating beasts that followed the floggings, when they were attacked by leopards, bears of all kinds, wild boars, and bulls goaded with hot irons; and at the incredible courage of these noble people in facing each of the beasts?

I myself was there when this was happening, and I saw the divine power of our Savior Jesus Christ himself—the object of their witness—clearly present and revealing itself to the martyrs: the man-eaters for some time did not dare to touch or even approach those who were God's beloved but attacked others who were goading them on from the outside. The holy champions, though they stood naked and waved their hands to attract the animals, as they were ordered to do, were left untouched. Or when the beasts did rush at them, they were stopped, as if by some divine power, and would retreat. For a long time this went on, astonishing the spectators, and when the first beast did nothing, a second and a third were released against one and the same martyr.

The dauntless courage of these saints in the face of these ordeals and the firm tenacity in young bodies was astounding. You would have seen a youth not yet twenty standing unchained, his arms spread in the form of a cross and his mind at ease, in leisure prayer to the Deity. While bears and panthers breathing anger and death almost touched him, he did not retreat an inch. Yet by a divine, mysterious power their mouths were seemingly muzzled and they retreated again. You would also have seen others—five in all—thrown to a maddened bull. When others approached from the perimeter he tossed them into the air with his horns and mangled them, leaving them to be picked up half dead. But when he rushed furiously at the defenseless martyrs, he could not even approach them, though he pawed with his hoofs and thrust his horns to and fro. Goaded on by hot irons into a snorting rage, he was dragged backward by divine providence, and other beasts had to be let loose against them in place of the harmless bull. At last, after a horrible variety of assaults by these animals, they were all butchered with the sword, and instead of an earthen burial they were cast into the waves of the sea.

Martyrs in Egypt

8. Such was the ordeal of the Egyptians who contended so gloriously for the faith at Tyre. But those of them who were martyred

Limestone relief of a leopard attacking a gladiator in a Roman amphitheater (left), while someone goads a lion to attack (right) as a victim falls to the ground (*Museo Nazionale, Rome*).

in their own land are also admirable, countless numbers of men, women, and children, disdaining this passing life to endure a variety of deaths for the sake of our Savior's teaching. Some of them were scraped, racked, ruthlessly whipped, and tortured in ways too terrible to describe and finally given to the flames or drowned in the sea. Others courageously bared their necks to the executioners or died of torture or hunger. Some again were crucified as criminals usually are, while others, even more cruelly, were nailed in the opposite way—head downward—and kept alive until they died of hunger on the cross.

9. The outrageous agonies endured by the martyrs in the Theban area, however, defeat all description. Their whole bodies were torn to shreds with clawlike potsherds until they expired. Women were tied by one foot and swung high in the air, head downward, by machines, their bodies totally naked without a stitch of clothing—the most shameful, cruel, and inhumane of all spectacles for onlookers. Others died fastened to trees: they bent down their strongest branches by machines, fastened one of the martyr's legs to each, and then let the branches fly back to their natural

position, instantly tearing apart the limbs of their victims. This
went on not for a few days but for some whole years. Sometimes
ten or more, at times more than twenty were put to death, or
thirty, or almost sixty; at other times a hundred men, women,
and little children were condemned to a variety of punishments
and killed in a single day.

I myself saw some of these mass executions by decapitation
or fire, a slaughter that dulled the murderous axe until it wore
out and broke in pieces, while the executioners grew so tired
they had to work in shifts. But I also observed a marvelous eagerness and a divine power and enthusiasm in those who placed
their faith in Christ: as soon as the first was sentenced, others
would jump up on the tribunal in front of the judge and confess
themselves Christians. Heedless of torture in its terrifying forms
but boldly proclaiming their devotion to the God of the universe,
they received the final sentence of death with joy, laughter, and
gladness, singing hymns of thanksgiving to God until their last
breath.

Wonderful as these were, even more admirable were those
distinguished for their wealth, birth, and reputation, as well as
for learning and philosophy, who yet put everything second to
true piety and faith in Jesus Christ. One such was Philoromus, an
important officer in the imperial administration at Alexandria,
who daily conducted judicial investigations and had a military
bodyguard befitting his Roman rank. Another was Phileas, Bishop
of Thmuis,[6] as famed for his patriotism and public service as
for his command of philosophy. A host of relatives and friends
begged them, as did high-ranking officials, and even the judge
himself urged them to have mercy on themselves and spare their
wives and children. Yet all this pressure was not enough for them
to favor the love of life over our Savior's warning about confessing or denying him. So with a brave and philosophic determination—or rather with a reverent and God-loving spirit—they stood
firm against all the judge's threats and insults, and both were
beheaded.

Phileas on Martyrdoms in Alexandria

10. Since I said that Phileas was well known also for his secular
learning, let him appear as his own witness to reveal his character

---

6. A town in Lower (northern) Egypt.

and also to describe, more accurately than could I, the martyrdoms that took place in Alexandria.

FROM THE WRITINGS OF PHILEAS TO THE THMUITES

With all the examples from sacred Scriptures before them, the
blessed martyrs did not hesitate, but, with the eye of the soul toward
God and a resolve to die for their faith, they held fast to their calling, knowing that our Lord Jesus Christ became man for our sakes,
to destroy sin and enable us to enter into eternal life. Equal with
God, he emptied himself to assume the form of a servant who humbled himself unto death, even death on the cross [Phil. 2:6–11]. So,
eagerly desiring the greater gifts, the Christ-bearing martyrs endured
suffering and torture devices of every kind, not once but twice in
some cases. And though their guards competed in all their threats
against them in deed as well as word, they never faltered, because
perfect love casts out fear [1 John 4:18].

When all were given a free hand to insult them, some hit them
with clubs, some with rods, others with scourges and straps, and
still others with whips. In this ever-changing spectacle of odious
torments, some, with hands tied behind them, were hung from the
gallows and all their limbs were pulled apart by machines. Then,
as they lay helplessly, their tormenters were ordered to use the
instruments of torture not only on their sides, as with murderers,
but also on their bellies, legs, and cheeks. Others were suspended
by one hand from a colonnade and hauled up with excruciating pain
in their joints and limbs. Others were lashed to pillars, facing them,
with their feet off the ground and their body weight pulling the ropes
tighter and tighter. This they endured not only while the governor
was speaking to them at his leisure but for most of the day. Whenever he went on to others, he left his agents to watch the first in case
anyone seemed to be surrendering to the tortures. Only at the last
gasp were they to be taken down and dragged off. They were not to
have the least regard for us but were to treat us as if we no longer
existed, another torture added to the rest. Even after such torment,
some were put into stocks and had both feet stretched to the fourth
hole, forcing them to lie on their backs since they were unable [to
sit upright] due to their wounds. Others were hurled to the ground
and lay there, a display of tortured flesh more horrible to spectators
than the punishment it reflected.

Some died under torture, their endurance putting the Adversary
to shame. Others were locked into prison half dead and soon found

fulfillment because of their agonies. The rest in time recovered and gained confidence from their imprisonment. But when they were ordered to choose between touching the abominable sacrifice and gaining an accursed freedom, or not sacrificing and incurring death, without hesitation they went to their death gladly. They knew what the sacred Scriptures have ordained for us: "Whoever sacrifices to other gods shall be destroyed" [Ex. 22:20], and "You shall have no other gods but me" [Ex. 20:3].

Such are the words of the martyr, true lover of both wisdom and God, that he sent to the brethren in his diocese while he was still in prison before the final sentence, describing his own circumstances and also urging them to stay firm in the faith, even after his imminent fulfillment.

Martyrs in Asia Minor, Syria, and Elsewhere

But why need I give example after example of the godly martyrs' contests throughout the world, especially those who were no longer attacked under common law but as enemies in war? **11.** A little town in Phrygia, for instance, all of whose inhabitants were Christian, was surrounded by armed infantrymen who set it on fire and burned to death men, women, and young children as they were calling on almighty God. The reason? All the townspeople, from the mayor himself and the magistrates to the entire populace, confessed their Christianity and refused to commit idolatry.

There was also a high Roman official named Adauctus, who came from a prominent Italian family. He had advanced through all the ranks of honor under the emperors, providing irreproachable service in the general administration of what they call the magistracy and ministry of finance. Besides this, since he was esteemed for his godly conduct and his confessions of Christ, he faced his ordeal and was adorned with the crown of martyrdom while still serving as finance minister.

12. Need I cite the names or numbers of the rest or the varieties of their martyrdoms? Sometimes they were killed with an axe, as was the case in Arabia, or had their legs broken, as those in Cappadocia. At other times they were hung upside down over a slow fire, so that smoke rising from the burning wood suffocated them, as in Mesopotamia. Sometimes noses, ears, and hands were mutilated and the other parts of the body butchered, as was the case in Alexandria.

At Antioch they were roasted on hot gridirons for prolonged torture, not seared to death. Rather than touch the cursed sacrifice, some stuck their hands directly into the fire. Others, to escape such trials, threw themselves down from the roofs of tall houses before they were caught, regarding death as a prize snatched from the wicked.

A certain saintly person,[7] whose woman's body contained an admirable soul, was widely known at Antioch for her wealth, birth, and sound judgment. She had raised on pious principles two virgin daughters whose youthful beauty was in full bloom, evoking a great desire to find out their hiding place. When it was learned that they were living in a foreign country, they were purposely recalled to Antioch, where they were at the mercy of the soldiers. When the woman saw that she and her daughters were in great jeopardy, she alerted them to the dreadful things that awaited them, including the most terrible of all: the threat of fornication. She persuaded her girls—and herself—to shut their ears to the least whisper of such a thing and said that surrendering their souls to demonic slavery was worse than any form of death. The only way to escape from it all was to flee to the Lord. Agreeing on this, they arranged their clothes, and when they came to the midpoint of their journey they modestly asked the guards to excuse them for a moment and threw themselves into the river that flowed by.

Another pair of girls also lived in Antioch, true godly sisters of eminent birth, admirable life, youthful charm, pious conduct, and splendid devotion. As if the earth could not stand such perfection, the demon-worshipers ordered them thrown into the sea.

In Pontus, others suffered things horrifying to hear: sharp reeds were driven into their fingers under the nail ends, or molten lead was poured down their backs, scalding the vital parts of their bodies. Others endured shameful, pitiful, unmentionable suffering in their private parts and intestines, which the noble, law-abiding judges eagerly invented, trying to outdo one another in devising new tortures, as if contending for a prize.

These torments came to an end when their gruesome wickedness wore them out. Tired of killing and sated with blood, they

---

7. Her name was Domnina, according to Chrysostom, and her daughters were Bernice and Prosdoce.

turned to what they deemed mercy and humanity in no longer harming us—or so they thought. To pollute the cities with the blood of its own citizens was hardly in good taste, they felt, or to render the supreme rulers vulnerable to a charge of cruelty, a government that was mild and favorable to all. Rather, the kindness of the humane imperial authority should be extended to everyone and the death penalty no longer imposed. It had been stopped, thanks to the humanity of the rulers.

Instead, orders were now issued that their eyes be gouged out and one of their legs maimed—"humanity," in their opinion, and "the lightest of punishments." As a result of such philanthropy on the part of godless men, it is now impossible to report the vast number of people who first had their right eye sliced out with a sword and cauterized with fire and the left foot rendered useless by branding irons applied to the joints. After this they were condemned to the copper mines in the province, less for work there and more for the abuse and hardship they received, as well as other ordeals too numerous to report. Their dauntless deeds exceed all calculation.

In all these trials the magnificent martyrs of Christ were so distinguished throughout the world that eyewitnesses of their courage were astounded. They provided in themselves clear proof that the power of our Savior is divine and ineffable indeed. To mention each by name would be a long if not impossible task.

Churchmen Proved Through Blood

13. Among church leaders martyred in well-known cities, the first name we should record on monuments to the saints as a martyr of Christ's kingdom was Bishop Anthimus of Nicomedia, who was beheaded. Of the martyrs at Antioch, the noblest throughout his life was Lucian, a presbyter, who, when the emperor himself was at Nicomedia, proclaimed the kingship of Christ there first by an oral defense of the faith and then also by deeds. Of the martyrs in Phoenicia, the most famous are the beloved pastors of Christ's flocks: Tyrannion, Bishop of Tyre; Zenobius, presbyter at Sidon; and Silvanus, Bishop of Emesa and vicinity. The last became food for wild beasts, as were others at Emesa itself, and was taken up into the chorus of martyrs. The other two glorified the Word of God at Antioch by enduring to the end, the bishop thrown into the depths of the sea, while Zenobius, that finest of physicians, died bravely under tortures applied to his sides.

Of the martyrs in Palestine, Silvanus, Bishop of Gaza, was beheaded, with thirty-nine others, at the copper mines of Phaeno, where also the Egyptian bishops Peleus and Nilus, along with others, suffered a fiery end. Here we must mention also the great glory of the community at Caesarea, the presbyter Pamphilus, the most extraordinary man of my time, whose valiant achievements I shall relate at the proper time.

Of those gloriously fulfilled at Alexandria, the Theban area, and the rest of Egypt, the first to be recorded is Peter, Bishop of Alexandria, a devout example of the teachers of godliness in Christ, as well as the presbyters with him—Faustus, Dius, and Ammonius, fulfilled martyrs of Christ—and Phileas, Hesychius, Pachymius, and Theodore, bishops of the churches in Egypt. Countless other cel-

Constantius Chlorus, the father of Constantine. He was appointed Caesar in 293, Augustus in 305, and he died at York, Britain, in 306 (*Museo Torlonia, Rome*).

ebrated people are also commemorated locally in their own areas.

To record in detail the ordeals of those who fought throughout the world for reverence toward the Deity would be a task for eyewitnesses rather than for me. But those I did see I will set down for posterity in another work.[8] In this book, however, I shall add to the above the recantation of the edicts against us and what followed the beginning of the persecution, material of most importance to my readers.

Diocletian, Constantius Chlorus, and Constantine

Before the Roman government went to war against us and whenever the emperors were friendly and peacefully disposed toward us, it enjoyed an inexpressibly bountiful har-

8. Eusebius's *Martyrs of Palestine*.

vest of good things, the rulers of the worldwide empire reaching their tenth or twentieth year and passing their days in festivities, public games, the most joyful banquets, and merriment during total, secure peace. But as their authority increased day by day without check or hindrance, they suddenly canceled their peaceful attitude toward us and started a perpetual war. Less than two years later, a revolution took place that overturned the entire government. An ill-fated disease attacked the foremost of the previously mentioned emperors [Diocletian], which deranged his mind, so he returned to ordinary private life, along with the one who 305 was in second place after him [Maximian]. And this had not yet happened when the whole empire was split in two, something that had never occurred before.[9]

Not long afterward, the emperor Constantius [Chlorus], who was always kindly disposed toward his subjects and friendly to the divine Word, died, leaving his lawful son Constantine emperor and Augustus in his place. He [Constantius Chlorus] was the first [of the tetrarchs[10]] to be proclaimed one of the gods, judged worthy of every posthumous honor that might be accorded an emperor as one of the kindest and mildest. He was the only one in my day who spent his whole reign in conduct worthy of his exalted office, showing favor and benevolence to all. He took no part at all in the war against us—in fact, he even rescued the godly among his subjects from injury and abuse—and he neither demolished church buildings nor caused us any other harm. So he won a happy and thrice-blessed end of life,

Seated statue of Helena, the mother of Constantine (*Capitoline Museum, Rome*).

---

9. For the meaning of this paragraph and a guide to the complicated politics of the Roman Empire at this time, see the commentary at the end of this chapter.

10. The first of the four rulers at this time: Diocletian and Galerius in the East, Maximian and Constantius Chlorus in the West.

Colossal head of Constantine the Great (*Conservatori, Rome*).

for he alone died while still emperor, with a lawful son, wise and godly in every way, to succeed him.

The legions immediately proclaimed his son Constantine **306** supreme emperor and Augustus, as did God himself, the King of all, long before them. And he [Constantine] resolved to emulate his father's reverence toward our beliefs.

Later, by a common vote of the rulers, Licinius was declared **307** emperor and Augustus—a bitter blow to Maximin [Daia], whom all recognized only as Caesar. So, as a tyrant to the core, he arrogantly usurped the honor and appointed himself Augustus. Meanwhile, the man who had abdicated and then resumed office [Maximian] devised a plot to kill Constantine but was discovered and died a most shame- **310** ful death. He was the first to have his laudatory inscriptions and statues toppled as reminders of a wicked and godless person.

Maxentius

14. His son Maxentius, who set himself up as tyrant at Rome, at first pretended our faith in order to please the Roman populace. He commanded his subjects to stop persecuting the Christians, put- ting on a show of piety to appear more friendly and moderate than his predecessors. Yet his actions belied people's hopes. He plunged into every sort of wickedness, and no abominable, depraved deed escaped him, including adultery and rape of all kinds. He would take lawfully married women from their husbands, insult and fla- grantly dishonor them, and send them back to their husbands. Targets of his besotted behavior were not the unknown or obscure but the most distinguished of those who had attained the highest place in the senate. All groveled before him, commoners and mag- istrates, celebrated and obscure, worn out by his horrible tyranny. Even if they stayed quietly subservient there was no escaping the tyrant's lethal cruelty. On a trivial pretense he once ordered his bodyguard to massacre the people, and thousands of Roman citi- zens were killed in midcity not by Scythian or barbarian spears and weapons but by those of their fellow citizens. How many sena- tors were slaughtered because of their wealth it is impossible to say: countless numbers were eliminated for various sham reasons. But the nadir of all the tyrant's crimes was his resort to witchcraft: obsessed with magic, he would rip open pregnant women, examine the entrails of newborn babies, slaughter lions, or invent horrific rites to invoke demons and thereby avert war—all means by which he hoped to achieve victory.

One cannot even speak of what this tyrant did at Rome to enslave his subjects. They were reduced to such extreme need of even essential food as has never been known before either at Rome or elsewhere, according to my contemporaries.

Maximin Daia

Maximin, the tyrant in the East, formed a secret alliance with the tyrant of Rome—a brother in wickedness—and thought for a long time that it was not known. (In fact, he was later discovered and paid a just penalty.) A cousin in crime with the Roman despot, he actually outdid him and won first prize for corruption. Leading frauds and magicians gained his highest esteem, every noise terrified his superstitious self, and he dreaded any error regarding idols and demons. Without divinations and oracles he would not dare to move a nail's breadth. For this reason he persecuted us with more power and persistence than his predecessors, ordering [pagan] temples built in every city and the sacred sanctuaries that time had ruined to be carefully restored. He appointed priests for idols in every city and district, and as high priests over them in every province he selected those most distinguished in every area of public service, with a military bodyguard. He recklessly conferred governorships and the highest privileges on impostors as if they were beloved of the gods.

Henceforth he oppressed not a city or district but whole provinces through the heaviest assessments of gold, silver, and goods, as well as a variety of fines. Depriving the wealthy of their ancestral property, he lavished a fortune on his train of flatterers. He drank so excessively that he became deranged while drunk, issuing commands that he regretted the next day when sober. In wild debauchery he allowed none to surpass him but appointed himself a teacher of corruption to those around him. He inclined the army to lassitude through licentious excesses of every kind and encouraged governors and commanders to attack their subjects through plunder and extortion as if they were his fellow tyrants. Need one recall his scandalous lust or count the multitude of those he raped? He could not pass through a city without ravishing women and carrying off virgins.

He succeeded in all this with one exception: Christians, who scorned death and nullified his odious tyranny. The men endured fire, sword, and nailings; wild beasts and submersion in the sea; branding and cutting off of limbs; stabbing, gouging out of eyes, and mutilation of the whole body; and, in addition, starvation, chains, and the mines. They preferred to suffer for the faith rather than transfer to idols the reverence due to God. As for the women, inspired by the divine Word, they showed themselves as manly as the men. Some were subjected to the same ordeals as the men and won the same prizes for valor; others, while dragged away to seduction, surrendered their spirits to death rather than their bodies to dishonor.

Among those whom the tyrant ravished at Alexandria, a most esteemed Christian woman[11] bravely conquered Maximin's lust as the sole exception. Though celebrated for her birth, wealth, and education, she put modesty first. Despite his propositioning her repeatedly, he could not put her to death—though she was willing to die—because his lust was stronger than his anger, so he punished her with exile and confiscated her property. Countless others, refusing even to listen to a threat of fornication from provincial governors, underwent every sort of torture, racking, and mortal punishment.

While these were wonderful, the most wonderful of all was a woman at Rome[12] who was the noblest and most chaste of all, the intended prey of that Maximin-like tyrant, Maxentius. She also was a Christian, and when she learned that the tyrant's procurers were at her house and that her husband, though a Roman prefect, through fear had given them permission to take her away, she asked to be excused for a moment, as if to beautify herself. Alone in her room, she impaled herself on a sword and died quickly. Her corpse she left to the procurers, but by deeds more eloquent than any words she announced to all that the only invincible and indestructible possession is a Christian's virtue. To such depths of parallel wickedness sank the two tyrants who had divided the East and West between them. Anyone seeking a cause for these crimes[13] would find it in the persecution against us, especially since this outrageous chaos did not cease until Christians regained their freedom.

Civil War

15. Throughout the decade of persecution, their plotting and warfare against each other continued unabated. The seas were

---

11. Dorothea, according to Rufinus.

12. Sophronia, according to Rufinus, though possibly the name derived from the Greek *sophronestate* ("most chaste") in the context.

13. Here Eusebius also has in mind the turmoil within the Roman Empire, as the next clause and paragraph demonstrate.

unnavigable, and none, no matter where they set sail, could elude torments of every kind: the rack, their sides torn open, interrogation under torture as potential enemy agents, and finally crucifixion or fiery punishment. The manufacture of shields and armor, javelins, spears, and other weapons of war boomed, as well as the building of triremes and naval armament, and all expected an imminent enemy attack. Later on, famine and plague also ravaged them, which I shall describe at the proper time.

The End of Persecution

16. By the grace of God, the persecution came to a complete end in its tenth year, though it began to die down after the eighth. For when divine grace showed that it watched over us, our rulers changed their minds and recanted in a most amazing manner—the very men who had long waged hostilities against us—and they quenched the blazing fire of persecution through humane edicts and ordinances. This, however, was not due to human initiative or to the compassion or humanity of the rulers, as one might assume. Quite the contrary. From the start they were daily plotting more and harsher measures against us, fresh attacks through a greater variety of schemes. It was rather due to divine providence, which became reconciled with the people but attacked the perpetrator of these crimes [Galerius], angry with him as the prime instigator of the whole evil persecution. Even if it was destined that it should take place as a divine judgment, the Scripture says, "Woe to him through whom the offense comes."[14]

Divine punishment overtook [Galerius], which started with his flesh and went on to his soul. An abscess suddenly appeared in the middle of his genitals, then a deep ulcerous fistula that ate into his inner intestines incurably. From them came a great mass of worms and a deadly stench, since gluttony had transformed his whole body, even before the disease, into a great blob of flabby fat that then decayed, offering a revolting and horrendous spectacle. Some of the doctors could not endure the excessive, unearthly stench and were executed. Others, who could give no help because the mass had swollen beyond any hope of recovery, were put to death without mercy.

---

14. Paraphrase of Luke 17:1.

The Imperial Recantation

17. Wrestling with this awful malady, he felt pangs of conscience   312
over his cruelties against the godly. After composing himself,
he first publicly confessed to the God of the universe and then
ordered his officers to halt the persecution against the Christians
immediately. By imperial law and edict, they were now to build
their churches and perform their customary rites, offering prayers
in behalf of the emperor. Action followed immediately, and imperial ordinances were announced in each city with the following
recantation. [*For clarity, the most recognizable in the chain of
names of each emperor is in boldface type.*]

> The Emperor Caesar **Galerius** Valerius Maximianus Invictus Augus-
> tus, Pontifex Maximus, Germanicus Maximus, Egyptiacus Maximus,
> Thebaicus Maximus, Sarmaticus Maximus five times, Persicus Maxi-
> mus twice, Carpicus Maximus six times, Armeniacus Maximus, Medi-
> cus Maximus, Adiabenicus Maximus, holding the tribunician power
> for the twentieth time, imperator for the nineteenth, consul for the
> eighth, pater patriae, proconsul. . . .
>
> And the Emperor Caesar Flavius Valerius **Constantine** Pius
> Felix Invictus Augustus, Pontifex Maximus, holding the tribunician
> power, imperator for the fifth time, consul, pater patriae, procon-
> sul; and the Emperor Caesar Valerius Licinianus **Licinius** Pius Felix
> Invictus Augustus, pontifex maximus, holding the tribunician power
> for the fourth time, imperator for the third, consul, pater patriae,
> proconsul—to the people of their provinces, greeting.[15]
>
> Among the other measures that we take for the use and benefit of
> the state, we have previously desired to correct anything not in accord
> with the ancient laws and public order of the Romans, so we made pro-
> vision that also the Christians who had abandoned the beliefs of their
> own ancestors should return to sound opinions. Through some strange
> reasoning, such presumptuousness and folly had possessed them that,
> rather than following ancient principles laid down possibly by their own
> forefathers, they made laws for themselves to suit their own inclinations

---

15. The elision after Galerius shows where Eusebius must have omitted Maximin
Daia's names and titles, since Lactantius claims that the edict was published by all four
emperors, which Eusebius also implies in 8.16. Whereas only civil titles are listed for
Constantine and Licinius, Galerius, as senior Augustus, includes also honorific names
of areas conquered or controlled by Rome.

and observed them as each one wished, assembling crowds in various places.

Therefore, when we issued an edict that they were to return to the practices of the ancients, vast numbers of them were placed in jeopardy, and many were harassed and endured death of all kinds. Most of them shared the same folly, neither paying the gods in heaven the worship due them nor honoring the god of the Christians. Thus, in view of our clemency and our consistent practice of granting pardon to all men, we thought it right also in this instance to offer our concession most cheerfully, so that Christians may exist again and restore the houses in which they used to assemble, provided that they do nothing against the public order. In another letter we shall show the judges how they are to proceed. Accordingly, in view of this our concession, [the Christians] will be obligated to implore their own god for our welfare and that of the state and of themselves, so that the welfare of the state may be preserved in every way and they may live unburdened in their own homes.

So read the edict in the [original] Latin, translated into Greek as best I could. It is now time to consider what happened subsequently.

Appendix to Book 8 [16]

313

A gold aureus coin of the emperor Maximian, struck at the Ticinum mint in A.D. 293.

After this confession, the author of the edict was released from his pain but died a short time later. He had been the prime originator of the calamitous persecution: long before the other emperors acted he had used force to purge Christians in the army, beginning with members of his own household. Some he had degraded in rank, others he insulted disgracefully or threatened with death.

16. This is found only in the following codices: Codex Parisinus 1430 in the Bibliothèque Nationale; Codex Laurentianus 70 in Florence; and the Codex Mosquensis in Moscow.

Finally, he had aroused his co-emperors to a general persecution of all.

To pass over their deaths in silence would be inappropriate. Of the four who had shared supreme power, the two who were more advanced in age and honor [Diocletian and Maximian] retired from rule less than two years after the persecution started, as I have already said, and spent the rest of their days as private citizens with the following ends. [Diocletian], who was first in honor and age, succumbed to a long and painful illness, while [Maximian], who was second to him, strangled himself for his many crimes and so fulfilled a demonic prediction. Of the rest, [Galerius], who was in last place—the originator of the whole persecution—suffered the fate mentioned above. But his immediate superior, Constantius [Chlorus], spent his entire reign in a manner worthy of his high office, most gracious and favorable to all. He desisted from the war against us, saving his godly subjects from injury and abuse, and he neither destroyed any church buildings nor troubled us in any way. So he won an end to life that was truly happy and thrice-blessed, since he alone died gloriously while still emperor, to be succeeded by a lawful son who was prudent and godly in all respects. He [Constantine] was immediately proclaimed the most perfect ruling emperor and Augustus by the armies, and he resolved to emulate his father's reverence toward our faith.

Such was the fate of the four. The last to survive was [Galerius], whom I mentioned previously. Along with his subsequent colleagues, he published the document cited above.

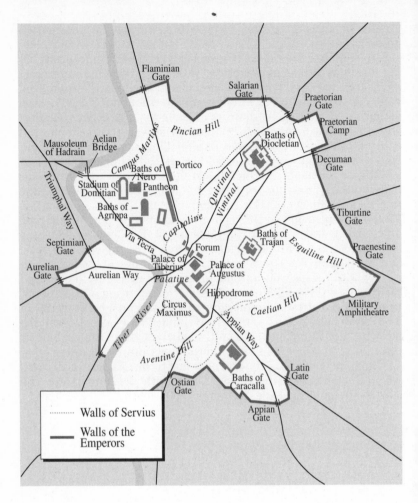

Imperial Rome. During the era of the Republic, the city extended only to the Servian Wall.

THE FOUR EMPERORS

The stylistic contrst in this book, compared to the others, is obvious. No longer anchored to past sources for his history, Eusebius was an eyewitness to much of what he reports in these pages, which take on a life sometimes missing in his previous books. Here he is the contemporary historian, reporting his own observations or using the reports of others, with due credit, as in the records of persecution in Egypt. That there had been previous horrific persecutions in these centuries is obvious to any reader who has come this far. But the added color, acuity, and lurid detail of the ghastly torments in Book 8 testify to both the final desperation of demonic emperors and the presence of eyewitnesses.

To account for all the horror, one might have thought that Eusebius would execrate the emperors in charge. He does delight in reporting the grotesque medical details of the death of Galerius (as he will that of Maximin Daia)—a pattern he likely learned from Josephus's account of the final illness of Herod the Great. And yet he finds also a higher, even astonishing, cause beyond the brutality of the emperors: it was the complacency, envy, hypocrisy, and quarreling within the church that incited divine justice to permit persecution. This was a remarkable admission by a writer usually faulted for his exuberant triumphalism.

Eusebius did not intend to provide a political history of his day but, where Rome was concerned, only a record of those points at which imperial policies involved the church. In terms of the way they would change the course of Western civilization, however, the imperial politics at this time were momentous, fascinating, and, above all, complex. While Eusebius's contemporaries had no trouble understanding the political background in this and the next two books, moderns may well find it bewildering. The following may help.

Diocletian (284–305), a Dalmatian of humble origins who rose in the cavalry, put an end to the half century of civil war that had torn the empire. He purged the legions of disloyal elements, reformed Rome's administration, and stabilized the economy. Above all, he tried to solve the imperial succession problem through a scheme designed to avoid the chaos of previous decades. Romans were to know long in advance who the next emperors would be, and by thus ruling out competitors a peaceful succession would follow. Convinced, furthermore, that the empire was too vast to be controlled by a single ruler, Diocletian now divided its administration into western and eastern halves, with the Adriatic Sea as the divider. Italy, Gaul, Britannia, Spain, and western North Africa were to be governed from Milan under his colleague Maximian, while Greece and all the eastern provinces Diocletian himself would rule from his new capital at Nicomedia (modern Izmit, at the easternmost finger of the Sea of Marmora in Turkey).

The two emperors, each called an *Augustus,* selected one subordinate each, who was termed a *Caesar,* and he would directly administer a portion of the half. When the Augusti retired or died, the two Caesars would become the new Augusti; they in turn would choose new Caesars, and the cycle would continue. Diocletian chose Galerius as his Caesar, and Maximian selected Constantius Chlorus, the father of Constantine, as his. Thus the pattern started as follows:

	West	*East*
Augusti:	Maximian	Diocletian
Caesars:	Constantius Chlorus	Galerius
	(ruling Gaul, Britain)	(ruling Syria, Palestine, Egypt)

Each Caesar married the daughter of the Augustus he would one day succeed, and thus the empire was divided among these four rulers.

Constantius had attractive qualities. He was a man of moderation who was sympathetic to Christianity and tried to blunt the force of the persecution in his domains. He pulled down a few token churches to comply with the letter of the persecution edict—Eusebius may not have known about this—but he permitted no executions in areas under his control. Galerius, in contrast, was a huge hulk of a man, boorish, brutal, and overambitious. He was the one who incited the great persecution of the Christians, persuading a Diocletian who would most probably have tolerated them. Eusebius reported the results in excruciating detail.

On May 1, 305, two years after the persecution began, an ailing Diocletian, under enormous pressure from Galerius, tearfully abdicated his office and retired to Dalmatia. Earlier, Galerius had persuaded Maximian to retire also. The new Augusti were Galerius himself and Constantius Chlorus, as planned, but then everything went wrong. Galerius chose both new Caesars: his nephew Maximin Daia for the East and his friend Severus for the West—this when Constantius's son Constantine or Maximian's son Maxentius might have been chosen instead for the West.

Constantine had been attached to the court of Diocletian at Nicomedia, but when the latter retired, Constantine asked Galerius for permission to join his father in the West. This was denied. Nevertheless, Constantine managed to escape and join his father after a furious horseback ride to Gaul. When they crossed into Britain and Constantius subsequently died at York, his troops immediately proclaimed Constantine as Augustus, in July 306. Galerius was furious, of course, but grudgingly accorded him the title of Caesar, instead, while raising his friend Severus to the rank of co-Augustus.

At Rome in October, however, Maximian's veterans revolted under his son Maxentius, who recalled his father to the throne. Severus then attacked them but was captured and killed. Maximian now formed an alliance with Constantine, awarding him the title Augustus and giving him his daughter Fausta in marriage on March 31, 307. After quarreling with his own son, Maximian sought refuge with Constantine, but later tried to take control of his army when he was absent. He died in 310, probably a suicide.

In the East, meanwhile, Galerius had replaced the dead Severus with Licinius, while Maximin Daia, resentful at being passed over, claimed the title of Augustus for himself. The five concurrent rulers dwindled to four when Galerius himself died of disease in 311, at which time power in the Roman Empire was divided as follows:

West	East
Constantine: Gaul, Spain, Britain	Licinius: Balkan peninsula
Maxentius: Italy and Africa	Maximin Daia: Asia Minor, Syria, Egypt

Given the normal ambitions of Roman emperors, one might well suspect that this arrangement would not long endure.

Book 9

THE GREAT DELIVERANCE

MAXIMIN, MAXENTIUS, AND CONSTANTINE

Apparent Relief

311 **1.** The revocation of the imperial will cited above was published throughout Asia and in the adjacent provinces. When this had been done, the tyrant of the East, Maximin [Daia], that totally irreverent creature who had been the most passionate enemy of piety toward the God of the universe, was not pleased with what was written, and instead of circulating the letter he gave verbal instructions to his subordinates to reduce the campaign against us. Since he could not oppose the judgment of his superiors in any other way, he stuffed the above edict in a corner, making sure that it would never see the light of day in his areas, and issued oral instructions instead. His subordinates put these in writing for each other. Sabinus, for example, whom they honored with the title Most Excellent Prefect, communicated the emperor's desires in the following letter to the provincial governors, as translated from the Latin:

> With the most brilliant and dedicated fervor, the Divinity of our divine masters, the emperors, has long aimed to guide all men's thoughts to the holy and proper way of life, so that even those who follow customs foreign to the Romans might accord the immortal gods the worship due them. But the unyielding resistance of some was such that the sound reasoning of the edict failed to deter them, and they did not fear the threatened punishment. Since, then, many endangered themselves by such behavior, the Divinity of our masters,

the almighty emperors, with noble piety regarding it alien to their divine purpose that they should imperil these men for such a reason, issued an order through my Dedication to write Your Intelligence[1] that if any of the Christians is found practicing their religion, you should shield him from molestation and danger and not punish him on this charge, since a long period of time has shown that they cannot in any way be persuaded to abandon their obstinate behavior. Let it be Your Carefulness's duty to write to the comptrollers, magistrates, and officials of every urban district that it is not necessary for them to pay any further attention to that document.[2]

The provincial governors, deeming the communication authentic, then wrote letters alerting the comptrollers, magistrates, and rural officers to the imperial decision. They implemented it not only in writing, but even more by action, setting free all who were incarcerated for confessing the Deity and even releasing those condemned to the mines, for they assumed that this was what the emperor intended.

When this had been done, it was as if a light had suddenly blazed out of a dark night. In every city, churches were thronged, congregations crowded, and rites duly performed. All the unbelieving heathen were astonished at the wonder of so great a transformation and hailed the Christians' God as alone great and true. Among our own people, those who had valiantly contended through the ordeal of persecution again enjoyed freedom with honor, but those whose faith had been anemic and their souls in turmoil eagerly sought healing, begging the strong to extend the right hand of rescue and imploring God to be merciful to them. Then, too, the noble champions of godliness, released from their misery in the mines, returned to their own homes, rejoicing and beaming as they went through every city, exuding an indescribable delight and confidence. Crowds of men went on their way, praising God with hymns and psalms in the middle of the thoroughfares and public squares. Those who a little earlier had been prisoners, cruelly punished and driven from their homelands, now regained their own hearths with smiles of elation, so that even those who had thirsted for our blood saw this unexpected wonder and shared our joy at what had happened.

---

1. These stilted phrases reflect Latinisms used among potentates of the time. Traces remain in such forms of address as "Your Excellency" and the like.

2. Literally, "letter" or "state paper," probably a previous document ordering persecution of the Christians.

Maximin's Renewed Repression

2. This was more than the Eastern tyrant could endure, who hated goodness and good men, and he tolerated this situation for less than six months. He tried in numerous ways to overturn the peace, first by finding a pretext to stop us from assembling in the cemeteries.[3] Then he sent to himself delegations of miscreants to oppose us, having prompted the citizens of Antioch to ask, as a great favor to them, that he forbid any Christian from living in their area and to arrange that others make the same request. The author of all this was an Antiochene named Theotecnus, a clever but evil fraud who belied his name.[4] Apparently he was the city comptroller.

3. Time and again this man [Theotecnus] engaged in hostilities against us, trying every means to hunt our people out of hiding as if they were thieving villains, using every subterfuge to slander and accuse us, and even causing death to countless numbers. Finally, with illusions and sorceries, he erected a statue of Zeus as god of friendship, and after devising demonic rites, initiations, and repulsive purifications for it, he displayed his magic even in the emperor's presence through whatever oracular utterances he pleased. Moreover, through flattery pleasing to the emperor, this fellow claimed that the god had ordered the Christians out of the city and its vicinity since they were his enemies.

4. This man acted first, but all the other officials in cities under the same rule quickly followed suit, the provincial governors seeing that this pleased the emperor and proposing that their subjects do the same. The tyrant gladly approved their petitions by a rescript, and once again the persecution against us was reignited.

Maximin himself appointed as priests and even high priests of the images in each city those most distinguished in public service, and they worshiped the gods they served with enthusiasm. The inane superstition of the ruler was clearly persuading all under him, governors and the governed alike, to curry his favor by a full-fledged assault on us. To thirst for our blood and find novel ways to show their hostility was the greatest favor they could bestow on him in return for the benefits they expected from him.

---

3. See 7.14, note 11.

4. Theotecnus means "child of God" in Greek.

5. In fact, they forged *Memoirs* of Pilate and of our Savior, full of all sorts of blasphemy against Christ, and sent them, with the approval of their superior, all over his realm with edicts that they were to be posted everywhere, both town and country, and assigned to children by their teachers to study and memorize instead of lessons.

At Damascus, meanwhile, an army commander—called *dux* by the Romans—arranged to have some loose women abducted from the city square and forced them, under threat of torture, to put in writing that they had once been Christians, knew about their [Christians'] criminal activities, and that in their very churches the Christians indulged in immoralities, and whatever else he wanted the women to say in defaming the faith. He also copied their words in his report to the emperor, who ordered him to publish the document in every district and city. **6.** But not long afterward, the commander became his own executioner and so paid the penalty for his wickedness.

New Martyrdoms

For us, however, exile, severe persecution, and cruelty from all provincial governors resumed, and some of the most prominent in the divine Word were sentenced to death, without mercy. Three confessed Christians in Emesa, a city of Phoenicia, were thrown to wild beasts as food, Silvanus among them, a very old bishop who had served forty years in office. Peter also, who presided admirably over the churches in Alexandria—a godly example of a bishop in the integrity of his life and his scriptural expertise—was suddenly arrested for no reason and beheaded, as if by command of Maximin, as were many other Egyptian bishops.

Lucian, a presbyter at Antioch of the finest, temperate character and adept in theology, was brought to Nicomedia, where the emperor was staying. After defending the faith in the presence of the ruler, he was sent to prison and put to death. So swift and brutal was the assault by Maximin, that hater of anything good, that this persecution seemed to us much worse than the previous.

7. In the urban centers, petitions against us from cities and rescripts of imperial replies were engraved on bronze tablets and posted—something that had never happened before—while children in the schools daily had the names of Jesus and Pilate on their lips and the insolently forged *Memoirs*. Here I think the document Maximin engraved on the tablets ought to be inserted so that the haughty arrogance of this hater of God may become obvious to all, as well as the divine justice that followed hard on his heels with its sleepless loathing of evil. (It was this that caused him to reverse his policy regarding us soon afterward and publish it in written laws.)

COPY OF A TRANSLATION OF MAXIMIN'S RESCRIPT
IN REPLY TO THE PETITIONS ATTACKING US,
TAKEN FROM THE TABLET AT TYRE[5]

At last the feeble boldness of the human mind has shaken off and scattered all the blinding fog of error that, until now, had assaulted the senses of people more miserable than wicked and shrouded them in the darkness of ignorance, and it now recognizes that the benevolent providence of the immortal gods governs and sustains it. Words cannot express how very grateful and delighted I am at the most splendid proof of your godly character, since even before this all knew of the reverence and piety you accorded the immortal gods, with a faith not of mere empty words but continual and marvelous in its deeds. Your city, then, deserves to be called a temple and domicile of the immortal deities, and many signs suggest that it flourishes because the immortal gods dwell there.

It was your city that totally ignored its private pursuits and earlier requests when it saw that the followers of that damnable folly were starting to spread once again, like a forgotten, smoldering pyre that rekindles into a blazing conflagration. Instantly you appealed to our piety, as to a mother city of all religious worship, for some healing and help, a salvific idea clearly implanted in you by the gods because of your faith and reverence to them. It was therefore he, the most high and mighty Zeus—defender of your illustrious city, the guardian of your ancestral gods, your women and children, your hearth and home from all destruction—who inspired you with this resolve for rescue, demonstrating how splendid and salutary it is to accord due reverence to the worship and sacred rights of the immortal gods.

Who is so senseless or stupid as not to grasp that only the benevolence of the gods prevents the earth from refusing the seeds

---

5. This is clearly the most prolix and bombastic document Eusebius records. To prevent the reader from despairing, I have pared away a bit of the excess verbiage in this translation, but the prose is still turgid, reflecting a disordered mind in Maximin. An oxymoron appears at the beginning.

committed to it and frustrating the hopes of the farmer? Or that impious war does not plant itself on the earth to drag grimy bodies off to death and pollute the healthy air of heaven? Or that the sea does not swell and storm under the blasts of wind? Or that typhoons do not strike in lethal destruction without warning? Or, again, that the earth, the nurse and mother of all, does not sink with a dreadful quake into its deepest hollows and her mountains collapse into the chasms that result? All these disasters, and those even worse, have often happened before this, as everyone knows. And all of them happened at once because of the error and folly of those immoral people, when it possessed their minds and nearly subverted the entire world through its shameful deeds. . . .

Let them see on the broad plains the crops ripe with waving ears of grain, the meadows glittering with flowers—thanks to timely rains—and the weather temperate and mild. Let all rejoice that through our piety, sacrifices, and veneration, the power of the mighty and uncompromising air[6] has been propitiated, and they may therefore enjoy the most tranquil peace in safety and in quiet. And let all those who have been saved from that blind folly and restored to a right state of mind rejoice the more, as if they had been delivered from an unexpected storm or critical illness, and let them reap life's future delights. But if they persist in their damnable folly, let them be driven out of your city and vicinity, just as you requested, so that, in accord with your laudable enthusiasm in this matter, your city may be purged of all pollution and impiety and follow its natural disposition to worship the immortal gods with due reverence.

That you may know how much we appreciate your request and how inclined we are to benevolence quite apart from petitions and pleas, we permit Your Dedication to ask whatever reward you wish in return for this godly intention of yours. Resolve now to do this and receive your reward without delay. Awarding it to your city will forever demonstrate your piety toward the immortal gods and a proof to your posterity that our benevolence duly rewarded your conduct.

This was engraved on tablets in every province, leaving us hopeless of any human help, so that, as in the divine saying, these things might cause even the elect to stumble [Matt. 24:24]. In fact, hope was fading among most when, suddenly, while those

---

6. The text is probably corrupt here. Shifting a vowel to alter *aeros* to *areos* in the Greek text would render the translation "the power of . . . Ares [Mars] has been propitiated," which makes far more sense in view of the subsequent context.

delivering the decree attacking us were on their way and had not yet arrived in some districts, God, the Champion of his own church, gagging the pompous boasting of the tyrant, showed himself as our heavenly ally.

Famine, Plague, and War

8. The usual winter rains and showers were denying the earth its normal downpour when famine struck, as well as plague and an epidemic of another sort of disease: an ulcer that was called a carbuncle[7] because of its fiery appearance. It spread very dangerously over the entire body but attacked the eyes in particular, blinding countless men, women, and children.

In addition to this, the tyrant was troubled with war against the Armenians, people who had been friends and allies of the Romans from early times. But since they were Christians and ardent in their reverence to the Deity, this God-hater tried to make them sacrifice to idols and demons and so turned them from friends into foes, enemies instead of allies.

The fact that all these things occurred at the same time completely refuted the tyrant's impudent boasting against the Deity, for he had had the gall to proclaim that in his day famine, plague, and war were averted by his enthusiasm for the idols and his attack on us. All of these impacting him at the same time served as prelude to his overthrow. He and his army were worn out by the Armenian war, while people in the cities under his rule were so ravaged by famine and plague that 2,500 Attic drachmas were given for a single measure of wheat. Countless numbers died in the cities and even more in the villages and countryside. Rural registers that were once full of names now were all but obliterated, since lack of food and disease destroyed almost the entire population at the same time. Some bartered their most precious possessions for the smallest scrap of food from those better supplied, while others sold their things little by little until they were reduced to desperation. Still others ruined their health and died from chewing wisps of hay and rashly eating poisonous herbs. As for the women, some ladies of the urban aristocracy were forced to beg shamelessly in the marketplaces, their embarrassment and their clothing revealing a noble upbringing.

---

7. *Anthrax* in Greek, which means coal, a precious red stone, or an ulcer resembling it. This is also the name of the disease in English.

Some, shriveled like ghosts of the departed, staggered about until they fell down, and as they lay in the middle of the streets they would beg for a small scrap of bread and, with their last gasp, cry out that they were hungry—anything more than this anguished cry was beyond them. The wealthier classes, astonished at the mass of beggars they were helping, changed to a hard and merciless attitude, since they assumed that before long they would be no better off. In the middle of the city squares and narrow lanes, naked bodies lay scattered about unburied for days on end—a most pitiful spectacle. Some were eaten by dogs, for which reason the living began killing dogs, for fear they might go mad and start devouring people. No less horrible was the plague that infected every house, especially those that had survived the famine because they were well stocked with food. The affluent, rulers, governors, and numerous officials, as if intentionally left by the famine for the plague, suffered a sudden, bitter death. Moaning was heard everywhere, and funeral processions were seen in every lane, square, and street, with the usual flute playing and breast beating. Death, waging war with the two weapons of plague and famine, quickly devoured whole families, so that two or three bodies might be removed for burial in a single funeral procession.

Such was the recompense for Maximin's arrogant boasting and the cities' petitions against us, while the zeal and piety of the Christians were obvious to all the heathen. In this awful adversity they alone gave practical proof of their sympathy and humanity. All day long some of them tended to the dying and to their burial, countless numbers with no one to care for them. Others gathered together from all parts of the city a multitude of those withered from famine and distributed bread to them all, so that their deeds were on everyone's lips, and they glorified the God of the Christians. Such actions convinced them that they alone were pious and truly reverent to God.

After all this, God, the great, heavenly Champion of the Christians, having displayed his wrath to all men in return for their brutal assaults against us, restored his providence to us again and caused the light of peace to shine on us out of black darkness, as it were, making it clear to all that God himself had constantly been overseeing our affairs. Sometimes he scourged his people and in due time corrected them through trials, but after enough chastening he showed mercy and kindness to those who had hope in him.

The Death of the Tyrants

9. Thus Constantine, emperor and son of an emperor, devout and son of a most devout and prudent father, and Licinius, his next in rank—both honored for their wisdom and piety, two men beloved by God—were incited by the King of kings, God and Savior of the universe, to declare war against the two most irreligious tyrants. God proved to be their ally in a most marvelous manner: at Rome, Maxentius fell at the hands of Constantine, while he of the East [Maximin] did not long survive him and was put to a most disgraceful death by Licinius, who had not yet gone mad.

312   Constantine, the superior in imperial rank and dignity, was the first to take pity on the victims of tyranny at Rome. Praying to God in heaven and his Word, Jesus Christ the Savior of all, as his ally, he advanced with all his forces to restore to the Romans the liberty of their ancestors. Maxentius, however, relied on magical schemes rather than on the good will of his subjects and did not dare advance outside the city gates. With a vast throng of heavy infantry and countless companies of legionaries, he instead secured every district or town in the vicinity of Rome and anywhere else in Italy that he had reduced to slavery. Relying on God's help, the emperor attacked the first, second, and third of the tyrant's forces, easily defeated them, and then advanced across a large part of Italy until he arrived close to Rome itself. Then, so that he would not have to fight against Romans because of the tyrant, God himself dragged the tyrant with chains, as it were, far outside the city gates. And what sacred Scripture said long ago against the wicked—words deemed mythical and unbelievable by most but credible to believers—now by their clarity evoked belief in the believer or unbeliever who witnessed the miracle. As in the days of Moses himself and the godly race of ancient Hebrews:

> The chariots of Pharaoh and his forces he has cast into the sea;
> His chosen horsemen, his captains were sunk in the Red Sea;
> The sea covered them [Ex. 15:4-5].

In the same way, Maxentius and his armed guards and pikemen "went down into the depths like a stone"[8] [Ex. 15:5] when

---

8. Here Eusebius is describing the battle of the Milvian Bridge at Rome in 312, one of the extraordinary turning points of history. While the modern reader might well prefer an uninterrupted account, the author cannot resist portraying the battle as analogous to Israel's exodus from Egypt.

he turned back in the face of Constantine's God-given power and was crossing the river [Tiber] in his path, which he himself had well spanned by lashing boats together, and in so doing prepared a device for his own destruction. So it might be said:

> He made a pit and dug it and shall fall into the ditch he made
> His effort shall rebound onto his own head,
> And his wickedness shall come down on his own crown [Ps. 7:15-16].

Similarly, when the bridge of boats broke up, the crossing of the river collapsed, and the boats, men, and all went down into the deep at once, first that most evil wretch himself, then the shield bearers around him "sank like lead in the mighty waters," as foretold in the sacred writings [Ex. 15:10]. So, if not in words at least in deeds, like the great servant Moses and his followers, those who had gained victory with God's help might well sing the same words as were sung about the evil tyrant of old:[9]

> Let us sing unto the Lord, for gloriously has he been glorified:
> The horse and its rider he has thrown into the sea.
> The Lord, my helper and protector, became my salvation.

And

> Who is like you among the gods, O Lord? Who is like you?
> Glorified among saints, awesome in praises, working wonders?

These and many similar things Constantine sang by his very deeds to God the Ruler of all and Author of his victory. Then he entered Rome with songs of triumph, and all the senators, high notables, women, children, and all the people of Rome, beaming with insatiable joy, received him with praises as a deliverer, savior, and benefactor. But he, with inborn reverence for God, was neither thrilled by their shouts nor elated by their acclaim, knowing that his help came from God. He immediately ordered a trophy of the Savior's passion placed in the hand of his own statue, and when it was erected in the most public spot in Rome, holding the Savior's sign in his right hand, he had them engrave this inscription in Latin:

---

9. The Egyptian pharaoh of the Exodus, prototype of Maxentius. The song of Moses and the Israelites that follows is quoted from Ex. 15:1-2.

The Milvian Bridge still spans the Tiber River at the north of Rome. Here, in 312, Constantine defeated Maxentius in one of the most crucial battles in the history of Western civilization.

> By this saving sign, the true proof of valor, I saved your city from the yoke of the tyrant and liberated her. I also freed the senate and people of Rome and restored their ancient fame and splendor.

After this, Constantine and the emperor Licinius, whose mind was not yet deranged by the madness that later possessed him, acknowledging God as the Author of all their success, drew **313** up a most precise ordinance in the most complete terms in behalf of the Christians.[10] Then they sent a report of the magnificent things that God had done for them, of their victory over the tyrant, and the ordinance itself to Maximin, who still ruled the eastern provinces and pretended to be their friend. Tyrant that he was, he was most disturbed by what he learned. He neither wanted to seem to yield to others nor to suppress the order for fear of those who had commanded it. Accordingly, as if on his own initiative, he wrote this first letter on behalf of the Christians to his governors, in which he lies and claims to have done things he never did.

COPY OF A TRANSLATION OF THE TYRANT'S LETTER

Jovius Maximinus Augustus to Sabinus. It must be obvious to Your Firmness and to everyone that our masters Diocletian and Maximian,

---

10. The famous Edict of Milan, drawn up in January 313. See 10.5.

our fathers, when they noted that almost everyone had abandoned the worship of the gods and affiliated with the tribe of the Christians, justifiably ordered that all who deserted the worship of the immortal gods should be called back to the worship of the gods by public correction and punishment. But when I came so auspiciously to the East for the first time and learned that at certain places many who could serve the public were being exiled by judges for this reason, I ordered each of the judges that henceforth none was to deal harshly with the provincials but instead to recall them to the worship of the gods through cajolery and persuasion. The judges followed my directives, and no one in the eastern sectors was either exiled or insulted but rather recalled to the worship of the gods, since no harsh treatment was accorded them.

Last year, however, when I had gone auspiciously to Nicomedia, citizens there approached me with images of the gods and a plea that under no circumstances should such people be allowed to live in their city. But when I learned that many of this religion lived in that very district, I replied that I was pleased and thanked them for their request but noted that it was not unanimous. Therefore, if some persisted in this superstition, let each do as he wished and acknowledge the worship of the gods if they so desired. Nevertheless, to the Nicomedians and the other cities that have so earnestly pleaded that no Christian live in their cities, I was obliged to give a friendly reply, because the emperors of old had observed this principle and it pleased the gods themselves, by whom all people and state government itself exist, that I should confirm such a request made in behalf of the worship of their deity.

In the past, instructions and ordinances have informed Your Dedication that provincials who persevere in such a custom should not be treated harshly but with patience and moderation. Still, lest they suffer insults or blackmail at the hands of the *beneficiarii*[11] or anyone else, I send this letter to alert Your Firmness to use cajolery and persuasion to induce our provincials into proper respect for the gods. Therefore, if anyone resolves to worship the gods, welcome such people; but if some wish to follow their own worship, you should leave it up to them. Your Dedication should carefully accede to these orders and give no one authority to harass our provincials with insults and blackmail, since, as stated, it is better to coax and persuade them back to the worship of the gods. And so that our

---

11. Officers granted special privileges, probably in the entourage of a provincial governor.

provincials may learn of our mandate, you must publish what we
have commanded in an edict of your own.

Since he issued these orders under compulsion and not of
his own free will, it was now clear to all that he was neither
truthful nor trustworthy, for after making a similar concession
on a former occasion, he had proven to be a changeable hypocrite. So none of our people dared to convene a meeting or
appear in public, since the letter did not permit even this, stipu-
lating only that we be shielded from harsh treatment but with
no directives regarding meetings, building churches, or perform-
ing any of our regular activities. And yet the defenders of peace
and piety [Constantine and Licinius] had written him to permit
these very things and granted them to all their subjects through
edicts and laws. Indeed, this irreverent wretch had determined
not to give in on this issue—until divine justice forced him to do
so against his will.

The Fate of Maximin

10. These are the circumstances that surrounded him. He was
unable to manage the vast government that had so undeservedly
been entrusted to him and administered his affairs foolishly for
want of a prudent, imperial mind. Above all, an inane and boastful
arrogance inflated him against his colleagues in the empire, who
were his superiors in birth, upbringing, and education, in character and intelligence, and—most important of all—in self-control and
reverence for the true God. He began to posture insolently and
publicly proclaim himself first in rank. Next, pushing his mania
to the point of insanity, he broke the treaty he had made with
Licinius and brought on implacable war. Soon he created universal confusion, threw every city into turmoil, formed an immense
army, and marched out to fight [Licinius], his hopes placed in
demons (whom he regarded as gods!) and his confidence in myriads of infantry.

When the armies clashed, he found himself divested of God's
oversight, and victory went to Licinius, as directed by the one and
only God of all. The heavy infantry in which he had trusted was
destroyed first, and when his bodyguard deserted him and went
over to his conqueror, the wretched man quickly discarded the
imperial insignia that so ill suited him, and in cowardly, abject,
and unmanly fashion, he slipped into the crowd. Then he fled

this way and that, hiding in fields and villages, and with all this concern for safety he barely escaped his enemies, his very deeds declaring the truth of the divine sayings:

> No king is saved by great power,
> Nor a giant by his great strength.
> Vain is a horse for safety,
> It will not save by its great power.
> Behold, the eyes of the Lord are on those who fear him,
> On those who hope in his mercy
> To deliver their souls from death [Ps. 33:16–19].

Similarly, the tyrant, loaded with shame, returned to his own territory. First, in his mad rage, he executed many priests and prophets of the gods whom he had once revered and whose oracles had induced him to declare war, on the ground that they were charlatans and impostors and, above all, betrayers of his safety. Next, he gave glory to the God of the Christians and drew up a decree granting them full and final liberty. Shortly afterward, no interim being granted, his life ended in a painful death.   313

The law he enacted is as follows:

COPY OF THE TYRANT'S ORDINANCE IN BEHALF OF THE
CHRISTIANS, TRANSLATED FROM LATIN INTO GREEK

The Emperor Caesar Gaius Valerius Maximinus, Germanicus, Sarmaticus, Pius Felix Invictus Augustus. All who know the facts are aware that we pay constant attention in every way to the well-being of our provincials and wish to grant them whatever redounds to the advantage of all. We have learned that, using the excuse that our most divine fathers Diocletian and Maximian ordered the termination of Christian assemblies, public officials had engaged in much extortion and robbery, which increased as time went on to harm our provincials—whose good must be our strong concern—and to destroy their personal possessions. This past year, therefore, we sent letters to the governors in each province, decreeing that if anyone wished to follow such a custom or form of worship he might do so without hindrance by anyone and that they should have freedom to do exactly as each pleased without fear or suspicion. Yet it has not escaped our notice that some of the judges have disregarded our injunctions and caused our people to doubt our directives, rendering them rather hesitant to join in those religious rites that pleased them.

So that in the future all suspicion or doubt due to fear may be eliminated, we have decreed that this ordinance be promulgated, clarifying to all that those who wish to follow this sect and worship are free to do so as each wishes and desires, in accordance with this our boon, and to join in the religious rites he was accustomed and desired to practice. Permission to build "the Lord's houses" has also been granted them. In addition, so that our bounty may be still greater, we decree this also: if any houses or lands that once belonged to the Christians have through command of our predecessors been added to the public treasury or been confiscated by any city—whether these have been sold off or conferred on anyone as a gift—all these shall through our command be restored to the Christians as the former legal owners, so that all may appreciate our piety and concern here also.

These were the tyrant's words that came less than a year after he posted his anti-Christian edicts on tablets, the man who a short time earlier regarded us as impious, godless blights on society who were not allowed to live in the country or desert, much less the city—this same man now drew up ordinances and laws in behalf of Christians! And those who shortly before were victims of fire and sword, and food for wild beasts and birds—as he looked on—and who suffered every sort of punishment, torture, and death, as if they were godless and evil—these he now permits to worship as they wish and to build the Lord's houses, the tyrant himself confessing that they have some legal rights!

When he had conceded all this he received a reward for it, so to speak, suffering less than he should have suffered when he was suddenly struck by a scourge of God and died in the second clash of the war. Yet his death was not that of generals who fight bravely for virtue and friends before fearlessly meeting a glorious end in battle but as an impious enemy of God, hiding at home while his army still held the field. All at once God's scourge struck his entire body, and he fell prone in terrible pain and agony. He withered from hunger, his flesh was consumed by an invisible fire, and his bodily shape dissolved into an assortment of dry bones, like some phantom reduced over time to a skeleton, so that attendants could only think that his body had become the tomb of his soul, interred in what was now a corpse. As his fever burned ever hotter from the depths of his marrow, his eyes protruded and fell from their sockets, leaving him blind. Even in this condition he still breathed and made confession to the Lord, pleading for death. After acknowledging that he justly suffered for his ferocity against Christ, he breathed his last.

The End of the Enemies

11. After Maximin was removed—the last and worst of the enemies of godliness—the renewal of the churches from their foundations was undertaken, by the grace of almighty God, and the Word of Christ was proclaimed with greater freedom than before, while the impious enemies of godliness were shrouded in vile shame and dishonor. Maximin had been the first to be proclaimed by the rulers a common enemy of all and a most impious, despicable, and God-hating tyrant, as posted in public edicts. Of the portraits hung in his and his children's honor in every city, some were hurled to the ground and smashed to pieces, others had their faces blackened over with dark paint and ruined. All the statues that had been erected in his honor were similarly toppled and shattered, serving as targets for joking and sport to those who wanted to insult and revile them.

Next, all the honors of the other enemies of godliness were also stripped away, and all partisans of Maximin were executed, in particular those high in government who had violently persecuted our teaching to coddle him. One such was Peucetius, whom he honored over everyone, the truest of his friends, consul three times, whom he appointed as chief finance minister. Another was Culcianus, who had held every office in government, a man who delighted in the murder of countless Christians in Egypt. There were many others who had been prime facilitators in reinforcing and extending Maximin's tyranny.

Justice also summoned Theotecnus, determined that what he did to the Christians should never be forgotten. After he had set up the idol at Antioch, he seemed to enjoy great success and, indeed, was awarded a governorship by Maximin. But when Licinius came to Antioch, he made a search for impostors and tortured the prophets and priests of the new idol to find out how they contrived their frauds. When, under torture, they revealed that the entire mystery was a deception contrived by Theotecnus, he [Licinius] inflicted a long series of tortures on them and put them to death, first Theotecnus and then his partners in fraud.

To these were added the sons of Maximin, with whom he had already shared imperial honors and whose features he had displayed publicly in portraits. Those who previously had boasted

The triumphal Arch of Constantine at Rome, which was erected next to the Colosseum (right edge).

that they were related to the tyrant and tried to lord it over others endured the same sufferings and disgrace, for they did not accept correction or understand the precept in the sacred books:

> Put not your trust in princes,
> In the sons of men who cannot save.
> His breath shall depart and he shall return to his earth.
> In that day all his thoughts shall perish [Ps. 146:3-4].

When the impious were thus removed, the rule that belonged to them was preserved secure and undisputed for Constantine and Licinius alone. They had made it their priority to purge the world of hostility to God, and, acknowledging the blessings he had conferred on them, they showed their love of virtue and of God, their devotion and gratitude to the Deity, through their edict in behalf of the Christians.

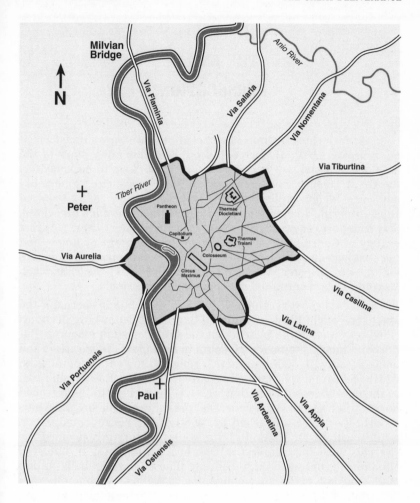

The principal roads surrounding Rome as a hub. The Battle of the Milvian Bridge took place where the Via Flaminia crosses the Tiber at the northern edge of this map. Paul reached Rome by means of the Via Appia (lower right), and was most probably buried along the Via Ostiensis (lower left center). Peter was likely interred in the Vatican Valley across the Tiber west of Rome.

THE END OF PERSECUTION?

Just as the lengthy links of persecution since Nero's time formed no unbroken chain of horror—indeed, Eusebius fairly sings of the freedoms enjoyed by Christians before what came to be known as the Great Persecution—so the end of state-sponsored torment did not come in any clear and orderly fashion. How many imperial edicts ordering a cessation of persecution has Eusebius presented, only to report renewed repression a few pages later? Even the great victory of Constantine at the Milvian Bridge, north of Rome, and the ensuing edict of toleration in 313, the usual popular benchmark for the end of persecution, did not take effect in the East when Maximin Daia determined to renew the oppression.

Eusebius devotes much of Book 9 to Maximin—perhaps too much, one might think, with detail that might better have been lavished on Constantine instead, as the first Christian emperor. But Eusebius richly supplies such detail in his *Life of Constantine*, and his concern with Maximin merely reflects the vantage point from which he wrote: the again-persecuted Christian East in contrast to the now-liberated Christian West. As eyewitness to the resumed horror after the Eastern churches' premature rejoicing, Eusebius reports the havoc unleashed by "the tyrant"—his repeated, favorite designation for Maximin Daia, whom he correctly deemed the church's most implacable foe. One has the impression that even Maximin's gruesome death—can any illness cause eyeballs to pop out?—was not catharsis enough for Eusebius. A contemporary historian, Lactantius, even claims that Maximin died a lingering death from self-administered poison, although his book, *De Mortibus Persecutorum* ("On the Deaths of the Persecutors"), has divine anger against all who persecuted the church as its theme.

Eusebius, however, will have to reopen his thesaurus of censures one last time, in Book 10, for Licinius. The eastern Augustus, Constantine's former ally who had begun his reign so favorably, would end his days as the very last in the long cavalcade of Eusebius's villains.

In the complex of Roman politics, the last chapter had ended with the following configuration of Roman rulers:

West	*East*
Constantine: Gaul, Spain, Britain	Licinius: Balkan peninsula
Maxentius: Italy and Africa	Maximin Daia: Asia Minor, Egypt

With such an array of rivals, all aspirants to supreme power, civil war in both West and East was inevitable. Constantine and Licinius formed an alliance against Maxentius and Maximin, which was potentially felicitous from the church's point of view since it placed the two worst enemies of Christianity, Maxentius and Maximin, on the same side. Thus Christians could unreservedly support Constantine and Licinius. For his part, Constantine seems to have inherited from his father a policy of moderation toward the Christians and had joined in Galerius's edict of toleration in 311.

In the summer of 312, Constantine invaded Italy with an army inferior in number to Maxentius's but with better training. And in probably the most pivotal decision in Roman history, Constantine placed himself and his forces under the protection of the Christian God. Eusebius claims that he was responding to the vision of a cross of light that he and his army had seen one afternoon on the march, followed by a dream in which Christ appeared to him. Defeating Maxentius's forces at Turin and Verona, he advanced southward until he arrived, just north of Rome, at a bend of the Tiber River where the Milvian Bridge crossed it. Maxentius, however, had cut the bridge as a defensive tactic and remained inside a well-fortified Rome, where it would have been difficult for Constantine to dislodge him. When the city populace rioted against him, however, Maxentius trusted a pagan oracle predicting that "the enemy of the Romans would perish" and marched his forces out of the city to meet Constantine, crossing the Tiber by means of a bridge of boats. And so, on October 28, 312, they fought the battle of the Milvian Bridge, one of the most momentous events in church or secular history.

According to Lactantius, Constantine had a dream the night before the battle in which he saw the first two letters—the *chi* and the *rho*—of Christ's name in Greek superimposed and heard the words *In hoc signo vinces,* "By this sign you will conquer." The next morning he had his soldiers paint this symbol on their shields and on his helmet, a monogram that was later incorporated into the imperial standard. When the battle was joined, Constantine's forces attacked from a low ridge running parallel to the Tiber that Maxentius had foolishly failed to occupy. Soon Maxentius's troops broke and fled back toward the severed Milvian Bridge in disarray, so many of them crowding onto the bridge of boats that it collapsed and thousands drowned, including Maxentius himself. The victor, probably a convert to Christianity even before the battle but certainly after it, deemed himself the servant God had chosen to convert the Roman Empire to the Christian faith.

Perhaps Christianity might have triumphed apart from Constantine's victory at the Milvian Bridge, but surely that triumph would have been delayed substantially. Had Maxentius won instead of Constantine, the subsequent history of the Roman Empire—certainly of Christianity—might have been bleak indeed. It would have been even worse had Maximin Daia conquered the forces of Licinius in the East and then been equally successful against those of Constantine in the West.

Constantine's subsequent political and religious policies have been engrossing themes for a host of studies, some listed in the bibliography. Here it remains only to sketch how a tetrarchy of four emperors—three after the battle of the Milvian Bridge—became a monarchy once again.

In the spring of 313, Licinius visited Constantine at Milan, where he married Constantine's sister Constantia, thus cementing their alliance. Here the two Augusti also agreed on a policy of toleration for both Christians and pagans in the empire—often mistakenly called the Edict of Milan—which was proclaimed at Nicomedia in June of 313. This accorded full toleration for all religions as well as restitution for Christians. In the West, Constantine supplied this restitution on a lavish scale with large donations to the church and generous immunities to the Christian clergy.

Months earlier, however, Maximin Daia had tried to revive paganism and resumed a vicious persecution of Christians in the East, which Constantine vigorously opposed and succeeded in moderating. Maximin then invaded Licinius's European territories while he was meeting with Constantine at Milan, but Licinius hurried back and routed Maximin's forces near Adrianople. Maximin himself fled to Asia Minor, where he died of a loathsome disease at Tarsus.

Now only a dyarchy was left: Constantine supreme in the West and Licinius in the East, a truce that persisted for the next eleven years. Their relations, however, deteriorated when Licinius became devoted to the cult of Sol Invictus and began persecuting Christians again, claiming that he was unsure of their loyalty. Constantine attacked him victoriously at Adrianople in July, 324 and again in September at Chrysopolis, across the Bosporus from Byzantium. Honoring the pleas of his sister, Constantine spared Licinius's life and exiled him to Thessalonica, but the following year he was executed on a charge of rebellion. Constantine now ruled as sole Augustus of a reunited Roman Empire until his death in 337. This summary of the Roman political background, however, takes us beyond 324, the year in which Eusebius concludes his *Church History* with Book 10.

The monogram of Christ that Constantine had his troops paint on their shields became a classic Christian symbol. In the panel of this fourth-century sarcophagus, it is surrounded by a victor's crown and attended by doves of peace (*Lateran Museum, Rome*).

Book 10

CONSTANTINE
AND PEACE

1. Thanks be to God, the almighty King of the universe, and to Jesus Christ, the Savior and Redeemer of our souls, through whom we pray that peace from troubles external and internal may be preserved for us intact and undisturbed.

Along with my prayers I now add Book 10 to the *Church History* and dedicate it to you, my most consecrated Paulinus,[1] and blazon you as the seal of the whole work. It is appropriate that in a perfect number[2] I shall here provide a completed account in celebration of the restoration of the churches, in obedience to the divine Spirit who urges us:

> Sing to the Lord a new song, for he has done marvelous things;
> His right hand and his holy arm have wrought salvation for him.
> The Lord has made known his salvation:
> His righteousness he has revealed in the sight of the heathen [Ps. 98:1-2].

Accordingly, let me now sing the new song, since, after those grim and horrifying scenes and narratives, I was now privileged to see and to celebrate what many righteous men and martyrs of God before me desired to see but did not see, and to hear but did not hear. But they hurried on to far better things in the heavens, caught up into a paradise of divine bliss, while I, admitting that even the present circumstances are more than I deserve, have been totally astonished at the magnitude of grace he has conferred and offer him my total awe and worship, confirming the truth of the prophecies that declare:

---

1. The Bishop of Tyre who urged Eusebius to write this history. Later he became Bishop of Antioch, his native city. Eusebius also dedicated his *Onomasticon* to him.

2. Perfect because after ten there are no new numerals, just combinations of the previous ones.

Come and behold the works of the Lord,
What wonders he has brought on the earth,
Making wars to cease to the ends of the world.
He will break the bow and shatter the spear,
And the shields he will burn with fire [Ps. 46:8-9].

Rejoicing that all this has been clearly fulfilled, let me proceed with my narrative.

The whole race of God's enemies was destroyed, as stated before, and disappeared in a moment, fulfilling another divine saying:

I saw the wicked in great power, lifted up like the cedars of
    Lebanon.
And I passed by, and lo, he was not;
And I sought his place, and it was not found
    [Ps. 37:35-36].

From now on, a cloudless day, radiant with rays of heavenly light, shined down on the churches of Christ throughout the world, and there was no reluctance to share even with those outside our society the enjoyment, if not of equal divine blessings, at least of their effects.

Restoration of the Churches

2. All people, then, were set free from the tyrants' oppression, and, rescued from their former miseries, they acknowledged in various ways that the Champion of the godly was the only true God. But especially we who had hoped in Christ had inexpressible happiness, and a divine joy blossomed in all our hearts as we saw places that had, a little earlier, been laid waste by the tyrants' malice now reviving as if from a long and deadly injury and cathedrals rising again from their foundations to lofty heights, far exceeding the magnificence of those that had been demolished.

And emperors too, the most exalted, further confirmed God's blessings to us through a succession of decrees in favor of the Christians, while bishops received many personal letters, honors, and gifts of money from the emperor. At the proper place I shall insert these documents into this book, translated from Latin into Greek, so that they may be preserved for all who come after us.

Church Dedications Everywhere

3. Next came the spectacle for which we all prayed and yearned: festivals of dedication in the cities and consecrations of the new houses of worship, conferences of bishops, assemblies of representatives from distant lands, friendship among the laity, and unity among the members of Christ's body as they joined in complete harmony. In accordance with the prophecy that mystically predicted what was to be, bone combined with bone, and joint joint,[3] and all that was foretold in the divine oracles. There was one power of the divine Spirit infusing all the members, who were of one soul, showing the same enthusiasm for the faith with one hymn of praise on the lips of all. Indeed, our leaders conducted flawless ceremonies, while ordained priests observed the sacred, stately rites of the church, singing psalms, offering prayers, and ministering the divine liturgy, all under the symbols of the Savior's passion. Male and female of every age together gave glory to God, the Author of their happiness, with all their hearts, souls, and minds.

[Here Eusebius makes an abrupt transition from general Christian celebrations to a particular one at Tyre. What follows is not history but panegyric, a literary form no longer used, though it was popular in the ancient world at this time. Many readers may find it too long, adulatory, or outright boring for modern tastes. They are urged to pass on to section 5.]

Each of the church dignitaries present delivered a panegyrical oration, inspiring the assembly as he was able. **4.** One of those moderately capable[4] came forward with a prepared address, to which the many pastors present gave a quiet, orderly hearing as in a church assembly. Addressing a single bishop, a most excellent man beloved by God, through whose zeal the most magnificent cathedral in Phoenicia had been erected at Tyre, he delivered the following oration:

PANEGYRIC ON THE BUILDING OF THE CHURCHES,
ADDRESSED TO PAULINUS, BISHOP OF TYRE

---

3. Ezek. 37:7, though Eusebius added the comment about joints for literary purposes.

4. Eusebius himself.

Friends of God and priests clothed with the sacred robe and the heavenly crown of glory, the divine unction of the Holy Spirit, and you, O youthful pride of God's holy temple, honored with mature wisdom from God yet famed for deeds of youthful virtue, on whom he who comprehends all has bestowed the unique privilege of building his house on earth and restoring it for Christ his only begotten and firstborn Word, and for Christ's holy bride [the church]: Shall I call you a new Bezalel, the architect of a divine tabernacle [Ex. 35:30], or a Solomon, king of a new and better Jerusalem, or a new Zerubbabel, who brought to the temple of God a glory that was greater than the old?[5] And you also, nurslings of the sacred flock of Christ, known for good works, self-control, and godliness:

Long ago, as we listened to the reading of passages from Holy Scripture that told of miraculous signs from God and the wonders performed by the Lord, we could sing hymns to God in the words taught us:

> We have heard with our ears, O God, our fathers have
>   told us
> The work that you did in their days, in the days of old
>   [Ps. 44:1].

But now it is no longer by hearing that we learn of the right hand of God but by deeds, as we see with our own eyes that the traditions of long ago are credible and true. And so we can sing a second hymn of victory in the words:

> As we have heard, so have we seen
> In the city of the Lord of hosts, in the city of our God
>   [Ps. 48:8].

And in what city if not this new city built by God, his church, the pillar and ground of truth, about which Scripture says, "Glorious things are spoken of you, O city of God" [Ps. 87:3]? Since the all-merciful God has convened us in this city through the grace of his Only Begotten, let each of the guests sing, no, shout: "I was glad

---

5. In the classical world at this time, such formal orations were typically extravagant in their praise of a person or thing. Since the panegyric that follows is so flowery and verbose as to be almost unreadable, I have pared away some excessively eulogistic verbiage but translated every word of historical significance. Clearly Eusebius has exchanged his role as historian for that of an orator in this document.

when they said to me, we will go into the house of the Lord" [Ps. 122:1], and "Lord, I have loved the beauty of your house and the place where your glory dwells" [Ps. 26:8].

Not just individually but all of us together, with one spirit, give glory and praise, saying, "Great is the Lord and highly to be praised in the city of our God, in his holy mountain" [Ps. 48:1]. He is truly great, and great is his house, lofty and expansive and beautiful. Great is the Lord who does countless glorious and marvelous things, who changes the times and seasons, removes kings and installs them, raises the poor from the ground and lowers princes from their thrones, feeds the hungry, and breaks the arms of the proud. He has proved the ancient narratives true not only for the faithful, but also for the faithless. Let us then sing the new song to the Doer of wonders, the Lord of the universe, Creator of the world, the almighty, the all-merciful, the one and only God:

> To him who alone does great wonders,
> For his mercy endures forever,
> To him who struck down great kings,
> For his mercy endures forever.
> For he remembered us in our low estate,
> And freed us from our enemies.[6]

May we never cease to offer the Father of the universe such loud praise. As for the second source of our blessings, teacher of the knowledge of God, destroyer of the wicked, killer of tyrants, reformer of humanity, savior from despair—namely, Jesus, let us honor his name on our lips. For he alone, the only Son of the Father, willingly assumed our corrupt nature, as the Father willed it out of love for us. Like the best doctor, who, to cure the sick, "though he sees the horrible ills still touches the foul areas, and for someone else's troubles brings suffering on himself,"[7] so he saved us, who were not merely sick or afflicted with terrible ulcers and festering wounds but lying among the dead, for no one else in heaven could undertake the salvation of so many. He alone endured our sorrows, taking on himself the penalty for our sins when we were not half dead, but decaying in tombs, and he raised us up and saves us now, as in the days of old, out of ardent love for humankind, sharing with us the Father's blessings—our lifegiver, enlightener, great physician, king, and lord, the

---

6. Adapted from Ps. 136.
7. Hippocrates *On Breaths* 1.

Christ of God. When he saw the whole human race sunk in demon-inspired darkness, his appearance alone tore apart the chains of sin as easily as wax melts in the sun.

But when the demon that loves evil, enraged at this great grace, marshaled his lethal forces against us, he first was like a mad dog that bites the stones thrown at him, venting on lifeless missiles his fury at those trying to drive him off: he aimed his ferocity against the stones of the houses of prayer, ruining the churches, as he thought. Then he hissed like a serpent through the threats of godless tyrants and the blasphemous edicts of impious rulers, vomiting out death and infecting the souls he snared by his soul-destroying poisons and almost killing them with his death-inducing sacrifices to dead idols, releasing against us every beast in human form and every sort of savagery.

Once again, however, the great commander-in-chief of the host of God suddenly appeared, whose greatest soldiers proved their training through faithful endurance and caused all hostility to disappear into nameless oblivion. But those near and dear to him he advanced beyond all glory in the sight of all: men, sun, moon, stars—the entire heaven and earth. Now the most exalted emperors, aware of the honor they received from him, spit on the faces of dead idols, trample on the unholy rites of demons, and laugh at the old lies they inherited from their fathers—something that never happened before. But they acknowledge as the one and only God, the Benefactor of all and Christ as Son of God and sovereign King of the universe, naming him "Savior" on monuments and inscribing in imperial characters in the center of the city that is empress among the world's cities an indelible record of his victories over the wicked. Thus Jesus Christ our Savior is the only person in history to be acknowledged—even by earth's most exalted—not as an ordinary human king but worshiped as the true Son of the God of the universe and as himself God.

Small wonder. For what king ever attained such greatness as to fill the ears and mouths of all humankind with his name? What king ever made laws so wise as to have them proclaimed to the entire world? Who annulled the barbarous customs of uncivilized nations through his civilized and most humane laws? Who was attacked by everyone for ages yet remains in his youthful prime? Who founded a people not heard of since time began that now is not hidden in some corner of the earth but is found everywhere under the sun? Who so equipped his soldiers with weapons of faith that their souls proved stronger than adamant in struggles with their enemies? Which of the kings has such power, leads his armies after death, puts up trophies over his foes, and fills every place, district, and city, both Greek and foreign, with votive offerings: his royal houses and divine temples, such as this cathedral and its splendid ornaments and offerings? These things are awesome and astonishing and themselves clear proof that our Savior is sovereign, for now also "He spoke, and they were made; he commanded, and they were created" [Ps. 33:9; 148:5].

What could oppose the will of the Word of God himself? That would require a separate discourse. Of greater importance is how God looks at the living temple we all comprise, formed of living stones firmly set on the foundation of the apostles and prophets, Jesus Christ himself being the chief cornerstone [Eph. 2:20]. . . . This is the greatest sanctuary, whose innermost sanctums are hidden from humanity as a true Holy of Holies, which only the great High Priest of the universe can enter to search out the mysteries of each rational soul.

But perhaps it is possible for one other, alone among equals, to take the second place after him, namely, the commander of this army [Paulinus], whom the first and great High Priest has honored with the second place in the ministry here, the pastor of your spiritual flock, whom the Father appointed over your people, the new Aaron or Melchizedek, maintained by God through your prayers. Let him alone, then, after the first and greatest High Priest, be permitted to examine the innermost recesses of your souls, since his long experience, enthusiasm, care, and religious instruction qualify him.

Our first great High Priest tells us that whatever he sees the Father doing, that he does also [John 5:19]. This one in turn looks to the first as a teacher, and whatever he sees him doing becomes the patterns from which, like an artist, he has molded the closest likenesses to the best of his ability. He is then not inferior to Bezalel, whom God himself filled with wisdom, understanding, and knowledge of the crafts and sciences, calling him to be the architect for the [tabernacle as] symbol of the heavenly temple. In the same way, this man, bearing the image of Christ in his soul, has erected this magnificent structure for God most high, similar in nature to the pattern of that better, invisible one. Words cannot describe his generosity and determination or the enthusiasm you all showed in contributing so lavishly to match him in this respect.

This site, it should first be said, which had been covered with all kinds of filthy rubbish thanks to our enemies, he did not abandon to their hostility, though he could have chosen another site—the city has countless others—to avoid effort and trouble. Instead, he stirred up and unified the people with his enthusiasm, for he felt that [the church] that had been attacked by the Enemy and suffered the same persecutions as we—earlier ones too, like a mother bereft of her children—should share in the blessings of the all-gracious God. For since the great Shepherd had driven away the wild beasts and wolves and broken the teeth of the lions, it was most fitting that he should also erect the fold of the flock, putting the Enemy to shame and condemning his crimes.

Now these haters of God no longer exist, having paid to Justice the penalty of destroying themselves, their friends, and their families, proving the sacred predictions of long ago to be true, in which the divine Word says:

The wicked have drawn the sword and bent the bow
To topple the poor and needy,
To slay the upright in heart.
May their sword enter their own hearts,
And may their bows be broken [Ps. 37:14-15].

And again: "Their memory has perished with a crash," and "Their name you have blotted out forever and ever" [Ps. 9:6, 5, LXX]. For indeed, when they were in trouble:

They cried (but there was none to save)
To the Lord, and he did not hear them.
They were tied hand and foot and fell;
But we rose and stood upright [Ps. 18:41; 20:8].

And the words, "Lord, in your city you shall obliterate their image" [Ps. 73:20], have been shown true before everyone.

Fighting against God like giants, they have brought their lives to a miserable end. [The church] that was rejected by men has endured, as we have seen, so that the prophecy of Isaiah calls to her as follows:

Be glad, thirsty desert; rejoice and blossom like a lily;
The desert places shall blossom forth and rejoice.
Be strong, drooping hands and weak knees,
Take courage, you timid-hearted, be strong, do not fear.
Behold, our God dispenses justice and will do so,
He will come and save us.

> For water broke out in the desert, and a stream in thirsty soil.
> And the desiccated place shall become wetlands,
> And on thirsty ground shall be a spring of water [Isa. 35:1-7].

Foretold long ago, this has come down to us no longer as hearsay but as fact. With axes they cut down the gates of this desert, this defenseless widow, and tore her down with hatchet and hammer, destroying her books, setting the sanctuary of God on fire, and desecrating the ground of his dwelling place. All who passed by broke down her fences and plucked her fruit; the boar ravaged her, and the wild beast devoured her. Now, by the miraculous power of Christ, as he wills, she has become like a lily. She was also disciplined at his command, as by a father who cares, "For whom the Lord loves, he chastens, and he whips every son whom he acknowledges" [Prov. 3:12]. Appropriately corrected, she is now called to rejoice again, and she blooms like a lily, shedding her fragrance on all humankind, for water did indeed burst out of the desert, the stream of divine regeneration through baptism. The weak hands are strengthened, as witness this splendid structure, and the feeble knees firmed to march on the road to the knowledge of God. If the tyrants' threats have dulled some souls, the saving Word does not give up on these but heals them with divine encouragement, saying: "Take courage, you fainthearted, be strong and fearless."

The word that foretold how she who was desert would be blessed after bitter captivity was understood by our new and excellent Zerubbabel,[8] who did not pass by the body as dead, but, with the approval of you all, he interceded with the Father. With the only Resurrector of the dead as his ally, he raised her up after cleansing and healing her, dressing her not in her old clothes but such as followed the divine instructions: "The glory of the new house shall be greater than the former" [Hag. 2:9].

Accordingly, the area that he enclosed was much larger,[9] and he surrounded it all with a protective wall for safety. Then he set a portico, wide and lofty, to catch the rays of the rising sun, providing a broad view of the interior even to those outside the sacred precincts and catching the attention even of strangers to the faith, who might

---

8. After the Babylonian captivity of the Jews, he led one of the groups returning to Jerusalem, where he supervised the rebuilding of the temple. See Hag. 1:1-15. The "new . . . Zerubbabel," of course, was Paulinus.

9. Than the previous structure. The paragraphs that follow provide the earliest known description of a Christian church building and its furnishings.

be astonished at the miraculous transformation of what had been ruins and [be] lured inside. Whoever goes through the gates cannot pass immediately with unhallowed and unwashed feet into the holy places inside: he has left a very wide space between the entrances and the church itself, adorning the perimeter with four colonnades to form a quadrangle of columns. Between these are wooden screens of latticework and in the middle an area open to sun and sky. There, directly in front of the cathedral, he placed fountains flowing with fresh water for entrants to purify themselves. This is the first stopping place for those who enter, enhancing the splendor and serving as a point of first instruction for those requiring it.

Among porticoes leading to the cathedral, he placed three gates on one side, the center one much higher and broader than the outside pair, and plated it in bronze trussed with iron and detailed reliefs so that it resembles a queen flanked by two bodyguards. Colonnades along both sides of the structure have similar gateways, with openings atop the colonnades, adorned with exquisite wood carvings, to admit still more light.

The basilica itself he constructed sturdily of even costlier materials, sparing no expense. Here I need not give the dimensions of the building or describe its radiant beauty, indescribable vastness, dazzling workmanship, the loftiness that touches heaven, or the costly cedars of Lebanon that form the ceiling. The sacred Word tells us even about them: "The trees of the Lord shall be glad, the cedars of Lebanon that he planted" [Ps. 104:16].

I need not now detail the perfection of the design and the extraordinary beauty of each part, for evidence to the eye obviates that to the ear. After finishing the structure he adorned it with lofty thrones to honor the prelates and also with convenient benches throughout. In the middle he placed the holy of holies—the altar—excluding the congregation from this area by surrounding it with wooden latticework of marvelous artistry.

Not even the floor escaped his notice, which he brightened with marble of every kind. Outside the building, he erected large halls and rooms on both sides that were skillfully attached to the sides of the basilica and shared its light. Our most peaceful Solomon built these for those still in need of sprinkling with water and the Holy Spirit, so that the prophecy cited previously is no longer word but fact, since the glory of this house is indeed greater than the former.

It was appropriate that [the church], since her Lord had suffered death on her behalf, after which he had assumed his glorious body and transformed his flesh from corruption into incorruption, should benefit from the Savior's labors. Having received his promise of much better things than these, she yearns to receive the new birth in the resurrection of an incorruptible body, with the choir of angels in the kingdom of God, with Christ Jesus himself, her great Benefactor and Savior. For the present, she who was long widowed and deserted has been clothed by God's grace with these blossoms to become as a lily, as prophesied, and, once again in bridal dress with a garland of beauty, she is taught by Isaiah to dance, as it were, giving thanks to God the King in words of praise:

> Let my soul rejoice in the Lord;
> For he has clothed me with the garment of salvation and the
>   cloak of gladness,
> He has wreathed me like a bridegroom and adorned me
>   like a bride,
> And like the soil that makes its flower grow
> And as the garden causes what is sown to spring up,
> So the Lord will cause righteousness and joy to spring up
>   before all nations [Isa. 61:10-11].

With these words she dances. And how does the Bridegroom, Jesus Christ himself, answer her? Listen to the Lord as he says:

> Do not fear that you have been put to shame or reproach,
> For you will forget the shame and reproach of your widowhood.
> The Lord has called you, not as a wife deserted and hated,
>   says your God.
> For a little while I forsook you, but with great mercy will I
>   comfort you.
> A little angry, I hid my face from you, but my mercy will be
>   everlasting, says the Lord who delivered you.
> Awake, awake, you who have drained the cup of the Lord's
>   fury!
> Among all the children you bore, there was none to comfort
>   you or take you by the hand.
> See, I have taken from your hand the cup of staggering, the
>   bowl of my fury, and you will not drink it again.
> I will put it into the hands of those who wronged and humbled
>   you.
> Awake, awake, put on your strength and glory; shake off the
>   dust and arise, loosen the band from your neck.
> Raise your eyes and see your children gathered together.

As I live, says the Lord, you will clothe yourself with them all
  like a bridal ornament.
For your desolate ruins will be too narrow for your inhabitants,
  and those who devour you will be removed far from you.
The sons whom you lost will say, "This place is too narrow for
  me; give me a place to live."
And you will say in your heart, "Who has produced these for
  me? I am a childless widow, but who has raised these?"[10]

Isaiah prophesied all this, but it was necessary that we should
some day learn their truth through facts. And since the Bridegroom—
the Word—speaks to his bride, the holy church, in this way, how
appropriate that this bridal attendant[11] stretched out your hands in
common prayer and, by the will of God and the power of Jesus Christ,
awakened her who lay desolate and dead. And, after raising her, he
restored her according to the precepts of the sacred oracles.

A mighty, breathtaking wonder is this [cathedral], especially to
those who pay attention only to externals. But far more wonderful
are the archetypes or divine patterns of material things; I mean
the renewal of the spiritual edifice in our souls. This edifice the
Son of God himself created in his own image and divine likeness:
an incorruptible nature, a spiritual essence alien to earthly matter,
and endowed with intelligence. He brought it into being and made it
a holy bride and sacred temple for himself and the Father. This he
clearly reveals in the confession: "I will dwell in them and walk in
them; and I will be their God, and they shall be my people" [2 Cor.
6:16]. Such is the perfect, purified soul, created from the beginning
to bear the image of the heavenly Word.

But when, through the jealousy of the demon that loves evil,
she became of her own free will a lover of sensuality and evil, the
protecting Deity departed from her, and she fell prey to the snares of
those who envied her. Toppled by the battering rams of her spiritual
enemies, she crashed to the ground, leaving not one stone of her
virtue standing on another as she lay dead, bereft of innate thoughts
about God. As she lay prostrate, she was ravaged by spiritual wild
beasts who inflamed her with passions, as with fiery arrows of wickedness that set on fire the divine sanctuary of God, totally profaning
the dwelling place of his name. Then she was buried under a great
mound of earth, hopeless of any salvation.

---

10. Adapted from Isa. 54:4, 6–8; 51:17–18, 22–23; 52:1–2; 49:18–21.
11. Paulinus.

But when she had paid the penalty for her sins, the saving Protector—the Word—restored her once again, through the grace of his Father. First he chose the souls of the supreme emperors, most beloved by him, and through them he cleansed the whole world of all the wicked and noxious and of the dreadful God-hating tyrants themselves. Then he brought out into the open his disciples, who all their lives had been dedicated to him yet concealed in the storm of evils by his sheltering concern, and he gave them a worthy reward with his Father's bounty. Through them he cleansed the souls that had been fouled with rubbish of all kinds and the trash of impious decrees, using pickaxes and mattocks—his penetrating teachings. And when he had made this place bright and clear, he entrusted it to this all-wise and God-beloved leader, so discerning and prudent regarding the souls committed to his care. From the start he has never ceased to build, setting in place the shining gold, the pure silver, and the precious stones among you all, fulfilling the sacred prophecy that says:

Behold, I prepare for your stone the carbuncle
And for your foundations the sapphire,
And for your battlements jasper,
And for your gates crystal,
And for your wall choice stones,
And all your sons taught by God,
And in perfect peace your children;
And in righteousness shall you be built [Isa. 54:11-14].

Building truly in righteousness, he divided the people according to their ability.[12] With some, a majority of the people, he fenced only the outer enclosure with a wall of unwavering faith. To others he entrusted the entrances to the church, where they are to guide those entering. Others he made supports for the first columns that surround the quadrangle around the courtyard, bringing them to their first touch with the letter of the four Gospels. Still others he joined to the basilica along both sides, those advancing under instruction and not far from the innermost divine vision of the faithful. Choosing from these the pure souls that have been cleaned like gold by divine washing, he makes them supports for columns much grander than the outermost, using the innermost mystic teachings of the Scrip-

---

12. The following two paragraphs use the physical church as model for the spiritual rank of its members.

tures, while others he illuminates with openings toward the light. The whole temple he adorns with one mighty gateway: the praise of our one and only God and King, flanking the Father's supreme power with the secondary beams of the light of Christ and the Holy Spirit. As to the rest, throughout the structure he shows clearly the truth that is in everyone by including the living and secure stones of human souls. Thus he has constructed from them all a great and royal house, luminous inside and out, since not only their souls and minds but even their bodies have been glorified with the many-blossomed adornment of chastity and temperance.

In this shrine are also thrones and countless seats, the souls on which rest the Holy Spirit's gifts, such as appeared to the holy apostles and their associates long ago as divided tongues of fire. In [Paulinus] the ruler of them all, the entire Christ resides, and in those second to him in proportion to each one's capacity to receive the power of Christ and the Holy Spirit. The souls of some might even be seats of angels committed to the teaching and guarding of each. As to the great and unique altar, what might it be but the spotless Holy of Holies of [Christ], the common priest of all? Standing beside it on the right side, the great High Priest of the universe, Jesus, the only begotten of God, joyfully receives the sweet-smelling incense and prayers of all and forwards them to the heavenly Father and God of the universe. Adoring the Father, he alone renders him the honors due and implores him to continue favorable toward us forever.

Such is the great temple that the Word, great Creator of the universe, has built throughout the world so that his Father might be honored and worshiped. But as for the realm above the skies, the Jerusalem above, as it is called, the heavenly Mount Zion and celestial city of the living God, where hosts of angels and the first enrolled in heaven offer ineffable praise to their Maker—these things no mortal can hymn worthily, for indeed "eye has not seen and ear has not heard" the things that God has prepared for those who love him [1 Cor. 2:9]. Partially deemed worthy of these things, let us all—men, women, and children, small and great, with one spirit—offer eternal thanks and praise to the Author of all our blessings. He shows mercy on our offenses, cures our diseases, redeems our life from destruction, crowns us with compassion, and satisfies our desires with good things. He has not dealt with us according to our sins, but as far as east is from west he has removed our iniquities from us. As a father pities his sons, so the Lord has pitied those who fear him.[13]

---

13. Adapted from Ps. 103:3-5, 10-13.

Now and for all time to come, let us rekindle the memory of these things. Let the Author of the present assembly and of this joyful, most glorious day—the Lord himself—be ever in our minds night and day, through every hour and every breath. Let us cherish and revere him with all the power of our souls. And now let us rise and implore him with a loud voice to shelter and preserve us to the end in his fold and confer on us his eternal, unbreakable peace in Christ Jesus our Savior, through whom be glory to him for ever and ever. Amen.

Imperial Decrees

5. Here let us quote the imperial ordinances of Constantine and Licinius, as translated from the Latin.

313   COPY OF IMPERIAL ORDINANCES,
                          TRANSLATED FROM LATIN[14]

We have long intended that freedom of worship should not be denied but that everyone should have the right to practice his religion as he chose. Accordingly, we had given orders that both Christians and [all others] should be permitted to keep the faith of their own sect and worship. But since many conditions of all kinds had evidently been added to that rescript in which such rights were accorded these same people, it may be that some of them were shortly thereafter deterred from such observance.

When under happy auspices I, Constantine Augustus, and I, Licinius Augustus, had come to Milan and were discussing all matters that concerned the public good, among the other items of benefit to the general welfare—or rather, as issues of highest priority—we decided to issue such decrees as would assure respect and reverence for the Deity; namely, to grant the Christians and all others the freedom to follow whatever form of worship they pleased, so that all the divine and heavenly powers that exist might be favorable to us and all those living under our authority. Here, therefore, is the decision we reached by sound and prudent reasoning: no one at all was to be denied the right to follow or choose the Christian form

---

14. This is the famous Edict of Milan, drawn up by Constantine and Licinius at Milan but announced at Nicomedia in June, 313. It was then dispatched to the governors of the Roman provinces. Its superiority to Galerius's edict is that this one accorded freedom to all religious beliefs.

of worship or observance, and everyone was to be granted the right to give his mind to that form of worship that he thinks suitable to himself, so that the Deity may show us his usual care and generosity in all things. It was appropriate to send a rescript that this is our pleasure, so that with all conditions canceled in the earlier letter sent to Your Dedication about the Christians,[15] whatever seemed unjustified and foreign to our clemency might also be removed and that now everyone desiring to observe the Christians' form of worship should be permitted to do so without any hindrance. We have decided to explain this very thoroughly to Your Diligence, so that you may know that we have granted to these same Christians free and limitless permission to practice their own form of worship. And when you note that we have granted them this permission unrestrictedly, Your Dedication will understand that permission has also been given to others who wish to follow their own observance and form of worship—something clearly in accord with the tranquility of our times—so that everyone may have authority to choose and practice whatever form he wishes. This we have done so that we might not appear to have belittled any rite or form of worship in any way.

As regards the Christians, in the previous letter sent to Your Dedication, definite instructions were issued regarding their places of assembly. We now further resolve that if any should appear to have bought these places either from our treasury or from any other source, they must restore them to these same Christians without payment or any demand for compensation and do so without negligence or hesitation. If any happen to have received them as a gift, they must restore them to these same Christians without delay, provided that if either those who have purchased these same places or those who have received them as a gift appeal to our generosity, they may apply to the prefect of the district, so that they may also benefit from our kindness. All this property must be handed over to the body of the Christians immediately, through zealous action on your part and without delay.

And since these same Christians not only owned places of assembly, but are also known to have had others belonging not to individuals but to the corporation of the Christians, all such property, under provisions of the above law, you will order restored without any question whatever to these same Christians, that is, to their corporation and associations, provided, again, that those who restore the same without compensation, as mentioned above, may seek to indemnify their losses from our generosity.

---

15. The edict of Galerius.

In all these matters you should expend every possible effort in behalf of the aforesaid corporation of the Christians so that our command may be implemented with all speed, in order that here also our kindness may promote the common public tranquility. In this way, as mentioned earlier, the divine care for us that we have known on many prior occasions will remain with us permanently. And in order that our generosity and enactment may be known to all, what we have written should be announced by your order, published everywhere, and brought to the attention of all, so that the enactment incorporating our generosity may escape the notice of no one.

COPY OF ANOTHER IMPERIAL STATUTE, SHOWING
THAT THE FAVOR WAS GRANTED ONLY
TO THE CATHOLIC CHURCH

Greetings, our most honored Anulinus.[16] In keeping with our benevolence, we desire that whatever belongs by right to another should not only suffer no harm but even be restored. Therefore it is our wish that when you receive this letter you will arrange that if any of the property that belonged to the catholic church of the Christians in any city or place is now in the possession either of citizens or any others, that these should be restored immediately to these same churches, inasmuch as we have determined that whatever belonged to these same churches should rightfully be restored to them. Since, therefore, Your Loyalty notes that the intention of this our command is perfectly clear, you must earnestly see to it that everything—gardens, buildings, or whatever—that rightfully belonged to these same churches be restored to them as soon as possible, so that we may learn of your most careful compliance with this our command. Farewell, most honored and esteemed Anulinus.

COPY OF AN IMPERIAL LETTER ORDERING A SYNOD
OF BISHOPS TO BE HELD AT ROME FOR UNITY
AND CONCORD OF THE CHURCHES

313   Constantine Augustus to Miltiades, Bishop of Rome, and to Mark. In view of the numerous documents sent to me by Anulinus, the illustri-

---

16. Proconsul of Africa, who had to deal with the Donatist controversy. The "catholic church" in this document refers to the universal or mainstream Christian church as opposed to such schismatics as the Donatists, who taught that the rites of the church depended for their efficacy on the officiant.

ous Proconsul of Africa, in which it appears that Caecilian, Bishop of Carthage, is accused on many accounts by some of his colleagues in Africa,[17] I deem it a very serious matter that in those provinces that divine providence has entrusted to My Dedication and where there is a great number of people, the multitude should be found taking the wrong course in splitting up, as it were, and the bishops divided among themselves. It seemed good to me that Caecilian himself, with ten bishops who seem to be accusing him and ten others whom he thinks necessary for his case, should set sail for Rome, where, in the presence of yourselves and your colleagues Reticius, Maternus, and Marinus, whom I have directed to hasten to Rome for this purpose, he may be granted a hearing through such a procedure as you think accords with the most sacred law. So that you may have complete information on all these matters, I have attached to my letter copies of the reports Anulinus sent to me and have dispatched them to your colleagues above. When you have read them, Your Constancy will decide how the aforementioned case can most carefully be investigated to reach a just verdict, for, as Your Diligence is well aware, my respect for the lawful catholic church is so great that I want no schism or division of any kind anywhere. May the divinity of the great God keep you safe for many years, most honored sirs.

COPY OF AN IMPERIAL LETTER ORDERING
A SECOND SYNOD TO BE HELD TO HEAL
ALL DIVISIONS AMONG THE BISHOPS

Constantine Augustus to Chrestus, Bishop of Syracuse. When on a former occasion base and perverse motives led some to create divisions regarding the worship of the holy and heavenly Power and the catholic religion, I wished to cut short such dissensions among them. I gave orders that certain bishops should be sent from Gaul, that the opposing parties who were quarreling stubbornly should be summoned from Africa, and that the Bishop of Rome be present also. The issue might then receive a fair resolution through their careful examination of every particular. As it happens, however, some have forgotten both their own salvation and the reverence they owe their

314

---

17. The Donatists in Africa claimed that Caecilian had been consecrated by Felix, a bishop who had become a *traditor* in the Diocletianic persecution, that is, one who had surrendered the Scriptures to persecutors. Deeming Caecilian's consecration invalid, they appointed Majorinus, another bishop, in his place, who was soon succeeded by Donatus, from whom the Donatist schism is named.

most holy religion and have not ceased even now fostering their private hostilities. They refuse to accept the judgment already reached, claiming that only a few persons offered their views and opinions or that they were in a great hurry to pass judgment without first having investigated all matters thoroughly. Consequently, the very people who ought to be unified in fraternal concord are separated from each other in a disgraceful, no, abominable manner, providing those who are strangers to this most holy religion a pretext for scoffing. I was therefore bound to arrange that what should have ended by voluntary agreement after the judgment already passed might now, if possible, be settled once and for all in the presence of many persons.

Inasmuch, therefore, as we have ordered a great many bishops from numerous places to assemble at Arles by the Kalends [first] of August, we thought it good to write to you also. You should obtain from the illustrious Latronian, the *corrector*[18] of Sicily, a public carriage, and add to your company two others with second rank [presbyters] of your choice. Take three servants along who will be able to look after you on the journey, and be present at the place and date named above. Both by Your Constancy and the united wisdom of others assembled, this quarrel too—disgracefully and miserably prolonged—may, however belatedly, be replaced by genuine religion, faith, and fraternal concord when all has been heard, also by those who are at variance with each other, whom we have also commanded to be present. May God Almighty keep you in good health for many years.

COPY OF AN IMPERIAL LETTER GIVING
GRANTS OF MONEY TO THE CHURCHES

6. Constantine Augustus to Caecilian, Bishop of Carthage. Since it has been our pleasure that in all provinces—namely, Africa, Numidia, and Mauretania—certain specified ministers of the legal and most holy catholic religion should receive some contribution for expenses, I have sent a letter to Ursus, the most eminent finance officer of Africa, directing that he pay three thousand *folles*[19] to Your Constancy. When you have received this sum, you will arrange that it is distributed among all the above-named persons according to the

---

18. Governors of certain fourth-century provinces had the title *konrektoros* or corrector.

19. The *follis* was a double denarius.

schedule sent you by Hosius.[20] If later on you find that you lack anything to fulfill my intentions regarding them, do not hesitate to ask
Heraclides our procurator for whatever you need. When he was here
I gave him orders that if Your Constancy should ask any money from
him, he was to hand it over without question.

And since I have learned that certain people of unstable mentality
are eager to lead the laity of the most holy catholic church astray by foul
inducements, know that when they were here, I instructed Anulinus, the
proconsul, and also Patricius, the vicar of the perfects,[21] that especially
in this matter they are not to overlook such incidents. Therefore, if
you observe any such men persisting in this madness, you must not
hesitate to bring this matter before the aforementioned judges so
that, as I instructed them when they were here, they may turn these
people from their error. May the divinity of the great God keep you
safe for many years.

COPY OF AN IMPERIAL LETTER ORDERING THAT
THE HEADS OF THE CHURCHES BE EXEMPTED
FROM ALL PUBLIC DUTIES

7. Greetings, our most honored Anulinus. Many facts prove that the
vitiation of religious worship, by which the highest reverence for the
most holy, heavenly [Power] is preserved, has greatly endangered
public affairs and that its lawful restoration and preservation have
conferred the greatest good fortune on the Roman name and extraordinary prosperity on all humankind—blessings bestowed by divine grace.
It has therefore seemed good that those men who give their services
to conduct divine worship with due holiness and observance of this
law should receive the rewards of their own labors, most honored Anulinus. So I desire that those in your province in the catholic church,
over which Caecilian presides, who devote their services to this sacred
worship—those whom they customarily call clergymen—should once
and for all be kept entirely free from all public duties. Then they will
not be drawn away from the worship owed to the Divinity by any error
or sacrilege but instead strictly serve their own law unencumbered.
In so rendering total service to the Deity, they will clearly confer

---

20. Hosius was Bishop of Cordova in Spain and the most influential theological
adviser to Constantine.

21. At this time the vicar governed a group of provinces and the prefect governed
one of the four major administrative divisions of the empire. The vicar of Africa was
under the prefect of Italy.

immense benefit on the affairs of state. Farewell, our most honored and esteemed Anulinus.

The Folly and Fate of Licinius

8. Such, then, was the divine and heavenly grace accorded us by our Savior's appearance, and so great was the abundance of good things that peace provided for all humankind. And so our happiness was celebrated with joyous festivities. But the envy that hates what is good, the demon who loves what is evil, could not stand the sight, and the fate of the tyrants mentioned above [Maxentius and Maximin] was not enough to strike sense into ·Licinius. He had been honored with emperorship at a time of prosperity, second to the great Constantine, and had become related through marriage to this most exalted person. Yet he abandoned the example of good men and imitated the wicked folly of impious tyrants, preferring to follow those whose end he had seen with his own eyes rather than remain in friendship and esteem with his superior. Filled with envy of the common benefactor, he waged an unholy and total war against him, paying no respect to the laws of nature, sworn treaties, ties of blood, or pledges. For Constantine, all-gracious emperor that he was, had given him true tokens of good will, not begrudging him kinship with himself or refusing him a brilliant union with his sister. He, rather, thought him worthy to share in his ancestral nobility and the imperial blood he had inherited, conferring on him, as a brother-in-law and joint emperor, a share in sovereign power and equal rule over lands under Roman control.

317–324   Licinius, however, behaved in the exact opposite: day by day he devised schemes against his superior, inventing plan after plan to reward his benefactor with evil. At first he tried to conceal his plots and posed as a friend, hoping to achieve his goal through treachery and deceit. But God became Constantine's Friend, Protector, and Guardian, who exposed the intrigues devised in secret and frustrated them—such power has the great weapon of godliness to fend off the enemy and safeguard its own. So protected, our emperor, most beloved by God, eluded the plots of this notorious schemer. When he saw that his clandestine intrigue was not going according to plan—God revealed every trick and ruse to his beloved emperor—he made war openly, unable to conceal himself any longer. In deciding to fight Constantine, he was already rushing into battle also with the God of the universe, whom he knew [his opponent] worshiped. So he planned an attack, quietly and discreetly at first, against his godly subjects, though they had never shown any disloyalty to his rule. He did this because an inborn corruption had afflicted him with a terrible blindness that neither kept before his eyes the memory of those who had persecuted Christians before him nor of those whom he himself had destroyed for their evil deeds. Turning from the path of prudence and reason, he became totally mad and determined to make war on God himself, as Constantine's Protector, instead of on him who was protected.

First, he dismissed every Christian from his household, depriving himself, poor fool, of the prayers to God in his behalf that their fathers had taught them to make for everyone. Next, he ordered that, city by city, soldiers be singled out and stripped of their rank if they failed to sacrifice to demons.

But these were petty when compared with more drastic measures. To mention one by one the deeds of this hater of God is hardly necessary, or how illegal laws were devised by this most lawless of men. He actually decreed that no one should treat humanely those suffering in prison by giving them food or take pity on those in chains who were starving to death. No one was to show any kindness, even if prompted by a natural inclination to sympathize with neighbors.

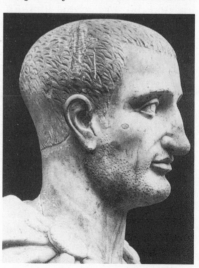

Of his laws, one was patently shameless and cruelest of all in its subversion of every civilized feeling: it specified that those who showed pity should suffer the same punishment as those whom they pitied, and those who provided humane assistance should be chained and imprisoned to share the punishment of those enduring it. Such were the ordinances of Licinius.

Need I list his innovations regarding marriage or his radical changes concerning those who departed this life? He dared to rescind the ancient and well-founded Roman laws,

Licinius, Constantine's final opponent in the East (*Museo Torlonia, Rome*).

replacing them with some that were barbarous, uncivilized, and truly illegal. There were countless assessments to the detriment of his subject peoples, many demands of gold and silver, revaluations of land, and the gain from fines imposed on rurals no longer living but long since departed. Then there were the innocents that this hater of humankind banished and the arrests of noble, esteemed men, whose wedded wives he separated and handed over to some vile members of his household for insult and humiliation. As for the many married women and unmarried girls with whom this drunken old dotard satisfied his limitless lust, why should I expand on these things when his final outrages make those earlier seem trivial and negligible?

In the ultimate stage of his madness he took action against the bishops, assuming their opposition to his deeds as servants of the supreme God. He started plotting against them, not openly at first for fear of his superior but, again, with secret cunning: conspiring with the governors, he put the most highly esteemed of these to death. The way they were murdered was grotesque and unheard of, and what was done at Amasea and the other cities of Pontus surpassed every excess of cruelty. Some of the churches there were again torn down from top to bottom, while others were locked up to prevent any of the worshipers from meeting and giving God the service due him. He did not think their prayers were offered on his behalf—the reasoning of a guilty conscience—but that all our supplications were for the emperor whom God loved. This is why he vented his wrath on us. Convinced that they were doing what the wretch wanted, sycophants among the governors arrested entirely innocent bishops as if they were criminals and executed them, without pretext, like murderers. Some suffered an even more novel form of death: their bodies were cut into many pieces by a sword, and then, after this brutal, horrifying spectacle, they were thrown into the depths of the sea as fish food. This caused the men of God to flee again, and once more the fields, deserts, valleys, and mountains welcomed the servants of Christ.

When the impious fellow had succeeded also in these measures, he then planned to renew a general persecution against all. He had the power to do this, and nothing prevented his carrying it out—had not God, the Champion of his souls, quickly foreseen the impending danger. Out of the dark and murky night, He caused a great light and savior for them all to shine forth, his uplifted arm leading his servant Constantine to that spot. **9.** To him, as the worthy fruit of his devotion, God conferred from heaven above the trophies of victory over the wicked. But the guilty one he struck down, with all his advisers and friends, prone beneath the feet of Constantine.

Constantine Victorious

When Licinius had carried his madness to the limits, the emperor, friend of God, would endure this no longer. With sound reason and tempering the demands of justice with humanity, he determined to save those savaged by the tyrant and hurried to rescue the bulk of the human race by putting a few ravagers out of the way. Previously, when his humanity alone had shown Licinius undeserved mercy, the man did not improve: he did not abandon his wickedness but accelerated his mad rage against his subjects, leaving his victims bereft of any hope for rescue from a wild beast tyrannizing over them.

Therefore, blending a love of goodness with a hatred of evil, the champion of the good set out with that most humane prince, his son Crispus,[22] holding out a hand of rescue to all who were perishing. Then, with God the supreme King and God's Son the Savior of all as Guide and Ally, father and son divided their forces against the haters of God on every side and easily won the vic- 324 tory, God facilitating all in accord with his purpose.[23] Suddenly, those who yesterday had been breathing threats and death were no more: even their names were forgotten, while their portraits and honors were appropriately disgraced. What Licinius had seen with his own eyes happen to the wicked tyrants before him he endured himself, neither corrected nor enlightened by the blows that fell on his neighbors. He followed the same path of iniquity as they and deserved to topple off the same precipice.

---

22. Crispus was the eldest son of Constantine and was given the title *Caesar* in 317. In the campaign against Licinius he won a naval victory at the Hellespont in 324. Two years later, however, he was executed. Since his stepmother, Fausta, was also executed soon afterward, rumors circulated that she had accused Crispus before Constantine of attempted seduction, only to be herself denounced by Helena, mother of Constantine. With Eusebius portraying Crispus so favorably in this passage, Book 10 and the final version of the *Church History* must be dated before 326 and was most probably published c. 324–325.

23. Licinius was defeated in July 324 at Adrianople and again at Chrysopolis (Üsküdar, Turkey) in September. After his surrender he was exiled to Thessalonica and was executed in 325 for attempted rebellion.

Head of Constantine. Only the face is ancient (*Louvre, Paris*).

His enemy prostrate, the mighty victor Constantine, outstanding in every virtue godliness confers, as well as his son Crispus, a ruler most dear to God and like his father in every way, won back their own eastern provinces and combined the Roman Empire into a single whole, as in former days, bringing it all under their peaceful rule, from the rising sun to the farthest dusk, in a wide circle from north to south. People now lost all fear of their former oppressors and celebrated brilliant festivals—light was everywhere—and men who once were dejected greeted each other with smiling faces and sparkling eyes. With dance and song in city and country alike, they gave honor first to the supreme God, as they had been instructed, and then to the pious emperor and his sons, dear to God. Old troubles were forgotten, all impiety vanished; the good things present were enjoyed, those yet to come anticipated. Everywhere the victorious emperor published humane ordinances and laws that reflected liberality and true piety. And so all tyranny was eradicated, and the kingdom that was theirs was preserved, secure and undisputed, for Constantine and his sons alone. They, having first cleansed the world of hatred to God and knowing all the good He had conferred on them, showed their love of virtue and of God, their devotion and gratitude to the Almighty, by their actions for all to see.

EUSEBIUS AND CONSTANTINE

Eusebius is regularly roasted for his triumphalism and the adulation that he lavishes on Constantine. Beyond all debate, such flowery epithets as "the emperor beloved by God" become cloying to the contemporary reader. Eusebius's *Life of Constantine*, the biographical panegyric that he published after the emperor's death in 337, will continue in the same vein. Rather than add to the chorus of criticism, one would do well to stand in Eusebius's sandals instead. Not only did the man write of persecutions in times yore, but also the final books of his *Church History* reflect the torments and repressions against Christians that he witnessed and experienced in his own imprisonment. Victims included the one man he apparently valued even above Origen or Constantine: his beloved teacher in Caesarea, Pamphilus. When someone finally put an end to all this horror—outrageous persecutions that kept reappearing in the East after several edicts of toleration—it is hardly surprising that Eusebius would be inclined to surround Constantine with a nimbus of awe.

Constantine himself, the first fully attested Christian emperor, had a complex personality that included some negative traits not cited by Eusebius. These would be enlarged upon by detractors in later generations, beginning with his nephew Julian the Apostate, emperor from 361 to 363, who tried unsuccessfully to restore Roman paganism. His snide insinuations about his uncle were enlarged by Eunapius of Sardis into assigning Constantine blame for the decline of the Roman Empire—long before Edward Gibbon. Around 500, the pagan Byzantine historian Zosimus used Eunapius to warp Constantine's portrait even further in this respect, and his caricature received some support at the time of the Renaissance.

More recently, some historians, like Jacob Burckhardt in the last century, disputed Constantine's conversion, claiming that his actions in behalf of Christianity were done on the basis of cold political calculation rather than conscientious conviction, a strategy to use the church for partisan support to serve his personal ambitions. They point to the title Constantine retained as *pontifex maximus* of Roman paganism, the *Sol Invictus* ("Unconquered Sun") emblem on his coinage, his public subsidies to the cults of ancient paganism at Rome, the executions in his own household, and the delay in his baptism until his deathbed.

Most historians, however, conclude that Constantine's conversion was genuine. As for the negative evidence cited, Constantine felt that he had to be emperor for *all* Roman citizens, including the pagan majority, and he put no stock in his role as high priest. Pagan emblems on his coinage ceased after several years. The executions of his son Crispus and the (probably assisted) suicide of his wife, Fausta, are mysterious tragedies that have never been solved, though the latter's false accusation of the former seems to have been involved. That Constantine's personal and domestic life did not always reflect Christian ideals is obvious, but not more so than we might expect from a ruler involved in a transition from paganism to Christianity. And delaying one's baptism until the end of life in order to purge all previous sins was a convention at that time, however mistaken theologically.

The evidence that Constantine was sincere in his Christianity is overwhelming. It should first be remembered that in the ancient world nearly everyone practiced a religion of some sort: there was hardly a secularist alternative to religion, as there is today. If pagan polytheism was failing the Roman state—and it surely was, in view of the civil upheavals and decline of the empire—Christian monotheism became a superior religious substitute for many Romans in the fourth century, not only for Constantine.

Once he became emperor, Constantine's favors in behalf of Christianity are too numerous for listing here beyond several highlights, some of which have been obvious from Eusebius's text. Constantine gave the Christian clergy dramatic legal advantages, immunities, and exemptions in the Roman state, while bishops regularly dined at his table and accompanied his entourages. He not only restored property confiscated from the churches, but also built or rebuilt Christian basilicas in both West and East, including those on the Mount of Olives and Bethlehem (prompted by his mother, Helena), as well as the Church of the Holy Sepulcher in Jerusalem. He supported Christian charities, prescribed Sunday as a holy day, and strengthened the institution of marriage, while condemning pagan divination, crucifixion, and gladiatorial combat. Above all, he remained an active lay Christian for the rest of his life, as his correspondence and activities more than demonstrate. He called the Council of Arles into being to settle the Donatist controversy in 314 and even presided at the celebrated Council of Nicea in 325, which dealt with the Arian heresy and formulated the Nicene Creed.

He warned colleague emperors not to persecute Christians and claimed that his campaigns against these emperors was as a champion of the church to stop such persecution, which was more than pretext. He consecrated his new city on the Bosporus, Nova Roma (New Rome, later named Constantinople), to "the God of the Martyrs" and erected splendid churches there. Even his foreign policy on the northern and eastern frontiers of the empire reflected Christian principles, and he joked with bishops at a dinner after the Council of Nicea that he too was a bishop "of those outside the church." At the close of his masterful study, Timothy D. Barnes summarizes Constantine's career:

> After 312 Constantine considered that his main duty as emperor was to inculcate virtue in his subjects and to persuade them to worship God. . . . With all his faults and despite an intense ambition for personal power, he nevertheless believed sincerely that God had given him a special mission to convert the Roman Empire to Christianity.[24]

Eusebius never intended to provide a balanced, critical portrait of Constantine—in the convention of the day he wrote a panegyric instead—and so the skepticism of a Burckhardt may have served a worthy purpose as a necessary counterpoise. Yet, Eusebius's representation of Constantine the Christian is much truer than Burckhardt's, and his is the image that would capture the future, as Christian kings and emperors henceforth would measure their success against that of Constantine.

Thus Eusebius's *Church History* closes on a note of triumph with the proverbial happy ending. To dismiss the first church historian as a mere triumphalist, however, would betray callous insensitivity to what Christians endured under persecution in the ancient world. Survivors of that horror, who survived because of Constantine, might even have faulted Eusebius for not being kind enough to that emperor. In any case, Eusebius saw a plan of divine destiny in it all—this saga from Christ to Constantine—and readers in subsequent centuries caught his vision also. Otherwise the *Church History* would never have survived word for word through many manuscript recopyings, as it clearly did—before the age of printing.

---

24. Timothy D. Barnes, *Constantine and Eusebius* (Cambridge, Mass., and London: Harvard University Press, 1981), 275.

APPENDIX 1

EUSEBIUS'S CITATION
OF JOSEPHUS ON JESUS

In 1.11 of his *Church History* Eusebius quotes the famous passage from Josephus's *Antiquities* (18.63) that mentions Jesus, the longest non-Christian reference to him in the literature of the first century A.D. For comparison purposes, the passage is again reproduced here, with several extraordinary phrases that I have italicized:

> About this time lived Jesus, a wise man, *if indeed one ought to call him a man.* For he was the achiever of extraordinary deeds and was a teacher of those who accept the truth gladly. He won over many Jews and many of the Greeks. *He was the Messiah.* When he was indicted by the principal men among us and Pilate condemned him to be crucified, those who had come to love him originally did not cease to do so; for *he appeared to them on the third day restored to life,* as the prophets of the Deity had foretold these and countless other *marvelous things* about him. And the tribe of the Christians, so named after him, has not disappeared to this day.

In *Antiquities* 20.200, Josephus makes a second reference to Jesus in reporting the death of his half brother James, which is also cited by Eusebius in 2.23. Because Josephus remained a Jew who did not convert to Christianity, the preceding passage has provoked much scholarly literature, especially in view of the italicized phrases.

Scholars fall into three camps regarding this celebrated reference:

1. It is entirely authentic, occurring as it does in the middle of Josephus's description of Pilate's administration and in all the manuscripts of Josephus.
2. It is entirely a Christian forgery, since Origen asserted that Josephus never converted.
3. It contains Christian interpolations in what was Josephus's authentic report on Jesus.

The first option would seem hopeless: no Jew could have claimed Jesus as the Messiah who rose from the dead without having converted to Christianity. The second is hardly tenable, since the passage occurs in all Greek manuscripts of Josephus and the undisputed reference to Jesus in 20.200 would doubtless have supplied more identifying material if this were the first mention of Jesus. Accordingly, a large majority of scholars today favor the third option, that the passage has been interpolated.

Jesus is portrayed as a "wise man," *sophos aner* in Greek, a phrase not used by Christians but employed by Josephus for such Old Testament figures as David and Solomon. Furthermore, the claim that Jesus won over "many of the Greeks" is not paralleled in the New Testament and thus is hardly a Christian addendum but rather something Josephus would have noted in his own day. And there is new evidence that the italicized phrases were indeed Christian interpolations.

In 1972, Professor Schlomo Pines of the Hebrew University in Jerusalem announced his discovery of an Arabic manuscript of Josephus written by the tenth-century Melkite historian Agapius, in which the passage in question translates as follows:

> At this time there was a wise man called Jesus, and his conduct was good, and he was known to be virtuous. Many people among the Jews and the other nations became his disciples. Pilate condemned him to be crucified and to die. But those who had become his disciples did not abandon his discipleship. They reported that he had appeared to them three days after his crucifixion and that he was alive. Accordingly, he was perhaps the Messiah, concerning whom the prophets have reported wonders. And the tribe of the Christians, so named after him, has not disappeared to this day.[1]

Clearly this version of the passage is expressed in a manner appropriate to a non-Christian Jew, and it corresponds almost precisely to previous scholarly projections of what Josephus actually wrote.

Accordingly, the interpolations in Josephus's text on Jesus must have come early, for Eusebius quotes the standard or

---

1. While the final sentence is not in Agapius, Pines justifiably concludes that it was in the original Josephan text. See Schlomo Pines, *An Arabic Version of the* Testimonium Flavianum *and Its Implications* (Jerusalem: Israel Academy of Sciences and Humanities, 1971).

traditional version when he published the first seven books of his *Church History,* probably before 300. That he did not detect the Christian interpolations, however, underscores the fact that he was not a critical historian. Since, however, he did not expand on the apologetic potential in this passage, using it only against forgeries of his own day, he may have had some qualms about its authenticity.

Appendix 2

THE SUCCESSIONS OF EMPERORS AND BISHOPS

(Dates are the years of accession of the emperors. Their reigns terminated at the next date following. Some of the earlier churchmen were not bishops in the later sense.)

Roman Emperors	Bishops of Jerusalem	of Antioch	of Alexandria	of Rome
27 B.C. Augustus				
A.D. 14 Tiberius				
37 Gaius Caligula				
41 Claudius				
	James			
54 Nero		Peter		
			Mark	
	Symeon	Evodius	Annianus	Peter?
68 Galba				Linus
69 Otho, Vitellius Vespasian				
79 Titus				Anencletus
81 Domitian			Abilius	
				Clement
		Ignatius		
96 Nerva				
98 Trajan			Cerdo	

Roman Emperors	Bishops of Jerusalem	of Antioch	of Alexandria	of Rome
	Justus I			Evarestus
	Zacchaecus			
	Tobias			
	Benjamin	Hero	Primus	Alexander
	John			
117 Hadrian				
	Matthias			Xystus
	Phillip		Justus	
	Seneca			
	Justus II			
	Levi			
	Ephres			Telesphorus
	Joseph		Eumenes	
	Judas			
	Mark	Cornelius		
138 Antoninus Pius				Hyginus
	Cassian			Pius
	Publius		Mark II	
	Maximus I			
	Julian I	Eros		
	Gaius I			
	Symmachus			
	Gaius II			
			Celadion	Anicetus
161 Marcus Aurelius	Julian II	Theophilus		
	Capito			
	Maximus II			Soter

Roman Emperors	Bishops of Jerusalem	of Antioch	of Alexandria	of Rome
	Antoninus		Agrippinus	
	Valens			
	Dolichian			Eleutherus
180 Commodus	Narcissus			
	Dius	Maximin	Julian	
	Germanion			Victor
	Gordius			
		Serapion		
193 Pertinax				
			Demetrius	
193 Septimius Severus				
		Asclepiades		Zephyrinus
211 Caracalla	Alexander			
217 Macrinus				
218 Elagabalus				Callustus
222 Alexander Severus				Urban
		Philetus		
		Zebennus	Heraclas	Pontian
235 Maximinus Thracian				
				Anteros
238 Gordian				Fabian
		Babylas		
244 Philip				
			Dionysius	
249 Decius				Cornelius
	Mazbanes	Fabius		

Roman Emperors	Bishops of Jerusalem	of Antioch	of Alexandria	of Rome
251 Gallus		Demetrian		
253 Valerian + Gallienus				Lucius
				Stephen
	Hymenaeus	Paul of Samosata		Xystus II
				Dionysius
260 Gallienus alone				
			Maximus	
268 Claudius II		Domnus		Felix
270 Aurelian				
				Eutychian
276 Probus	Zabdas			
		Timaeus		
282 Carus			Theonas	
	Hermo			Gaius
284 Diocletian		Cyril		
286+ Maximian				
				Marcellinus
			Peter	
305 Galerius, Constantius Chlorus		Tyrannus		
307 Galerius, Licinius, Constantine, Masimin, Maxentius				
311 Death of Galerius				

Roman Emperors	Bishops of Jerusalem	of Antioch	of Alexandria	of Rome
312 Death of Maxentius				
313 Death of Maximin				
324 Death of Licinius				
337 Death of Constantine				

BIBLIOGRAPHY

A. Writings by Eusebius

The works of Eusebius appear, often in a series, in many of the major Western languages. Individual titles and editions of the original Greek texts are listed in the introduction, as are important English translations of the *Church History* (McGiffert, Lake and Oulton in Loeb, and Williamson). As indicated, the translation in this book was based on the Greek text edited by Eduard Schwartz in *Die Griechischen christlichen Schriftsteller der ersten Jahrhunderte* (Leipzig: Hinrichs'sche Buchhandlung, 1897).

English translations of the *Church History* have also been published by Augsburg, Baker, Barnes & Noble, Bell, Catholic University of America, Eerdmans, Harvard University Press and Heinemann (Loeb), Penguin, SPCK, and Kregel. Other translations appear under such titles as *Histoire ecclesiastique* (French), *Die Kirchengeschichte* (German), *Storia della chiesa* (Italian), and *Kirkehistorie* (Danish). These merely represent other languages into which Eusebius has been translated.

B. Works about Eusebius

The following are books and monographs on Eusebius published in the twentieth century. Numerous articles on aspects of Eusebius's life and writings have also appeared in periodicals, collections, series, and *Festschriften*. Many unpublished doctoral dissertations have also examined various themes in Eusebius's works.

Attridge, Harold W., and Gohei Hata, eds. *Eusebius, Christianity, and Judaism*. Detroit: Wayne State University Press, 1992.
Barnes, Timothy D. *Constantine and Eusebius*. Cambridge, Mass., and London: Harvard University Press, 1981.
Bauer, A. *Beiträge zu Eusebios und den byzantinischen Chronographen. Sitzungsberichte der kaiserlichen Akademie der Wissenschaften in Wien*. 162.3. Vienna: 1909.

Berkhof, Hendrikus. *Die Theologie des Eusebius von Caesarea.* Amsterdam: Uitgeversmaatschappij Holland, 1939.

Chesnut, Glenn F. *The First Christian Histories: Eusebius, Socrates, Sozomen, Theodoret, and Evagrius.* Paris: Beauchesne, 1977.

Cuneo, Bernard H. *The Lord's Command to Baptize: An Historico-critical Investigation with Special Reference to the Works of Eusebius of Caesarea.* Washington, D.C.: Catholic University of America Press, 1923.

Daniele, Ireneo. *I documenti Costantiniani della "Vita Constantini" di Eusebio di Cesarea.* Rome: Gregorian University, 1938.

Dempf, Alois. *Eusebios als Historiker.* Munich: Bayerische Akademie der Wissenschaften, 1964.

Des Places, Edouard. *Eusèbe de Césarée Commentateur: Platonisme et Ecriture Sainte.* Paris: Beauchesne, 1982.

Doergens, Heinrich. *Eusebius von Caesarea als Darsteller der griechischen Religion.* Paderborn: Schoningh, 1922.

——. *Eusebius von Caesarea als Darsteller der phonizishen Religion.* Paderborn: Schoningh, 1915.

Drake, Harold A. *In Praise of Constantine: A Historical Study and New Translation of Eusebius' Tricennial Orations.* Berkeley: University of California Press, 1976.

Farina, Raffaele. *L'impero e l'imperatore Cristiano in Eusebio di Cesarea. La prima teologia politica del Cristianesimo.* Zürich: Pas Verlag, 1966.

Foakes-Jackson, F. J. *Eusebius Pamphili, Bishop of Caesarea in Palestine and First Christian Historian: A Study of the Man and His Writings.* Cambridge: W. Heffer & Sons, 1933.

Fritze, E. *Beiträge zur sprachlich-stilistischen Würdigung des Eusebios.* Leipzig: Borna, 1910.

Godecke, Monika. *Geschichte als Mythos: Eusebs "Kirchengeschichte."* Frankfurt and New York: Peter Lang, 1987.

Grant, Robert M. *Eusebius as Church Historian.* Oxford: Clarendon, 1980.

Gressman, Hugo. *Studien zu Eusebs Theophanie.* Leipzig: Hinrichs, 1903.

Hardwick, Michael E. *Josephus as an Historical Source in Patristic Literature Through Eusebius.* Atlanta: Scholars Press, 1989.

Heikel, Ivar A. *Kritische Beiträge zu den Constantin-Schriften des Eusebius.* Leipzig: Hinrichs, 1911.

Helm, Rudolf. *Eusebius' Chronik und ihre Tabellenform*. Berlin: de Gruyter, 1924.

Henry, Paul. *Recherches sur la "Préparation Évangelique" d'Eusèbe et l'édition perdue des oeuvres de Plotin publiée par Eustochius*. Paris: Leroux, 1935.

Keller, E. *Eusèbe, historien des persécutions*. Geneva and Paris: 1912.

Laqueur, Richard A. *Eusebius als Historiker seiner Zeit*. Berlin: de Gruyter, 1929.

Lawlor, Hugh J. *Eusebiana: Essays on the Ecclesiastical History of Eusebius, Bishop of Caesarea*. Oxford: Clarendon, 1912.

Luibheid, Colm. *Eusebius of Caesarea and the Arian Crisis*. Dublin: Irish Academic Press, 1978.

Lyman, J. Rebecca. *Christology and Cosmology: Models of Divine Activity in Origen, Eusebius, and Athanasius*. New York: Oxford University Press, 1993.

McGiffert, A. C. "The Life and Writings of Eusebius of Caesarea." In P. Schaff and H. Wace, eds., *The Nicene and Post-Nicene Fathers*. Series 2, vol. 1, Eusebius, 3–72, plus notes. 1890. Reprint, Grand Rapids: Eerdmans, 1961.

Mosshammer, Alden A. *The Chronicle of Eusebius and Greek Chronographic Tradition*. Lewisburg, Penn.: Bucknell University Press, 1979.

Nordenfalk, C. *Die spätantiken Kanontafeln: Kunstgeschichtliche Studien über die eusebianische Evangelien-Konkordanz in den vier ersten Jahrhunderten ihrer Geschicht*. Göteborg: 1938.

Sant, Carmel. *The Old Testament Interpretation of Eusebius of Caesarea: The Manifold Sense of Holy Scripture*. Malta: Royal University of Malta, 1967.

Schoene, Alfred K. I. *Die Weltchronik des Eusebius in ihrer Bearbeitung durch Hieronymus*. Berlin: Weidmann, 1900.

Schwartz, E. "Eusebios von Caesarea." In *Realencyclopädie der classischen Altertumswissenschaft* 6, ed. F. Pauly and G. Wissowa. Stuttgart: 1909.

Sirinelli, Jean. *Les vues historiques d'Eusèbe de Césarée durant la période prénicéenne*. Dakar: University of Dakar, 1961.

Stevenson, James. *Studies in Eusebius*. Cambridge: Cambridge University Press, 1929.

Wallace-Hadrill, D. S. *Eusebius of Caesarea*. London: A. R. Mowbray, 1960; Westminster, Md.: Canterbury, 1961.

Weber, Anton. *APXH: Ein Beitrag zur Christologie des Eusebius von Caesarea*. Munich: Neue Stadt, 1965.

Winkelmann, Friedhelm. *Eusebius von Kaisareia: der Vater der Kirchengeschichte*. Berlin: Verlags-Anstalt Union, 1991.

———. *Die Textbezeugung der Vita Constantini des Eusebius von Caesarea*. Berlin: Akademie Verlag, 1962.

INDEX OF PERSONS

A

Abdus, 48

Abgar Uchama, 45–48, 49–50, 53

Abilius of Alexandria, 92, 96

Abraham, 23–25, 31–32

Acacius, 11

Achaeus, judge, 237

Achillas, 254

Achion, 37

Adamantius (Origen), 199

Adauctus, 269

Aelian, 247

Aelius Hadrian, 119, 121, 126

Aelius Publius Julius, Bishop of Debeltum, 175

Aelius Spartianus, 223

Aemilianus, 225, 232–34, 256

Aemilius Frontinus, 174

Africanus, Julius, 34, 35, 38, 49, 209

Agabus, 56, 59, 172

Agapius, 253, 337, 337n

Agathonice, 135

Agrippa Castor, 121

Agrippa, Herod, I. See Herod Agrippa I

Agrippa, Herod, II. See Herod Agrippa II

Agrippina, 79

Agrippinus, 138, 166

Albinus, 73, 89

Alburnus, idol, 55

Alce, 134

Alcibiades, anti-Montanist. See Miltiades, anti-Montanist

Alcibiades, martyr, 160

Alcibiades, Montanist, 160, 160n. 7

Alexander of Eumenia, 172

Alexander Severus, 204–5, 208, 224

Alexander the Great, 192

Alexander, alabarch, 56

Alexander, Bishop of Alexandria, 11

Alexander, Bishop of Jerusalem, 16, 194, 196–99, 203–4, 207–8, 212, 222, 228

Alexander, Bishop of Rome, 118, 119

Alexander, martyrs named, 216, 235

Alexander, Montanist, 174

Alexander, physician martyr, 157–58

Alexas, 40

Ambrose, 200, 205, 208

Ammes, 206

Ammia, 172

Ammon, Bishop of Bernice, 245

Ammon, martyr, 217

Ammonarion, 216

Ammonius Saccas, 202, 202nn. 12–13

Ammonius, martyr, 272

Ananias, courier, 45–46, 89

Ananus, son of Ananus (Annas), 41, 73

Anatolius, 250–53

Anchialus, 175

Andrew, 80, 101, 112

Anencletus, 92–93, 96, 162

Anicetus, 125–26, 128–29, 138–39, 162, 180–81

Annas (Ananus), 41–42, 42n

Annianus, 74, 92, 96

Anteros, 208

Anthimus, Bishop of Nicomedia, 263, 271

Antinous, 123, 123n. 7, 196n. 5

Antipas, Herod, 37, 40, 43, 56, 61

Antipater, 34, 37, 40

Antoninus (Caracalla), 194–95, 200, 203, 204, 224

Antoninus (Elagabalus), 204

Antoninus Pius, 62, 119n. 3, 123–24, 126, 128n, 129, 129nn. 20–21, 135, 144, 146, 148

Antoninus Verus (Marcus Aurelius), 137, 150, 161, 161n. 8, 166

Antony, Mark, 32, 32n, 37, 50, 50n

Anulinus, 324–25, 327–28

Apelles, 167–68

Apion, grammarian, 56, 90, 110

Apion, writer, 182

Apollinarius, Bishop of Hierapolis, 115, 139, 142, 145, 161, 161n. 11, 169

Apollo, 34, 37

Apollonia, marytr, 215

Apolloniades, 184

Apollonius, anti-Montanist writer, 173–75

Apollonius, martyr, 177–78

Apollophanes, 202

Aquila of Pontus, 165

Aquila, associate of Paul, 68, 78
Aquila, governor of Alexandria, 190–91
Aquila, presbyter, 235
Aquila, translator, 200, 200n. 9
Arabianus, 182
Archelaus, 34–35, 40
Aretas, 43
Aristarchus, 69
Aristides, apologist, 119, 119n. 3, 147–48
Aristides, correspondent of Africanus, 35, 209
Aristion, 112–13
Aristo of Pella, 121
Aristobulus II, high priest, 34, 37
Aristobulus, philosopher, 198, 252
Aristotle, 184
Arius, 11–12
Artaxerxes, 91, 165
Artemas. 249. See also Artemon
Artemisius, 89
Artemon, 182, 249n. 22
Asclepiades, Bishop of Antioch, 196, 204
Asclepiades, heretic, 184
Asclepiodotus, 183
Asterius Orbanus, 171
Astyrius, 236–37
Ater, 216
Athanasius, 255
Athenodore, 209, 236, 246
Attalus, 154, 156–58, 160
Atticus, Bishop of Synnada, 203
Atticus, consular, 106, 106n. 36
Augustine, 14, 223
Augustus, 10, 21, 32, 34, 40, 50–51, 50n, 78, 144
Aurelian, 225, 246, 249, 249n. 23, 257
Aurelius Quirinius, 175, 236

Autolycus, 142
Avircius Marcellus, 169

B

Babylas, Bishop of Antioch, 208, 212
Bacchius, 126
Bacchylides, 140
Bacchyllus, 178–79
Balbinus, 225
Bar-Cabbas, 122
Bar-Coph, 122
Bar-Kokhba, 62n. 16, 120–21, 123, 148
Bardesanes, 50, 146
Barnabas, 44, 53, 55–56, 59, 62, 101, 198, 244
Barsabas, 44, 112–13
Bartholomew, 166
Basilicus, 168
Basilides, Bishop in Pentapolis, 245
Basilides, heretic, 121–22
Basilides, martyr, 191, 193
Benjamin, 120
Bernice, 116
Beryllus, 204, 210
Besas, 216
Bezalel, 311, 314
Biblis, martyr, 153
Bishop of Ancyra, 12, 13
Bishop of Antioch, 110, 142, 175, 178, 196, 207, 220, 222, 250, 308n. 1
Bishop of Athens, 82, 140
Bishop of Bernice, 245
Bishop of Bostra, 210
Bishop of Caesarea, 11, 17, 208, 223, 246
Bishop of Carthage, 325, 326
Bishop of Corinth, 140, 178, 179
Bishop of Crete, 139
Bishop of Emesa, 271
Bishop of Ephesus, 105, 178
Bishop of Gaza, 271

Bishop of Gortyna, 142
Bishop of Hierapolis, 108, 175
Bishop of Jerusalem, 53, 82, 105–6, 222
Bishop of Laodicea, 235
Bishop of Lyons, 155, 162
Bishop of Nilopolis, 217
Bishop of Pentapolis, 245
Bishop of Rome, 75, 80, 82, 92–93, 105, 116, 119, 120, 125–26, 138, 146, 150, 160, 182, 204–5, 207–8, 230, 324–25
Bishop of Sardis, 128
Bishop of Smyrna, 108, 128, 148
Bishop of Syracuse, 325
Bishop of Tarsus, 222, 246
Bishop of Thmuis, 267
Bishop of Tyre, 271, 308n. 1, 310
Blandina, 154, 156, 158
Blastus, 169, 175
Bolanus, 247
Britannicus, 79

C

Caecilian, 325, 325n, 326–27
Caesar, the philosopher. See Marcus Aurelius
Caiaphas, 41–42, 41n. 17, 42n
Caligula, 56–58, 77–78, 224
Callirhoe, 39
Callistus, 204, 229n. 2
Camithus, 41
Candidus, 182
Capito, Bishop of Jerusalem, 167, 167n. 26
Caracalla, 194, 200, 203n. 14, 204, 224
Caricus, 175, 197
Carinus, 225, 249, 257
Carpocrates, 122, 163n. 14
Carpus, 135

Carus, 225, 249, 257
Cassian, 167, 198
Cassius, Bishop of Tyre, 181
Castor, 121–22
Celadion, 126, 138
Celerinus, 218
Celsus, anti-Christian writer, 211, 211n
Celsus, Bishop of Iconium, 203
Cephas, 44–45, 44n. 22
Cerdo, Bishop of Alexandria, 96, 118,
Cerdo, heretic in Rome, 125
Cerinthus, 102–3, 129, 243
Chaeremon, Bishop of Nilopolis, 217
Chaeremon, deacon of Alexandria, 232–33, 235
Chaeremon, Stoic, 202
Chlorus, Constantius. See Constantius Chlorus
Chrestus, Bishop of Syracuse, 325
Christ. See Jesus of Nazareth
Chrysophora, 142
Clarus of Ptolemais, 181
Claudius II, 225, 257
Claudius, emperor, 59, 59n. 10, 61, 62, 63, 64, 66n, 68, 78–79
Clemens, Flavius, 94, 94n. 20, 117
Clement of Alexandria, 44, 44n. 22, 52, 59, 64, 71, 73, 77, 96–97, 99, 103, 104, 104n. 32, 115, 143, 166–67, 182, 193, 197–99
Clement of Rome, 82, 93, 96, 108, 111, 115, 116–17, 139, 141–42, 162, 207
Cleobius, 139
Cleopatra, 32, 32n
Clopas, 72n. 25, 92, 105–6, 139

Colon, Bishop of Hermopolis, 221
Commodus, 144, 166, 171n, 177, 178, 182, 186, 193
Constantia Augusta, 15, 306
Constantine (the Great), 14, 15, 16, 225, 275, 284–85, 294–96, 298, 302, 322, 322n, 324–26, 328–32, 331n. 22; at Council of Nicea, 11–12; and battle of Milvian Bridge, 294–96, 304–7; conversion of, 333–35; and edict of toleration, 11, 304–5, 322–24; proclaimed emperor, 273–75, 281
Constantius Chlorus, 272–73, 273n. 10, 281, 284–85
Coracion, 242
Cornelius, Bishop of Antioch, 139
Cornelius, Bishop of Rome, 212, 218, 220, 222, 227, 256
Cornelius, centurion, 11, 55
Cornutus, 202
Crescens, companion of Paul, 82
Crescens, Cynic opponent of Justin, 135–36
Crispus, 16, 331, 331n. 22, 332, 334
Cronion (Eunus), 216
Cronius, 202
Culcianus, 301
Cyprian of Carthage, 218, 228, 256
Cyril, 250

D

Daia, Maximin, 40n. 14, 238n, 275, 276–77,

279n, 283, 285, 286, 304–6
Damas, Bishop of Magnesia, 109
Damnaeus, 73
Daniel, 26–27, 35, 145, 193, 206, 209
Decius, 212–13, 214, 225–26, 227, 227n, 234, 241, 261
Demetrian, 222, 228, 236, 245, 249
Demetrius, Bishop of Alexandria, 178, 188, 190, 194, 203, 208, 209, 236
Demetrius, Hellenistic Jew, 198
Demetrius, presbyter, 235
Didius Julianus, 186
Didymus, 234, 239
Diocletian, 11, 15, 249, 257, 262, 262n. 2, 272–73, 273n. 10, 281, 283–85, 296, 299
Dionysia, martyr, 216
Dionysius (Areopagite), 82
Dionysius, Bishop of Alexandria, 16, 103, 199, 211, 213–14, 213n. 24, 220–22, 227–31, 229n. 4, 232–35, 236, 238, 242, 242n, 245, 246, 247, 250, 254, 255
Dionysius, Bishop of Corinth, 75, 139, 140–42
Dionysius, Bishop of Rome, 230, 231, 245, 246–47, 249
Dioscorus, confessor, 216
Dioscorus, presbyter, 235
Dius, Bishop of Jerusalem, 196
Dius, martyr, 272
Dolichian, 167
Domitian, 92, 93–96, 105, 106, 117, 144, 164n. 19
Domitilla, Flavia, 94, 94n. 20, 117

Domitius, 234, 239

Domnus, Bishop of Antioch, 249, 250

Domnus, Bishop of Caesarea, 236

Domnus, lapsed from faith, 197

Donatus, 325n

Dorotheus, imperial servant, 259, 262–63

Dorotheus, presbyter of Antioch, 250

Dositheus, 139

Dystrus, 252

E

Elagabal, 224

Elagabalus, 204

Eleazar, 41, 86

Eleutherus, 126, 139, 150, 160, 162–63, 178

Elpistus, 140

Ephres, 120

Epimachus, 216

Eros, Bishop of Antioch, 139

Estha, wife of Matthan, 37

Euclid, 184

Euelpis, 203

Eumenes, 120, 126

Eunapius of Sardis, 333

Eunus, 216

Euphranor, 245

Eupolemus, 198

Euporus, 245

Eusebius, Bishop of Caesarea, 9–10, 310, 336–38; on the canon of Scripture, 116; and church history, 15–17; and Constantine, 305–7, 333–35; concerning the Apostles, 77–79; concerning Christian agonies and arguments, 185–87; concerning the defenders and defamers of the faith, 147–49;

concerning Dionysius of Alexandria, 255–57; concerning the end of persecution, 304–7; concerning the four emperors, 283–85; concerning Jesus, 49–51; early life, 10–11; horizons, 223–26; at Nicea, 12; sources, 115–17; writings of, 12–15

Eusebius, deacon and Bishop of Laodicea, 232, 235, 250–53

Eustathius, 12

Eutychian, 250

Eutychius, 247

Evarestus, 108, 118, 162

Evodius, 96

Ezra, 145, 165, 206

F

Fabian, Bishop of Rome, 208–9, 211, 212

Fabius, Bishop of Antioch, 212, 214, 218, 220, 222, 236

Fadus, 62, 62n. 14

Fausta, 285, 331n. 22, 334

Faustinus, 235

Faustus, deacon, 214, 232–33, 235

Faustus, presbyter, 272

Felicitas, 223

Felix, Bishop of Rome, 249–50, 325n

Felix, procurator of Judea, 11, 68–69

Festus, 11, 69–70, 73

Firmilian, 208, 222, 228, 236, 246–47

Flavia Domitilla, 94, 94n. 20, 117

Flavius Clemens, 94, 94n. 20

Flavius Josephus. See Josephus

Flavius, unidentified, 239

Florianus, 225, 249n. 23, 257

Florinus, 169, 175–77

Florus, 75

Fundanus, 124, 144, 148

G

Gaius Caligula, 56–58, 57n. 5, 59, 61, 68, 78

Gaius, Bishop of Jerusalem, 167

Gaius, Bishop of Rome, 250

Gaius, companion of Dionysius of Alexandria, 214, 235

Gaius, martyr, 172

Gaius, presbyter of Rome, 75, 77, 102, 105, 204

Galba, 80, 82, 82n, 116

Galen, 184

Galerius, 15, 259, 262, 262n. 2, 273n. 10, 278–79, 279n, 281, 283–85, 305, 322n, 323n

Gallienus, 225, 231, 233, 236, 241, 241n, 246, 256–57

Gallio, 79

Gallus, 225, 227, 231, 256

Gamaliel, 61, 62n. 14

Germanicus, 130, 279, 299

Germanion, 196

Germanus, 213, 213n. 24, 232, 234

Geta, 224

Gnaeus Pompey, 34

Gordian I, 208, 225

Gordian III, 225

Gordius, 196

Gorgonius, 259, 263

Gorthaeus, 139

Gothicus, Claudius, 246, 257

Granianus, Serennius, 124

Gratus, proconsul of Asia, 41, 42n, 170

Gregory, 209, 209n. 19, 236, 246

H

Hadrian, 119, 119n. 3, 120–24, 123n. 7, 126, 144, 148, 162, 167, 196n. 5, 257

Hegesippus, 16, 71, 73, 77, 92–95, 106, 115, 122, 126, 138–40

Helen, companion of Simon Magus, 63

Helena, mother of Constantine, 331n. 22, 334

Helena, queen of Adiabene, 62, 62n. 16

Helenus, Bishop of Tarsus, 222, 228, 246–47

Heli, legal father of Joseph, 36–38

Heliodorus, 228

Heliogabalus (Elagabalus), 224

Heraclas, 190, 200, 202, 207–9, 211, 229, 230

Heraclides, martyr, 191

Heraclides, procurator, 327

Heraclitus, 182

Herais, martyr, 191

Hercules, 124

Hermammon, 227, 231, 241

Hermas, 81, 101

Hermo, 254

Hermogenes, heretic, 142

Hermophilus, 184

Hero, martyr, 110, 139, 191, 216

Herod Agrippa I, 11, 56, 59–62, 61n. 13, 68

Herod Agrippa II, 68, 73, 92, 116

Herod Antipas, 37, 40, 43, 56, 61, 100

Herod of Ascalon, 33–34

Herod the Great, 10, 37–41, 41n. 16, 109, 283

Herod, chief of police, 131

Herodias, 43, 56

Hesychius, 272

Hierax, 239, 247

Hippolytus, scholar, 204, 222

Hoshea, 27

Hosius, 327, 327n. 20

Hyginus, 125–26, 162

Hymenaeus, 236, 246–47, 254

Hyrcanus, 34, 37

I

Ignatius, Bishop of Antioch, 96, 108–10, 111, 115, 117, 147, 165

Ingenuus, 217

Irenaeus, 16, 63, 93, 96, 101, 103, 109, 111–13, 115, 121–22, 125, 128–29, 138–40, 142, 145–47, 160–66, 175–77, 179–82, 198

Isaiah, 29, 72, 72n. 24, 145, 206, 209, 232, 315, 318–19

Ischyrion, 217

Ishmael, 41

Isidore, 216

Israel. See Jacob

J

Jacob, natural father of Joseph, 36–38

Jacob (Israel), 24–25, 31

James the Just, Bishop of Jerusalem, brother of Jesus, 45, 52–53, 70–74, 77, 88, 92, 120, 139, 238, 255, 336

James, apostle, 53, 59, 82, 112, 167, 243–44

Jeremiah (Jeremias), 28, 72, 145, 206, 260

Jeremias. See Jeremiah

Jesus of Nazareth (Christ), 10–13, 38, 50, 72, 86–90, 100, 121, 123, 125, 133, 152, 156, 163, 176, 180, 212, 229, 238, 255, 265, 268, 308, 312–14, 317–19, 321–22; advent of (incarnation), 30, 31–35, 52; advent of (second coming), 105, 176, 179; ascension, 15, 45, 46, 63, 82, 103, 113; Christ of God, 22, 29, 31, 41, 86, 313; citation by Josephus, 44, 336–38; correspondence with Abgar, 45–46, 49; creation by, 23; crucifixion of, 78, 337; Eusebius on, 49–51; genealogies of, 14, 35–38, 49; known in Old Testament, 27–30; nature of, 22–27; relatives, 93–96; resurrection, 45, 54, 102–3, 109, 178–80; Son of God, 12, 23, 47, 49, 71, 134, 163, 248, 313, 319; theophany, 13, 31; trial by Pilate, 77

Jesus, son of Ananias, 89

Jesus, son of Damnaeus, 73

John Mark, 244

John the Baptist, 41, 43–44, 99, 116, 152n. 2

John the Presbyter, 112–13, 112n. 46, 244, 255

John, apostle, 9, 53, 59, 80, 93, 96–101, 103, 104–5, 111–12, 116–17, 129, 138, 164, 167, 175, 177, 179, 181, 199, 207, 231–32, 243–45, 255

John, Bishop of Jerusalem, 120

Jonathan, 69

Joseph Caiaphas, 41–42

Joseph, 36–38, 40, 52, 92, 165, 200

Joseph (Barsabas, Justus), 44, 112–13

Joseph, Bishop of
Jerusalem, 120
Josephus, Flavius, 9, 16–17,
20, 32–34, 39–40, 41n.
15, 42n, 43, 44n. 21, 49,
56–57, 58n. 7, 60–61,
60n. 11, 68–69, 73, 73n.
26, 75–76, 77, 87–89,
89n. 10, 198, 252, 283;
life of, 90–92; passage
on Jesus, 44, 336–38;
on Pilate in Jerusalem,
57–58; as source for
Eusebius, 83–85, 115;
and succession of high
priests, 41–42; on
Theudas, 61–62; writings
of, 90–92
Joshua, 24, 27, 27n. 5, 34,
145, 206
Judas (Thomas), 46
Judas the Galilean, 32–33,
33n. 7
Judas, betrayer of Jesus,
44, 52, 113, 171
Judas, Bishop of Jerusalem,
120
Judas, brother of Jesus.
See Jude
Judas, writer, 172
Jude, brother of Jesus,
45n, 74, 94, 101, 106,
193, 198
Julia Mamaea, 204, 224
Julian the Apostate, 238n,
333
Julian, Bishop of
Alexandria, 166, 178,
188
Julian, Bishop of Apamea,
171
Julian, Bishop of Jerusalem,
167
Julian, martyr at
Alexandria, 216
Juliana, 200
Julius Africanus, 34, 49,
209
Justin Martyr, 16, 20,

62–63, 63n, 77, 101, 115,
123–24, 126–28, 135–
38, 135n. 25, 145–46,
147, 149, 165, 182, 186
Justinian, 176
Justus (Barsabas, Joseph),
44, 112–113
Justus, Bishop of
Alexandria, 119
Justus I, Bishop of
Jerusalem, 108, 120
Justus II, Bishop of
Jerusalem, 120
Justus of Tiberius, 91

K

Kallistio, 168

L

Lactantius, 279n, 304–5
Laetus, 188
Lagus, 165
Lampridius, 224
Latronian, 326
Leonides, 188
Licinius, 15–16, 236, 275,
279, 279n, 285, 294,
296, 298, 301–2, 304–7,
322, 322n, 328–31,
331nn. 22–23
Linus, 80, 82, 92, 96, 162
Longinus, 202
Lucian, martyr, 231, 271,
289
Lucius, at synod of
Antioch, 247
Lucius, Bishop of Rome,
227
Lucius, martyr, 137
Lucius, presbyter of
Alexandria, 235
Lucius Verus, adopted son
of Pius, 126, 129, 129n.
20, 148, 161n. 8
Lucuas, 118
Luke, 14, 32, 35–37, 41,
42, 50, 59, 61, 62n. 14,
69–70, 81–82, 87, 99–

100, 105, 109n. 41, 111,
164, 198, 207, 209
Lupus, 118
Lusius Quietus, 119
Lysanias, 40–41, 41n. 16,
56

M

Macar, martyr, 216
Macrian, 197, 231–32,
232n. 8, 241, 241n, 256
Macrinus, 204, 224
Majorinus, bishop, 325n
Malchion, 246–47
Malchus, 235
Mamaea, Julia, 204, 224
Mani, 14, 250
Marcella, 191
Marcellinus, 250
Marcellus, confessor in
Egypt, 169, 233
Marcellus, Bishop of
Ancrya, 12, 14
Marcian, heretic at
Rhossus, 182
Marcion of Pontus, 140,
142, 145–46, 165, 167–
68, 168n. 27, 172, 235
Marcius Turbo, 118
Marcus Aemilius, 55
Marcus Aurelius, 127, 129,
129nn. 20–21, 137, 138,
143, 145, 148–49, 150,
157, 161–62, 161n. 8,
161n. 10, 166, 186, 224
Marcus, heretic, 125
Marinus, Bishop of Arles,
325
Marinus, Bishop of Tyre,
228
Marinus, martyr at
Caesarea, 236–37
Mark Antony, 50
Mark, Bishop of
Alexandria, 126
Mark, Bishop of Jerusalem,
121, 167
Mark, evangelist, 64, 74,

353

99, 100, 113–14, 164,
199, 207
Mark, of Rome, 324
Mary (the Virgin), 38, 52,
102, 165, 200
Mary, daughter of Eleazar,
86
Mary, wife of Clopas, 106
Maternus, 325
Matthan, 36–38
Matthew, evangelist, 14,
35, 37, 99–100, 112, 114,
164, 166, 200, 206, 209
Matthias, apostle, 44, 52,
101, 104, 113, 120
Matthias, father of
Josephus, 90
Maturus, 154, 156
Maxentius, 275, 277, 285,
294, 295n, 306, 328
Maximian, 273n. 10, 275,
281, 284–85, 296, 299
Maximilla, 169, 170n,
171–72, 174
Maximin Daia, 15, 40n.
14, 238n, 275, 276–77,
279n, 283, 285, 286,
288–90, 290n, 293, 294,
296, 298–301, 304–6,
328
Maximin, Bishop of
Antioch, 142, 175
Maximinus Thracian,
emperor, 208, 225
Maximus, author, 182
Maximus, Bishop of
Alexandria, 246, 254
Maximus, Bishop of
Bostra, 246
Maximus, Bishop of
Jerusalem, 167, 167n. 26
Maximus, presbyter, 218,
232–33, 235, 247
Mazabanes, 212, 228, 236
Melchi, 36–38
Melchizedek, 29, 314
Meletius, 253
Melito, Bishop of Sardis,
115, 128, 128n, 139,

142–45, 147, 149, 179,
182, 198
Menander, 101–2, 121
Mercuria, martyr, 216
Meruzanes, 222
Metras, 214
Metrodorus, 134
Miltiades, anti-Montanist,
172, 172n, 182
Miltiades, Bishop of Rome,
324
Miltiades, Montanist, 169,
172, 182, 324
Minucius Fundanus, 124
Moderatus, 202
Modestus, 139, 142
Montanus, 145, 145n, 160,
169–74, 170n
Moses, 23–27, 31, 33–34,
38, 67, 90–91, 145–46,
166, 198, 201, 239, 252,
294–95, 295n
Moses, presbyter at Rome,
220
Musaeus, 252
Musanus, 139, 145–46

N

Narcissus, Bishop of
Jerusalem, 167, 167n. 26,
178–79, 181, 194–96
Natalius, 183
Nathan, 36–38
Nebuchadnezzar, 165
Nemesion, 216
Neon, 203
Nepos, 241–43
Nero, 9, 50, 68–70, 70n,
73–75, 74n, 79, 80, 82,
82n, 93, 96, 105, 116,
144, 164n. 19, 304
Nerva, 96, 117
Nicetes, 131, 134
Nicolaus, 102–4
Nicomachus, 202
Nicomas of Iconium,
246–47
Nilus, 272

Novatus (Novatian),
217–18, 218n, 220–22,
228, 230
Numenius, 202
Numerian, 225, 249, 257

O

Onesimus, Bishop of
Ephesus, 109
Onesimus, friend of
Melito, 144
Origen, 13–14, 16, 19,
58n. 9, 73n. 26, 80, 80n.
2, 191, 193, 204, 208–9,
210, 211n, 212, 213n.
23, 222, 223–24, 227,
227n, 236, 333, 336; and
biblical scholarship, 199–
200; and the bishops,
207–8; commentaries on
the Scriptures, 205–7,
209–10, 211; early years,
188–91; and heretics,
200–201; influence of,
11; opinions on, 201–3;
orchiectomy of, 193–94
Otacilia Severa, 225
Otho, 82, 82n, 116

P

Pachymius, 272
Palmas, 140, 179
Pamphilus, 11, 13, 16, 210,
223, 253, 272, 333
Pantaenus of Alexandria,
166, 193, 197, 199, 199n.
7, 203
Papias, Bishop of
Hierapolis, 64, 108,
111–14, 112n. 47, 115
Papirius, 179
Papylas, 135
Patricius, 327
Paul of Samosata, Bishop
of Antioch, 182, 245–49,
250, 253, 256–57
Paul, Alexandrian heretic,
189

Paul, apostle, 9, 11, 44–45, 53–54, 55–56, 59, 62, 68, 70n, 75nn. 29–30, 77–79, 81–82, 96, 97, 100–101, 104, 104n. 31, 110, 118, 129, 140, 146, 162, 167, 207, 212, 229n. 3, 238, 244–45; as author of Hebrews, 198–99, 204; and defense in Rome, 69–70; epistles of, 66, 81, 99, 102, 111; martyrdom of, 75, 80; ministry in Rome, 164

Paul, companion of Dionysius of Alexandria, 214, 235

Paul, presbyter, 247

Paulinus, Bishop of Tyre, 308, 310, 314, 316n. 8, 319n. 11, 321

Paulinus, lay preacher, 203

Peleus, 272

Perennius, 178

Perpetua, 223

Pertinax, 182, 186

Peter, apostle, 9, 20, 44, 44n.22, 53–54, 55, 59, 75n. 29, 96, 108–9, 111, 112, 118, 167, 182, 238, 244; children and wife of, 104; epistles of, 80–82, 129, 207; and John Mark, 64, 114, 164–65, 199, 207; martyrdom of, 75, 77, 79, 104; pseudo writings, 100–101, 197–98; and Simon Magus, 62–64

Peter, Bishop of Alexandria, 254, 272, 289

Peter, companion of Dionysius of Alexandria, 214, 235

Peter, imperial servant and martyr, 263

Peucetius, 301

Phabi, 41

Phileas, Bishop of Thmuis, 267–69, 272

Philemon, 228–29

Philetus, 204–5

Philip the Arab, emperor, 210–12, 210n. 21, 215n. 25, 225

Philip, apostle, 104–5, 105n. 34, 112, 179

Philip, Asiarch, 133

Philip, Bishop of Gortyna, 139, 140, 142

Philip, Bishop of Jerusalem, 120

Philip, evangelist, 53–54, 105

Philip, tetrarch, 40–41, 41n. 16, 56, 61

Philo, 56–58, 64–68, 64n, 65n, 66n, 77, 198, 252

Philoromus, 267

Philoumene, 168

Pierius, 253

Pilate, Pontius. See Pontius Pilate

Pinnas, 236

Pinytus, 139, 140–41

Pionius, 134, 135n. 24

Pius, Bishop of Rome, 126, 180

Plato, 202

Pliny, 107–8, 108n, 117

Plutarch, 190–91

Polybius, 16, 109

Polycarp of Smyrna, 103, 108–11, 115, 128–35, 129n. 21, 131n, 135n. 24, 147–48, 162, 176–77, 179, 181

Polycrates, Bishop of Ephesus, 105, 178–79

Pompey, 34, 37

Pontian, Bishop of Rome, 205, 208

Ponticus, 158

Pontius, churchman, 175, 197

Pontius Pilate, 11, 19, 40–43, 40n. 15, 44, 54, 55n, 56–58, 58n. 9, 77–78, 163, 289, 336–37

Porphyry, 13, 201–2

Potamiaena, martyr, 191, 193

Pothinus, 155, 162

Potitus, 168

Primus, Bishop of Alexandria, 118, 119

Primus, Bishop of Corinth, 139

Priscilla, 68, 78, 169, 170n, 173, 175

Priscus, father of Justin Martyr, 126

Priscus, martyr at Caesarea, 235

Priscus, presbyter at Alexandria, 254

Probus, 225, 249, 249n. 23, 257

Proclus, bishop, 247

Proclus, Montanist, 75, 105, 204

Protoctetus, 208

Protogenes, 247

Ptolemy Philadelphus, 165n. 23, 252

Ptolemy Soter, son of Lagus, 165, 165n. 23

Ptolemy, martyr, 136–37, 217

Publius, 140, 167, 175, 236

Pythagoras, 56, 122

Q

Quadratus, Bishop of Athens, 140

Quadratus, prophet and apologist, 110, 115, 119, 119n. 3, 147–48, 172

Quinta, 214

Quintus, 130

Quirinius, 32, 175, 236

R

Reticius, 325

Rhodo, 115, 167–68

Rufinus, 13, 277nn. 11–12
Rufus, companion of Ignatius, 110
Rufus, governor of Judea, 120
Ruth, 37, 145, 206

S

Sabellius, 229n. 2, 245
Sabinus, Praetorian Prefect, 286, 296
Sabinus, Prefect of Egypt, 213, 213n. 24, 234
Sagaris, 143, 179
Salome, 40
Sanctus, martyr, 154–56
Saturninus, 121, 145–46
Saul, 34
Sejanus, 57, 57n. 4
Seneca, 70n, 79
Seneca, Bishop of Jerusalem, 120
Septimius Severus, 150, 171n, 182, 187, 188, 193, 223–24
Serapion of Alexandria, 221
Serapion, Bishop of Antioch, 175, 178, 196–97
Serapion, martyr, 215
Serennius Granianus, 124
Serenus, martyr, 191
Servillius Paulus, 143
Severa, 211, 225
Severus, heretic, 146
Sextus, 182
Shapur I, 236n, 256
Sidonius, confessor, 218
Silas, 172
Silvanus, 272, 289
Simon Magus, 53–54, 62–64, 63n, 77, 101, 121–22, 125, 139, 256
Simon Peter. See Peter, apostle
Simon, son of Camithus, high priest, 41

Socrates, Bishop of Laodicea, 250
Socrates, philosopher, 135, 135n. 25
Solomon, 25, 36–38, 140, 145, 165, 182, 198, 206, 317, 337
Sosthenes, 44
Sotas, 175
Soter, Bishop of Rome, 138–39, 141, 146, 150, 162, 165n. 23, 180
Stephen, Bishop of Laodicea, 253
Stephen, Bishop of Rome, 227–28
Stephen, one of the seven deacons, 52–53, 55, 82, 103, 159
Susanna, 209
Symeon, 92, 96, 105–7, 106n. 36, 108, 120, 139
Symmachus, Bishop of Jerusalem, 167
Symmachus, translator, 200, 200n. 9
Syneros, 168

T

Tacitus, historian, 16, 41n. 15, 59n
Tacitus, emperor, 225, 249n. 23, 257
Tatian, 50, 136, 145–46, 167–68, 182, 198
Telesphorus, 120, 124–25, 162, 245
Tertullian, 9, 55, 55n, 74, 74n, 77, 96, 108, 108n, 115, 161–62, 223
Thaddeus, 45–48, 53
Thelymidres, 222, 228
Themiso, 171, 173
Theoctistus, 203, 208, 222, 228, 236
Theodore, lay preacher, 203
Theodore, martyred

Egyptian bishop, 247, 272
Theodore, student, 209
Theodotion, 165, 200, 200n. 9
Theodotus, banker, 183
Theodotus, Bishop of Laodicea, 253
Theodotus, Montanist, 160, 171
Theodotus, shoemaker, 182–84
Theonas, 254
Theophilus, bishop, 247
Theophilus, Bishop of Antioch, 142
Theophilus, Bishop of Caesarea, 178–79, 181
Thebouthis, heretic, 139
Theophilus, martyr, 217
Theophrastus, 184
Theotecnus, Bishop of Caesarea, 236–37, 246–47, 252–53
Theotecnus, comptroller, 288, 288n. 4, 301
Theudas, 61–62, 62n. 14
Thomas, 45–46, 53, 80, 101, 112
Thraseas, 175, 179
Thucydides, 16
Tiberius, 40–41, 41n. 16, 50–51, 54–56, 55n, 56–57, 57n. 4, 77–78
Timaeus, 250
Timothy, associate of Dionysius of Alexandria, 213–14, 245
Timothy, associate of Paul, Bishop of Ephesus, 70, 80–82, 162
Titus Flavius Clement, 197
Titus, Bishop of Crete, 81
Titus, emperor, 82, 85, 91n. 17, 92, 116–17
Tobias, 46–47, 120
Trajan, 95, 96–97, 105–6, 106n. 36, 107–8, 108n, 117, 118, 119, 148, 162

Trypho, 137–38
Tymion, 173
Tyrannion, 271
Tyrannus, 250

U

Urban, Bishop of Rome,
  204–5
Urban, confessor, 218
Urbicius, 136
Ursus, 326

V

Valens, 167
Valentinian, 139, 146, 175
Valentinus, 125, 129, 146,
  200
Valerian, emperor, 225,
  227n, 231–35, 236,
  236n, 241n, 256–57, 261
Valerius Gratus, 41, 42n,
  170
Vespasian, 58, 73, 82, 82n,
  87, 90, 92, 93, 116, 162
Vettius Epagathus, 152
Victor, Bishop of Rome,
  105, 178–81, 182–83
Vitellius, 82n, 116

X

Xerxes, 91
Xystus I, Bishop of Rome,
  119–20, 162, 181
Xystus II, Bishop of Rome,
  228, 230–31, 236, 245,
  245n. 18, 256

Z

Zabdas, 254
Zaccheus, 120
Zacharias, father of John
  the Baptist, 152
Zadok, 32
Zebedee, 82, 243
Zebennus Philetus, 205,
  208
Zeno, 217

Zenobia, 257
Zenobius, 271
Zephyrinus, Bishop of
  Rome, 75, 182–83, 199,
  204
Zerubbabel, 311, 316,
  316n. 8
Zeus, 288, 290
Zosimus, 110, 333
Zoticus of Cumane, 171
Zoticus of Otrous, 169,
  171, 174

INDEX OF PLACES

A

Achaia, 79
Acrocorinth, 141
Actium, 200
Adiabene, 62, 62n. 16
Adrianople, 306–7, 331n. 23
Adriatic Sea, 284
Aelia Capitolina, 62, 62n. 16, 121, 148, 203, 228. See also Jerusalem
Africa, 186, 218, 254, 285, 305, 325–26
Alexandria, 11, 15–16, 19, 51–52, 56–57, 64–65, 73–74, 92–93, 96, 103, 116, 118–21, 126, 136, 138, 143, 165–66, 178, 181, 185, 188–90, 192–94, 197–99, 203, 205, 207–9, 211, 214, 220, 222, 226–27, 230, 233–35, 238–39, 245–47, 250–51, 253–56, 267–69, 272, 277, 289
Amasea, 330
Amastris, 140
Amphitheater of the Three Gauls (Lyons), 153
Ancyra (Ankara), 12–13, 169
Antinoöpolis, 123, 123n. 7, 196n. 5
Antioch, 11–12, 16, 19, 44, 51, 53, 55, 59, 62, 93, 96, 102, 108–10, 116–17, 139, 142, 147, 175, 178, 196, 204–5, 208, 212, 214, 218, 220, 222, 224, 228, 236, 245–47, 249–50, 253, 259, 270–71, 288–89, 301

Apamea, 171–72
Appian Way (Rome), 224
Arabia, 203, 210–11, 217, 228, 269
Arch of Constantine, 302
Ardabau, 170
Areopagus (Athens), 82
Arles, 326, 334
Armenia, 222
Arsinoe, 242
Ascalon, 34, 37
Asia, 80, 96, 105, 108, 112, 124, 127–29, 133, 135, 143–44, 148, 152, 160, 164–65, 169–70, 174–75, 177, 179, 185, 244, 286
Asia Minor, 68, 80n. 1, 113, 152, 176, 185, 223, 255, 262, 269, 285, 305–6
Athens, 82, 140, 144, 210
Attica, 253
Aurelian Wall (Rome), 257

B

Babylon, 34
Babylon (Rome), 64, 207
Balkan Peninsula, 285, 305
Bathezor, 86
Bernice, 245
Bethlehem, 32, 38, 40, 51, 334
Betthera, 121
Bithynia, 13, 80, 108, 117, 228
Bosporus, 307, 335
Bostra, 204, 210, 246
Britain, 78, 224, 272, 284–85, 305

Byzantium, 307

C

Caesarea (Cappadocia), 208, 236, 246–47
Caesarea Maritima, 9–12, 15–17, 19, 55, 59, 60, 79, 105, 178–79, 194, 203, 205, 207–10, 212, 223, 226, 228, 235–37, 252–53, 272, 333
Caesarea Philippi, 237, 255
Callirhoe, 39
Caparattea, 101
Cappadocia, 80, 196, 208, 222, 228, 236, 246–47, 269
Capri, 78
Carthage, 176, 223, 228, 256, 325–26
Catacombs of Domitilla (Rome), 95
Cephro, 233–34
Chalcedon, 264
Chrysopolis, 307, 331n. 23
Church of the Holy Sepulcher, 15, 334
Cilicia, 148, 222, 228
Cochaba, 38
Colluthion, 234
Colosseum, or Flavian Amphitheater (Rome), 116, 302
Constantinople, 12, 14–15, 335
Corinth, 75, 75n. 30, 79, 82, 93, 116, 139–41, 162, 178–79
Crete, 81, 139, 140
Cumane, 171

Cyprus, 53
Cyrene, 118, 148

D

Dacia, 117, 257
Dalmatia, 284
Damascus, 289
Danube River, 149, 186
Dead Sea, 39
Debeltum, 175

E

Edessa, 45, 47, 49–50, 53
Egypt, 11, 13, 32, 37, 38,
    40, 50, 62, 64, 87, 118,
    121, 148, 167, 185, 188,
    192, 203, 213, 223,
    233, 234–35, 239, 241,
    255–56, 264–65, 272,
    283–85, 301, 305
Emesa, 271, 289
Ephesus, 80–81, 96–97,
    105, 109, 112, 128–29,
    137, 164–65, 174–75,
    178–79, 244
Ethiopia, 54
Eumenia, 172, 179
Euphrates River, 45, 47, 49

F

Flavia Neapolis, 126
Flavian Amphitheater, or
    Colosseum (Rome), 116,
    302
France, 151, 185

G

Galatia, 80, 169, 228
Galilee, 40, 68, 100
Gamala, 32
Gate of Mithridates
    (Ephesus), 98
Gaul, 43, 82, 150–52,
    157, 160, 162, 179–80,
    185–86, 223, 284–85,
    305, 325
Germany, 162

Gittho, 63
Gomorrah, 24
Gortyna, 140, 142
Greece, 86, 167, 205, 284

H

Herculaneum, 117
Hierapolis, 64, 105, 108,
    112, 142, 169, 175, 179

I

Iconium, 203, 230, 246
Illyricum, 68, 80, 207
India, 166
Ionia, 167
Israel, 35, 72n. 25, 140,
    239, 260
Istanbul, 264
Italy, 75, 167, 185, 218–19,
    223, 249, 257, 284–85,
    294, 305
Izmit, 264, 284

J

Jericho, 24, 39, 200
Jerusalem, 11, 14–16, 19,
    34, 45–46, 51, 52–53,
    55, 57–58, 62, 68–69,
    71, 73, 75, 77, 80,
    82–83, 86–87, 89–90,
    92–93, 96, 103, 105,
    106, 115–16, 119–21,
    138, 148, 165, 167, 173,
    175, 178, 179, 194, 196,
    203, 207–8, 212, 222,
    236, 238, 244, 246,
    253–54, 255, 311, 321,
    334, 337
Jordan, 225
Jordan River, 39, 62, 88,
    237

L

Lake Mareotis, 65, 192
Laodicea (in Asia), 143,
    179
Laodicea (in Syria), 222,

    228, 235, 250–51,
    253–54
Laranda, 203
Lebanon, 167, 309, 317
Lechaion Road (Corinth),
    141
Leptis Magna, 187
Library of Celsus
    (Ephesus), 98
Libya, 233, 235
Lugdunum. See Lyons
Lyons, 150–53, 155, 160,
    162, 185–86, 223

M

Machaerus, 43
Magnesia, 109
Mamre, 24
Mareotis, 235
Mauretania, 264
Meander River, 109, 172
Mediterranean, 10, 47, 61,
    192, 223, 256
Melitene, 161, 263
Mesopotamia, 47, 49, 117,
    118, 146, 148, 228, 269
Milan, 284, 306, 322
Milvian Bridge, 296, 303,
    304–6
Mt. of Olives, 69, 334
Mt. Vesuvius, 117
Mt. Zion, 321
Mysia, 170

N

Nazareth, 10, 38, 51
Nicea, 12, 14–16, 264,
    334–35
Nicomedia, 262–64, 271,
    284–85, 289, 297, 306
Nicopolis, 200
Nile River, 239
North Africa, 187, 284
Numidia, 326

O

Osrhoene, 179

Ostian Way (Rome), 75

P

Palestine, 10, 13, 37, 54–55, 126, 167, 178, 179, 185, 194, 203, 205, 212, 222, 223, 235–36, 252–54, 264, 272, 284
Palmyra, 257
Pamphylia, 244
Paneas (Paneion), 237
Paphos, 244
Paraetonium, 236
Parthia, 80, 224
Patmos, 93, 97, 117, 244
Pella, 82, 121
Pentapolis, 229, 245
Pepuza, 173–74
Perea, 68, 82, 86
Perga, 244
Pergamum, 136, 154
Persepolis, 256
Persia, 14, 91, 165, 250, 256
Phaeno, 272
Pharos lighthouse, 192
Philadelphia, 109, 134, 172
Philomelium, 130
Phoenicia, 11, 53, 264, 271, 289, 310
Phrygia, 130, 152, 160, 169, 173, 176, 269
Pirucheum (Alexandria), 251
Pompeii, 117
Pontia (island), 94
Pontus, 80, 125–26, 140, 165, 168, 179, 209, 236, 238, 246, 253, 270, 330
Ptolemais, 181, 229

R

Red Sea, 239, 294
Rhine-Danube (frontier), 50, 256–57
Rhone River, 150–51, 158
Rhossus, 197
Rome, 9, 11, 16, 19–20, 34, 50–51, 56–57, 62–64, 68–70, 74–75, 77–79, 80, 82, 92–96, 106, 108–9, 111, 116–17, 118–20, 125–26, 128–29, 138–39, 141, 146, 148–49, 150, 160, 162, 164, 167–69, 175, 177–82, 185–86, 199, 204–5, 207–8, 211–12, 218–20, 222, 223–26, 227, 230–32, 245–46, 249, 256–57, 266, 276–77, 283, 285, 294–96, 302–5, 324–25, 334–35

S

Salim, 100
Salonina, 257
Samaria, 53, 68
Samosata, 182, 245, 256–57
Sardis, 128, 142, 149, 179, 333
Scillium, 186
Scythia, 80
Sea of Marmora, 284
Sicily, 201, 326
Sidon, 271
Smyrna, 97, 108–9, 128, 130, 132–34, 147–48
Sodom, 24, 85, 183
Spain, 116, 284–85, 305
Strato's Tower (Caesarea), 11, 60
Synnada, 203, 230
Syracuse, 325
Syria, 11, 32, 75, 108–10, 121, 126, 170, 185, 223, 228, 236, 250–51, 256, 263, 269, 284–85

T

Taposiris, 213
Tarsus, 222, 228, 246–47, 306
Thebaid (Theban area), 188, 264, 266, 272

Thessalonica, 144, 307
Thmuis, 267
Thrace, 175
Tiber River, 63, 295–96, 303, 305
Ticinum, 280
Tralles, 109
Tripoli, 187
Troas, 109
Turin, 305
Turkey, 113, 176, 284, 331n. 23
Tyre, 11, 15–16, 63, 181, 228, 250, 264–65, 271, 291, 310

V

Vatican, 75
Vatican Valley (Rome), 303
Verona, 225, 305
Via Appia, 303
Via Flaminia, 303
Via Ostiensis, 303
Vienna, 186
Vienne (Gaul), 43, 150–52, 154, 186
Vindobona. See Vienne

Y

York (England), 224, 272, 285,

Z

Zion, 260, 321

INDEX OF SUBJECTS

A

Abomination of
Desolation, 83
Acts of Paul, 81
Acts of Pilate, 40–41,
40–41n. 14, 55n. 2
Acts of the Apostles, 146
Against Apion (Josephus),
90
Against Heresies (Irenaeus),
63, 93–94, 96–97, 103,
125, 138, 145–46, 162
Against Hierocles
(Eusebius), 13
Against Marcellus
(Eusebius), 13–14
Against Porphyry
(Eusebius), 13
Against the Greeks (Justin
Martyr), 137
Against the Greeks (Tatian),
136, 146, 198
*Against the Heresy
of Hermogenes*
(Theophilus), 142
Against the Manicheans
(Eusebius), 14
*Allegories of the Sacred
Laws* (Philo), 67
amillennialists, 186
angels, 60, 60n. 11, 183
Antichrist, 164, 164n. 19
Antinoites, 196, 196n. 5
Antiochenes, 121, 189, 248
apostles, 42–43, 44–45,
61–64, 77–79, 88, 112–
13, 126–28, 166, 175;
apostolic succession,
166–67; daughters
of, 105; in Jerusalem,

52–54; and marriage,
104; paintings of, 255;
renunciation of property
by, 65; in Rome,
69–70; scattering of
throughout Asia Minor,
80, 82; as *Therapeutae*
and *Therapeutrides*
("healers"), 65, 65n.
19. *See also* apostles,
writings of
apostles, writings of,
80–82, 99–100, 109,
122–24, 182, 204,
205–7; of Apolinarius,
145; canonical and
noncanonical writings,
100–101; of Clement,
111; of Musanus, 145; of
Papias, 111–14; of Tatian,
145–46
Arianism, 11–12, 334
Arminian War, 292
ascetics, Egyptian, 64–67
Augustan History
(Spartianus), 223–24

B

bandits, 69, 256
baptism, 219, 219n. 30,
230. *See also* heretics,
rebaptism of
bishop of Alexandria, 11,
96, 103, 118, 120, 126,
138, 166, 178, 190, 208,
246, 254; as pope, 229,
229n. 4
bishop of Ancyra, 12
bishop of Antioch, 96,
108, 117, 139, 142, 178,

196, 212; succession of,
208, 250
bishop of Armenia, 222
bishop of Athens, 82, 140
bishop of Caesarea, 11,
178, 208, 236, 246, 253
bishop of Cordova, 327n.
20
bishop of Corinth, 75, 139,
140–42, 178, 179
bishop of Crete, 139
bishop of Emesa, 271
bishop of Ephesus, 105,
178
bishop of Gaza, 271
bishop of Gortyna, 142
bishop of Hierapolis, 64,
142–43
bishop of Jerusalem, 53,
82, 92, 105, 119–20,
167, 178, 212, 222;
succession of, 167, 167n.
26, 254
bishop of Laodicea, 222,
250–51, 253
bishop of Lyons, 162
bishop of Nicomedia, 271
bishop of Nilopolis, 217
bishop of Rome, 75, 80,
82, 93, 96, 119, 125,
138, 146, 150, 160,
245; succession of, 126,
162–63, 204, 208
bishop of Sardis, 128,
142–43
bishop of Smyrna, 128
bishop of Tarsus, 222
bishop of Thmuis, 267
bishop of Tyre, 181, 271
bishopric succession, 16,
92–93, 96, 108, 119–20,

124–26. *See also* bishop of Antioch, succession of; bishop of Jerusalem, succession of; bishop of Rome, succession of

C

cannibalism, 25–26, 86, 154, 154n. 3, 155; of children, 122n. 6
catechetical schools, 189–90, 199n. 7, 207
celibacy, 140
cemeteries, 233, 233n. 11
Cesti (Julius Africanus), 209
Christendom, 17, 223; four great sees of, 19–20
Christian apologetics, 147–48
Christianity, 13, 23, 66n. 20, 149, 157n. 4, 161n. 9, 257, 284; among Roman rulers, 225; benefits of heretical challenges to, 148; characteristics of, 66–67; defenders of, 55, 147; growth of after the end of Roman persecution, 301–2; history of, 9–10; objections to, 49; spread of, 55–56, 259, 287
Christians, 28–29, 30, 55, 108–10, 144, 293; bravery of, 130; churches of, 65–66; internal strife among, 259–60; prayers of, 161–62; as "prophet killers," 170–71; writings of, 203–4. *See also* Christians, persecution of
Christians, persecution of, 59, 79, 122n. 6, 123, 129, 130, 143–44, 223–24, 231–35, 284; edict of Trajan against hunting Christians, 107–8; in

Egypt, 255; ending of under Galerius (the imperial recantation), 279–80, 279n. 15, 281, 286–87; ending of under Gallienus (edict of toleration), 236, 241, 257; response of Christians to persecution, 147, 226, 265; under Decius, 212–13, 225–26; under Diocletian, 11, 15; under Domitian, 93–96; under Maximin Daia, 276–77, 288–92, 298–300; under Maximinus Thracian, 208; under Valerian, 256; in various parts of the Roman Empire other than Rome, 185. *See also* churches, destruction of; martyrs/martyrdom
Chronicon (Eusebius), 13
Chronography (Julius Africanus), 209
churches, 50, 65–66, 109–10, 141, 159–60, 236, 308–9; Asian dioceses, 180; and Christian clergy, 334; church dedications, 310–22; description of early church architecture and furnishings, 316–18, 316n. 9; destruction of, 260–61; and distribution of property to the needy, 110; at Ephesus, 97; exemptions of church leaders from public duties, 327–28; internal challenges of, 185–86; organization of, 67, 219; the physical church as model for the spiritual rank of its members, 320–21; rebuilding of Christian basilicas, 334;

restoration of, 309; Roman grants of money to, 326–27; at Rome, 75n. 29
circumcision, 31
civil war (Roman), 257, 277–78, 283, 298–99
Collection of Ancient Martyrdoms (Eusebius), 13, 150, 161
Commentary on Genesis (Origen), 80
Commentary on Holy Scriptures (Origen), 205–7
Commentary on the Psalms (Eusebius), 14
Concerning Easter (Clement), 143
Concerning Easter (Melito), 143
Concerning Fate (Bardesanes), 146
Concerning Knowledge (Irenaeus), 182
Concerning the So-Called Gospel of Peter (Serapion), 197
Concerning Virtues (Philo), 68
Council of Antioch, 12
Council of Arles, 334
Council of Asia, 127–28, 127n. 17
Council of Nicea, 12, 334

D

Defense of Origen (Eusebius), 13, 210, 223
Defense of Our Faith, A (Justin Martyr), 123, 126, 136, 137
Defense of the Christians (Tertullian), 55
Defense of the Faith (Tertullian), 161–62
demons, 63, 89, 237, 276; expulsion of, 163. *See also* magic (sorcery)

Demonstration of Apostolic Preaching (Irenaeus), 182

Dialogue Against Trypho (Justin), 137–38

Diatessaron (Tatian), 146

disciples. *See* apostles

divine justice, 39–40, 43, 59–61, 259–60, 278, 283, 293

divinity, 22, 23, 45, 100, 286; of Roman gods, 54–55

Docetists, 197, 197n. 6

Donatists, 160n. 6, 325n. 17

E

Easter, 128, 143n. 31, 180n. 37, 251–52; controversy concerning, 178–81; and the "festival letters," 238–39; and the zodiac, 252

Ebionites, 102, 102n. 29

Edict of Milan, 322–24, 322n. 14

Embassy, The (Philo), 57, 57n. 5

Encratites, 145–46

epistle of Barnabas, 198

eunuchs, 193–94, 250

evangelical life, 66

evangelists, 110–11, 209

Evocatus, 94, 94n. 21

F

faith, 32–33, 185; antiquity of, 30–32; defenders of, 9–10; defense of, 119

famine, 59, 59n. 10, 62, 292–93. *See also* Siege of Jerusalem, famine during

fasting, 180, 180n. 37, 181n. 38

Feast of Purim, 131n. 23

Feast of Tabernacles, 89

Feast of Unleavened Bread. *See* Passover (Feast of Unleavened Bread)

Frumentarii, 213, 213n. 24

G

Gentiles, 53, 121, 167, 173; and the statue of Jesus, 238, 255–56

geometry, 183–84

Gnosticism, 14, 21n. 1, 147, 148, 175n. 35; and modern ultrafeminism, 186; as taught by Basilides, 121–22

Gospel of the Hebrews, 102, 140

Gospels: order of, 199; Synoptic Gospels, 116

"great Sabbath," 131, 131n. 23

H

Harmony of Moses and Jesus, The (Ammonius), 202

Hebrews. *See* Jews

Hebrews, epistle to, 198–99

heresies, 109, 121–22, 125, 139–40, 147, 200, 229–31; after the era of the apostles, 106–7; at Antioch, 246; of Apelles, 168; Arabian, 211–12; of Artemon and Theodotus, 182–84, 249, 249n. 22; of Beryllus, 210; Cerinthian heresy, 102–3, 129; Helkesaite heresy, 212; Manichean heresy, 250; Marcion heresies, 126, 138, 167–68, 168n. 27, 172; of the Nicolaitans, 103–4; Novatian heresy, 160n. 6, 217–20, 221, 230; origins of, 139–40; Phrygian heresy, 169–72, 186; Roman schismatics, 175–77; schism of Nepos, 241–43. *See also*

Christianity, benefits of heretical challenges to; Gnosticism; heretics

heretics, 142, 189, 200–201; conversion of, 129; rebaptism of, 227–28

Hexaemeron, 168, 182, 204

Hexapla (Origen), 200, 200n. 9

high priests, 27, 27n. 4, 28–30, 34–35, 42n. 19, 288, 314; tenure of hereditary priests, 41, 41n. 17

historical documents, veracity of, 49–50

Holy Scripture, 90–91, 91n. 13, 99–101, 164–66, 201, 242, 320–21; as a base for Christianity, 13; commentaries on, 205–7, 209–10, 211; corruption of, 183–84; scholarship concerning, 199–200

humanity: punishment of, 26; wickedness of, 25–26

Hypotyposes (Clement), 44n. 22

I

idolatry, 55, 63, 123, 288, 301

imperial (Roman) decrees, 322–28

imperial (Roman) politics, 273n. 9, 283; and the problem of imperial succession, 283–85, 304–5, 306–7

incest, 122, 154, 154n. 3

J

Jewish Antiquities (Josephus), 39, 40, 41, 43, 68, 73, 90, 336

Jewish War, The (Josephus), 39–40, 69, 83, 90

Jews, 30–31, 34, 80, 138, 173; anointing of, 35; and art, 255–56; Babylonian captivity of, 316, 316n. 8; and the crucifixion of Christ, 77–78, 115; expulsion of from Jerusalem, 148; expulsion of Jewish leaders from Rome, 68, 78–79; genealogies of, 35–38; rioting of, 56–57, 68; war of with Rome, 75–76, 116. See also Jews, persecution of; Jews, revolts of

Jews, persecution of, 40, 58, 92, 115; under Gaius, 56–57; under Nero, 74–75. See also Siege of Jerusalem

Jews, revolts of, 58, 76, 118–19; the Bar-Kokhba revolt, 62n. 16, 120–21, 120n. 4, 123, 148

L

Law of the Prophets, 125
Letter to the Corinthians (Clement), 142
Life of Constantine (Eusebius), 12, 13, 304
Life of Pamphilus (Eusebius), 11, 13

M

Maccabaikon, 91
Macedonians, 165
magic (sorcery), 63, 101–2, 122, 125, 275, 276, 288
marriage, 104, 104n. 31, 140, 329
martyrs/martyrdom, 9, 53, 70, 75n. 30, 117, 134, 135n. 24, 136–37, 160–61, 171–72, 174, 261–62, 289; in Alexandria, 214–17, 267–69; of Apollonius, 177–78; in Asia Minor, 262–64; 269–71; of Blandina, 154, 155, 156–57, 158; at Caesarea, 235; of church leaders, 271–72; in Egypt, 265–67; in Gaul, 150, 152, 154–59, 186; and the "humanity" of the persecutors, 270–71; of James, 70–74; of John, 104–5; of Justin, 135–36; in Lyons, 185, 186; mass executions, 267; of Metrodorus, 134; in Nicomedia, 263; of Paul, 69–70; in Pergamum, 135; of Philip, 105; in Phoenicia, 264–65; of Polycarp, 129–30, 129n. 21, 131–34, 148; in Smyrna, 134–35, 135n. 24; student martyrs, 191–93; of Symeon, 105–6, 106n. 36; women martyrs, 135, 191, 191–93, 216, 235, 266, 270, 276–77

Martyrs of Palestine (Eusebius), 13
Massacre of the Innocents, 38
Memoirs (Hegesippus), 71
Memoirs (Pilate), 289
millennialists, 186
Milvian Bridge, battle of, 294–96, 294–95n. 8, 305–6
miracles, 45–48, 112–13, 163–64, 195
Miscellanies (Clement), 104, 193, 198
monasticism, 65n. 19
Montanism, 148, 170, 172–75, 186
Mosaic law, 168

N

Nicene Creed, 12, 334
Nicolaitans, 103–4
nomenclature, in antiquity, 10

O

Ogdaod (Irenaeus), 175–76, 175n. 35
On Martyrdom (Origen), 208
On Peace (Dionysius), 222
On Promises (Dionysius), 103, 241–42
On Repentance (Dionysius), 221–22
On Schism (Irenaeus), 175
On the Nomenclature of the Book of the Prophets (Eusebius), 15
On the Numerous Progeny of the Ancients (Eusebius), 13
On the Paschal Festival (Eusebius), 14, 198
On the Sole Sovereignty (Irenaeus), 175
On the Soul (Justin Martyr), 137
On the Theology of the Church: A Refutation of Marcellus (Eusebius), 14
On the Virtues (Philo), 57
Onomasticon (Eusebius), 14
Outlines (Clement), 59, 64, 166, 197–98
owls, 60n. 11

P

paganism/pagan polytheism, 55, 202, 333–34
panegyric (to the Emperor Constantine), 12, 310, 311n. 5
Parthians, 34
Passover (Feast of Unleavened Bread), 83,

88–89, 128, 252. *See also*
  Easter
Patripassianism, 13
Phrygians, 170
pirates, 256
plague, 239, 239n. 14,
  240–41, 256, 292–93,
  292n. 7
Praetorian Guard, 186, 187
Preparation for the Gospel
  (Eusebius), 13
priestesses, 66
priests, 68–69, 288. *See
  also* high priests
Problems (Tatian), 168
*Problems and Solutions
  in Genesis and Exodus*
  (Philo), 67
Proof of the Gospel
  (Eusebius), 13
prophecy, 35, 160, 171,
  310
prophets, 27, 146, 170,
  171, 174; and ecstatic
  speaking, 172; false
  prophets, 62, 69, 88,
  122; prophetesses, 169,
  173–74
Proverbs (of Solomon),
  140

R

Rechabites, 72, 72n. 25
Refutation, A (Justin
  Martyr), 137
*Refutation and Overthrow
  of Knowledge Falsely So-
  Called* (Irenaeus), 163
Refutation of the Allegorists
  (Nepos), 242
repentance, 220–21
resurrection, 53, 178–79;
  and the kingdom of
  Christ, 113
Revelation of John, 100,
  103, 138, 164, 174, 207,
  231, 241–42, 242n. 17,
  243–45, 255

Revelation of Peter, 198
Rich Man Who Is Saved, The
  (Clement), 97

S

Sabellianism, 12, 13, 229,
  229n. 2
Samaritans, 63
Sanhedrin, 73
Saracens, 217
*Sayings of the Lord
  Interpreted, The* (Papias),
  111–14
Scripture. *See* Holy
  Scriptures
Septuagint, 165–66, 166n.
  24
Severians, 146
Shepherd of Hermas, The
  (Hermas), 81
Siege of Jerusalem, 82;
  atrocities during, 83–84,
  86; famine during,
  83–86; Jesus' predictions
  concerning, 86–87; lives
  lost during, 87
Siege of Pirucheum, 251
Sol Invictus, 257, 333
sovereignty of God, 26–27
Sovereignty of God, The
  (Justin Martyr), 137
"spiritual brides," 248
Synod of Antioch, 246
Synod of Constantinople,
  12
Synod of Rome, 218,
  324–26
Syriac Gospel, 140

T

Ten Evangelical Canons
  (Eusebius), 14
Tetrapla (Origen), 200
Theophany (Eusebius), 13
"Thundering Legion" (the
  "Thundering Twelfth"),
  161–62, 161n. 11

To Constantia Augusta
  (Eusebius), 15
triumphalism, 283, 333
True Word, The (Celsus),
  211, 211n. 22
*Two Books of Objection and
  Defense* (Eusebius), 13

W

weapons, manufacture of,
  277–78
witchcraft, 275

INDEX OF PHOTOGRAPHS, MAPS, AND CHARTS

A

Alexandria, map of, 192
Amphitheater of the Three Gauls, Lyons, 153
Antoninus Pius, head of, 127
Arch of Constantine, 302
Asia Minor, map of, 176
Augustus, statue of, 33

C

Caesarea, 10;
reconstructed theater at, 61
Caracalla, bust of, 195
Catacombs of St. Sebastian, Rome, 226
centers of early Christianity, map of, 113
Christian Martyrs' Last Prayer, The, by Jean-Léon Gérôme, 222
Chi-Rho symbol, 226, 307
Christian symbols, Catacombs of St. Sebastian, 226
Colosseum, or Flavian Amphitheater, 302
Constantine, head of, 274, 332
Constantius Chlorus, head of, 272
Corinth, looking south along the Lechaion Road, 141

D

Decius, bust of, 213
Diocletian, head of, 260
Domitian, head of, 94

E

Eastern empire under Diocletian, map of, 264
Eastern Mediterranean world, map of, 47

F

Flavia Domitilla, head of, 95
Flavia Domitilla, name on marble slab in Catacombs, 95

G

Gate of Mithridates, Ephesus, 98
Gaul, map of, 151
gladiator, limestone relief carving of, 266

H

Hadrian, statue of, 120
Helena, mother of Constantine, statue of, 273

I

Imperial Rome, map of, 282

J

James, early mosaic of, 51
Jesus Christ, genealogy chart of, 36
Joseph Caiaphas, limestone ossuary of, 42
Julia Mamaea, bust of, 205

L

Library of Celsus, Ephesus, 98
Licinius, head of, 329
Lyons, site of persecutions, 153

M

Marcus Aurelius, statue of, 130
Maximian, coin of, 280
Milvian Bridge, Rome, 296

N

Nero, head of, 74

P

Paul, early mosaic of, 51
Philip the Arab, bust of, 211
Pompey, head of, 35

R

Rome, map of principal roads, 303

S

Septimius Severus, bust
  of, 187
Smyrna, Roman
  colonnade, 132
spread of Christianity, map
  of, 258

T

Tiber River, Rome, 296
Titus, statue of, 93
Trajan, bust of, 107

V

Vespasian, statue of, 88

Also by Paul L. Maier

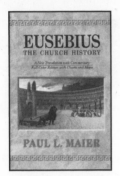

This hardcover edition includes Paul L. Maier's clear and precise translation; historical commentary on each book in *The Church History*; and more than 150 full-color photographs, maps, and illustrations. Coupled with four helpful indexes and the Loeb numbering system, these features promise to liberate Eusebius from previous outdated and stilted works, creating a new standard primary resource for readers interested in the early history of Christianity.

Eusebius: The Church History
Translated and edited by Paul L. Maier
ISBN 978-0-8254-3328-3   416 pp.   hardcover

Josephus's *Jewish Antiquities* and *The Jewish War* take on brilliant new dimensions in this revised edition of the award-winning translation. Now with commentary and full-color photographs, charts, and maps.

Josephus: The Essential Works
Translated and edited by Paul L. Maier
ISBN 978-0-8254-3260-6   416 pp.   hardcover

Also available

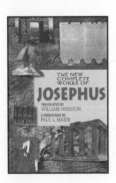

This unabridged volume of the complete works of Josephus has been revised and expanded to include commentary by Paul L. Maier. Also includes a harmony of Greek and English numbering systems, a table of Jewish weights and measures, Old Testament text parallels, twenty full-page illustrations, and an updated index.

The New Complete Works of Josephus
Translated by William Whiston
Edited by Paul L. Maier
ISBN 978-0-8254-2924-8   1,152 pp.   hardcover
ISBN 978-0-8254-2948-4   1,152 pp.   paperback